AN
INVISIBLE
SPECTATOR

ECCO PRESS BOOKS BY PAUL BOWLES

The Delicate Prey (STORIES)

A Distant Episode (STORIES)

Jean Genet in Tangier by Mohamed Choukri
(TRANSLATION)

Points in Time (FICTION)

Their Heads Are Green and Their Hands Are Blue
(ESSAYS)

Up Above the World (NOVEL)

Without Stopping (AUTOBIOGRAPHY)

AN INVISIBLE SPECTATOR

A Biography of Paul Bowles

CHRISTOPHER SAWYER-LAUÇANNO

THE ECCO PRESS
New York

First published in 1990 by The Ecco Press
26 West 17th Street, New York, NY 10011
Published simultaneously in Canada by
Penguin Books Canada Ltd., Ontario
Printed in the United States of America
Designed by Irving Perkins Associates

This edition by arrangement with Weidenfeld & Nicholson.

Due to limitations of space, permissions and credits appear on page 502.

Library of Congress Cataloging-in-Publication Data

Sawyer-Lauçanno, Christopher, 1951-
An invisible spectator: a biography of Paul Bowles
Christopher Sawyer-Lauçanno.
p.   cm.
Reprint. Originally published: New York:
Weidenfeld & Nicolson, 1989.
Includes bibliographical references.
1. Bowles, Paul, 1910-   —Biography.
2. Authors, American—20th century—Biography.
3.Composers—United States—Biography.
I. Title.
[PS3552.O874Z89   1990]   813'.54—dc20   [B]   90-30333   CIP

ISBN 0-88001-257-9

10 9 8 7 6 5 4 3 2 1

The text of this book is set in Baskerville

To V.O.L.

ACKNOWLEDGMENTS

I AM INDEBTED to many. I first want to thank Paul Bowles, who cooperated, in his own fashion, with this undertaking. Of his long-time friends, William S. Burroughs, Buffie Johnson, Bruce Morrissette, Edouard Roditi, Ned Rorem, and Virgil Thomson were exceedingly helpful, generous of both their time and memories. Others, too, were of great assistance: Andreas Brown, Rudy Burckhardt, Mark Dery, Kenward Elmslie, Lawrence Ferlinghetti, Edward Field, Allen Ginsberg, James Grauerholz, Maurice Grosser, Robert Jones, Ned Leavitt, Richard Leavitt, John Lehmann, Bennett Lerner, William Mackay, Irving Malin, Felicity Anne Mason, William McBrien, Margot Miflin, Dorothy Morrissette, Bradford Morrow, Mohammed Mrabet, Jonah Raskin, Rodrigo Rey Rosa, Robert Sharrard, William Targ, and Regina Weinreich. Cathy Henderson and Ken Craven of the Harry Ransom Humanities Research Center at the University of Texas, and Kendall Crilly of the Music Library at Yale University provided expert assistance in helping me work my way through their excellent archives. I also want to acknowledge the support of friends and family: James and Nancy Sullivan first introduced me to the works of Paul Bowles and have continually encouraged me in the writing of this book. Patricia Pruitt never wavered in her constant belief in me and in this enterprise. No words are sufficient to thank her. Sarah Diane Pruitt and Jessica Chelsea Pruitt always managed to keep me grounded in reality, while the Garcías—Anna, César, Erin, María Elena, and Martín—were always there to cheer me on. At MIT, Karen Bushold went far beyond her duties as the administrative officer of the Foreign Languages and Literatures section in order to facilitate this project. Her assistants, Chris Pomieko, Carol Watson, Richard Larraga, and Cynthia Wooley, followed her lead. Finally, this book would not have been possible without the tremendous enthusiasm and able guidance of my agent, Roslyn Targ, and my editor, Mark Polizzotti. Thank you all.

CONTENTS

INTRODUCTION

PAUL BOWLES is the consummate artist: fiction writer, composer, translator, North African folklorist. Although perhaps best known as a writer since the early 1950s, when his first novel, *The Sheltering Sky,* made the best-seller list, Bowles actually began his artistic career as a composer, a protégé of Aaron Copland and Virgil Thomson. But his considerable body of music, much of it excellent, is now nearly forgotten by all but a small number of twentieth-century music aficionados, and even his fiction has not been popular in the United States for the last thirty years.

Gore Vidal, among others, has speculated that the reason for the lack of acceptance in his own country is that he doesn't write about America or American themes. He does write about Americans, but his Americans are of the sort rarely encountered on the main streets of the United States. His characters are often rootless and soul sick, spiritual outcasts wandering through remote wastelands in search of nothing or everything. His major theme is often the surreal and ultimately fatal encounter of these voluntary exiles with an alien culture. At his best, Bowles is a master of charting inner disintegration, madness, and terror, at laying bare the morally empty souls of his characters. His vision, rendered in prose as precise as cut crystal, is unrelentingly agonizing, frequently violent, as black as a starless night. One does not just read a story by Paul Bowles; one is consumed by it. As the malevolent dark overtakes his characters, it overtakes his readers.

I first came under the spell of Paul Bowles in 1980, when some friends lent me *The Collected Stories.* I had heard of Bowles before then and was vaguely aware that the Beats had considered him some sort of patron saint. I was also aware that he had lived for many years in Tangier. But I had never read a word of his writing.

I began with the story "Pages from Cold Point" and was immediately mesmerized; within a few days I had read the other thirty-eight stories in the volume, not savoring them—that would happen later—but gorging myself on the feast. As I began to recover from the headiness induced by the stories, I was certain that Bowles was no less than a modern master, an extraordinarily gifted craftsman, a fabulous voyager through nightmare landscapes into an equally uncharted geography of the imagination.

About that same time I bought a few song scores and unearthed in library archives a few scratchy recordings of his piano pieces. The music was thoroughly enchanting, buoyant, harmonic, as full of light as the fiction was of dark. It was almost as if the composer were a totally different person from the writer. The more I read, the more music I played or listened to, the more interested I became in the man himself.

His autobiography, *Without Stopping,* while entertaining, gave very few clues as to who Bowles really was, and was nearly devoid of commentary on either his writing or his music. I dug a bit deeper, finding that some of Bowles's most gifted contemporaries had been more than willing to laud his achievements, but even these accolades contributed more to the enigma than to its decipherment:

TENNESSEE WILLIAMS: Paul's work? I guess it's about as good as anything is now.

NORMAN MAILER: Paul Bowles opened the world of Hip. He let in the murder, the drugs, the incest, the death of the Square (Port Moresby), the call of the orgy, the end of civilization: he invited all of us to these themes a few years ago, and he wrote one short story "Pages from Cold Point," a seduction of a father by a son, which is one of the best short stories written by anyone.

NED ROREM: (when asked, upon receiving the Pulitzer Prize in music, which American composer he most loved): Paul Bowles.

GORE VIDAL: "Carson McCullers, Paul Bowles, Tennessee Williams are, at this moment at least, the three

> most interesting writers in the United States."
> A quarter century has passed since I wrote
> that sentence. . . . All in all, I see no reason not
> to support my youthful judgment of Paul
> Bowles. As a short story writer, he has had few
> equals in the second half of the twentieth cen-
> tury.

By the fall of 1984 Bowles had become an obsession. The following summer I made the pilgrimage to Tangier, after receiving a
letter of invitation from him. Day after day I made the trek from
my hotel out to his little three-and-a-half room apartment on the
edge of the city. Contrary to what I'd expected, Bowles was warm,
talked easily, patiently and frankly answering innumerable questions about himself and his work.

When I arrived back in Boston in the fall of 1985, I began to plan
this book. I wrote to Bowles about it. He replied almost immediately:

> I hope no biography will be written during my lifetime. . . . In any
> case, I hope you will come to Tangier in the summer and discuss the
> project with me, so I can have some sort of idea of what it includes.
> I'm delighted that you find the music of interest, since I already
> know you approve of the writing. It's almost impossible to find a
> person who takes both writing and music with equal seriousness.
> Those who like the music regret my having left it; those who like the
> writing generally are ignorant of the music, or find it old-fashioned.

Naturally, I felt crushed. Both my agent, Roslyn Targ, and my
editor at Weidenfeld & Nicolson, Mark Polizzotti, urged me not to
give up but to write back to Bowles explaining the project in
further detail. More letters were exchanged. In each of his, Bowles
both expressed resistance to the idea of a biography and encouraged my interest in him and his work; he also asked for further
information on the project and exhorted me to come to Tangier.

In late May of 1986 I returned to visit Bowles. After a few days
of further conversation, we came to an agreement on the terms.
Bowles consented to my writing what he termed an "unassisted,
synthetic biography." By "unassisted" he meant that he would
neither actively help nor hinder me; "synthetic" he defined as
information relating to his life or work privately or publicly availa-

ble from outside sources such as manuscripts, letters, and interviews. To facilitate my research, he granted me blanket permission to quote from all of his published or unpublished writings, but at the same time asked that I include the following statement: "P.B. found it so difficult to write the autobiography that he was unable to face getting involved in the same material, and thus asked to be excused from all participation in the project."

I spent some more time in Tangier that summer, visiting him daily, conversing freely about a thousand topics—music, magic, literature, Morocco. Of these conversations, some were obviously not germane to the book, but quite often he would tell an anecdote about his life or work. Over the next year I visited him twice more; we exchanged letters in the interim.

In the United States I began to look up Bowles's old friends. Many enthusiastically responded to my requests for information, while noting that I had set an arduous task for myself. Bowles himself had already warned me in a letter: "I don't envy you your task, but it may not be as difficult as my imagination paints it." William Burroughs, commenting on Bowles's legendary reserve, wrote in a similar vein, "All best wishes for success with a most difficult subject." A score of others also pledged their support, but were quick to echo Burroughs's sentiments that Paul Bowles was not an easy subject for any biographer. Indeed, not only had Bowles's peripatetic existence left few documents behind, but over the last quarter century, largely as a consequence of his Tangier exile, he had become an enigma.

Little by little, though, Bowles began to emerge, not as an austere, gloomy recluse sending out manuscripts from some Saharan hideaway, but as even more multidimensional than I had first perceived. His almost obsessive refusal ever to explain himself, his work, or his emotions left me with the task of trying to sort out what Bowles thought about certain matters and why. I do not think for a moment that I have been able to illuminate all of the inner Paul Bowles, but I have attempted, without resorting to fanciful psychoanalysis, to unravel who this man is and what motivated him to do what he did.

My original goal in writing this biography was to provide a comprehensive portrait of Paul Bowles as a creator, to place his work within the larger frame of the age itself so that his accomplishments—in both words and music—may finally earn their rightful place as major artistic achievements of this century. In this aim I never wavered. If my biography is able to attract even a few new listeners to Bowles's music, or new readers to his prose, then I have succeeded in my own personal mission. As such, this book is really for Paul Bowles—a visible homage to the invisible spectator.

I wish I could have been present at a reunion of the Japanese fan club. Perhaps not exactly present, but an invisible spectator.

Letter from Paul Bowles to the author, 1985

PART I

The Invented Cosmos

CHAPTER 1

It was unseasonably warm in New York City on the morning of December 30, 1910. Fog encircled Manhattan, obscuring the tops of the three or four newly erected skyscrapers. As a light rain fell, streetcars and taxis, mostly horse drawn, plied their way through the congested city streets. Underneath the city the tunnel crew was busy excavating another few yards of subway line. The new year was coming and a festive mood flowed in and around the city.

At Mary Immaculate Hospital in the recently incorporated town of Jamaica, borough of Queens, Rena Winnewisser Bowles was having a baby. This was her first child and the labor was prolonged. Her husband, Claude Dietz Bowles, a thirty-two-year-old dentist, waited impatiently. He had had to take time off from the practice he was working hard to build and was agitated that the delivery was taking so long. He became even more upset upon learning that the baby was not emerging correctly and that it would have to be a forceps delivery. Finally, early in the afternoon, Rena was etherized and the baby pulled forcefully from her womb. It was a boy, and he weighed eight-and-a-half pounds. He was named Paul Frederic after his mother's brothers, Paul and Fred Winnewisser.

Coming out from under the anesthetic, Rena was delighted. Her baby was alive, and despite a large gash on the side of his head, a result of the forceps delivery, he seemed normal and healthy. Claude, after learning that he was now the father of a blond-haired, blue-eyed son, went back to work. The baby was placed in a basinet in Rena's room.

Although weakened from the delivery, Rena lifted Paul into her arms, marveling at the tiny creature. She was holding him when, at around 4:30 that afternoon, the nurses came to remove the baby, announcing that he must be baptized, as it was unlikely he would live through the night. Rena refused; the nuns persisted and tried to pry Paul out of her arms. The confrontation continued for

3

some minutes, Rena emphatically stating that she would take responsibility for her son's soul. When that failed to dissuade them, she pulled herself up and in a fury proclaimed: "If you take that child out of the room, I'll follow you on my hands and knees screaming." The sisters finally relented, leaving the "madwoman" to nurse her baby, a baby that without baptism was surely already on his way to hell. When recounting the incident to Paul years later, she added: "Agh! Dirty creatures, with their old crosses dangling! They give me the shivers. Of course, some of them *are* very fine women, I make no doubt. But those black capes!"

It was not just the nuns that Paul and Rena had to fear. Claude was not terribly happy over the arrival of his son, either. It was another responsibility that he felt he really didn't need with all that he was trying to do to become a successful dentist. In addition, Rena seemed totally preoccupied with little Paul. The attention, support, and sympathy Claude counted on from his spouse was now all going to his tiny son. Life was no longer the same; the child, in fact, was making him quite miserable. After mulling over the situation for about six weeks, Claude apparently decided to act.

According to a persistent family legend, one night in mid-February, during a terrible snowstorm, Claude came into his son's room and opened the window. Then, lifting Paul from his crib, he stripped him and placed him in a wicker basket perched on the windowsill. A bit later, awakening to cries of distress, Paul's maternal grandmother, Henrietta Winnewisser, went into her grandson's room to investigate. Finding him exposed and with the snow falling on top of him, she sounded the alarm. After bundling Paul in a blanket, she turned to Claude and told him: "I know what you want. You shan't do it. You'll harm this baby over my dead body." Years later when she recounted the story to Paul, she added that Claude reminded her of the "old tomcat that comes back and eats his own kittens." It is an arresting description, intended to shock. Its overtones of cannibalism, even if not precisely calculated to instill dread in the mind of an impressionable young boy, could not have done otherwise.

Whether this incident actually occurred in the way Henrietta related it to Paul—or even occurred at all—is impossible to say, but Bowles has always believed it to be true. There is reason for skepticism, however, as Bowles also notes that his grandmother never wasted an opportunity to villify her son-in-law: "I discovered in her an inexhaustible lode of spleen against Daddy." Since he did not want to doubt its veracity ("The thing seemed only too possible. You could never be certain of what anyone really had in his mind"), and even found the account "exciting," the effect on Paul was substantial. Told to him when he was around six years old, the tale cemented Paul's considerable dislike of his father—for which, he felt, there was already sufficient cause. Claude's active animosity did not abate after this incident, nor did he seem to forgive Paul for having been born. At the same time, with such faithful informants filling his ears with tales of terror, Paul hardly had a chance ever to know his father on his own terms. Throughout Paul's childhood, Claude would always be viewed as a monster, a personification of evil itself. But Claude did little to present a different picture; indeed, he seemed to revel in the role.

Another incident sticks in Bowles's mind from those early years. When he was four, Rena was again in the hospital, this time in Exeter, New Hampshire. Exeter was the home of Henrietta's sister and brother-in-law, Edward and Jenny Green. Paul, despite having his mother in the hospital, was enjoying himself: his great-uncle and aunt gave him a lot of attention; and even better, his father had not yet come up from New York. Even at this age, the very presence of his father meant misery. One afternoon, under the supervision of Aunt Jen, he had been allowed to shape and bake cookies to take to his mother, an activity that greatly pleased him. A shadow suddenly darkened the kitchen. His father had arrived, chasing away the atmosphere of goodwill. Taking Paul aside he told him, with all the vehemence he could muster: "Your mother is a very sick woman, and it's all because of you, young man. Remember that."

Although stunned by his father's accusation, he took it for granted that somehow he was, indeed, responsible. Not understanding quite how, however, he finally asked his mother for an explanation. Rena brushed aside his father's spiteful admonition, telling him that Claude had not really meant what he said. She offered as an excuse that she had had a difficult time with Paul's birth and that it had taken her a while to recover from it. Although Paul didn't really see how this clarified his father's statement, it did help to reduce his sense of guilt. A pattern, though, was already established: Claude could be counted on to be spiteful, to lash out, to accuse; Rena, while not openly contradicting her husband, would comfort, explain, intervene. The polarity would be a constant in Bowles's childhood world, the roles played out again and again.

Paul Bowles spent the first five-and-a-half years of his life living on the third floor of an old brownstone at 108 Hardenbrook Avenue in Jamaica, New York. The second floor was taken up by his father's dental office, the first floor by the dental laboratory, which reeked of gas burners and hot metal. Paul's life was strictly regimented. His father did not permit him to play with other children, and he generally spent his days entertaining himself. For one hour each day he was sent into the small, fenced-in backyard, but even this activity often resulted in conflict. If he stood still in the yard, he would hear his mother pounding on the window, motioning him to move around and "play"; if he obeyed her, he would soon hear his father or his father's receptionist relaying Dr. Bowles's message to "calm down." Even on days when Paul managed to please both his mother and father, he was still under the tyranny of a large clock placed in the third-floor window, which legislated how much time remained for his outdoor "play."

Utterly tyrannized, Paul began quickly to retreat into himself, to invent his own universe, a world that was not subject to the dictates of his parents. By the age of three or four he hit upon two stratagems to escape the repressive routine. The first escape was through illness; the second through reading, writing, and drawing.

Despite his father's suspicion that Paul liked to be sick, it was one aspect of his existence that Claude could not forbid. When ill, or (as was often the case) feigning to be so, Paul could remain in the private sanctum of his imagination for long stretches of time without interruption and without fear of remonstrance. By the age of four, using alphabet blocks, he had taught himself how to read and write. Although it was risky and needed to be done on the sly for fear that his father would interfere, reading gave him access to an enchanted world far beyond his third-floor apartment in Jamaica; writing allowed him to transfer his own imaginary wanderings into concrete form. His earliest surviving notebook, printed in pencil and containing illustrated animal stories, is dated 1915. No doubt influenced by the stories he was reading or having read to him, it tells of fanciful creatures who have adventures in the world—something Paul was strictly prevented from having.

Paul, naturally, also had toys, but once his father came upstairs at 6:00 they had to be completely packed away in the toy chest. Writing and drawing, too, would have to be suspended until his father was back at work the next day. The one great pleasure of the evening during these early years was the half-hour before bedtime, when his mother would read to him, a practice she had begun when he was two. The stories, at first, were typical childhood ones, but by the time Paul was about seven, Rena moved on to Hawthorne and Poe.

> I remember wanting to stay in Hawthorne's *Tanglewood Tales* and the combination of repugnance and fascination I felt at hearing the stories of Poe. I could not read them aloud; I had to undergo them. Mother's pleasant, low voice and thus, by extension, her personality took on the most sinister overtones as she read the terrible phrases. If I looked at her, I did not wholly recognize her, and that frightened me even more.

Rena's choice of Poe as bedtime reading reflected her own adolescent thrill at his particular brand of horror. The effect on young Paul was considerably different: rather than eliciting excitement, the stories terrified him and caused him to have repeated nightmares. But Poe would stick in his imagination, and the sleepless nights would eventually yield Bowles's own fictionalized tales of terror. Thirty years later, he acknowledged his debt to both Poe and Rena by dedicating his first volume of short stories, *The Delicate Prey,* to his mother, "who first read me the stories of Poe."

Paul and his mother enjoyed each other's company, particularly when his father was not around. She encouraged him in his writing and drawing, paying great attention to his work and commenting critically on whatever he read or showed her. Her guide to child rearing was *Child Psychology* by a Dr. Riker. Riker advocated patience, understanding, and encouragement, values completely opposite those held by his father. Arguments about how best to raise Paul, therefore, frequently erupted between his mother and father. His father's main line was: "A kid will always go as far as you let him." The doctrine of absolute authority was for him the only way to curb undesirable behavior, to create an unspoiled, "unsissified" young man. No one ever seemed to win the arguments; Paul's mother continued to follow Dr. Riker when Claude was not around; his father insisted on total obedience in his presence. The seesaw continued until Paul left home.

It was a different matter when Paul visited his grandparents in the country. August and Henrietta Winnewisser lived at the Happy Hollow Farm, a 165-acre site of hills, brooks, and meadows near Springfield, Massachusetts, dominated by an imposing two-story house built at the turn of the eighteenth century. But it was the woods and surroundings that Paul loved most. Outside, he could wander at will among the maples and carefully venture into a series of old dark and rustic sheds that ran from the main house to the springhouse. Despite the natural beauty of the setting, it was the sheds that most attracted Paul, possibly because they contained a variety of mysterious objects and smells: "freshly cut wood . . . mildewed burlap, apples, and damp earth."

In a short story written in 1957, "The Frozen Fields," Bowles described a farm much like Happy Hollow as seen through the eyes of the young protagonist, Donald:

> Everything connected with the farm was imbued with magic. The house was the nucleus of an enchanted world more real than the world other people knew about. During the long green summers he had spent there with his mother and members of her family he had discovered that world and explored it, and none of them had ever noticed that he was living in it.

For Paul, as for Donald, one of the major advantages of these visits to the grandparents was that his father often remained behind in the city. And even when he did come, his wrath was somewhat held in check by the presence of his in-laws.

Paul's maternal grandparents were originally from Bellows Falls, Vermont. August Winnewisser, "a moody and violent man, subject to sudden surges of temper" (as Bowles later described him), had owned the only department store in the little Vermont town but had been forced into an early retirement following an accident with a runaway horse that had left him with a bad leg. It was then, in 1906, that he had bought Happy Hollow and moved to western Massachusetts. A second-generation American (his father, an anti-government radical, had emigrated from Germany in 1848), August was a freethinker and individualist who took every opportunity to rail against religion, organizations, and, of course, the government. Bowles remembers his grandfather as being a frightening, stern man, prone to frequent outbursts that alternated with long stretches of silence. His face was marred by a discolored and crooked nose, the result of a blow his own father had given him with a hammer when he was young (a practice August perpetuated, on his sons). Father of five children—Ulla, Emma, Rena, Paul, and Frederic—August appears to have been a classic patriarch. By contrast, Henrietta Winnewisser was extraordinarily warm, kind, and conciliatory, "the principal counterbalance to the latent emotional violence that often seemed about to engulf her family." For Paul, she represented an ideal mother, always patient, calm, and cheerful. Although not religious, she would often quietly chide August when he launched into one of his anti-Christian speeches. It wasn't the sentiment that bothered her, but the manner in which it was expressed.

There was no love lost between August and Claude: Paul's father considered his father-in-law a bit unbalanced and avoided contact with him as much as possible; Paul's grandfather, in turn, disliked Claude, even down to his "sissy" name. As a result of August's opposition to Claude, Paul sought out his grandfather as an ally and a silent partner in his own struggle against his father. What was lacking in genuine affection was compensated for by August's dislike of the person who Paul perceived to be a far greater evil.

Claude's own parents lived in upstate New York. Their main residence was on West Church Street in Elmira, but they also owned three houses on the shore of Seneca Lake in Glenora, New York. It was in Glenora that most of the vacation time was spent, and Glenora was, for Paul, the preferred residence. These grandparents, called Daddypapa and Daddymama to distinguish them from the Winnewissers, were an interesting contrast to his mother's parents.

His grandfather, Frederick Bowles, was a descendant of the well-established and rather distinguished Bowles family, of whom the most famous was Samuel Bowles, a Springfield newspaper editor and abolitionist. According to the family records, the Bowles family first emigrated to America from England in the mid-seventeenth century. Frederick, an independent businessman, was a strong-willed, staunch New Englander, proud of his ancestry and of his role as a soldier in the Civil War, which he always referred to as "the war," or "the War of the Rebellion." As a father, he too seems to have been something of a tyrant, concerned with forcing his sons into respectable careers. Claude, for instance, had wanted to become a concert violinist, but Frederick forbade such dilettantism, insisting instead that he study dentistry, a career into which he had already channeled Claude's older brother. As a grandfather, however, Daddypapa was the affectionate, understanding one. He was also, for Paul, the most intriguing relative. Studious and intense, he would spend his days alone in his den, reading. One of his particular intellectual preoccupations was American Indians. In the course of his study, he would pause now and then to snip an article on the topic from a magazine, which he would then file in a cabinet filled with such clippings. At some point in his later years he had taught himself French so as to read Hugo, Dumas, and Balzac in the original, and in his seventies took up Spanish, continuing to study it for the rest of his life. It is evident that these twin interests of language and other cultures, including "primitive" cultures, left their mark on young Paul, nurturing in him a desire to follow his grandfather's example.

Grandmother Bowles, on the other hand, seems to have been more like Paul's father: distrustful, prone to finding fault in everyone, Paul included. Paul's image of her, though, was certainly colored by Rena's insistence that her mother-in-law was inordinately suspicious—a trait, she continually insisted to Paul, that had been passed on to Claude.

Despite the allure of the woods and the lake, of Daddypapa's den where Frederick addressed young Paul in French and always had some amazing array of mysterious objects and pictures on hand to astonish his grandson, the visits to upstate New York were not all pleasant. A favorite pastime of the Bowles family was discussing Paul's supposed defects. In that, the family shared his father's philosophy that strong criticism and "suggestions" for improvement were the keys to building character. The most common pronouncement regarding Paul's involvement with reading or his tendency to enjoy being by himself seems to have been "it's not natural." As at home, Paul quickly began to distrust the world of his extended family, began to adopt two distinct modes of being, roughly equivalent to two identities. The private self was that of an isolated, imaginative, and sensitive youngster; the public self was one of altered facial expressions and mien, of postures opposite those of his true feelings. It would be a way of getting by for years to come.

During the summer of 1916, when Paul was five years old, the family moved into a new house at 207 De Grauw Avenue in Jamaica. Compared to the dark, cramped quarters on Hardenbrook Avenue, the new house, surrounded by woods, seemed open, remote, and airy. Overlooking the center of town, the house was situated on a ridge dubbed "The Hill," the site of the Battle of Long Island. A two-family house, the first floor was occupied by the owners, a young architect who had designed the house and his wife. The place seemed to Paul a major improvement over his first lodgings. Here, in open space filled with dogwood and pine, thrushes and robins beckoned. Even better for Paul, though, was that inside the house he had the third floor all to himself.

Despite the newness and lightness of his new quarters, Paul's world was much the same as it had been in the old house, except that his father no longer worked at home, thereby allowing Paul more freedom during the day. In the evenings and on the weekends, however, Claude and Rena continued their battle over how best to raise their son. During these times Paul usually managed to retreat to the third floor and his own private universe. Dinner, however, was sacred and unavoidable. It was especially difficult for Paul because his father imposed on him a method of chewing food called Fletcherization. Named after its proponent, Horace Fletcher (also known as the "Moses of Mastication"), the method essentially advocated chewing each mouthful of food at least forty times before swallowing. Claude began to insist that his son Fletcherize at the age of five and relentlessly imposed the practice on him until he left the house. If Paul failed to chew each mouthful the required number of times, Claude, ever watchful, would hit him in the face with his linen napkin. Although Paul would beg his mother to allow him to eat in the kitchen, she never was willing to cross her husband on this matter.

While Claude's enforcement of the practice was extreme, Fletcherization was not confined only to the Bowles household. Indeed, in the early part of the century the method was touted by such notable adherents as William and Henry James, John D. Rockefeller, Upton Sinclair, and John Kellogg, "the breakfast king." Henry James even went so far as to write Fletcher in 1906 that Fletcherization "makes my life possible, and it has enormously improved my work. You really ought to have a handsome percentage on every volume I sell."

Another boon to the method was decreased food consumption, an aspect of the practice that Claude also heartily endorsed. In his notes for *Without Stopping,* Bowles also recounted his father's stinginess in regard to food:

> The lack of nourishment at home was not due to poverty, but to an excessive preoccupation on my father's part with regard to my diet. If I said I was hungry, he would reply: "That's just indigestion. Wait two or three hours and you'll see that the pangs will go away." If I asked for a second helping, he often refused me on the grounds that I hadn't chewed the first properly.

Such experiences characterized Paul's relationship with his father. In Claude's presence, Rena was nearly as helpless as her son, acquiescing to her husband's whims and demands, but in his absence she continued to encourage Paul. She was particularly supportive of his literary and artistic projects, and after Paul began school the following year, also bolstered him in his scholastic endeavors.

Paul was enrolled at the age of six at the Model School, which had been established as a training institution for several hundred new public school teachers. The emphasis was on modern instructional methods, the teachers theoretically representing "model teachers," and the students, "model pupils." For Paul, going to school was important for one principal reason: it was his first excursion into the world of other children, for before his enrollment he had never played with or spoken to another child. Paul, however, was bothered by the way in which his attendance at school interrupted his own imaginative work. He did not care much for the world of other children, a world he quickly concluded was one of "unremitting warfare." Being small, aloof, smart, and inexperienced at the sociology of play, Paul became an immediate victim of the larger boys. Arriving home bruised and beaten earned him no sympathy from his father, however. "This is what he needs to bring him down to earth," Claude would remark to Rena.

Paul's precociousness and well-established command of reading and writing resulted in near-immediate advancement to second grade, but he did not get along with his new teacher, Miss Crane. He resented her authoritative style and rapidly began to devise ways of not complying with her wishes. He adamantly refused to take part in class singing and as a method of revenge devised a system to do what to him were meaningless assignments without really doing them: he simply wrote everything perfectly, but backward. This eventually resulted in a call to Paul's mother, who convinced him to conform to Miss Crane's strictures, mainly by suggesting that his father would be less than pleased if he found out about his behavior.

After doing his homework, and during vacations, Paul continued to work on his own projects. Among his favorite pastimes of these early years was the invention of places and place names. One small notebook contained page after page of entries detailing this preoccupation. The title page, in Paul's neat printing, read:

Appointment Book

The ALL of
WAYS Book.
For Young and Old

THE LAWREN
STEN BOOK
FOR ONLY OLD. 1

Inside, numerous lists detailed stops on various imaginary railroad lines: "Staitions [sic] on the Scranton Railroad," "Stations on the Garwood Railroad," "Stations Edison Railroad." The names were almost all invented, although occasionally real towns did appear, but not necessarily in their correct geographical locations.

On one vacation in Glenora, Paul decided to carry this penchant for inventing place names into reality by printing the names on small pieces of paper and carefully placing them at regular intervals in the woods surrounding his grandparents' home. Catching sight of them, his father demanded that Paul dismantle his creation. Daddypapa intervened, however, saying that there was no harm in allowing them to remain in place until the following day. Suddenly, to his surprise, Paul noticed that his father seemed amused by one of the names assigned the edge of a dry creek bed, "Notninrivo." Explaining to Rena that the name meant "nothing in the river," Claude actually allowed that it was a fairly clever invention. To Paul, his father's explanation seemed "crass and ridiculous." In reality, Notninrivo was simply the name of the preceding station, O'Virninton, spelled backward. When Paul objected that the interpretation was incorrect, Claude became enraged, seized his son by the collar and began shaking him, demanding that he confess the true meaning of the name. Paul refused; his father continued to shake him, denouncing him to the others as a "conceited little rotter." Finally his grandmother intervened, but even after Claude had stopped shaking his son, Paul refused to tell the grownups the true meaning of the name. Instead, he ran into the woods, picking up all of the signs, and then, on the shore of the lake, burned them, grinding the ashes into the mud.

In this, as in so many similar incidents in Paul's early years, the conflict revolved around Claude's desire for control over his child and Paul's fervent resistance to such control. For Paul, it was a struggle for his own private identity. To yield to his father would mean a loss of self. The obsessive behavior on both of their parts can be seen as being the result of a profound and essential distrust. Paul could not trust his father to appreciate or respect his individuality; Claude could not trust Paul to accept his ideas and therefore attempted to impose his views on his son through force. The more Claude tyrannized Paul, the more Paul resisted, became entrenched in his own imaginary universe. The cycle would never be entirely broken, and though it is not entirely clear what either of them gained from the struggle, it does seem that for Paul the positive consequences were that he developed a tremendous belief in his own self, in his power to resist the dictates of an external code of behavior. Never seeming to realize that his authoritative attempts to impose his will on Paul were doomed to failure, Claude seems merely to have lost the opportunity to impart any of his values to his son. The irony is that this was the goal to which he was probably most dedicated.

"The hostility involved with my father was very real," Bowles recalled. "It started on his side and became reciprocated, naturally, at an early age. I don't know what the matter was. Maybe he didn't want children. . . . My maternal grandmother told me it was simply because he was jealous. She said he couldn't bear to have my mother pay attention to this third person, me."

To Paul's mother, another reason for Claude's behavior stemmed from the fact that, since he was so maniacally working at building up his dental practice, he was under tremendous personal strain to succeed. Indeed, having "chosen" to become a dentist, he now had to prove to himself that he had made the correct move. But he was further confounded even in this when, at about the time Paul was nine, Claude woke up one morning unable to see out of his left eye. Going to the ophthalmologist, he was told that he had had a hemorrhage and would be permanently blind in that eye as a result. He was ordered to stop working so hard, to relax, enjoy himself more. Although he did join a country club and began to play golf, he was even more moody than usual at the house. He became increasingly preoccupied with his health, developing a fairly substantial case of hypochondria. It was all, Rena assured Paul, a result of Claude's worry about losing the sight in his good eye, which would have ended the dental practice he was working so hard to build. Paul wasn't so sure. His irrational behavior had hardly begun with becoming blind in his left eye.

CHAPTER 2

When Paul was seven, Claude decided that his son needed braces to straighten his teeth. As the orthodontist's office was in Manhattan, Paul began making his first excursions into the city. For the first year he was always accompanied, but by the time he was eight it was decided that he was old enough to go on his own. The treatment required two visits a week, on Tuesday and Friday afternoons. Wandering at will along the busy streets, Paul quickly began to enjoy the freedom and exhilarating ambience of the big city. The highlight of the trips, though, was his once-a-month visit to the New York Public Library. Working as head of the Children's Section was Annie Carroll Moore, a friend of his father's sister, Adelaide Bowles, who also worked at the library. Miss Moore always managed to spend a few minutes chatting with Paul and took great interest in guiding him in his reading. Often she had a book for him to keep. These books, frequently signed and inscribed to him, ranged from Hugh Lofting's *Dr. Dolittle* to Carl Sandburg's *Rootabaga Stories.* He occasionally was also able to visit Miss Moore in her Greenwich Village apartment while on family outings to visit his Aunt Adelaide. For Paul, her place epitomized exoticism. Decorated in a "Japanese" motif, full of screens and lanterns and candlelight, it was Paul's favorite place to visit when in the city. It was made all the better because the visits were officially sanctioned, as Miss Moore was a friend of the family's.

During the winter of 1918–19 an epidemic of the Spanish flu hit the United States. Tens of thousands became ill; thousands died. Paul and both of his parents caught it, as did his Aunt Adelaide. Unlike Paul's family, however, Aunt Adelaide did not recover; complicated by pneumonia and pleurisy, her illness became fatal. Paul's mother, trying to protect him, simply said: "Your Aunt Adelaide has gone away. You'll never see her again." "Where? Why not?" asked Paul. His mother would not respond and simply walked out of the room. Understanding intuitively that his aunt was dead, Paul was infuriated. His anger fastened upon his mother, both for telling him and not telling him. Not being able to discuss it with anyone, as he wasn't supposed to understand death, he internalized the event. But for the next seven years he could not mention Adelaide's name.

Another major event for Paul that year was the introduction of music into the house via his father's purchase of a phonograph. The initial collection, begun naturally by Claude, featured only classical music. Paul liked it, but decided to extend it a bit. On one of his excursions into New York, he went to a record store and bought "At the Jazz Ball" by the Original Dixieland Jazz Band. Upon hearing it, his father became livid, calling the music "trash" and forbidding Paul ever to bring any more of it into the house. Paul complied, in his own way: after that he purchased records of military bands playing Latin American pieces. From military marches he moved on quickly to big band music. "I used to buy a new dance record every week up until the time I was twelve," he recalled later. "I used to get more pleasure from Whiteman than anyone, because he orchestrated his pieces so much more interestingly. From 1919 to 1924 he was God himself to me."

It was a small leap from listening to music to playing it. Shortly after the purchase of the phonograph, it was decided that Paul should begin studying piano. His mother insisted on a grand piano which Claude, over numerous protests, finally bought; the services of a Miss Chase were enlisted. The lessons were given privately. On Tuesdays Paul studied theory, solfeggio, and ear training; on Fridays, piano technique. Paul remembers enjoying the lessons. Practicing was also a delight, as it was one activity that could be done publicly but without anyone invading his privacy. Only when he improvised or composed his own little pieces was he interrupted by his mother, who would gently inquire if what he was playing was his assigned work. But as long as he had put in a sufficient amount of time on his lesson, no one bothered him while he was experimenting with his own melodies and improvisations.

Unfortunately the lessons were interrupted about a year later, when the sounding board on the piano buckled and split. His father, knowing that he had been right in not wanting to buy a grand in the first place, railed against the shoddy workmanship of the postwar era, returned the piano to Wanamaker's department store, and refused to buy another one. After a hiatus of nearly a year, his grandparents sent an old Chickering upright from Elmira. This pleased Claude as it had been gotten for free, but greatly distressed his mother, who felt that the old piano was unsightly. As far as Paul was concerned, it was perfectly fine, as it had an excellent tone. Piano and theory lessons resumed and Paul became more and more interested in music, particularly in creating his own works. He learned rapidly and made remarkable progress in a short amount of time; as a result, he was soon tackling increasingly difficult pieces and expanding his repertoire far beyond that expected of a nine year old.

Almost from the beginning, he began to experiment with creating music himself. Aided by the classes in theory, he found it fairly easy to reproduce on manuscript paper the melodies that ran through his head. His first major composition was an "opera." Composed when Paul was about nine, the work was entitled *Le Carré: An Opera in Nine Chapters.* The plot was quite "adult." It dealt with two men who want to exchange wives. They finally manage, around the end of the first chapter, to do so by procuring divorces, but once the new arrangement has been made the wives find themselves unhappy and endeavor to get their husbands back. More of a story with occasional lyrics set to music than a real opera, the "libretto" features an aria in the second chapter with the following text:

Oh, lala,
Oh daba,
Oh honeymoon!
Say, oh say when . . .
But she got no further
For there was her ex-husband
Glaring at her like a starving pussycat.

Quite proud of *Le Carré,* Paul performed the piece over and over again for anyone who would listen. Upon realizing, though, that the enthusiasm for his work was due to its being perceived as uproariously funny, he put it away, steadfastly refusing ever to perform it again.

As *Le Carré,* with its highly literary component, shows, Paul was still quite engaged with words. Each night after doing his homework and music lessons he would make entries in a diary. Paul did not record the events of the day, however, but instead filled up notebook after notebook with the adventures of imaginary characters. Each entry was generally made in a third-person cryptic style:

Sun
Mavis Dies. Marshelle weeps and weeps.
Mon
Mavis is cremated. Marshelle weeps more.
Tues
Someone steals Mavis' bones in golden urn.
Marshelle swears she will find the brute.
Wed
Marshelle gets a package. In it is the golden
urn, but no bones. She faints.
Thur
Marshelle marries Dukol Canna.
Fri
Dukol Canna and Marshelle invite Queedol Canna, his brother to
live with them.
Sat
Abbie has a death fit. Adele cries. Clement
faints. Marshelle goes on a hunt late at night
for the vandal who stole bones.
Sun
She arrives in Centerville and sees a huge snake.
Hears nothing of search.
Mon
In Notninrivo she hears of man who was riding on
horse back wildly with golden urn.
Tue
Arrives in Virninton and finds man in hotel. She
shoots him dead and recovers the bones.

From just this brief excerpt (the entire narrative contained around 450 entries) we can see a number of Paul's early preoccupations. Chief among them are illness and death, travel and adventure, and, of course, the invention of names, both for his characters and places. Possibly the most striking feature of the narrative, though, is the adeptness with which this young writer is able to fabricate a story that mixes, rather convincingly, the most fantastic adventures with commonplace reality. Thirty years later this would become a hallmark of the Bowles style. It should also be evident that the language is quite sophisticated: the punctuation, grammar, and spelling are nearly impeccable, the vocabulary rich. What is also remarkable is Paul's ability to sustain characters and plot over many pages. Although some of the early diaries appear to be lost, it is possible to reconstruct the basic outline and genealogy contained in the amazing saga Paul worked on for at least a year:

Dukol and Marshelle are lost forever. . . .

Queedol sails safely to WenKog. . . .

Queedol Canna changes his name to Dukol Whitman. . . .

Dukol Whitman builds a castle for himself to shut out the Green Horror. . . .

Dukol Whitman wishes for a wife.
Bluey Morain the most beautiful girl in the world comes to Clifton. . . .

Dukol Whitman takes Bluey away to his castle to escape the Green Horror. Dukol Whitman and Bluey Morain marry. . . .

Dukol and Bluey. They get a baby girl. They name it Marjorie. They give Marjorie postage hypodermic. Makes her 15 years old. . . .

Marjorie Whitman buys a Marmon. Takes Dukol and Bluey to ride in it.

Marjorie drives very recklessly. Bluey asks Dukol to take the car away from her. He does. Marjorie gets furious and takes another postage hypodermic. She is 30 years old. Late at night Marjorie decides to leave home. . . .

Dukol Canna and Marshelle are found. . . .

Dukol Canna marries Marjorie Whitman. . . .

Marshelle sues Dukol for Bigamy and desertion.

Marshelle gets Green Horror.
Marshelle dies of Green Horror. . . .

Dukol Whitman dies of Green Horror. . . .

Marjorie has a baby girl names it Bluey Laber Dozlen.

Drugs, bigamy, desertion, lawsuits, the plague: these are hardly the elements one expects to find in the writings of a nine year old. Much of this must have come to Paul through his reading; some of it may have come from listening to the talk of adults. More than anything else, though, it reveals how "adult" the world was in which Paul lived. Despite the naïve relation, there is a matter-of-fact quality to the events, a reflection perhaps of Paul's feeling that the world was, in fact, a rather ghastly place in which unrestrained anarchy reigned. It is also interesting to note that all of these fabulous adventures (with numerous side plots omitted) take place over a three-year period. Marjorie, therefore, is really only three, but thanks to the "postage hypodermic" has become thirty-one by the time Bluey Dozlen is born. Paul's invention of the "postage hypodermic" no doubt reflected his own desire to grow up more quickly, to be less dependent on irrational adults.

But the narrative does not end here. Indeed, these events only pave the way for the amazing series of episodes recounted in the tales of Bluey Laber Dozlen, who sets sail to begin a new life in a place called Wen Kroy (New York spelled backward). Nearly twenty-five years after writing the Bluey diaries, Paul published a small section of it in *View* magazine, under the title "Bluey: Pages from an Imaginary Diary." *View*'s editor, Charles-Henri Ford, introduced the piece to his readers with the following preamble:

This *chef d'oeuvre* of the primitive style was created by its author at the age of nine. For pure comedy, dramatic tension, and harmonic development of theme, it seems unequalled by any other work by a writer of the same age, and needless to say, is far more persuasive than the writing of most adults.

Ford might have also mentioned that the style was decidedly (albeit inadvertently) surrealistic. Irrational juxtaposition, arresting imagery, comic incongruity—in short, the trademarks of the surrealist style—are all present in "Bluey." But then, readers of *View* would have not needed this pointed out to them, as the review's contributors included André Breton, Marcel Duchamp, Max Ernst, René Magritte, André Masson, Pablo Picasso, and Salvador Dalí, among the better-known surrealists.

The story essentially follows Bluey through a series of up-and-down escapades: numerous illnesses, two love affairs, a gigantic snowstorm, and near starvation. In addition to the "adult" themes, though, many elements of Paul's childhood are also present: frequent illness (mostly pneumonia—there's no Green Horror here); irrational behavior on the part of adults, including frequent fighting and bickering; escape to the nearly idyllic countryside; fear of robbers; and admiration for flashy objects (Bluey buys a Pierce Arrow, Packard, and an airplane). Significantly missing, as in the earlier narrative, are children, the only mention being in the following entries:

> [Feb.] 21. It starts snowing again. 34 degrees. Bluey wants a child.

> [Feb.] 22. Henry says they cannot have a child until they get married. 31 degrees.

Throughout "Bluey" there is great attention to small detail. We get a continual running commentary, for instance, on the temperature and the amount of snow, which eventually reaches 201 feet. Nearly every entry, in fact, gives a brief weather report, which often seems of as much, or even more, significance than the events. Although "Bluey" continues the saga begun in the earlier notebooks, it is tighter, less fantastic than the entries made the year or so before. More of Paul's daily reality seems to have crept into the "Bluey" pages too. The preponderance of illness and death is no doubt due, in part, to the very real illnesses and deaths that surrounded Paul during the time of its composition. Somewhat prior to beginning the work, his Aunt Adelaide had died of influenza and his Aunt Emma had spent a long period of convalescence in the Bowles household. During the actual writing of the piece his father and maternal grandparents had all come down with serious cases of pneumonia. The other major theme in "Bluey" is the difficulty of relationships between the sexes. Paul needed only to listen to the bickering of his mother and father to realize that marriage was not necessarily a state of bliss.

Aside from the imaginary diaries, Paul also produced a daily "newspaper." Printed in pencil and crayon and issued in an edition of one copy, the paper was, like the diaries, fictional. A daily feature was a report made by the newspaper's "correspondents" on a long sea voyage. Aided by a loose-leaf atlas of the world, Paul charted the journey from port to port, island to island, country to country. The trip, it seems, was more of an excuse to study the maps—which Paul did for hours—than to recount startling adventures in exotic locales.

Another major project for Paul at the time was the creation (on paper) of a gigantic real estate development. This activity seems to have come out of his earlier preoccupation with place names, but is greater in scope and scale. Much of a small red notebook, which has survived the years, is filled with drawings of houses, to which Paul appended the price, location, and imaginary purchaser. Typical entries consist of a two-dimensional, but detailed drawing of a house, and underneath the picture, information like this:

Pinetops Ave 514 to 523 West
    1,0,000,000 Dollar House

Land 1,000 Acres
Money 1,0,000,000

Also included in the journal are a detailed map of the fictional Wen Kroy and a list of addresses; various financial entries in ledger fashion; a list of holidays, among them Candy Day, Clock Day, and Mountain Day; and a poem entitled "In the Pickled Woods":

Oh Do you know? I saw
            a lovely Plan—
Plant I mean. It had the
beautifulest Pink blosse—Blossems,
Did you know that

CHOREZ [Chorus]
I had a sour walk
in the pickled woods
in the bitter town.

At the end of the diary is a detailed index that gives page numbers for the various entries.

All of this creative work had to be done on the sly. Indeed, such activities were subject to total disapproval by his father. One morning in July, probably when Paul was about eight years old, his father surprised him in the act of drawing houses. Initially angered because Paul had locked his bedroom door, Claude then proceeded to interrogate his son about what he was doing. When Paul informed him that he had locked the door because he didn't believe that his father would approve of his drawing before breakfast, Claude became enraged at what to him seemed Paul's utter impertinence. Seizing his son, he began to spank him relentlessly for several minutes, shouting repeatedly, "Had enough?" As Paul refused to reply, the spanking continued. Finally Claude stopped, demanding that Paul hand over all of his notebooks. Tucking them under his arm, his father carried them downstairs. Later that day Paul learned from Rena that he was to be deprived of them for two months, "the shortest sentence" his mother could obtain. "I was considerably relieved, having expected them to be destroyed once and for all. I also felt stronger, because I knew that no matter what physical violence was done to me, I would not have to cry; it was something I had not realized until that day."

Claude's violent reaction, far out of proportion to the provocation, suggests that he was responding not just to the incident, but to what it represented: Paul's refusal to acknowledge Claude's authority over his son's artistic activities. At his father's insistence, Claude had reluctantly stifled his own desire to become a violinist, and had even suffered a nervous breakdown in the process. Given his frustration at having been denied a creative career as a young man, it appears quite possible that the true focus of his wrath was Paul's obstinacy in continuing to create, in not allowing himself to be thwarted as Claude had been. In a sense, Paul was a victim of displaced rage, which was actually directed at Frederick Bowles (whose name, coincidentally, the young Paul Frederic bore, even though he had been named for his maternal uncle). But because the child proved to be stronger willed than Claude had been, the situation ultimately only culminated in increased frustration on the father's part and engendered further animosity in his son: "This was the only time my father beat me. It began a new stage in the development of hostilities between us. I vowed to devote my life to his destruction, even though it meant my own—an infantile conceit, but one which continued to preoccupy me for many years."

How long is "many years"? It is impossible to say. But even in 1957 the childhood anger and emotion were close enough to Paul that he could infuse a short story with them. "The Frozen Fields" is a vivid portrayal of a tyrannizing father and a precocious son. The story is about a Christmas visit by six-year-old Donald and his parents to his grandparents' farm. Although the gathering begins as a happy one, by the end of the story the family unity has been ripped asunder. The main culprit, predictably, is Donald's father. After a day of receiving a mixture of warm approbation from his relatives and strong disapproval from his father, Donald is trying to go to sleep:

> On his way through the borderlands of consciousness he had a fantasy. From the mountain behind the farm, running silently over the icy crust of the snow, leaping over the rocks and bushes, came a wolf. He was running toward the farm. When he got there he would look through the windows until he found the dining-room where the grownups were sitting around the big table. Donald shuddered when he saw his eyes in the dark through the glass. And now, calculating every moment perfectly, the wolf sprang, smashing the panes, and seized Donald's father by the throat. In an instant, before anyone could move or cry out, he was gone again with his prey still between his jaws, his head turned sideways as he dragged the limp form swiftly over the surface of the snow.

Later on, Donald accompanies his uncle on an excursion to the hen house but is forced back by his father who challenges him to a snowball-throwing contest. Ever mindful of the possibility of wolves, Donald refuses to engage in the competition. For refusing to obey, his father pushes him to the ground and rubs snow in his face, finishing up by pushing handfuls of it down his back. Like Paul, Donald holds back his tears. Writes Bowles:

> Donald moved forward, looking at the white road in front of him, his mind empty of thoughts. An unfamiliar feeling had come to him: he was not sorry for himself for being wet and cold, or even resentful at having been mistreated. He felt detached; it was an agreeable, almost voluptuous sensation which he accepted without understanding or questioning it.

The story concludes this way:

> When she had left him, he lay in the dark listening to the sound of the fine snow as the wind drove it against the panes. The wolf was out there in the night, running along paths that no one had ever seen, down the hill and across the meadow, stopping to drink at a deep place in the brook where the ice had not formed. The stiff hairs of his coat had caught the snow; he shook himself and climbed up the bank to where Donald sat waiting for him. Then he lay down beside him, putting his heavy head in Donald's lap. Donald leaned over and buried his face in the shaggy fur of his scruff. After a while they both got up and began to run together, faster and faster, across the fields.

Although the account is fiction, the emotions are not. In these brief passages the adult Bowles is describing how young Paul was not only systematically and irrationally persecuted by his father, but also how he managed to cope with it through entrance into the realm of the imagination. The image of the wolf is a powerful one, representing an external force, also irrational, but a force far greater than that of his father. It also profoundly illustrates the powerlessness of the child against the menacing adult. No allies exist in the adult world; despite the understanding and sympathy of his mother and other relatives, the young Donald clearly realizes that they are not powerful or persuasive enough to triumph over his father. Only an impossible creature from fantasy can actually deliver him from the clutches of tyranny.

"The Frozen Fields" also contains other characters and details drawn from life. The most striking is the way in which the family members relate to one another. Initially, the adults allow superficial politeness to mask thinly an extraordinary amount of tension. After being together a while, however, the sub-rosa feelings break through the surface in quiet explosions of denunciation, anger, and anxiety, only to recede again into a false calm.

Donald's problem with his father is not the only matter of concern for the family, though. There is also the "problem" of Uncle Ivor's understated, but clearly homosexual relationship with Mr. Gordon, who also comes to the Christmas gathering along with Ivor's wife, Louisa. While the other relatives remark on how terrible it is ("I don't see how Louisa stands it"), there is no direct confrontation. Here, too, there is a parallel with Paul's own family, who apparently never publicly acknowledged that Rena's sister, Emma, was married to a homosexual, Guy Ross.

Early in 1921 Paul was sent to Springfield, Massachusetts, as his father had come down with a severe case of pneumonia. The house having been turned into something like a hospital, with nurses and the doctor coming and going, Paul's mother thought it best to get him "out of the way." Paul, of course, leaped at the opportunity to travel all by himself to his grandparents, the first time he had ever been allowed to make a visit on his own: "The idea of an indeterminate stretch of freedom ahead was intoxicating. I saw that life is potentially pleasant, and gained great respect for the unforeseen." The idea of making the trek unaccompanied also delighted him. Within two weeks of arriving at Happy Hollow Farm, however, both of his grandparents had also come down with pneumonia. He was, therefore, sent to nearby Northampton, Massachusetts, where Emma and Guy lived.

This second removal turned out to be full of even greater excitement and "unforeseen" events. First, Paul discovered that although his aunt and uncle lived in the same apartment building, they occupied separate apartments, an arrangement that struck Paul as being a bit odd. Second, it was decided that he should stay with Guy instead of Emma, an arrangement that did not displease him in the least, as he found his uncle a rather fascinating and unusual character, or as Bowles put it, "a novelty." Guy's apartment was filled with Oriental decor, particularly with a great number of incense burners in the shape of bronze dragons and Buddhas. Uncle Guy, for his part, wore Japanese kimonos while lounging around the house and had an abundant supply of Sax

Rohmer novels, which Paul proceeded to devour, enjoying them with a conspirator's glee. In addition, each afternoon Paul was taken to the movies—a tremendous and heretofore largely prohibited thrill.

There were also visits to the shop of a mysterious Mr. Bistany, a friend of Uncle Guy's. To Paul, Mr. Bistany's "oriental store" was a source of wonder, filled with Turkish rugs and also heavily perfumed with incense. Mr. Bistany insisted on giving a small gift to Paul each time he visited. Uncle Guy, in turn, would give back the gift, at which point the two would become engaged in argument, much to Paul's embarrassment. Finally, Guy stopped bringing Paul with him to the shop.

Being unused to dealing with children, Guy simply treated Paul as an equal. As a result, Paul regarded his uncle as a friend, a true ally. Things changed, however, when Guy decided one Saturday night to give a party in Emma's apartment. Paul was told to go to bed early and to stay behind in his room. Annoyed that suddenly he was being treated like a child, he went to his aunt's apartment, quietly opened the door, and peeked in. In the few seconds before a hand clutched his shoulder and spun him around, he glimpsed a crowded room with "pretty young men dancing together." The hand belonged to Uncle Guy and he was furious. He took Paul back to his own apartment and locked him in.

Paul felt betrayed: in the end Guy was "like all the others." For Paul, there seemed nothing unusual about men dancing together. What stood out in his mind was that he was being prevented from joining in on the celebration. In a rage, he smashed his fist into a large photograph of a girl that hung above the bed. Somewhat satisfied that he had gotten even, he fell asleep, heedless of his bleeding knuckles. The next morning, he confessed his crime to his uncle, offering to pay for new glass. Instead of being angry, Guy simply smiled. The response was quite disconcerting to Paul, who was more accustomed to anger. Relations restored, Paul never mentioned the party to anyone. A short time after this incident, Rena summoned Paul back to New York, and although he wrote her a pleading letter to allow him to stay longer, permission was not granted.

Back in Jamaica, with Claude recovered, life was decidedly less interesting. The major event of the year was that Paul was promoted from fourth grade to sixth grade. This placed Paul two years ahead of where he would normally have been, but by this time he was becoming accustomed to being "smart" and took the advancement in stride.

The following year the Bowleses moved again, this time to their own house at 34 Terrace Avenue, just a few blocks from the house on De Grauw. The new home was a great deal more spacious, necessitating numerous furniture purchases. As before, Paul had a room on the second floor, but in addition, had the run of the largely unfinished third floor.

From all indications, Paul was at this time learning to straddle several worlds simultaneously. Despite his precociousness and involvement with the world of adults, he was also becoming an active participant in normal boyhood activities. As usual, for young men, he was even called upon to prove his "boyhood" at about this time. The proof came in the form of a fight. Although not new to childhood violence, having often been a victim of bigger boys, Paul was decidedly uninterested in fighting; his involvement was strictly limited to a few feeble gestures of defense. One winter day, probably around 1922, however, Paul was finally forced to respond to the taunts of the local bully, who had approached him while he was shoveling snow and named off a great number of horrible things he could do to him. Entering the house, Paul expressed his anger to his grandmother Winnewisser. She responded by saying that she would give him a dollar if he went back outside and beat up Buddy the bully. Astonished, Paul at first protested, saying he didn't know how to fight, but finally decided to give it a try. Approaching Buddy, he gave no warning of his intent, but simply leaped upon him, throwing him to the ground. After a few minutes of intense choking and pummeling, Paul banged his opponent's head against the ground and let him go. Buddy lay in the snow in a daze. Paul walked back into the house and collected his dollar; Buddy staggered off to lick his wounds.

Probably the most important event for Paul, though, during his first year in the new house was an experience with psychic phenomena. Following upon the heels of a burglary in which all of his gold cuff links and a treasured gold watch were stolen, Paul dreamed that he was in the living room staring at the curtains. Upon pulling them back he noticed the window broken and the screen cut. At that moment he realized that he had been discovered, but before he could escape, a hand slipped between the curtains, the lights went out, and he found himself being strangled. This awakened him.

Needing to put his mind at rest, he went downstairs and examined the window. He was shocked to see that there had indeed been a second burglary attempt. But even more disturbing, the window was broken and the screen cut in precisely the same manner as in his dream. The experience remained with Paul as a vivid indicator that the universe was not as knowable as he had assumed. Or as he put it in his autobiography: "For me it was an unsettling experience and one that temporarily shook my stubborn faith in a rationally motivated cosmos."

Among the more immediate consequences of the incident was a poem entitled "Air," one of Paul's earliest uses of the unconscious for the purposes of literary creation:

> At night, when all is still,
> When all are entombed in slumber,
> I wake, and glide to the window.
> The window, my sweet window.
> The heavy silk curtain is rustling
> Rustling with sad, sickening whir.
> It must be pulled back—it must be pulled back—
> I am smothering, choking, gasping—
> Gasping for air.
> I must pull and push and rip and tear—
> At last! Ah! Ah! My sweet, sweet air!

Paul was also busy working on fiction at about this same time, embarking on writing a series of "long melodramatic" stories with titles such as "Their Just Desserts" and "A Cry in the Fog." One day, while in the seventh grade, he took one to school and deposited it on his teacher's desk. Mrs. Woodson, obviously impressed, asked Paul to read a portion in class; after two or three weeks, the supply of stories still not exhausted (mainly due to constant writing each night), Mrs. Woodson suggested that he conduct his readings after school, with attendance optional. Apparently the tales were of such interest to his classmates that most of the students remained after the 3:00 dismissal to hear the next installment. Although Paul had long paraded his works before receptive adult audiences, this was the first time he had exposed his creative writing to his peers.

The readings would no doubt have continued for the entire year, had it not been for an incident that incurred Mrs. Woodson's disapproval: Paul remarked to some of his friends that one of the girls in the class had a mustache between her legs. The offending statement was promptly reported to Mrs. Woodson, who kept Paul after school to discuss the matter. Upon being questioned about why he would say such a thing, Paul had no answer. His bewilderment was not feigned, for he was in truth ignorant, believing indeed that both sexes were anatomically identical (a perception he held until studying biology in high school). Finally, getting nowhere with her inquisition, Mrs. Woodson dismissed Paul, simply saying that she had expected better of him. Future readings were canceled.

In January 1924 Paul graduated from the Model School. The previous summer, he had spent time in Exeter, New Hampshire, with his great-uncle and -aunt, Edward and Jen Green. Uncle Edward proudly showed Paul around Phillips Exeter Academy, located across the street from his house. Much to the dismay of his mother and uncle, Paul was not at all interested in attending the school. Or as he remarked later, "I could not summon any spark of enthusiasm at the prospect of spending the next four years in such a place. I suspected that attending classes there would be like being in church." His mother persisted, responding simply: "Well, you're going." His father, however, balked at the idea, claiming that Exeter was a "snob factory." For once, Paul unexpectedly found his father on his side, and in the end he was enrolled at a public high school in Flushing, New York.

Going to school in Flushing demanded of Paul a daily one-and-a-half-hour trolley ride, which he spent reading and studying. He soon discovered, though, that high school demanded much more of him than grammar school had. Latin, algebra, and biology all presented their difficulties and required him to devote less time to "escaping reality" through his own creative pursuits. Surprisingly, he made the transition to scholastic engagement rather easily. Scholarly by nature, happy in study, he quickly became engaged in the day-to-day business of attending high school. He also began to read beyond the curriculum.

One of these readings was Arthur Waley's *A Hundred and Seventy*

Chinese Poems, published in 1923 in a Knopf "popular edition."
Paul bought it shortly after its appearance, the first book of poetry
he had ever purchased himself. It had a tremendous impact on
him:

> Poetry had never interested me; in school I had been made to memo-
> rize a bit of verse by Bryant or Whittier or Longfellow, and then as
> soon as possible, I had forgotten it. Waley's compact little pellets,
> however, suggested the existence of a whole series of other purposes
> for which the poetic process could be used. I began to look at the
> real world around me with the idea of defining it in as few words as
> possible. In the middle of doing my homework I would stop and
> tackle the problem of foghorns . . . on Long Island Sound or the
> poplars rustling outside my windows.

A small, carefully handwritten book of poems survives from
these years. Entitled *Air to the Sea,* and containing poems written
between 1922 and 1927, the volume includes numerous poems
reflecting Waley's influence: economy of expression, repetition of
phrases, often with a slight but key variation, and the poetic defini-
tion of nature.

In *Without Stopping,* Bowles commented at length on how the
discovery of Chinese poetry was an integral part of a rather peculiar "mental formation":

> When I had kept the imaginary diaries and printed the daily newspa-
> per, I had thought of myself as a registering consciousness and no
> more. My nonexistence was a *sine qua non* for the validity of the
> invented cosmos. Now with the poetic definitions it was very much
> the same psychic mechanism at work. I received and recorded them;
> others were people and had "lives." Perhaps two years later I found
> an even more satisfactory way of not existing as myself and thus
> being able to go on functioning; this was a fantasy in which the entire
> unrolling of events as I experienced them was the invention of a vast
> telekinetic sending station. Whatever I saw or heard was simulta-
> neously being experienced by millions of enthralled viewers. They
> did not see me or know that I existed, but they saw through my eyes.
> This method enabled me to view, rather than participate in, my own
> existence.

Viewing rather than participating in one's own existence is an
extraordinary concept, for not only does it allow for aloofness, it

also implies an essential detachment and estrangement from one's own life. For young Paul, the universe consisted overwhelmingly of a conflict between the inner self, the creative force behind the stories, poems, and music, and the outer self, the mask worn while operating in the world. The Paul who lived in the world, went to school, did homework, and Fletcherized at his parents' table was only a facade protecting a hidden identity, one allied to an infinite cosmos that stretched far beyond the walls on Terrace Avenue.

CHAPTER 3

T HE BEGINNING of 1924 saw not only Paul's graduation from the Model School, but also the death of Grandmother Winnewisser. This was the second death for Paul of a family member, his Aunt Adelaide having died five years earlier. This time no one attempted to hide the death from him, but little time was allowed for grieving or reflection, either. After Rena had read out the telegram sent by her father, and the news briefly digested, Claude simply told Paul to go upstairs and do his homework. As when Aunt Adelaide died, Paul was left on his own to sort out his emotions.

Another couple of incidents stood out for Paul that year. One was the discovery in biology class that men and women had sex differences. Paul deduced this fact from his studies, made in class, on the reproductive systems of mice. When he asked his teacher whether the same differences were found in humans, the class broke into snickers and Miss Vickers snapped, "That's enough out of you." This was all the proof he needed.

The second event was on a psychological level. One summer evening he decided to go down to Roth's soda fountain to have something to drink. But upon reaching the shop, he was overtaken by a compulsive desire. "As I pushed open the screen door, something happened to me," wrote Bowles. "The best way of describing it is to say that the connection between me and my body was instantaneously severed." Rather than being able to go in and sit down at the fountain, he simply walked through the store and out the other side. Twice more he repeated this circular course until he was finally snapped back to reality by the sight of his parents' car approaching in the distance. Not being able to understand what had happened to him, he felt he could not talk about it, but added that "the experience frightened me, and I suspected that if I were to put it into words, it would somehow become more threatening and true." Although a psychoanalyst might be inclined to describe such behavior as schizophrenic dissociation, for Paul it simply served as an indication that he was not totally in control of his own self, or of his own actions. Eventually he connected this experience with the dream of the broken window. As a result, this incident was probably more bothersome than it would ordinarily have been, for it indicated to him that despite his attempts to rationalize his existence, the universe also had its own irrational aspects. This knowledge would stay with him; the power of the unconscious had manifested itself as an enormous force to be reckoned with.

When Paul was very young, he was introduced to the Hoagland sisters—Anna, Jane, and Sue—who, during the summer, lived at Glenora and were longtime neighbors of Paul's grandparents. The rest of the year they occupied a large house in Brooklyn. From about the time Paul was ten he was allowed occasional weekend visits to their home in the city, which delighted him, as they often took Paul to the movies, to a concert at the Academy of Music, or to the Brooklyn Museum of Art. Artistically inclined themselves, they were quite sympathetic to Paul's creative projects and welcomed his visits as much as he enjoyed visiting them. During the summer, Paul also managed to spend a considerable amount of time at their Glenora house, called Lasata. It was through them, in the summer of 1925, that Paul met Mary Crouch.

Half Cree Indian, with black hair, a husky voice and an imperious manner, Mrs. Crouch, as Paul always referred to her, fascinated him. She became even more interesting when she was dubbed by his grandfather as an "immoral woman" and by his grandmother as "an unscrupulous adventuress" who "had a stranglehold on poor Sue." These comments seem to have been earned largely because Mrs. Crouch had spent much time abroad—in France, England, and South Africa—and because she smoked and drank and allowed her children, both in their late-teens, to do so as well.

Despite the Bowleses' disapproval, Paul was not prohibited from visiting; indeed, he began to spend more and more time at Lasata, basking in the liberal atmosphere and reading out loud to his hostesses a group of crime stories, "The Snake-Woman Series," that he was writing at the time. In each tale, someone died, possibly of natural causes, possibly not—it was left to the reader to determine. Present, however, at the scene of each crime was a mysterious woman named Volga Merna, who presumably had something to do with the death.

In addition to the Hoaglands and Mrs. Crouch, there was also his Aunt Mary, the sister of his maternal grandmother. Since Paul's early childhood, Aunt Mary had always struck him as being one of the more interesting members of the family. Part of this allure came from her interest in theosophy, particularly in Krishnamurti, and in spiritualism. The spiritualist practice caught Paul's attention, as it involved burning incense with the initials HPB, Helena Petrovna Blavatsky, whom Aunt Mary had known. According to his aunt, the smoke from the incense cubes could induce a trancelike state in the believers. She lived alone in an old house, called Holden Hall, in Watkins Glen, New York, near her brother Charles, also a practitioner. The house itself, a rambling old place built by her grandfather, had high ceilings and a mysterious tower room, used for meditation, which easily conjured up in Paul's mind the realm of the spirits. When Paul was fourteen, Mary invited him and his cousin Elizabeth, who was seventeen, to spend several weeks with her at Holden Hall. Paul was extremely pleased, as he was quite fond of spending time in the mysterious house with both Mary and Elizabeth. He particularly held Elizabeth in high regard, as she always took him seriously and treated him with respect.

On this occasion, however, things were different. One night, shortly after his arrival, he overheard Mary and Elizabeth conversing in the library. They were talking about him. Fragments of the conversation drifted from the room; one phrase particularly disturbed him. Said Aunt Mary: "Paul has all the earmarks of a boy who has started on the downward path." The next morning he asked Elizabeth what Aunt Mary had meant. She replied: "She thinks you have the wrong friends." Paul was astonished, as he didn't believe himself to have any friends. He was further upset because he felt that he was being judged on who he was rather than on anything he had done.

As illustrated by the anecdote, Paul, despite his obvious attempts to detach himself from the family, still very much wanted to be accepted by them, at least by those whom he felt should understand him. Aunt Mary's pronouncement filled him with dread: already he was less than confident that he was or could be an acceptable member of society. It was one thing to hide his self from his father, another to have his very identity questioned by someone he trusted.

This notion of something being wrong at the core of his being stayed with Paul for at least a few more years. In a poem written in early December 1927, Paul expressed the idea this way:

> A slowness of water delayed by centuries
> Could not flow less meaninglessly
> As do my fast brass words ring turbid.
> Shall this by what all I were
> Have meaning as deep as they wish?
> For they have lived more years than I
> And know they how to search.
> Ah, yes, says wisdom, it is for such smut
> That you must learn to seek
> For a soul is not a soul sans it have
> a dark recess
> Wherein lie the worms of ruin.

It is a concept that would never entirely disappear, but in the young man's mind it was an overpowering idea, for he truly believed that somewhere deep inside his own self lurked demons. In some ways, he would spend the rest of his life transforming the demons into art, creating fiction as a way of dealing with fear; or as he put it sixty years later: "Writing about such things is a way of keeping the evil outside, away from me." At this point, though, he was still engaged in the continual struggle to keep the darkness from surfacing.

In the spring of 1925, tired of the long trolley ride to Flushing, Paul decided to enroll at nearby Jamaica High School. When he informed his parents, his father's only comment was simply: "I know why he wants to change schools. Because here they don't know yet what a damned fool he is." At Jamaica High, Paul actually began to like school. Up until then he had tolerated it as another nuisance that had to be coped with, and while he had certainly done exceptionally well in his studies, it was always his own private work that had far greater appeal. But at Jamaica High School, the two worlds began to come together. Joining the school magazine, *The Oracle,* during his first term, he was quickly appointed humor editor. His chief task was to find and solicit jokes, droll stories, and nonsense rhymes to print in the magazine. Although the post was not of particular interest to him, he took the position as a way of working up to the editorial job he truly coveted, that of poetry editor.

During this time Paul continued to explore the bookshops and expand his reading in several directions. Among his major discoveries was the work of the English writer Arthur Machen. Although now largely forgotten, Machen had a brief flurry of fame and popularity in the 1920s, when Knopf began to bring out his works in the United States. It was these editions that Paul bought and devoured. Machen's specialty was psychological horror, but he also published a number of quest-inspired novels and translations, chief of which was Casanova's *Memoirs.* Above all else, Machen was a decadent and his books were often roundly condemned as "unwholesome," "unnatural" and, not surprisingly, "diabolical"— just the sort of publicity to attract a host of readers. To the imaginative Paul, they represented an extraordinary departure from the normal schoolboy novels.

They helped, as well, to underscore his profound belief in the soul with its dark recess. Standing between Poe and Lovecraft, Machen's world is sinister and labyrinthine, filled with secret codes, necromancy, alchemy, torture, terror, and death. The books would remain in Paul's memory for a long time, with the themes markedly re-echoing in some of his later fiction.

Even at fourteen or fifteen, however, there were many elements with which Paul could strongly identify. First were the details of Machen's life, itself. The following passage from the first part of Machen's autobiography, *Far Off Things,* must have resonated in Paul's head:

> I was an only child. Add to this statement that I had no little cousins available as play-fellows . . . that it was only by the merest chance and on the rarest occasions that I ever saw any children at all. . . . I grew up, therefore, all alone so far as other children were concerned, and though I went to school, school did not seem to make much difference to my habit of mind. . . . I came back, then, again and again to solitude. . . . I loved to be by myself, with unlim-

ited leisure for mooning and loafing and roaming and wandering from lane to lane, from wood to wood. . . . Wondering at these things, I never ceased to wonder.

The novels also provided points of identification. *The Secret Glory,* for example, tells the tale of Ambrose Meyrick, a sensitive, intelligent boy and a Poe devotee. Orphaned at an early age, he is sent to study at an English boarding school, where his uncle, the sadistic Mr. Horbury, is headmaster. At first brutally mistreated by both Mr. Horbury and his schoolmates, Meyrick eventually finds a way to fend off his persecutors through a combination of stratagems: he learns to fight and to excel at both academics and sports, therefore putting himself beyond reproach. But this is, of course, simply a front, a sham played out in order to survive the indignities of his daily existence. Thus, on the eve of graduation, with the expectations for his success high, he runs off to London. There he takes up with a chambermaid, writes an obscene, vilifying letter in Rabelaisian French to Mr. Horbury, and travels to the Continent. He finally ends up in Kevir, Turkey, where, having become a mystical Christian, he is captured by the Turks or Kurds (it isn't clear which) and crucified for his faith. Although the book rambles considerably and the ending is just plain silly, it is clear why Paul felt drawn to the novel.

Not only did Paul glean these notes of recognition from Machen, but the themes of much of Machen's other fiction, with their emphasis on mystery, the supernatural, and the unconscious, also found a receptive audience in Paul. Machen's novella, *The Terror,* for instance, deals with a series of unsolved murders, all seemingly impossible to decipher as to either the mode of death or the motive for the killings, a plot not terribly unlike Paul's "Snake-Woman Series." Unlike Paul's stories, however, Machen's story has an eventual denouement: the beasts have revolted against mankind, killing their supposed masters in a variety of ingenious and often horrible ways.

Paul also discovered Gide that year via the Knopf edition of *The Vatican Swindle* (subsequently retitled *Lafcadio's Adventures*). What primarily appealed to Paul was Lafcadio's "gratuitous act," the murder of a stranger for no purpose. It was not the murder itself that was so intriguing, but the amorality embodied in the act and

Lafcadio's ability, so impossible and foreign to Paul at that time, to translate his dark imaginings into action; or as Gide, through Lafcadio's voice, puts it:

> It's not about events that I'm so curious, but about myself. Many think they are capable of anything, but pull back at the last minute . . . There is such a distance between the imagination and the act . . . And no more right to take back one's move than at chess. Bah! If all the risks were known, the game would lose its interest.

Thus in Machen and Gide, Paul began to find writers who expressed his own concerns, who gave form to the dichotomy between his inner and outer self. And like Gide and Machen, Paul was beginning to find an exit through words.

There was also *The New Masses*. When it started in May 1926 under the guidance of Michael Gold, the monthly magazine was a mix of intellectual Marxism, revolutionary idealism, leftist interpretation, and cultural criticism, as well as "progressive" art and literature. It also represented the spirit of revolt, albeit in a different way from Gide or Machen. One day Paul brought a copy of the magazine to school and passed it around. Suddenly, after class, a fellow student named Goldberg informed Paul that *The New Masses* was not for him, the implication being that a thoroughly middle-class suburban WASP, the son of a dentist, could never possibly understand the proletarian struggle. Paul, as he did not associate himself with his origins, was mystified. For months, he "replayed the scene," never quite comprehending Goldberg's point.

Goldberg's dismissal of Paul mirrored Paul's rejection of most of his peers. While he generally got on well enough with his classmates, he felt himself to be more "advanced" than the majority. Indeed, most of his social life took place outside of school, in the company of usually much older acquaintances. This became even more pronounced when, at about this time, he began to explore Greenwich Village. Jane Hoagland, in particular, who knew a number of painters, poets, and intellectuals, would often take Paul around to visit the "Bohemians" in their "studios." One day in 1926, Miss Jane, as Paul always called her, took him to see Buckminster Fuller, who had just designed his Dymaxion house, of which an enormous model stood in the center of the room. A polyhedron that rotated on its axis so as to face any direction desired, the Dymaxion house totally intrigued Paul. Arriving back home, he began enthusiastically to describe Fuller and his house to his parents, emphasizing Fuller's genius. Characteristically, his parents were skeptical, his mother exclaiming that she would want no part of a house whose walls could become transparent. His father, sure that the inventor was not American, was taken aback when Paul informed him that the genius's name was Fuller. "What's in a name?" he retorted, obviously bothered.

Despite his enthusiasm for Fuller, Paul failed geometry. It seemed no matter how much he studied, he simply couldn't grasp the concepts. Conversely, however, he excelled in English, history, and French; as with many students it was probably more a matter of interest than ability. His study of French also got an extra boost about that time through his friendship with a young French teacher who lived near Paul on Long Island and taught high school in New York, Daniel Burns. He first met Burns through the Hoaglands, but soon the two began to develop a close friendship of their own. Burns was about ten years older than Paul. About six feet tall, round but not fat, urbane and witty, "continental" in his manners and mannerisms, with refined, almost "gay" speech (he was in fact homosexual), Burns quickly became Paul's mentor. He began to introduce Paul to a greater variety of French literature than was being studied in the high school curriculum and encouraged his creative efforts in music, writing, and drawing. For Paul, Burns seems to have represented the ideal father, a person he could talk with, get advice from, and from whom he could learn about the world. Burns spoke French fluently, had spent a considerable amount of time in France, and was eager to pass on his enthusiasm to Paul. Paul was enormously receptive. He began to read more and more French writers under Burns's tutelage and even attempted a few translations.

Not only was Paul expanding his knowledge of literature, but he was also broadening his musical awareness. Up until 1926, "serious" music, for him, had largely meant music written well before the twentieth century. Both his own studies and the concerts he had begun to attend regularly on Saturdays of the New York Philharmonic consisted largely of the standard repertoire, in particular nineteenth-century composers. Then one Saturday, the twentieth century arrived in the form of Stravinsky's *Firebird.* From the opening strains, Paul was mesmerized, astonished that an orchestra could produce such sounds. By this time he had acquired his own phonograph, and so on the way home he stopped into a record store and bought Victor's new release, on two 12-inch discs, of Stravinsky's ballet.

Alone in his room, Paul played the piece over and over, although softly so as not to disturb his father. The more he listened, the more delighted he became by its extension of the musical idiom, by its ingenious echoes of late nineteenth-century tendencies made new through a distinctive use of rhythmic variation and harmony. Although Stravinsky composed the *Firebird* shortly before Paul was born, for the boy from Jamaica it clearly represented absolute modernity. For the first time Paul became aware that music, paralleling art and literature, was taking a radical new direction in the first quarter of the twentieth century.

A second awakening to modernism would come the next year, when Paul discovered the following notice in Genêt's (Janet Flanner's) "Paris Letter," in the April 30, 1927, issue of the *New Yorker:*

> *Transition,* the new magazine edited here by Elliot Paul and Eugène Jolas, in its initial number contains, if not a feast, some good food for thought, the tastiest plate being the German Carl Sternheim's "Busekow," an excellent story of an amorous Potsdammerplatz policeman—this in despite of excerpts from Ludwig Lewisohn's "the Defeated" and "Opening Pages of a Work in Progress" by James Joyce, which goes thus: "riverrun brings us back to Howth Castle & Environs."

This brief description was enough to cause Paul to wander up and down Sixth Avenue on his next visit to the orthodontist's in Manhattan until he finally managed to put his hands on a copy of *transition.*

> No publication had ever made such a profound impression on me. Quite apart from the frontal assault of Surrealism, the existence of which I had not even suspected, I loved its concise format, the strange muted colors of the soft paper they used as covers, and the fact that each page had to be cut with a paper knife. Above all, each

month when I bought the new issue, I had the illusion of being in Paris, for the feeling of the city I got from reading its pages coincided with my own idea of what Paris must be like, where the people were desperate but sophisticated, cynical but fanatically loyal to ideas. Paris was the center of all existence; I could feel its glow when I faced eastward as a Moslem feels the light from Mecca, and I knew that some day, with luck, I should go there and stand on the sacred spots.

transition was indeed an extraordinary magazine. Its regular contributors included a host of prominent avant-garde writers. Its mission was to serve as a "transition" between the United States and Europe, bringing American writers to the attention of Europeans and European writers (in usually splendid translations) to the attention of Americans.

Having been promoted to poetry editor at *The Oracle,* Paul wrote almost daily in its small office during free hours, exploring the surrealist technique of automatic writing much favored by *transition's* editors. According to André Breton, who first codified the method in his *Surrealist Manifesto* of 1924, automatic writing was writing without any conscious intervention on the part of the writer. Its value was to be found in its dredging up from the unconscious the pure elements of poetry, or as Breton put it, "indefinitely opening up that box of multiple depths that is called man." By late that spring, Paul mastered the craft to his satisfaction. He prepared a manuscript of these new poems, taking special care so as not to reveal his youthful authorship, and sent them to *transition.* At about the same time, Eugène Jolas was writing his own poetic manifesto, which read in part:

Lyric poetry must be a primitive explosion of the enchained impulses of man. It must be against nature, and in itself a force of subversion. I will even go so far to say that, in order to create the true state of the subconscious, from which all possibility of destruction really comes, a poem might, under certain conditions, become merely an a-logical complexity of sounds, if the inspiration be really a sincere one.

The poems of the young "automatic writer" crossed the desk of one of the most fervent proponents of this technique. Minds met.

In the March 1928 issue of *transition*, alongside the work of James Joyce, André Breton, Gertrude Stein, Paul Eluard, Allen Tate, Francis Picabia and others, appeared "Spire Song," a poem by a totally unknown writer—Paul Frederic Bowles. A note from Jolas, dated March 30, 1928, accompanied the complimentary copy of *transition* sent to Paul. It read: "We are using Let Us Deny in our next number due to appear in June. No. 12 contained your Spire Song." In fact, the next issue featured a Bowles prose poem, "Entity," instead of the promised "Let Us Deny."

"Spire Song" is a somewhat long lyric—forty-eight lines divided into six unequal sections. It is essentially a poem of outer and inner observations, in which natural elements—a corn field, a thicket, a hill, a grove—inspire metaphysical questioning and often absurd reflections. The poem owes much to Paul's recent discovery of surrealism, employing as it does certain surrealist conventions as irrational juxtapositioning and anthropomorphism in lines such as these:

> A fresh mist drowns plantlice
> as sprucetrees dribble resin.

"Spire Song" doesn't really mean anything; it simply exists as a series of alternating observations and conjurings, the poet using the natural setting to describe his own sense of entrapment and isolation:

> here in this grove
> no one shall hear us.
> Moss clings to my shoulders
> and we are locked up in here
> refusing to see past the thicket.

It is by no means a great poem, yet it is easy to see why Jolas would have liked it: it champions no cause other than that of poetry itself, is basically anti-nature, is fundamentally a poem of the subconscious, and although coming from an American, reads almost as if it were a French poem in translation. Just as Paul had imitated Waley, he was now imitating the surrealists. Seen through surrealist eyes, natural phenomena have been relegated to forming a backdrop against which the psychological concerns are played out. Bowles has employed psychological tension, possibly a natural result of allowing the unconscious "to dictate" the lines, to break through the surface, invade the placid natural universe.

"Entity," incorrectly titled "Enlily" in the *transition* table of contents, is even more in the subconscious and surrealist vein than "Spire Song." As such, it must have represented to Jolas the cutting edge of the new poetics. From the distance of sixty years, however, it appears more confused than confusing, a hodgepodge of imagery held together only by syntax:

> The intimacy of spirals has become stone to him. This is in reality only the last prayer urge. As it is, all the crimson of stamps has resolved into loops. These fold up and seek sounds beyond lime rinds.

It is evident from just these lines that what we have here is a complete disjointing of natural observation, irrational association having become the actual (and only definable) subject of the poem. It must be noted, though, that the imagery produced by the process is absolutely new, or as Jolas puts it, "sincere." Unlike "Spire Song," which occasionally sinks into ponderous and even clichéd tones, "Entity" continually manages to present one arresting image after another. As a piece of automatic writing it is enormously successful in its "a-logical complexity of sounds." As a poem, it must also be judged against the avant-garde work of its time. As such, it is nothing short of a triumph of experimental form.

Bowles recorded his own reaction to seeing his work in print for the first time in a major publication:

> I arrived home one afternoon to find that a small packet had arrived for me from Paris. I tore it open. It was a copy of *transition* 12, with my name among those on the cover. I had imagined the moment so many times that the reality was almost like a *déjà vu.* I jumped into the air and let out a shout of triumph. . . . My joy and excitement were such that I remember little else about the spring of 1928.
>
> For months afterward I had only to remind myself of this great stroke of luck, and I would feel a momentary surge of euphoria. Now

when I sent poems out, I could add a note about myself, with my *transition* pedigree. At no point did I ask myself whether or not I had anything to say which could be of interest to someone else. My desire was to impose my personality by any means available; I did not conceive of anything beyond that.

Although Paul did share his literary success with his mother, he did not show his father *transition.* Indeed, Claude only learned of it when a friend of his called him the following year and said, "Congratulations! Paul's got a very nice poem in this important magazine!" "What's that?" Claude said. The friend then asked, "Well, didn't he show it to you?"

Paul was no longer a high school student when his poems appeared in *transition,* as he had graduated in January of that year. In the year and a half preceding graduation, however, Paul managed to establish a local literary reputation. Every number of the high school magazine contains some of his work, and in the January 1928 *Oracle,* the last issue of the magazine in which Paul was involved, he figures quite prominently. Along with "Spire Song" and another poem entitled "Tailpiece," there are the following entries. The first describes his academic career:

Bowles, Paul. "This strange disease of modern life." Chairman Prophecy Committee; By the Way, Oracle; Poet's Corner, Oracle; Honor Roll; President of Kinspirits; Vice-President Alliance Française; Literary Society of Flushing High School.

Another mention of Paul is in the Prophecy Column, which he edited. The prophecy, apparently authored by Paul himself, reads as follows:

Paul Frederic Bowles, graduate of most of the colleges in the United States, is now appointed poet laureate and private secretary in the royal court of King Edward. The immediate reason for this honor, was his acclaim received at the first successful attempt to swim the Atlantic, under water. Emerging triumphant but dripping, on British soil, he was immediately presented at court where he recited to his Royal Majesty the famous "Night Song at Papua" [Paul's own poem]. It didn't take his Majesty long to decide that this was the man he had been waiting for. Lord Paul Frederic instructs the royal family in swimming during his spare time.

Finally, there is this entry under the class chart:

Paul Bowles: He Is / A day dreamer; He Thinks He Is / A poet; He'd Like to Be / A Futuristic artist; Always Seen With a dazed expression; Hobby / Literature.

On the eve of graduation, the main question confronting Paul was what he would do with his life. As he would not be able to enroll in a university until September, it was necessary for him to find something to do with himself during the intervening nine months. There was also the question of college itself: where would he go and what would he study when he got there? As usual, he received little support from his father on making either decision. Claude, feeling that Paul had no objectives to speak of, at least career objectives, was not eager to waste money on his son's education. At the same time, he was not interested in having Paul loaf around the house.

The college question resolved itself shortly before graduation. Predictably, Paul received advice from outside the family. On one of his occasional visits to Annie Carroll Moore at the New York Public Library, Paul broached the subject of college. She suggested the University of Virginia, a school that immediately found favor with Paul, as one of his literary idols, Poe, had gone there. Furthermore, it was away from the family. The combination of advice from a trusted ally and his own predilections resulted in his sending off to Charlottesville for an application. Even before it was received, he had announced to his family his firm intention to enroll at the University of Virginia in the fall. Claude opposed the idea; Rena approved. Both, however, were concerned about what Paul would do in the interim and took a "wait and see" attitude regarding the choice of a university.

A possible answer to the question of how to spend the nine months between January and September had begun to form in Paul's head well before graduation, but he said nothing about it until the end of his high school term was imminent. All his life Paul had drawn pictures, and during high school he had begun painting. Therefore, fancying himself a painter, as well as poet, pianist and composer, Paul began to investigate art schools in Manhattan. The Art Students League intimidated him, chiefly because of its "official-looking entrance." Other schools seemed drab and depressing. He finally settled on the School of Design and Liberal Arts, a school of only about a dozen students located on the top floor of an old brick building at 212 Central Park South.

Having decided definitely to attend art school, he reasoned that he would need some proof of his ability as an artist, not only to gain entrance to the school, but to use as an arguing point with his father. It was, therefore, to the Hoagland sisters that he went, bearing a group of his latest paintings. They found the work of interest, and to show their enthusiasm arranged for some friends to come over and examine the work of the budding young artist. Several responded and he managed to sell two or three paintings.

With this "commercial success" under his belt, and with art school lined up, Paul decided to make the announcement at home. Although his father demanded to know what "liberal arts" amounted to, and his mother was sure that all her son would learn there was "expressionism," Paul, nonetheless, was given the tuition money. Part of the reason for his father's acquiescence was that he did not have to foot the bill. According to Bowles, in fact, from this time on Claude did not contribute either to his educational expenses or to his support, feeling that it was a "waste" of money to educate his son to be a "well-rounded dilettante." It was, instead, Winnewisser money that would be used to support Paul, leaving his father free from financial involvement in his son's future.

In February, Paul began classes at the School of Design and Liberal Arts. At first, the instruction focused on drawing objects— pitchers, urns, cylinders—and then progressed to sketching plaster casts of the human body in order to familiarize the students with human anatomy. Soon, drawing was to be done from life. It was a rather extraordinary experience for Paul the day the first model arrived. Having never seen a naked body before, save his own, he was repelled by both the idea and the reality: "It had not occurred to me that human beings could look so repulsive. The women had three times too much flesh, and the men were covered with body hair." Although the exercise continued for several weeks, he never could quite overcome his disgust for the human form. Seeing only the grotesque aspects of the nude figure, he elected to paint only in blue, thus deliberately creating outlandish representations of the models.

Paul also tried his hand at abstract painting. In March of that year he executed ten color abstracts, in oil, about six by eight inches each, with the series title of "Worm in D." The one recognizable element in the paintings is the worm, identified as being in "Danger," "Delight," "Distress," "Dreams," "Disillusionment," "Disgrace," "Detroit," "Death," and "Damnation."

Paul did not achieve great success at art school. At the end of the four-month course, though, he did receive an award for "greatest output and originality." A bit mystified as to what the prize meant, but suspecting that it had been invented specifically for him, he decided to inquire of the director, Miss Weir, as to how such an honor had come to be bestowed on him. She confirmed his suspicions, telling him simply, "You had to have a prize, but I couldn't give it for quality."

One side benefit of attending the School of Design and Liberal Arts, however, was that Paul had his first taste of romance. The subject of his attention was an English girl, Peggy, who also attended the school, majoring in fashion design and layout. Paul thought her particularly beautiful but was not quite sure how to approach her as he had never before had a date. He overcame his shyness and awkwardness, however, and asked her out. She willingly accepted as the attraction was apparently mutual. Indeed, it is easy to see why she would have found her fellow art student physically desirable. Photos from the period show an exceedingly elegant and well-groomed young man with delicate features: a long, thin, perfectly shaped nose, small mouth with full lips, wavy blond hair always neatly coiffed, blue eyes bright and attentive. A cautious courtship ensued, revolving around a shared dinner or trip to the theater or movies. Although Peggy had her own apartment in Greenwich Village on the floor below her father's, the relationship appears to have been wholly platonic. If Paul stayed too late, Peggy's father appeared. If he got home too late, he met with his own parents' disapproval.

Reconstructing sexual attitudes from the distance of sixty years is at best a suspect enterprise, but it seems clear that at this stage in his life, Paul was simply not interested in sex, or was very likely even afraid of it. While it is evident that he enjoyed the conventions of dating—eating out, going to events about town, sitting up talking until the last train left for Jamaica—sexual involvement was not considered by him to be a part of the relationship. Despite his penchant for "bohemianism," he was not ready or willing to embrace its code of sexual license. Part of this reserve, no doubt, had to do with his own sense of propriety and with the conventions of the period. But there was something stronger than either of these explanations operating in his makeup. One of his closest friends from that time, Bruce Morrissette, seems to have the best clue regarding Paul's attitude toward sex during his late adolescence. "He was basically antisexual," says Morrissette. "Interested in people, yes, but not sexually. Never." Virgil Thomson, who met Paul a few years after his high school graduation, confirmed Morrissette's assessment: "Paul had a very low sex drive. It just wasn't important to him." At this point in his life Paul's relationships, not only with his English "girlfriend" but also with others, were apparently not sexually charged.

With art school finished, and with almost four months remaining before he had to report to Virginia, his father decided that it would be a good idea for Paul to get some practical experience working in the real world. Claude arranged a summer job for Paul at the Bank of the Manhattan Company, whose manager was one of his patients. Paul began work in the transit department; his primary duty consisted of adding up columns of numbers on the adding machine. Paul rather enjoyed it—the task was simple, and he liked earning his own money, which he salted away to spend once he got to Virginia. There were also occasional courier duties—carrying a briefcase of checks from his branch to the main branch—which took him away from his desk for as much time as he could get away with. Some twenty years later he would assign the same position to the protagonist of his novel *Let It Come Down*.

During that summer, Paul continued to write poetry, compose music, and paint. A sense of the person whom he thought himself to be and whom he was trying to become is revealed in a letter to Daniel Burns, then in Europe. Written on small sheets of white stationery printed with his name, the letter straddles the boundary between adolescence and adulthood. It begins without salutation or date:

Jesus lives and Greenwich Village is most fascinating in August. Suffer the little kids to come unto me and I went avant-hier to the

Fifth Avenue Playhouse to see The City Without Jews. M. Royé seems to be acquainted with you, of which I may add $3.49 at a bargain. Brass is more sufficient que Elinor Wylie. Of which Jennifer Lorn is exquisite, but of what avail to utter faint praise. All of her romances are exquisite. Mr. Hodge and Mr. Hazard. The Orphan Angel. As to this The Gateway to Life by Frank Thiess, The Magic Mountain and Children and Fools by Thomas Mann are some Germanic literature I have read recently.

Attempt, while you are in London, to purchase transition 13, which so far is unattainable here.

May I retract some? It is when one is sleepy that unintelligibility arrives. I had never realized it before. Drowsiness is exactly the same in my head as Fever, Delirium and Tipsiness. The last mentioned I have experienced but once, and I do not need to go through it again, as I can attain the same effect by staying up to one o'clock. And I am positive I should write the same in both cases. Only when mine soul is weighted with physical illnesses do I become pensive and conventional.

As far as I can see, I haven't said anything, and so I may as well lay this aside. Or perhaps you enjoy this pathological ramble? I always fancied you had a morbid side. If my whim was correct, you must certainly be interested in watching me stagger along like this. And so I shall prod myself a bit farther for your benefit.

Tell me all about England, for I am extraordinarily excited about it. I feel as though the United States were only a temporary exile and England my true home. Which in a way is idiocy and in a way is the truth.

From these first paragraphs of Paul's letter a number of interesting facts and themes emerge. First, there is the eclectic reading list, composed of popular romances and Thomas Mann, seemingly of equal interest and value. Second, there is the aspect of self-preoccupation, particularly with exploring the terrain of the creative consciousness. What we see in the middle paragraphs is that Paul is attempting to use certain altered states of consciousness—induced through drowsiness, fever, delirium, or drunkenness—as a method of entry into the creative process. Years later, he would become legendary for writing drug-inspired works, but the tendency was already present at the age of seventeen. It was almost as if such an extreme alteration from the normal experience of reality was necessary for him to feel free enough to create.

Two other aspects of Paul's character are also revealed in the letter: First, it is evident, through his obvious desire to be stylistically artistic, that he already envisions himself as a writer. Second, he is already feeling alienated from the United States. This is made most explicit in his statements about England being his "true home." This sensation is more than adolescent alienation or involvement with a romantic idea of the "grass being greener" in Europe. It is, in fact, the outgrowth of a profound sense of separateness from the world of his parents.

In another letter to Burns written that summer, Paul expounded further on the concept of "unintelligibility" and the creative process:

> My not imaginary illness having long ago passed over, I now feel able to write as unintelligibly as I want to. Unfortunately, I find it slightly less easy to be thus than I used to. Perhaps that is because I have not *thoroughly* recovered. N'est-ce pas correct? You never seemed to be able to understand that pure inspiration is bound to be unintelligible, and that until it is refined into something legible or intelligible it is worth understanding, but afterward it is as nothing. The great majority of persons insist upon their brainfoods being refined, and go so far as to claim that the pure inspiration is worth nothing until refined—that thoughts must be chained, and trained into the narrow passages which society has chosen to "understand." You can understand anything if you leave your mind free. From this it is clear that a geologist cannot go on a picnic without stuffed eggs. Nor can Buddha go into the mountains without his barometer.
>
> How sorry I am to hear you admit that you prefer stupidity to unintelligibility. One should not prefer stupidity to anything. And since I very seldom feel like writing samples of stupidity and very often feel like writing samples of unintelligibility, I fear either you or I is at a loss. I having the advantage, in that I'm writing the letter, you are the unlucky person, for I am going to make no attempt after this preliminary explanation to write stupidity or perhaps if one might state it more clearly I am not going to make no attempt not to write unintelligibly.

It is obvious from Paul's highly intelligible remarks that he saw his doctrine of "unintelligibility" as being an antidote to conventional thinking, as somehow more directly related to poetic inspiration. To some extent, this is the position of an adolescent "poseur"; it is also a result of his love affair with surrealism and automatic writing, an involvement that, as far as he is concerned, has already brought him international fame through his poems in *transition*. On a deeper level, though, it is an embrace of freedom, a movement away from the rigid authoritarianism personified by his father. In another section from the first letter quoted above, Paul elaborates on this sense of apartness, a state of being which he seems to have almost relished (a marked contrast from his reaction to the remark made years before by his Aunt Mary):

> The same two discouraging ladies who in 1927 informed me that I am less than an amoeba, this year decided that I am at the end of a civilization, that I epitomize a decayed civilization, in its last feeble flares to resurrect itself in the eyes of other civilizations. They maintained that all my paintings and music merely strengthen the case for them, and were representative of imminent death: the final false energy of the moribund. Their absurdities are really the only absurdities of other people I can bear, and probably I can bear those only because they pertain to me. (They have been reading Spengler.)

As September neared and departure for Charlottesville became imminent, Paul's excitement about being on his own mounted. He wrote to Burns, now in France, the following sequence of (rather unintelligible) anticipatory statements about Virginia:

> O girl of my Sigma Chi the damned thing won't work o sugar babe! O Monticello! O dream river! O thick meals of grease lucky strike a coca cola why goddamn it o beloved thutty ayut mahls o beloved o red lips before me o camels o chesterfields o Virginia! O god o hell o damn o Virginia! O beloved beloved beloved beloved beloved . . .

Meanwhile, though, another small controversy erupted in the Bowles household over who (if anyone) would accompany Paul to the university. At last, his mother, over Paul's protests, decided that she would make the trip with him in order to get him settled in at school. The trip was made by train. Upon arrival, to Paul's surprise (and relief), he discovered that he was by no means the only freshman accompanied by his mother; indeed, the hotels were full of mothers and sons.

CHAPTER 4

CHARLOTTESVILLE IN 1927 was a small but prosperous and bustling town dominated by two institutions: the Tobacco Exchange and the University of Virginia. Situated at the foothills of the Blue Ridge Mountains, the city was exceedingly picturesque. The many elegant homes, including Thomas Jefferson's residence, Monticello, gave the city a gentrified atmosphere. The university itself, founded and designed by Jefferson, had about 2,000 male students (no women were admitted) and about 190 faculty members. The campus buildings, arranged around a large rectangular yard, many of which were also designed by Jefferson, reflected the largely bygone grandeur of the Old South.

For the young city boy it represented a major change. The town itself was entirely different from any Northern or New England town that Bowles had seen, and the Blue Ridge Mountains, looming in the west, were hardly comparable to the Berkshires of western Massachusetts and New York State. The ambience and attitudes were also different. On the first day of their arrival, Rena struck up a conversation with a woman in the lobby of the hotel. Names were exchanged. The lady then inquired as to whether Rena were a member of the "V'ginia Bowles." "No, the Massachusetts Bowles," his mother answered. Bowles adds: "The lady waited for just the amount of time it took to get the magnolias out of her voice before she said, 'I see.'" Following the incident Rena warned her son that "that's the sort of thing you're going to run up against here." In reality, though, Bowles's Yankee origins do not seem to have been held against him.

Bowles's first task was to find a place to live. Although the university did have dormitories, he elected, as did most of the students, to live off-campus. After a bit of searching, he secured a room in a lodging house run by the McMurdo family, only a short distance from the university. Five other students occupied other rooms in the house. For meals, he and his fellow lodgers had to go over to Mrs. Saunders's house, quite nearby the McMurdos' lodging house.

After getting her son settled in, Rena returned to New York, and Bowles was, at last, completely on his own. Euphoric, confident, ready to take on the challenge of managing his own affairs, he quickly began to make friends and explore Charlottesville and environs. He also had the beginning of school to occupy his attention. Although Bowles had no exact sense of what he intended to major in at the university, he enrolled in four classes his first term: English, French, geology, and history of music. He later wrote in his autobiography:

> In my French class one student wearing jodhpurs and boots regularly came in with his dog and gun. He stood the rifle by the door, and the setter went to lie quietly under Professor Abbott's desk. I made field trips with my geology class in search of hematite, schist, and crinoids. While some of the students straggled in order to stay far enough behind to be able to take quiet nips from their hip flasks, Professor Roberts explained ontogeny in phylogeny to those who had not fully understood it in class. . . .
>
> I came into contact with my first group of intellectual snobs and understood that their principal interest was not in literature and art, but in talking about these things. However, I learned from them. That autumn I first read *The Waste Land,* first heard Gregorian chant and Prokofieff, first listened with pleasure to Duke Ellington and his band from the Cotton Club. And I bought my first blues records at secondhand furniture stores in the black quarter of Charlottesville.

There were also excursions into the Blue Ridge Mountains. Not owning a car, Bowles occasionally hitchhiked into remote areas. When he couldn't get a ride he walked, enjoying immensely the beauty of the landscape. In fact, he became so enamored of these treks through the wilderness that he often neglected studying, an activity that, even without the natural distractions, was of less importance to him than experiencing life on his own.

All in all, Bowles did his best to fit into Charlottesville. At the McMurdos', Bowles seems to have gotten on well with his fellow students. Of the five who lived at the house, Bowles had difficulty with only one of them, a fellow named Andrews. The problem arose because Bowles always locked his door while studying and refused to answer when Andrews pounded on it. Andrews could not conceive of any reason Bowles could have for locking his door, except for one: he must be inside masturbating. And so he made a great show of circulating the rumor, hounding Bowles about it whenever an opportunity presented itself.

Happy on his own and in his new surroundings, Bowles recalled years later, when preparing his notes for *Without Stopping,* that "it was a pleasant life in Charlottesville," to which he added that he "felt well physically." This sense of physical well-being may have also come from the fact that for the first time in his life he was enjoying eating. It was not just that Mrs. Saunders was a great cook (rumored to be the best in Charlottesville serving meals to students), but, rather, that his father was not present and hence Bowles could actually take pleasure in food. No one in Virginia called upon him to Fletcherize while at table.

Bowles generally divided his time between studying, doing creative work, and socializing. In a letter to Burns written about midsemester, he described a bit of his life in Charlottesville and his activities:

Still *seventeen,* although the happy part of it is that down here everyone believes I'm nineteen. Not that I've told anyone such a lie, or even pretended to admit it when anyone remarks about it. In fact, I deny it vigorously, look extraordinarily (more than usual) innocent and say incredulously: but do I look nineteen? I have painted four things since I came. The first was called Sacrifice, and was done in black and white. I sold it to a student. The second was a portrait of Virgin Mary which shocked everyone. The third was Nausea and the fourth The Poet. You will undoubtedly be amazed at my new style, which is almost monochromatic and extremely heavy.

I have composed and written one piece, called Monotonal, and it bores almost everyone. I have made literally dozens of friends and most of them are intelligent and sympathetic. . . . Last night I saw Dracula. The Count was William Tilden the tennis player, if you can believe it. He behaved most hammily, I thought, although the mob cheered him as though he'd rescued Jesus from the cross.

One sees very little here. Concerts are infrequent. Maier and Pattison came and I heard *them.* The Barrere Little Symphony came and I heard *it.* And that's all. However, this weekend I am going down to Richmond and the Chicago Opera Company will be there for two nights. Don't you enjoy all these little provincialities?

Bowles had been invited down to Richmond by a newly acquired friend, Bruce Morrissette, a Richmond native and student at the University of Richmond. Morrissette distinctly remembers their first meeting: "At our first encounter we stole into a vacant University piano room, and Bowles played, among other pieces, his *Aubade pour l'avenir* [dedicated to Daniel Burns], with its rhythmic dissonances so prophetic of aspects of his later style."

The friendship with Morrissette was important, for Bowles felt little intellectual compatibility with either his fellow roomers or other students at the university. In Morrissette, though, he found a kindred sensibility and an intellectual curiosity that went beyond the confines of popular reading and entertainment. In his working notes for *Without Stopping* he commented on the general intellectual climate in Charlottesville:

This was the very end of the *College Humor* era. Everyone talked about Cabell, asking me if I had read *Jurgen.* I hadn't nor after looking at a page of it, did I have any intention of doing so. I liked the European writers of *transition* and that was about all. I used my reading hours to effect conscious escape from the meaning of any life I had known until then, into the mysterious, and for me irrational world of Lautréamont, Joyce, Kafka, Blok and Essenin [*sic*]. The fact that there was no one with whom to discuss any of these writers was perfectly acceptable because I assumed that any work which had reached the notice of the faculty or students of an American college was unworthy of serious attention on my part.

Despite Bowles's obvious snobbery, he did manage to partake, with delight it seems, of many of the less-than-intellectual activities engaged in by his fellow students. Caught up with expanding his experiences, he also began to indulge in the major student activity at the time: drinking. Despite Prohibition, there seemed to be no lack of moonshine alcohol. Bowles's excursions into the surrounding hills and countryside proved to be a great asset, for it was in the little farms scattered about the backroads that moonshine was sold. Bowles recalled: "You took along your empty gallon jugs, and they gave you new ones filled with colorless whiskey. When you got home, you drained off the fusel oil and added dried peaches and a bag of charcoal; the next night your whiskey was aged." Needless to say, the alcohol distilled in this manner was far from smooth, but as the idea was to get drunk, not savor the liquor, it sufficed.

Aside from drinking, Bowles also began to experiment with another method of intoxication. He briefly described it in a letter to Daniel Burns: "I am doing all manner of strange things, one of which is to inhale ether until I am quite drunk. It's a fad here among some circles." The basic method of using the anesthetic was to pour it into a small glass and sniff it between gulps of whiskey. Not quite satisfied with this method, Bowles decided to experiment. One night when the McMurdos were having a party he hung up in his room a sheet soaked in ether. The stench was so profound that the fumes leaked downstairs, invoking the wrath of his hosts whose party had been disturbed.

Bowles's infatuation with ether was not dampened, however. Shortly afterward, he visited Richmond to attend the opera. At that time, Morrissette was working as an usher at the theater and managed to sneak Bowles into the performance. Once the opera began, Morrissette joined Bowles in the audience. Suddenly, Bowles reached into his pocket and pulled out a vial of ether, which he silently unstoppered. The fumes immediately began to circulate around the hall. Within minutes, people became noticeably upset; many left their seats to escape the noxious odor. Finally, assured that he had sufficiently bothered everyone in the immediate vicinity of his seat, Bowles quietly replaced the stopper and put the vial back in his pocket. "He got a huge kick out of it," recalls Morrissette. "At that time Bowles would go a long way to *'épater le bourgeois.'* "

Bowles's life was full in Charlottesville. Adventures, intellectual stimulation (even if in the form of outside reading), friends his own age with shared interests, and freedom from irrational authority all combined to give him a sense of possibility. He summed up his enthusiasm in a letter to Burns:

> but as for the place here i think or perhaps feel that it is wonderful which as you know is rather strong language for me to use or isnt it? never from one weeks end to the other do i think of home except

through outside pressure. but of course i never have been able to understand what nostalgia is. i believe its the product of a mental hypochondriacs imagination. no one can feel homesick. . . .

the inhabitants of virginia seem to have a natural leaning toward smoothing hair. several of the boys i have met insist on rubbing their hands back and forth gently across my pate. that that is an emetic need i mention? or perhaps yes?

but as for the country roundabout i find it more beautiful than i had dared imagine it. from that you may deduce that each day i take long walks all alone in the mountains which is perfectly true. my studies will bleed from that practise but edgar poe went here and did the same thing didn't he? and what is good enough for edgar allan poe is good enow for me let me assure you or no?

During Christmas vacation Bowles returned to New York. The highlight of the visit seems to have been attending, on December 30, the night of his eighteenth birthday, one of the Copland-Sessions Concerts of Contemporary Music. It featured Henry Cowell's *Seven Paragraphs for String Trio,* Nikolai Lopatnikoff's *Sonatina for Piano,* Bernard Wagenaar's *Sonata for Piano, Four Songs for Baritone and Piano* by Marc Blitzstein (on texts by Walt Whitman), and George Antheil's *Second String Quartet.* For Bowles, the concert served as an introduction not only to contemporary music, but also to the whims of reviewers, who rather vehemently attacked Copland and his fellow composers. As Bowles was already aware of Copland's controversial music, having heard it criticized by several others, he decided "automatically that he was the most important composer in the United States."

Bowles remembers little else about the return to New York, except for the fact that the city enchanted him and that on New Year's Eve, the night before his return to Virginia, he drank too much speakeasy beer that had been needled with ether. As a result, he became violently ill and suffered the effects nearly all the way back to Charlottesville. Shortly after his return he developed a case of severe conjunctivitis, so severe, in fact, that he spent a week in the hospital, where he was treated with drugs and, to prevent him from rubbing his eyes and spreading the infection, had his hands strapped to his sides.

The combination of the trip to New York and the dismal episode with conjunctivitis left him with what he described as a "persistent malaise." His earlier euphoria dissipated, and he began to feel distinctly alien. Secretly, he began to agree with his father, who felt that the University of Virginia was not a college, but a country club. He did manage to do well on his semester exams in January and ended up on the dean's list. This was not only an honor: the college rules stated that any student on the list was exempted from attending classes. Bowles did not hesitate to take advantage of the opportunity, spending as much time as he could away from Charlottesville, either in the mountains or in Richmond. But despite diversions and a deepening friendship with Bruce Morrissette, Bowles could not shake his malaise. Years later he reflected on its probable cause:

> "There will come a day of reckoning," I told myself. "All this pleasure will have to be paid for, and it will be terrible."
>
> There was no use in trying to push it back into the dark part of my mind. It haunted me on my long walks through the back country, and darkened the winter sunshine around me. Certainly I did not believe that enjoyment was wrong, but some part of me believed it to be and I was aware of feeling it. Perhaps this phenomenon is the result of having one grandmother who had been born in New Hampshire and one in Rhode Island, one grandfather who had been born in Vermont and the other in Connecticut, and perhaps not. It didn't interest me then and it doesn't now. Causes are not very important to know unless one desires to use the knowledge to effect a change. I wanted to go on, not go back and start over again. I knew I was wasting time, but I had no idea how to employ it to any better advantage. The idea of attending classes and studying did not occur to me seriously because there was nothing in the classes I particularly wanted to learn.

Although disaffected, Bowles kept up the pretense, learned so well in his childhood, of being interested in what was going on around him. Morrissette, probably his closest friend at the time, doesn't recall that Bowles seemed really much different after his return from New York: "I knew he didn't feel he was getting much out of the academic experience, but then, the general consensus of both of us was that the students were more advanced than the faculty . . . that the teachers were a bunch of fuddy-duddys." But

Bowles could not escape his sense of discomfort. Scarcely a month into his second term, he had what he described as a "compulsive experience." He recorded the event in the working notes for the autobiography:

> About two months after my eighteenth birthday I ceased being a child. Possibly there was a whole period of transition which prepared the way for my sudden compulsive decision, but if there was I have forgotten the details of it, and remember only the evening when all at once I became aware that there were two possible choices to make. One was to swallow the contents of a bottle of sleeping pills, and the other was to disappear, that is, to go away, leaving no traces. When I looked at the little bottle, I knew I had no desire to be dead, so my decision was made. I remember leaping onto the bed with my shoes on, and jumping up and down with elation. Fortunately the springs were new: I had just bought them. When I had run through that phase of my good spirits I sat down and drew up a plan of action. First I made an inventory of all the saleable objects in the room. Then I wrote a letter to my mother in New York, saying that I needed $125 for textbooks and miscellanies and please to send it immediately. After this I spent a few minutes composing a telegram, put on my overcoat and went out.

In *Without Stopping,* Bowles recounted a similar, but slightly more dramatic version in which his decision was made by flipping a coin and allowing chance to determine the outcome. Regardless of the details, the act signified that Bowles, probably for the first time in his life, had made a decision entirely on his own. The other decisions—going to art school or the University of Virginia—were more in keeping with what others expected of him. To some extent, these other choices were also made in order to postpone having to decide what to do with his life. Now, he had made an "adult" decision, in that he had made the choice to take absolute control over his life. Coming on the heels of the guilt associated with "enjoying himself" too much, it was a radical step, a unique solution to his Charlottesville malaise.

The telegram he mentioned sending was destined for Mrs. Crouch, now in New York, having recently returned from Europe. In the wire, Bowles not only announced his decision, but asked her for a favor, namely helping him to get a passport. By "disappearing, going away" he meant well away, to Paris. To Bowles, Paris represented the center of the literary and musical world. *transition* was published there; Erik Satie and André Gide lived there; he fancied himself fluent in French. In short, it was the logical decision. As for Mrs. Crouch, not only did he feel he could trust her not to inform his parents, he also knew that "she could hardly be expected to resist such a splendid opportunity to shock all the members of my family at one fell swoop."

Bowles kept his departure a secret from everyone, including the university and Bruce Morrissette, although he did, shortly before departing, intimate to his friend that he was about to leave: "By all means you must visit me soon if I live long enough or if I remain here long enough." Morrissette did make arrangements to visit, but by the time he arrived, Bowles was gone.

Arriving in New York the third week in March, Bowles found a cheap, small, and crumbling hotel on Ninth Avenue where he checked in, paying in advance for a room for one night. Shortly after getting into bed he discovered that the mattress was infested with bedbugs, the first he had ever seen. He trudged down the stairs to complain to the proprietor, who simply shrugged and told him: "You don't like the room it's a free country." Bowles stayed the night, being acutely short of cash, and needing to save what little he had for the trip. The next morning he got up early and went over to Brooklyn to visit the Hoagland sisters and Mrs. Crouch. He was received enthusiastically and given assurances that he had made the right decision. "You'll fit into life over there," they told him.

The elation of escape quickly changed into practical planning, for before Mrs. Crouch could get him a passport, Bowles needed to obtain a copy of his birth certificate from the Bureau of Vital Statistics in Jamaica. As he had little time to spare, this meant going in person rather than soliciting the document by mail. This simple operation, naturally, was fraught with fear as there was always the danger that he might be spotted by either an acquaintance of his or, worse yet, of his parents. With considerable anxiety, therefore, he slipped into Jamaica and managed, with ease and anonymity, to obtain a photostat of the birth certificate. The next step involved getting the passport, a process that filled him with even greater uneasiness, as it was absolutely essential that it succeed in order for him to carry out his plan.

Both Miss Sue and Mrs. Crouch went in quest of the passport. Once at the office, they told the passport officials that they were his aunts and had been entrusted by Bowles's parents, who were both indisposed, to obtain a passport for their nephew. The deception worked and, passport in hand, Bowles went directly to the Holland-America Steamship Line to book passage on the next transatlantic steamer. The next sailing was on March 30, about a week away. The ship was the *Rijndam,* an old Dutch steamer making its last Atlantic crossing, calling at ports in England, Northern Ireland, France, and the Netherlands. Bowles bought a ticket to Boulogne-sur-Mer for $125, leaving him with less than $50 in his pocket. As he returned to Brooklyn he contemplated how he could live for another week without depleting his dwindling supply of cash. Again, Mrs. Crouch came to the rescue, giving Bowles the key to her daughter's vacant furnished apartment on Washington Square. As Mary Crouch Oliver was on her honeymoon in France, Mrs. Crouch saw no reason why Bowles shouldn't be able to use the apartment for the last week he was in New York. He moved in right away, but after a few days the owners came by and were quite upset to discover a stranger. They ordered him out, but after learning that he was sailing for Europe in a few days, permitted him to stay on. Bowles's charm, an asset on which he would soon need to rely extensively, had gotten him out of a scrape.

On Saturday morning, March 30, 1929, the day before Easter, Bowles took the ferry from the city to Hoboken, New Jersey. The temperature was in the 40s; a cold breeze blew briskly and mist encircled Manhattan. At the Fifth Street Pier, the *Rijndam* was getting ready to sail. With little cash, three letters of introduction to friends of Mrs. Crouch in Paris, a number of books (mostly given to him by his benefactors), an odd assortment of clothes, and a head full of dreams, Bowles arrived at the pier. Fearful that somehow his parents would have learned of the escapade, he kept an eye out for them. Instead, an unofficially adopted daughter of Miss Sue and Mrs. Crouch, Lucy Rogers, was there to bid him bon voyage. A few years younger than Bowles, Lucy had gotten to know Bowles in Glenora. Having studied in France, courtesy of Mrs. Crouch and Miss Sue, she was the ideal person to see him off. She also knew the three women for whom the letters of introduction were destined. She went on board with Bowles, talking with him, buttressing his decision, giving him advice about Paris and Parisian manners. She stayed with him until the announcement was made that all visitors had to go ashore.

At 11:00 A.M. the *Rijndam* blew its final horn and pulled away from the dock. Bowles was on his way to a new continent and a new life.

PART II

A Manufactured Savage

CHAPTER 5

THERE WERE eight other passengers on board the *Rijndam*. The most memorable was a young French woman named Christine, the wife of a French count, the Comte de Guendulaine, who had taken up residence in southern Mexico. Pregnant, she was returning alone to Paris to have her first baby at her mother's house. During the trip it was with her that Bowles talked most, picking up useful French slang and information about Paris. When not practicing his French with Christine, Bowles spent his time reading Gide's *Journal des Faux-Monnayeurs*. Two years before he had reviewed *The Counterfeiters* for *The Oracle*, writing that "It evokes more material for deep thought than any other book we have ever read. . . . A boy of sixteen leaves his home clandestinely to wander in the streets of Paris." It was therefore only fitting that he should follow it up with the *Journal*. Although eighteen, he was after all leaving his home clandestinely to wander the streets of Paris.

But the *Journal* is a different book, more cerebral, nonfiction. Nonetheless, it fascinated Bowles, but in a different way than the novel had stirred him. First, it showed him that art was not something that sprang whole from the creator's mind, but a process of working and reworking certain ideas. Second, Bowles saw in Gide's grappling with bringing a work into being a parallel with his own struggle to bring himself into being. The false starts, the dreams, the plans, the disconsolations, the elation at finally getting it right all found resonance in the young man's mind. Later, he too would keep journals, ponder on paper the development of his creations, but at eighteen he first had to create himself. Art would inevitably follow.

From on board the *Rinjdam* he wrote to Morrissette:

I'm sorry that I didn't wait to go until you had been up to see me. I suppose it's unethical for me to run off the way I did, without

67

apprising a soul of my intentions. I had to keep up the deceit until the last second, otherwise I should never have departed. The end justified the means, I think. . . . But at any rate I'm happy now where I wasn't at the university. I never should have been happy there, even if I'd stayed long enough to understand it. However, if everyone did the same things I do, there would be no "successes" in the world, I'm afraid. . . . I don't ever want to come back to the United States. I dislike it there. I may hate it in Europe. At any rate, I shall soon find out whether I was merely in the wrong environment or a misanthrope.

Bowles landed at Boulogne-sur-Mer the second week in April 1929. Now that he had made friends with Christine on board the *Rijndam,* she suggested they travel together up to Paris, a welcome suggestion to Bowles. At the Gare St.-Lazare they were met by Christine's mother, the Comtesse de Lavillate, and her brother, the Duc de Saint-Simon. They all insisted that Bowles accompany them back to their house on the rue St.-Dominique. As the taxi maneuvered through the streets of Paris, a chorus of blaring horns swelled up around the vehicle, causing the opening strains of *An American in Paris* to come to Bowles's mind. After listening for a bit to the general cacophony, he decided that Gershwin had done a marvelous job capturing with his trumpets the serenade of the Paris streets.

After an enormous lunch with Christine's large family, her brother brought Bowles to a pension run by a Madame Gaubert, where he took a room. Once alone, he counted his money: he had $24. It was clear that he needed to find work immediately. He consulted the letters of introduction given to him by Mrs. Crouch. One was to a Russian émigré, a Madame Daniloff; another was to an osteopath named Miss Lynch; the third was to an Irish actress, Madame Caskie. Bowles decided that his best bet for a job lay with Miss Lynch. The next morning he presented himself and the letter to the osteopath, who quickly turned him over to her receptionist, Monsieur de la Batut, who knew someone at the Paris *Herald Tribune.* Monsieur de la Batut took Bowles to lunch and then to one of the newspaper's offices on the rue du Louvre. He was told there to go to the main office on the Avenue de l'Opéra. After a brief interview he was given the job of switchboard operator at a salary of 200 francs (about $8) a week. Fortunately, since the *Herald Tribune* was an American company, he could start immediately rather than waiting the customary three months for a work permit.

It was April in Paris. Spring was in the air. Flowers were pushing their way skyward in the Jardin du Luxembourg and the buds were bursting into leaves on the trees along the Champs de Mars. The Champs Élysées was decked out for the annual fête of Jeanne d'Arc, the mid-season collections were previewing in the fashion salons, and Diaghilev's Ballet Russe was getting ready to perform Stravinsky's *Renard the Fox* and Prokofiev's *Le Fils Prodigue. Ulysses* was just out in Valéry Larbaud's French translation and selling briskly aside the original at Shakespeare and Company. Gertrude Stein was holding court at 27 rue de Fleurus and Natalie Barney was presiding over her rival salon at 20 rue Jacob. Harry Crosby, in the last months of his life, was struggling to finish a book of poems and had just become a financial backer and advisory editor of *transition.* Although Hemingway was not at his usual café table in Montparnasse, he was on a ship bound for France. The surrealist circle, under the autocratic guidance of André Breton, was in full bloom, with headquarters in Breton's apartment at 42 rue Fontaine; and *Le Journal de Paris* was hotly debating whether the wire sculptures of a young American, Alexander Calder, being shown at the Galerie Billiet, were sculptures at all. Everything seemed to be happening at once: art, music, literature, razzle-dazzle. The Great War was becoming a memory and prosperity seemed endless. Paris, in short, was a city of possibilities, of realizable dreams. And no one was more intent on realizing his dreams than Paul Bowles. With a job, a place to stay, and a few contacts, he could see stretching before him a life as an expatriate in Paris, in the grand tradition of so many others. Even with the small security he now had, he could see no reason to return to the University of Virginia, or even the United States. Life was going to be lived differently in Paris. He would no longer be Paul Bowles, son of a Long Island dentist, but Paul Bowles, poet, budding composer, painter, resident of Paris, contributor to *transition,* employee of the *Herald Tribune.*

Bowles started working at the paper the day after he was hired. The job, which consisted of standing in the operator's "cage" and watching the switchboard for a white "papillon" to light up, was less than glamorous. When the papillon blinked, Bowles had to plug in a line opposite it. The job, though monotonous, was also somewhat nerve-racking as he was continually concerned about making a mistake. "Since I was under the impression that I was proficient in French," he recalls, "it became a matter of personal pride never to give anyone a wrong number." "Anyone" could, in fact, have been Elliot Paul, who not only coedited *transition*, but also was on the staff at the *Herald Tribune*. Bowles would see him come and go day after day, but could not devise an easy way of speaking to him, letting him know that one of his *transition* contributors worked for the same newspaper. One afternoon an opportunity presented itself. Returning from lunch, the bearded editor walked straight to the cage and commanded Bowles to come outside where a taxi was waiting at the curb. "Look inside," he said. Bowles did. The interior was upholstered in fake snakeskin. "Do you see what I see?" he asked. Bowles confirmed that indeed the seat was covered with false boa-constrictor skin. At that, the old gentleman waved the driver on, and without bothering to converse anymore with Bowles, went inside and up the stairs. Bowles had missed the chance to announce his presence.

Nor could Bowles make himself known at *transition,* although he did one day go all the way to its offices and loitered for some time outside its door, only to conclude that no one on its celebrated staff would be at all interested in knowing who he was.

Choosing to remain anonymous, he decided, after work and on his days off, to discover Paris. The city delighted him. His main activity at the time, being extremely short of cash, was walking, learning the differences between one quarter and another:

> Paris was a continual joy—even walking to work in the morning. The era had not yet arrived when the traffic was thick enough to cancel the smells of spring in the air. Some nights the mere fact of being there excited me so much that there was no question of going to bed until I had walked all the way across the city, say from the Place Denfert-Rochereau to the Place Clichy. Then I would have to get back to whatever hotel I was living in. The next day I would feel voluptuously weary, in a vaguely floating condition. The day in the cage would pass more swiftly as a result.

Bowles also began to draw further on the letters given to him by Mrs. Crouch. Remembering that Lucy Rogers had told him that

Madame Daniloff could be counted on for a free meal, and being rather acutely in need of one, he quickly decided to present himself at her apartment, situated on the outskirts of Paris in Boulogne-sur-Seine. She had, in the meantime, received a letter from Mrs. Crouch informing her that Bowles would be calling on her. When he arrived at her door, she greeted him warmly, invited him in, and introduced him to her husband, a former officer in the White Russian army. Although Bowles had timed his visit to coincide with the dinner hour, the Daniloffs had already eaten. Upon being asked whether he would like something to eat, therefore, he protested weakly, saying that Madame Daniloff should not go to any great trouble for him. She nonetheless fixed him a Gruyère omelette and a salad, a repast better than any Bowles had had since his arrival in Paris. His obvious appreciation was such that Madame Daniloff decided to invite him again for dinner. Thus began a series of regular visits to the Daniloff apartment, for as Bowles later noted, "a stray cat returns to the place where it is fed."

In the meantime, back in Jamaica, his family began to wonder why they hadn't heard from their son in such a long time. Finally, becoming alarmed, Rena decided to investigate. Contacting the McMurdos, she learned that he had "disappeared" some time ago. Frantic with worry, she took the next train south to begin a personal search for her missing son in Charlottesville. Naturally, no one at the McMurdos' boardinghouse knew what had happened to Bowles. She did, though, discover what seemed to be a clue to his disappearance. In his room she found an unopened telegram from Bruce Morrissette which read: "CAN COME COLON SEE YOU SATURDAY." Deciding that "Colon" was Colón, Panama, and not a punctuation mark, she assumed that her son had fled to the tropics. She alerted the officials there to look for her runaway, then went back to New York to await any information that might be forthcoming. It would, in fact, be late April before she would learn of her son's whereabouts.

As for Bowles, he wasn't particularly concerned about whether his parents knew where he was or not: "I fully expected never to see my family again. I had taken matters into my own hands, and that they would not forgive." With this notion firmly in mind, he set about the business of getting on in Paris. Despite his enrapturement with the city, he had a major problem with finances. The pittance he received from the newspaper barely kept him in room and board. Indeed, finding a suitable room was proving quite difficult. Hating to spend what little money he had for rooms, he kept ending up in rather squalid hotels that teemed with bedbugs. At one hotel, at which he had paid a month's rent in advance, the bedbugs were so inventive that when the proprietress placed the legs of the bed in cans of kerosene to stem the attack, the bugs simply crawled up the wall, across the ceiling, and then dived onto the bed.

For meals, Bowles ate in cheap prix fixe restaurants and, whenever possible, at the Daniloffs. One day, while listening to Bowles's tales of his troubles with bedbugs and the like, Madame Daniloff decided that he should write to his parents and ask them for money. At this suggestion, Bowles had to admit that he had, in fact, never informed his parents of the trip and that they had no idea where he was. Madame Daniloff laughed, but decided to take matters into her own hands. Worrying about Bowles's health, she took him to an old Russian doctor, who made several tests to try to determine the cause of his excessive thinness and nervousness. At length, he came to the point: "Do you practice self-abuse?" he asked. Bowles, though embarrassed at being asked such a question, finally had to reply: "Once in a while." At this, the old doctor recommended that he take up running each day in the Bois de Boulogne. Madame Daniloff, however, decided that something more was needed, a rest in the country, perhaps. Using this as a pretext, she wrote to Bowles's mother, in English, telling her that Bowles needed money so that he could go away for a "cure."

Receiving the letter in New York, Rena was naturally delighted to learn that her son was alive and not lost in the jungles of Panama. But she was also concerned. To her, the word "cure" implied that Bowles had become a drug addict. She wrote to him immediately, telling him how glad she was to know where he was as well as urging him to use will power to break his habit, but enclosed no money. She also wrote to Madame Daniloff, thanking her for letting her know where Bowles was, but also to inform her that no financial help would be forthcoming. Madame Daniloff was shocked at the Bowleses' refusal to send aid. "She did not know the New England mentality, according to which reparations must accompany transgression."

Madame Daniloff persisted in her efforts to get monetary assistance for Bowles. On the heels of Rena's rejection she wrote to Mrs. Crouch's daughter, Mary Oliver, who was in London. Mary had just married a department store heir, Jock Oliver, and was quite well off at the time. She sent 2,500 francs (about $100) immediately, thus allowing Bowles to quit his job at the *Herald Tribune* and look for another. Rather than busy himself with job hunting, however, he decided to make some excursions into the countryside. At first, he made short trips out of the city, but finally bought a ticket for Chamonix, in the Alps. He spent the next ten days trekking through the mountains around Lake Geneva, walking from one village to the next, staying in country hotels. Finally, he decided to head south and took the train to Nice. The city greatly impressed him with its subtropical palms and mimosas lining the streets. He stayed on for a week, picking up his mail at American Express. One day he had a letter from Mary Oliver saying that she would be arriving in Paris soon. Bowles took this as a sign that he had better return to Paris and make some effort to find a job again.

Back in Paris, though, Bowles didn't immediately begin seeking employment. Instead he got some more money from Oliver and the Duc de Saint-Simon and spent the week or so Oliver was in the city accompanying her and her new husband to dinner and to see the sights. They also went to visit Madame Daniloff, who quite excitedly informed Bowles that she had spoken to her friend Sergei Prokofiev about giving Bowles composition lessons. This news frightened him, for he could not imagine what studying with such a master would be like. He became even more convinced that he was totally unworthy of being taught by the great composer after attending a performance of his *Pas d'Acier*, put on by Diaghilev's Ballet Russe. Madame Daniloff had already set the wheels in motion. An appointment was made for three o'clock on a Sunday afternoon. But by two, Bowles was at the train station, buying a ticket for Saverne, near the German border. Rather than having to face an interview with the master, he had decided to escape:

This was an act without conscious motivation; I was not able either at the moment or in retrospect to discover what determined my decision. Again and again I relived the afternoon in memory, hoping to catch the precise instant when I became aware that I was going to the Gare de l'Est, but I was never able to find it. Clearly I felt that the action precluded the necessity of making a choice, that once I was on the train there would be no question of my having to decide anything one way or the other.

Despite Bowles's growing sense of his own self as an artist, it is evident, both from this incident and from his inability to make contact with *transition*'s editors, that he was not nearly as confident of his abilities as he would have liked to have been. The bravado of his earlier letters to Burns aside, it was a great leap to go from being an "artist" among nonartists to being one among them. A genuine humility was operating that first season in Paris, a sense of not quite believing that he was good enough or advanced enough to have anything to offer the great masters.

He was, however, not at all shy at presenting himself through the mail and had gotten several poems accepted at little magazines. *Tambour,* a French-English publication put out in Paris, printed "Blessed Be the Meek" and "Poem." "Sonata and Three Poems" ("Sonata," "Along Brighter Lines," "Promenade des Anglais," and another poem entitled simply "Poem") were picked up by *Blues,* an experimental magazine edited in New York by Charles-Henri Ford. Another Paris-based magazine, *This Quarter,* accepted "Here I Am," "Halley's Comet," "International Poem," and "Stop That." Finally, *The Morada,* published in Albuquerque, New Mexico, took two poems, "The Church" and "Serenade au Cap." Before leaving the University of Virginia, he had also published "The Path to the Pond" in the college magazine. All of these poems were written in 1927 or 1928, with the exception of "Serenade au Cap," which dates from 1926. Most of them bear a heavy surrealist influence: word play, free association resulting in unusual pairings of real and imagined observation—in short, celebrations of the power of the unconscious.

He also began to write a few poems in French at this time, which he sent off to *Anthologie du Groupe Moderne d'Art,* a bimonthly journal issued in Liège, Belgium. Here, too, he was accepted. This particularly delighted him as he was a great admirer of French poets and could now count himself as a published poet in two languages. These poems are quite polished and carefully executed and, like his work in English, alternate between mundane observation and

marvelous revelation, in the process demonstrating a great awareness of contemporary trends in French poetry.

Despite his literary successes and the arrival of various acquaintances from the States, Bowles was becoming increasingly lonely
in Paris, and felt desperately in need of a true friend. In late June
he wrote a long letter to Morrissette, imploring him to come to
Paris:

> I'm . . . serious when I say your arrival might prevent an untimely
> suicide. You see—all I'm doing is borrowing money right and left,
> and it's discouraging. Not that your advent would stop the borrow-
> ing, but it would put an end to the discouragement. I have also no
> one to go anywhere with. All my acquaintances are the appointment
> kind. Between appointments I lie exhausted on my bed—not physi-
> cally exhausted but morally so. And besides, two together can live
> so extremely inexpensively. . . . And how much happier one is with
> a companion in Paris! It's not a city where you feel comfortable
> alone. Unless you have someone to talk to, the continual efferves-
> cence seems futile—the gaiety unnecessary, and one becomes in-
> voluntarily embittered.

Bowles's trip to Saverne, in northeastern France, turned into a
fairly long excursion. Getting off the train, he walked to Stras-
bourg, and from there crossed the Rhine into Germany, where he
spent a week in the Black Forest. Germany did not impress him.
Although he found the Germans friendly, they seemed wholly
uninteresting: "I understood why they stressed the word *Kultur:*
they had none and hoped to make one by dint of talking about it."

Returning to Paris, he avoided Madame Daniloff and set about
looking for work. Capitalizing on his previous banking experience
in New York, he succeeded in getting hired by the foreign department of the Banker's Trust, located on the Place Vendôme. Working, however, was not much to his liking. "Here I am working
pleasantly, being pleasant in the pleasant Banker's Trust," he
wrote Morrissette. "There is not time for anything but working,
eating, sleeping (a little), and keeping banal rendezvous. . . . I've
lost myself. I don't use my wits from one bedtime to another." Not
surprisingly, his banking career was short-lived. During the second
week of his employment he mistakenly gave an American woman

$1,000, rather than $100, worth of francs. The bank held him responsible for the missing $900. In a panic, he ran to the woman's residence at the Plaza-Athénée; she cheerfully refunded the money. The bank took a tolerant attitude now that the money was returned, but Bowles decided to use the incident to convince himself that he was not cut out for such work and quit the job that day.

Sitting on the terrace at the Dôme that night, pondering his future, he noticed two couples, one in their twenties and the other in their thirties, at a nearby table. Presently, the younger of the women, a Hungarian named Hermina, asked him to join them. They talked for a while. It turned out that they were going to spend the weekend camping beside the Seine. They invited Bowles to join them. The next morning, all five of them set off by car to the campsite about an hour and a half east of Paris. The following day, after lunch, Bowles and Hermina took a walk:

> I ran innocently into a patch of high nettles. Never having seen or heard of the plant before, I first thought I had brushed against a wasps' nest. We climbed through the woods and came out on top of a hill in a cherry orchard. The nettle stings were not the only initiatory experience for me that Sunday afternoon. There among hundreds of excited ants that rushed over us, while Hermina declaimed such sentiments as: "I'm the flower, you're the stem," I had my first sex. When I put my bathing suit back on, I realized that in addition to the nettles and ant bites I was painfully sunburned.

Bowles never saw Hermina again.

He did, however, meet up with Mrs. Crouch and Miss Sue, who had arrived in Paris on the way to the house near Arles. Mrs. Crouch, upon first seeing Bowles, expressed her dissatisfaction with Bowles's appearance: he looked the same as he had in New York. She had expected that he would at least be sporting a beret or cape or would have grown a little beard. The next day Bowles joined her for lunch at the American University Women's Club. Also present were Madame Daniloff and an American woman named Kay Cowen, who had just returned from Morocco. Mrs. Crouch and Madame Daniloff spent most of the lunch arguing about the Bolshevik revolution; Bowles talked with Cowen, who showed him pictures of what Bowles decided was one of the most exotic cities on earth: Marrakech. A few days later Cowen took him to see Tristan Tzara, who appeared to Bowles to be more like a doctor than a great Dada-surrealist poet.

Shortly after the departure of Mrs. Crouch and Miss Sue to Arles and Kay Cowen to the United States, Bowles received word that an unofficially adopted son of his paternal grandparents was on his way to Paris. A few years older than Bowles's father, Billy Hubert had grown up in the Bowles family after being orphaned at an early age. He was now a highly successful couturier with a salon on 57th Street and Fifth Avenue in New York. A flashy dresser and man of the world—his buying trips took him to Europe six times a year—Hubert, upon meeting his "nephew," immediately insisted that Bowles leave his meager hotel and move in with him at the Hotel Daunou. Bowles agreed, apparently not realizing that Hubert had other designs. The first evening together, Hubert, who had not seen Bowles in ten years, immediately began to compliment him on how handsome he had become. That night, as Bowles put it, he received "a further sexual initiation, equally cold-blooded and ridiculous."

This casual reference is the only comment Bowles has ever made about the affair, but it could hardly have been so insignificant at the time. Both Bowles and others have testified to his disinterest in, even fear of, sex. And yet, within the space of a month or so, Bowles apparently had two sexual encounters, one of them homosexual. Neither incident seems to have impressed him much. Perhaps it is best to view these sexual initiations within the context of Bowles's desire for new experiences, as necessary rites of passage for a young man. Further, as a passive recipient of the action, the one seduced, he could absolve himself of responsibility, could believe that he was not the one actively seeking the encounter. As such, he could see the sexual acts, like so many others in his life, as acts forced on him by stronger individuals. They were the ones who had acted, had led him into the new experience. While such reasoning, in an objective sense, is flawed, it was an interpretation of reality of which Bowles was quite fond, and which he would often use in the years to come.

The next day Hubert informed Bowles that Claude had sent a check for $200 to buy him clothes, but added, perhaps as a reward for his compliance of the night before, that he would foot the bill himself. That day he took Bowles shopping, ordering from his tailor a double-breasted chocolate-brown suit and bought him, as well, new shoes and a cane. Bowles, always one to enjoy being well-dressed, was delighted with the purchases. Hubert's "generosity" did not end there. He insisted that his "nephew" accompany him on a sojourn to the south of France.

After a few days in Paris, they set off on a short visit to St.–Moritz. From there, Bowles went on his own to Gueret, in the Creuse, where he had been invited by his first benefactors, the de Lavillates, to spend a week or so at their country house. From there it was to St.–Malo to rejoin Hubert, who whisked Bowles away to Dîves-sur-Mer so that he would have the experience of eating in a really fine restaurant. The Auberge de Guillaume le Conquérant had, in fact, figured in Proust, and the elderly proprietor, who walked about with a parrot on his shoulder, regaled the two with tales of Monsieur Proust who had been a regular customer. Since Bowles had not read *A La Recherche du Temps Perdu,* however, the stories were lost on him. Instead, he fixed most of his attention on the parrot.

Over lunch, and between listening to the owner's stories, Hubert began to try to persuade Bowles to return to the United States. Bowles, naturally, refused even to consider the proposal, as he felt that his parents would be considerably less than cordial, let alone conciliatory. Hubert tried to convince him otherwise, but soon let the subject drop. They went that evening to the casino, where Bowles managed to win about $250 at *petite boule.* His "uncle" meanwhile lost $4,000, the amount he had allowed for the night's gambling. Bowles was astonished at the sum lost and even more astonished by Hubert's attitude of nonchalance. That night Bowles got very drunk. Awakening the next morning with a tremendous hangover, he felt terrible, both physically and psychologically. Tired of being "kept," and feeling that he had come to the end of the line with Hubert, he asked him for his father's check, telling him, "I'll take the *Paris* on Monday." The older man was delighted that he had managed to persuade Bowles to return: "My, my! How glad your people are going to be to see their boy. And to think that Uncle Hubert is responsible for it!"

The next day Hubert drove Bowles to Le Havre, where that afternoon, on the 24 of July, he embarked for New York.

CHAPTER 6

$\mathbf{B}$OWLES DID not make his decision to return to New York without a considerable amount of anxiety. Now, on board the *Paris,* the consequences of his repatriation continued to worry him, particularly in regard to two matters. Uppermost in his mind was the question of how he would be received by his parents, or indeed, whether he would be received at all. Another nagging problem was what he would do once back in America. Upon arrival, the answer to the first question became clear; both Claude and Rena were at the dock to meet him. His mother seemed genuinely glad to see him. His father, characteristically taciturn, had little to say. Although neither rushed to criticize or interrogate him about his "escape," a few days after his arrival Claude did manage to express some emotion. In the car, alone, he declared, "That was a terrible thing you did to your mother. You've noticed her hair has gone gray as a result." When Bowles replied that he hadn't noticed, Claude angrily admonished him: "You're so busy thinking about yourself and what *you* want. You never see anything around you." No further words were exchanged.

Despite Claude's words, Bowles's overall impression was that he seemed to have earned from his parents a modicum of respect for acting so decisively, and on his own. As for the rest of the family, they were appreciative, even enthusiastic. Daddypapa marveled over his photographs and Aunt Mary exclaimed that the adventure had been a first-rate learning experience.

Bowles, however, now that the shock of arrival was over, began to feel increasingly "ashamed" of himself for returning. He wrote about it to Morrissette: "It's over. I'm going to remain here to become refined. . . . I'm ashamed. I do not have enough character to deny my mother's prayers. I do not blame her. It is entirely my fault."

His feeling of lacking in character was linked to his notion that

79

by leaving Paris he had betrayed his vision of becoming an expatriate artist. Indeed, now that physical reentry had been accomplished, he was able to turn himself once again to what was really
his major concern: finding a vocation, a direction for the future,
or as Bowles thought of it, "a civil status." Unable to decide what
to do with his life, he consulted a fortune-teller in the hope that
she might possibly pronounce him as being destined for something. It was in vain. "My future is tentative," he wrote Morrissette
in early September. " 'My dear, you have positively *no* fate line,'
said Madame Swenska, the palmist. 'Your career lies entirely in
your hands.' "

This knowledge did little to comfort him. While he would have
liked to have regarded himself as a poet or composer, it seemed
a bit too grandiose, or at least premature, to place such a label on
himself. As a result, he opted to get a job and continue working
at his creative endeavors on the side.

He first sought employment in a bank, as he remembered how
pleasant it had been working the summer before at the Bank of the
Manhattan Company. When a banking job failed to materialize, he
settled on a sales position at Duttons Bookshop on Fifth Avenue.
The commute to Manhattan, however, was long, and living at
home, now that he had experienced independence, was even less
desirable than before. After a few weeks and a couple of paychecks,
Bowles rented a room at 122 Bank Street in Greenwich Village.
Rather than inform his parents, however, he just disappeared.
Afraid that their son had either run back to Europe, or even worse,
eloped with his former girlfriend from art school, Peggy, whom he
had started dating again, his parents sought him out at Duttons.
When they questioned him as to where he had been and what he
thought he was doing, he informed them that he had simply taken
a room in the Village. Rena then shocked her son by inquiring if
he had gotten married. Flustered, he told her no, that he had
moved out only because he was tired of the commute. In reality,
though, he was infatuated with Peggy, as he recounted in an October 1929 letter to Morrissette:

> The only girl I have ever lost weight lying awake nights for is back
> in New York. . . . BAISERS INFINIS! Glory! Gorgeous! Preoccupa-
> tion quotidienne. . . . The only, the only, the only. 've given her

about three dozen of my favorite disks to play to herself in her room. 've lent her books, money everything. Because she really *is* only, only, only! (Strangely, her ma is lesb. and her pa an awful rake from his looks.) 's been expelled from every school she's ever attended here and en Angleterre. . . . 'Twas she who used to injure old Italian crones on Ninth Avenue by tossing empty bottles down from the elevated cars onto their pates. 'Twas she who used to Charleston on the edge of the parapet of the roof on Central Park South. 'Tis she who is intimate with drunks and subway guards, who masks as a boy and frequents men's toilets to read the inscriptions. Oh merveilleuse! Only! Only! Only!

In his autobiography, Bowles paints a picture of their relationship as being of benefit to him in largely domestic terms. He recounts how he had a key made for Peggy, who took it upon herself, much to Bowles's satisfaction, to let herself into his room in the afternoon. Often bringing in a load of firewood gathered from the banks of the Hudson River, she would start a fire in the fireplace, warming the apartment in advance of Bowles's return from work. They often would then go out to dinner together and occasionally to the movies or to a concert or to the theater. At other times, they would spend the evening talking; afterward Bowles would walk her home.

From letters, however, another picture emerges in which the romance threw him into something of a quandary regarding his own sexual identity:

I am too perverse. If I find I am doing a pleasing thing and that people like it, I switch; it must be bad what I am doing. . . . Perhaps you will say it is a part of "pan-emotionalism." Hooray! If it is, I can still be normal. (By that I mean either hetero or homo) but if not, then I must wander down life seeking something to fall definitely in love with, and it is quite likely it will be animals. That will be too bad because there we have a vice more vicious than ordinary indulgence with humans. But I was long ago aware that whatever I put my hand to is made into some sort of a vice. There can never be any love, any affection, even any satiation "in my life." Whatever is to please me must be a vice. True, really. Being beaten, for instance. A vice. But how enjoyable. How exquisite. Biding myself with the pain, all the more enjoyable than misbehaving with some girl or man. . . . At least

I am abnormal in a "different way" but it makes life unspeakably foul and deep. There is no other conception of my existence I can form.

Bowles's preoccupation with "vice" is a concern that was repeated over and over in letters of this period: "I have a conception of vice. I tried several forms in Paris, but it depressed me." And in another letter he wrote: "I should like to know intimately all forms of pleasure, knowing yes, ja, si, da, oui, yeah beforehand that to all I should remain equally indifferent. As of course under vices I list heterosexual or otherwise indulgence. Any form—a vice. We must have it thus."

For all of his pronouncements, he also acknowledged that " 'my indictment of desire' is a heritage from three centuries of the tightest-laced New England puritanism." And while he clearly wanted to rebel ("I insist that I am not 'revolted by the sight' of 'fornication' "), he went on to categorize sex as a "necessary evil," a classification that his forebears would no doubt have endorsed. In short, Bowles was trapped between wanting to be "modern," yet haunted by a very traditional conception of morality, of sexuality as being inextricably bound up with vice. Concomitantly, there was a rather profound feeling on his part that vice was unavoidable, that despite his misgivings he was destined to indulge himself in some sort of vice.

Others have also verified Bowles's attitude at this time toward sexuality. "Paul was never of an ordinary sexual temperament," Virgil Thomson recalls. "How much actual power of ejaculation there ever was in Paul I never knew but I always guessed it as low." Similarly, Bruce Morrissette remembers Bowles as being sexually aloof, "put off by the very idea of sex."

In addition to his New England heritage, there was also another major factor operating in his psyche, namely a basic fear of involvement with another human being. Although there is doubtlessly some posturing here, one can, in fact, read Bowles's statement that he feels destined to fall in love with animals, not as an indication of perversion, but as an expression of his deeply held belief that any intimate human relationship, by its very nature, had the potential for unmasking his emotional self. Indeed, Bowles's various denunciations of sex must be examined in conjunction with an identity forged from separateness and isolation. As Bowles had always prided himself on self-containment, on hiding emotions, his repugnance of the sexual act follows quite logically from a childhood devoted to the concealment of true feelings. It is also important to note that the two sexual encounters he had thus far experienced were purely physical events, not a result of any deep feeling on his part, therefore leaving him free from becoming emotionally involved with his partners.

With Peggy, though, as their relationship was based on some sort of mutual feeling, there was potential for emotional as well as sexual involvement. As a result, in spite of his obvious infatuation with her, he ended the relationship after a few months. Whether this was done to avoid sexual or emotional entanglement is not clear, but it seems likely that he feared that sex would complicate matters, perhaps causing him to become more intimately involved with her than he desired.

In the letters of this period there are also some rather clear statements regarding homosexuality, which evidently fascinated him. Characteristically, though, he chose to construct an elaborate abstraction regarding the subject, rather than deal with it in terms of his own sexual identity. Perhaps a result of Bowles's not having yet come to terms with "giving in" to Hubert, his attitude reflected an inability, or refusal, to confront his own sexuality directly. He preferred, instead, to look at homosexuality within a greater scheme of "vices." Again to Morrissette, he wrote: "Homosexuality is a thrilling subject to me, just as sanguinary killings are, and rapes, and tales of drug addicts. They are exciting because they are melodramatic. A struggle! And who would not give several years of his life could he but strangle someone with impunity?"

There is more to this linkage than simply adolescent interest in the forbidden, for in some ways it shows Bowles's unwillingness to discriminate between "vices." In his mind, at least, he could conceive of himself as being a murderer as easily as being a homosexual. In fact, his fascination with these themes—homosexuality, murder, rape, and drug addiction—would never abate, would become major components in his fiction, continuing to obsess his creative imagination. He learned later that he could commit murder and rape, indulge in homosexuality and drug addiction with true impunity, by doing so vicariously, on paper. It was, indeed, a natural imaginative avenue for him to explore, for even at this point in his development he did not really express anything but abstract interest in these "vices," seeing them as "thrilling subjects" upon which to muse, not as acts in which to be truly engaged. In many ways it was a convenient solution: he could indulge himself, without really indulging.

Despite the short-lived romance with Peggy and continual fear of emotional or sexual intimacy, Bowles's friendships were many. And many of them were quite deep. At that time, his closest friend in New York was undoubtedly Daniel Burns, who highly approved of Bowles's European escapade, and was, as usual, quite supportive of his literary endeavors. Burns also tried to help out in a practical way. Knowing that Bowles was short on cash, he offered him a job grading French papers. Bowles, however, felt that one job was enough and declined the offer. Bowles also began to see a lot of Dorothy Baldwin about this time. He had known Baldwin for years: like the Hoaglands, she had been a summer resident of Glenora and had originally been a friend of Grandmother Bowles. She had by this time, however, fallen out of favor with Daddymama, who judged her an "out-and-out radical," thus making her even more interesting to Bowles. Baldwin was married to the painter Maurice Becker, and their studio in the Village was a frequent gathering place for artists. Bowles enjoyed visiting, listening attentively to the conversation of painters such as Stuart Davis and John Marin, eagerly absorbing the "Bohemian" atmosphere.

Bowles's long-distance friendship with Bruce Morrissette, who was still in Richmond, also flourished. At that time Morrissette was editing the University of Richmond literary magazine, *The Messenger*. He asked Bowles for some work. Bowles quickly responded by sending him some poems, from which he picked "Lucidity" for the March 1930 issue. Morrissette was also the beneficiary of several books sent by Bowles courtesy of Duttons. According to Morrissette, these gifts were made possible through Bowles's filching selected volumes from his employer. He recalls: "Paul felt that stealing books was not a crime, that a literary person had a Gidean right to them. Paul, of course, never called it stealing; he simply said he was 'borrowing the book indefinitely.' "

Bowles's job at Duttons consisted largely of selling Everyman's Library volumes and travel books. It was a fairly relaxed position, allowing Bowles to take advantage of free moments to work on a book of fiction, which he entitled *Without Stopping*. (Forty years later, he would use the same title for his autobiography.) The narrative of those years was made up of a series of short pieces recounting, in somewhat fictional form, his adventures wandering "without stopping" through the countryside outside of Paris. One surviving fragment, called "In the Creuse," details aspects of a stay at the château of his first French friends, Christine's family, the de Lavillates, whose summer house was in Gueret, in the Creuse region of France. Stylistically reminiscent of some of Gertrude Stein's work and indebted, in terms of subject, to surrealism, the fragment, written in poetic prose, is in one continuous paragraph, with long sentences and only occasional periods for punctuation, and with dialogue unencumbered by quotation marks. It essentially tells of an outing with an unnamed member of the de Lavillate family. The tale begins with realistic, if lyrical observations of the house and countryside, but soon a surrealist note is interjected. Caught in a rainstorm, the narrator and his companion seek refuge in a farmhouse occupied by two women, one of whom is lying behind a stove, head bandaged, babbling incoherently:

> I looked again behind the stove at the old woman who was still talking to herself and I thought she is not crazy. It is you [the other woman] who are trying to make her that way but I suppose she really was but I felt sorry for her. It had suddenly stopped raining and so we thanked the woman and went out. The other woman was still peeling potatoes and did not look up. . . . As we started walking away we heard a rattling of chains at the side of the house and looked. It was a brown and white nannygoat and when she saw we were looking at her she began to bleat so that I felt as sorry for her as I had for the old woman.

Although Bowles's style would change dramatically by the time he was writing serious fiction fifteen years later, "In the Creuse" contains many of the elements found in his more mature work: attention to detail, particularly natural phenomena; detached observation of a rather incredible event; and the commingling of the real and the unreal. In many ways, "In the Creuse" reads like a dream narrative, events unfolding without any attempt on the part of the author to interpret them. Despite the use of the first person, which usually implies an intimate connection with the subject matter, there is a decided sense of separation from the reality being recounted. As much emotional attention, for instance, is given to the bleating nannygoat as to the old woman. The end result is that of a rather chilling sense on the part of the reader that the observer is incapable of any real involvement in the action. He is firmly neutral, a sharp-eyed recording machine, unable or unwilling to judge the very events that he is relating.

At this stage Bowles relied on the device of dream consciousness to keep himself out of the narrative. Although he ultimately abandoned the mask of the dream narrative, it would prove to be a useful mode for some time in establishing an essential distance between himself, as narrator, and the events narrated. Curiously, because they are not filtered through the author's subjective vision, these events become more intense, forcing the reader to encounter firsthand the raw elements, often terrifying, related by the narrator.

Although Bowles spent a considerable amount of time writing during that autumn, he was still ambivalent about what art to pursue; he decided to continue his creative efforts in two directions simultaneously—in words and music—until such time as someone would pronounce him either a writer or a composer. Perhaps because he was equally gifted and equally unformed, he could afford this stance, but it is also clear that he was awaiting approval from an outside authority. On his own, he seemed totally unable to know which creative course would be the better. Fortunately, he did not have to wait long: in February of 1930, in an attempt to propel Bowles's composing career forward, Dorothy Baldwin decided that he should show his music to an acquaintance of hers, Henry Cowell. Cowell, though only in his early thirties, was quite established at that time as a musical innovator and was regarded by most of his contemporaries as a rather outrageous avant-garde American composer.

Bowles greatly looked forward to the meeting, thinking that possibly Cowell would confer on him a definitive artistic direction, that of a composer, thus putting to rest his uncertainty as to profession. In a letter to Morrissette he vividly described the meeting:

The most breathtaking music I have heard is Cowell's. He played four pieces to me this morning. I sat gasping (really one does gasp) and was unable to do anything but shake my head silently. . . . Before

all this I played to him my stuff, and he found every flaw and criticized it. A very acute person. . . . "That's an amusing little piece! but
I always beware of music like yours." He said my pieces were all
completely French in outlook, which I don't understand. He said I
was not capable of writing serious music until my viewpoint
changed. He called my stuff facile, and worse, frivolous. On the latter
score, however, he said he thought if I wanted to make "frivolous
music" my forte, that it would be quite possible for me to become
a master at it. He said, "You have a fully developed frivolity." All
this, however, was discouraging. Even my so-called serious things he
called very delicate, amusing, or light. And, horrible, he termed me
reactionary and asked why I made the gesture of returning to the
eighteenth century for all my material. And then he said, "You
belong in the drawing rooms of the wealthy American set in Paris.
They would appreciate your music better than anyone." He quite
attacked me, and only ended by advising me to be intelligent in
writing music; to consider each theme as a thought rather than a
display of a bon mot or somesuch. He's quite right. . . . He asked
me if I would like to meet Copland and I jumped at the chance.
. . . At parting H.C. said: "I think Copland will be extremely pleased
with your music. He likes glittering stuff. I myself prefer substantial
food."

Cowell came through on his promise to introduce Bowles to
Copland, sending him a note of introduction, which read: "Dear
Aaron: This will introduce Paul Bowles. His music is very French,
but it might interest you." Given the way that Cowell had so stri-
dently criticized his music, Bowles was a bit unsure of what to make
of Cowell's ambiguous note. What he did not realize was that
Copland had spent three years in France, most of it studying with
Nadia Boulanger, and was quite sympathetic to "French" music.
Despite his misgivings, Bowles rang Copland to make an appointment and was invited to come over to his apartment hotel.

The prospect of meeting the man that he felt to be "the most
important composer in the United States" delighted Bowles. Although Copland was certainly a rising star, Bowles's assessment of
him was a bit premature, for it must be remembered that the
composer was not yet thirty at the time and had written few of the
pieces that would eventually establish his reputation. Young, supremely talented, energetic, the man Bowles was about to meet

was described by the critic Paul Rosenfeld as "a slim, beglassed, shy, and still self-assured young fellow with the aspect of a benevolent and scholastic grasshopper."

When Bowles arrived at the hotel, he waited a bit outside the door, listening to an occasional note issuing from a piano. Finally, he got up his nerve to knock; a voice called, "Come in," and Bowles walked into the room. A thin young man was sitting at the piano. Barely acknowledging Bowles's presence, he informed him that "Aaron will be back in a minute," and continued working. Copland shortly returned. Bowles gave him Cowell's note. Copland read it quickly, then burst into laughter. An almost instant bond was formed. Bowles wrote to Morrissette that "Copland . . . is jolly and swell. I had no opp. to play for him but he read the scores for over an hour to himself. Strange. He remarked at least half a dozen times about my 'painfully logical mind'. . . . I quoted Cowell's phrase—'well developed frivolity,' and he laughed saying 'priceless'! Next Saturday I am to play for him on the stage at Steinway Hall. He is having a concert there that night and has the auditorium for the entire day."

Bowles's "performance" was well received, and Copland invited Bowles to come around some more and play for him. Finally, after a few more sessions, Copland asked Bowles if he would be interested in having a daily composition lesson with him. "This went beyond my most sanguine expectations," Bowles recalled years later. "I ceased working at Duttons and even moved back home in order to have a piano at which I could work."

Bowles began studying doggedly. Copland's method of instruction was to examine in-depth the Mozart piano sonatas that Bowles had to learn to play and analyze formally. The idea was that if Bowles understood what Mozart was doing, he would have a better sense of what composition itself was all about. Aside from studying Mozart, Bowles also spent a considerable amount of time on his own compositions, mostly short pieces for solo piano. He was supremely happy. Not only was he studying with one of the most important young composers of the period, but he had finally acquired a "civil status" as well.

The euphoria was not to last long, however, for at home his parents were insisting that he return to the University of Virginia for the second term. Shortly before his departure he wrote Morrissette, "I have no desire to return to the university; only the Blue Ridge." But his mother, in particular, was insistent. He finally acceded to the demands and in March 1930 got on the train and headed back to Charlottesville. This time, rather than take a room in a boardinghouse, he decided to get an apartment, which he shared with an acquaintance from the year before, Rosser Reeves. Since Bowles was still on the dean's list, however, he did not have to attend classes. As a result, he spent a considerable amount of time away from school, either wandering in the hills, or in Richmond with Bruce Morrissette.

Music still occupied a good deal of Bowles's time. He continued, informally, his study of the masters and worked as well at composing. One music professor at the school, living on campus, allowed Bowles to practice on his grand piano, an instrument far superior to those in the practice rooms. But no one could take the place of Copland in Bowles's mind. For him the University of Virginia was not even on the map of modern music or letters; he could not bring himself to feel that there was anything to be learned there, nor could he accept a teacher of a caliber far less than that of Copland. He felt distinctly isolated, far from the scene of contemporary music and literature.

This impression was heightened shortly before Easter when Bowles discovered that Martha Graham was to appear with the Philadelphia Orchestra under the direction of Leopold Stokowski in Stravinsky's *Rite of Spring.* A friend, John Widdicombe, suggested that if Bowles wanted to attend the ballet, they could hitchhike; the two immediately set off for Philadelphia.

At the concert on Friday, April 11, 1930, Bowles took in Graham's debut in the Stravinsky masterpiece. He was as overwhelmed by the music as he had been years earlier when he first heard the *Firebird*—so overwhelmed that he barely noticed Graham's performance, concentrating most of his energy on listening rather than watching. There was much in the music to delight and inspire Bowles. The theme itself, of primitive brutality and self-annihilation, found resonance in the mind of the young composer. Its musical expression, where rapidly alternating rhythms overpower melodic and harmonic elements (the "primitive" force vanquishing the "refined" qualities of the classical tradition), also revealed to Bowles some musical possibilities that he would later attempt to incorporate into his own work. Finally, there was the use of folkloric quotation, which Bowles, in numerous compositions, would himself employ to great advantage.

Aside from the ballet, the most significant event of the trip was meeting Harry Dunham, a friend of Widdicombe's from Princeton. Dunham had a quick intelligence, a tremendous sense of adventure, a keen interest in all the arts, and a personality that was positively magnetic. Bowles and Dunham hit it off at once and although the encounter was brief, a friendship had begun. Within a year, in fact, the two would be traveling together, sharing adventures, and building an extremely close relationship.

The day following the concert, Dunham took Bowles and Widdicombe to his club at Princeton and introduced Bowles to a friend of his, another Princeton student who was starting a magazine. It was to be called *Argo: An Individual Review* and would feature experimental literature. The student asked Bowles for a contribution. Bowles naturally thought of poetry, but the young editor wanted fiction. The only fiction that Bowles had written had been the "Without Stopping" narratives. After his return he sent the editor a short selection entitled "A White Goat's Shadow." It was published in the December issue of the magazine.

Back in Charlottesville, Bowles immediately felt misplaced again. As a remedy, he decided to invite his mentor to visit. In late April, Copland arrived and Bowles proudly introduced him to members of the faculty. He also arranged for Copland to give a brief concert at which he played a movement from his *Jazz Concerto*. The audience was not appreciative; in fact, they felt that Copland's music was simply a series of noises, a hoax, and a joke. Bowles was enormously distressed but Copland, used to less-than-positive reaction to his work and confident in his own musical vision, was unmoved. Copland's self-confidence earned him further respect from Bowles, but it also convinced him that the University of Virginia was hopelessly provincial. He would finish out the term, he decided, but would not bother continuing after his freshman year. On a bright day in the middle of June, final exams over, he packed his bags, made his way to the train station and left the University of Virginia forever.

Back in New York, Bowles met with Copland again, but could not resume daily lessons because Copland had been invited to Yaddo, the creative arts colony in Saratoga Springs, New York. Bowles wangled a retreat of his own with his Aunt Mary at Holden Hall. There he worked daily on learning two new works: Hindemith's *Übung in Drei Stücke* and the piano version of Stravinsky's *Histoire du Soldat.* Although his Aunt Mary had a piano, he could not practice the two dissonant pieces there because of her penchant for meditation. She did arrange for him, though, to use the piano at a neighbor's house, where he went each day for his two-hour practice session.

The technique employed by Stravinsky in *Histoire du Soldat* of incorporating a variety of musical idioms into the piece, from American ragtime to Spanish paso doble to Argentine tango, would leave a distinct impression on Bowles. In his own later compositions, such as "Music for a Farce" or his ballet *Yankee Clipper,* Bowles would employ a similarly eclectic technique, borrowing freely. At this stage, though, he was simply attempting to understand what Stravinsky had managed to do; once gestated, he could begin to work the technique into his own compositions.

At his aunt's that summer, he also made the acquaintance of some distant cousins, Nina Smith and her two sons. The elder, Oliver, then twelve, spent most of his time designing houses, including floor plans and elevations. The skill with which he executed the drawings greatly impressed Bowles, who had, of course, spent a great deal of time in his early childhood engaged in a similar endeavor. Although neither could have foreseen it, ten years later Smith and Bowles would become close friends and collaborators in the theater, Smith designing sets, Bowles writing the music for the productions.

Finally, Bowles decided to join Copland at Yaddo. He wrote to Elizabeth Ames, the executive director of the foundation, and with Copland's help was invited down to spend September and October. Bowles spent his days composing or wandering in the woods, occasionally stopping outside Copland's turret studio, located some distance from the main house by a small pond, to listen to the composer's progress on his *Piano Variations.* At dinner he talked politics with the other residents and took pride in becoming the resident anagrams master. Despite the freedom to work, Bowles was not totally enthralled with the Yaddo community, nor as productive as he had hoped to be. In October he wrote to Burns: "there are people and people here and most of them get on one's nerves il faut admettre. . . . i am writing some songs you may like. the one i have completed i discover to be sentimental. isn't it a pity.''

In late October, Bowles returned to New York City, followed by Copland. Composition lessons resumed on an intermittent basis, but a new problem presented itself: Copland was planning to go to Berlin in late April and wanted Bowles to accompany him there and then take up study with the renowned teacher Nadia Boulanger in Paris in the fall. The problem was not so much with going to Europe as with acquiring the necessary funds. Since his parents could not be counted on for a loan, Bowles asked Harry Dunham, whom he had been seeing a lot of since their first meeting in Princeton. Dunham, however, had no money at the time, but was to come into a small sum on his birthday in November 1931, as long as he abstained from smoking until then. Ever resourceful, Dunham decided to ask his parents for an advance and took Bowles to meet them. The meeting did not go well. Dunham's parents had no sympathy for Bowles's plight; indeed, they seemed to feel that he was a rather objectionable character, "one likely to wield a destructive influence over their son." Dunham nonetheless persisted, and finally managed to extract the money from his parents, which he turned over to Bowles.

In December, Bruce Morrissette wrote to Bowles, asking him if he would like to be a guest editor of a special issue of *The Messenger.* Bowles quickly agreed and immediately sent out letters to some of the more famous names in avant-garde poetry at the time, including William Carlos Williams, Gertrude Stein, and Edouard Roditi, a foreign-born American poet whose work Bowles had admired in *transition.* His letter to Stein has survived:

I wonder if you could be persuaded to donate one or two things to a small revue published in Richmond, Virginia, called "The Messenger"? I am not the editor, but I have been selecting European material for my friend Mr. Morrissette, who is the editor. I cannot overemphasize the fact that I should like your pieces solely because of their literary value which I feel to be immense, and not to exhibit as curios (which I have discovered, alas, to be the motive underlying the printing of your work in one or two, at least, of our American "avant-garde" mags to whose editors I have talked. They are still unable to understand that anyone who writes English today with any degree of mastery owes you an inestimable debt). I sincerely hope you will have something to spare for us.

Bowles's request struck a sympathetic nerve in Stein. She sent him a contribution by return mail. Williams and Roditi also sent contributions; with Roditi and Stein, Bowles continued to correspond.

That winter, Bowles also gave his first public poetry reading. It came about through Charles-Henri Ford, who had published some of Bowles's poems that year in his little magazine, *Blues,* which now carried the subtitle "A Bisexual Bimonthly." Ford had organized a poetry reading of *Blues* contributors in Greenwich Village and invited Bowles. Feeling a bit shy and awkward, he decided to read only the poems he'd written in French. Using the foreign language to create a buffer between himself and the audience worked; no one apparently understood or responded to them. "You're way out over your head with these people, boy," remarked one of the listeners. As that had been Bowles's desire, he felt happy that he was suitably avant the avant-garde.

Having spent most of the last year and a half living on his own, in Charlottesville, at Holden Hall, and at Yaddo, Bowles found the readjustment to living at home difficult. No longer a child, he could not abide the tight control still exerted by his father. Although he attempted to minimize contact with him, the very presence of his father was enough to send his emotions into a tumult. Shortly before his twentieth birthday, the rage, held back for so many years, finally worked its way out:

> at the age of nineteen I was astonished one night to discover that I had just thrown a meat knife at my father. I rushed out of the house, shattering the panes of glass in the front door, and began to run down the hill in the rain. Before I had gone three blocks Daddy caught up with me in the car, then parked and came along behind me on foot. I stopped and turned around to face him.
>
> "I want to talk with you," he said. "You can't do this again to your mother. It wasn't my idea to come after you."

Bowles returned to the house, but did not speak to his mother. His father admonished him for not apologizing to Rena. At this,

Bowles screamed back: "You can't stand me because every time you look at me you realize what a mess you've made of me! But it's not my fault I'm alive. I didn't ask to be born."

In his room Bowles pondered his action. He was as upset by his outburst as by the act itself, feeling that by verbally expressing his rage he had revealed an essential weakness of being. But the violence also disturbed him:

> the throwing of the knife, which was now a fact rather than a fantasy, worried me with its implications of future danger. If it were so easy to lose control in this situation, it would be just as possible to lose it in one where the results might be tragic. As usual I reminded myself that since nothing was real it did not matter too much.

For Bowles, strength came from not disclosing one's true feelings. In this, he was the mirror image of his father, who similarly prided himself on never allowing his son the satisfaction of knowing that he was affected by Paul's actions. Bowles and his father were locked in an elaborate struggle in which the contest was measured in terms of how little or much personal emotion was revealed. That this was the real cause of Bowles's anger after the fact becomes clear through an examination of his own statement regarding the incident. He recalls feeling "like a person goaded by a provocateur into revealing what he should have kept to himself." Precisely because he was forced to reveal his emotions he felt vanquished, was troubled by an overwhelming sense that his father had gained the upper hand. Through the icy deflection of his own self-concern, Claude had scored a major victory in the battle of repressing personal emotions.

Despite the unpremeditated quality of his action, it is important to note that Bowles felt no regret for the act itself, but instead was upset by his blatant expression of emotion. He feared losing control, seeing in both the uncharacteristic outburst and in the act itself an essential weakness in his makeup; the shell that had for so many years held his anger in check had finally cracked, leaving him vulnerable. As long as Bowles believed that his inner core could not be penetrated (at least as far as his father was concerned), that the nearly constant scorn and derision could not reach beneath the surface, he felt strong. But with this act came the revelation that the long-suppressed anger was not as deeply repressed as he had believed. Now, unable to feel secure in his ability to control his rage, the concern entered: would it, could it happen again, just as unwillingly, as unpredictably? As an already devout believer in the power of the unconscious, there could be no certain answer. With this knowledge, the only consolation available was through a rather extraordinary act of self-deception: "Since nothing was real, it did not matter too much."

Tension in the house gradually subsided to the usual level. Bowles kept busy outside the house, stayed largely to himself when his father was at home. It was easy. He was getting ready to sail back to Europe in a few months and had much to do in the meantime, not the least of which was to try to learn German. He bought a grammar book and a dictionary and set down to study the language. But the ease with which he had learned French and a fair amount of Italian was not forthcoming with German. "I just didn't have an affinity for it," he recalled.

Despite his basic disinterest in German, he greatly looked forward to returning to Europe and began to make plans. It was decided that he and Copland would not sail together. Copland was engaged in putting together the final Copland-Sessions concert and the Philadelphia Orchestra was premiering his *Dance Symphony* in mid-April; thus he could not depart until after the middle of the month. Bowles, seeing no reason to stay longer in New York than he had to, decided to leave in late March, just after the concert, which that year revolved around a theme of music and film. They agreed to meet up in late April in Paris, then go on to Berlin in May. Bowles bought a ticket for Le Havre aboard the *McKeesport,* an old American freighter. On March 25 the ship lifted anchor, and Bowles found himself off on another European odyssey. Unlike his last voyage, however, he was going to something this time, not simply escaping from where he had been. Burns and a few others saw him off. No one, least of all Bowles, knew when they'd see him again on the American side of the Atlantic.

CHAPTER 7

THE VOYAGE over was not as pleasant as the trip on the *Rijndam* had been. On the first day, a severe storm began, which tossed the ship for two days, sending water cascading into Bowles's stateroom. In addition, he felt deprived of company, the only other passenger being a rather boorish Frenchman, who kept primarily to himself. Bowles busied himself reading and also began planning a new composition: setting some of Poe's poems to music. From the ship he wrote to Burns that he planned to use Poe's earlier poems. "His others, *because* of their Poesque quality, have 'lost something' by becoming well known. I like 'Ulalume' for instance, as well as any, but it would seem silly to set it to music. By setting to music I mean 'make songs of.' " In fact, he did not set Poe until 1935; once he disembarked in France, he found new sources of inspiration. But at this juncture, in the mid-Atlantic, he was still closer to America and American sources than he was to Europe.

In Paris once again, Bowles first checked into a small hotel, but quickly realized that if he could find a free place to stay it would enable him to economize even further. Having been corresponding regularly with Roditi, now in Germany, he wrote to him again telling him of his financial difficulties, and in particular complaining about the high price of lodging. Reading through the lines, Roditi wrote back to Bowles, referring him to a friend of his in Paris, Carlo Suarès, a French writer of Egyptian origin, who might be able to provide him with a place to stay. Bowles wasted no time in getting in touch with Suarès, who invited him to move in. Shortly afterward, Roditi learned from Suarès that Bowles was quite unobtrusive as a guest: "It was like keeping a cat. Paul would curl up and sleep on a sofa and as long as [Suarès] provided him with milk and a few other things he was a perfect guest."

The transition from American to expatriate American didn't take long. Emboldened by his recent accomplishments, Bowles no longer felt the shyness of the year before. Almost immediately upon his arrival in Paris, on April 10, 1931, he decided to look up Gertrude Stein. As he had had an amicable correspondence with her, and felt fairly confident that she would see him, he went to her apartment at 27 rue de Fleurus, rang the bell, and waited anxiously. A maid answered; he informed her that he had just arrived from America and needed to see Miss Stein, if only for a minute. After inquiring as to who he was, Stein invited him in, introducing him to Alice B. Toklas. The two seemed bemused by his appearance. Then Stein explained: "I was sure from your letters that you were an elderly gentleman of at least seventy-five." "A highly eccentric elderly gentleman," added Toklas.

Stein took an instant liking to Bowles, inviting him to dinner that night. The only other guest present was a Frenchman, Bernard Fay, a Harvard-educated history professor. Fay, too, had a very positive reaction to Bowles. According to Alice Toklas, Fay was impressed with his honesty: "Bernard was very pleased with the young boy, for when Bernard said to him, What does your father do? he answered, without any embarrassment or hesitation, My father is a dentist." During the dinner, Stein decided that Bowles was misnamed, that he really should be called Freddy. Names were important to Stein at that time. As she would write the following year in *Four in America*, "It is the first or Christian name that counts, that is what makes one be as they are." The other two concurred that Bowles's middle name was more appropriate than his given name, and from that time on Bowles was known in the Stein circle as Freddy. While the renaming is certainly amusing and illustrative of Stein's didactic and dogmatic personality, it also says something about the way she saw young Paul Frederic Bowles. For her, "Paul," with its Christian overtones, was a mask worn by a somber, elderly gentleman; the real person at her dinner table, youthful, alive, cocky, was a "Freddy."

Stein also decided that night that it was up to her to launch "Freddy." Accordingly, she, Toklas, and Fay talked about what people Bowles needed to meet in Paris, in the process compiling quite a list. Though it was never formally acted upon, by virtue of his having simply met Stein and company the doors of the avant-garde were opened to him.

Through Fay, for instance, he was introduced to Richard

Thoma, co-editor, with Samuel Putnam and Ezra Pound, of a magazine recently born in Paris, *The New Review*. And through Thoma he managed to meet Jean Cocteau. In a letter to Burns he recounted his first visit to the French poet:

> He rushed about the room with great speed for two hours and never sat down once. Now he pretended to be an orang outang [sic], next an usher at the Paramount Theater, and finally he held a dialogue between an aged grandfather and his young grandson which was sidesplitting. I think never have I seen anyone like him in my life. He still smokes opium every day and claims it does him a great deal of good. . . . His house is quite fantastic, giving one the feeling that outside are the tropics, and that these beige and taupe hangings and mattings are put out for coolness's sake. One room is devoted to a titanic Picasso which extends from one end to the other, and on an adjacent wall is Marie Laurencin's portrait of him.

Thoma also introduced him to Ezra Pound. He described that visit to Burns:

> Pound talked with me about an hour and a half about sound movies and the various methods of recording the soundwaves and I found I knew nothing about it whatever. I also found I knew nothing about opera when I mentioned that topic. At least I found that he did not know about it, and he went on to show to what degree. He said if he were a young musician he would aim straight at the talking picture without giving a thought to stage music. It is about the same idea that Hindemith has, I suppose, but somehow it seems rather sad and not nearly romantic enough for me. I am a reactionary in such respects.

The list of luminaries Bowles would meet in just the next couple of weeks was staggering. Stein could not have orchestrated a better "launching," or as she called it, a *"lancer*-ing." They included composer Virgil Thomson; the painters Pavel Tchelitchew and Bernard Fay's younger brother, Emmanuel; Marie Jolas, wife of Eugène Jolas, editor of *transition;* and even André Gide. Bowles recalls that the meeting with Gide lasted perhaps two minutes, but remembers nothing of the conversation. He was too awestruck during it, being face-to-face with his idol, even to know what it was they talked about during their brief encounter. Still, it made for an impressive fact to report back home and to tell Copland upon his arrival. Indeed, at this point in time, Bowles was quite earnest in meeting the famous, simply because they were famous. He recalled years later: "I was never aware of wanting to be part of a community, no I wanted to meet them. I suppose I simply felt that I was taking pot shots at clay pipes. Pop! Down goes Gertrude, down goes Jean Cocteau, down goes André Gide. . . . Apparently I thought such encounters were important or I wouldn't have bothered, because it involved a lot of work and sometimes a sacrifice of something I cared about."

Despite Bowles's growing sense of his own importance through association with the famous and their acceptance of him, his ego was dealt quite a blow by Stein's reaction to his poems. One afternoon he showed her his work. After careful perusal of his verse, she announced her verdict: "Well, the only trouble with all this is that it's not poetry." To Bowles's demand as to what it was, if it was not poetry, she replied, "How should I know what it is? You wrote it." She went on to tell him why:

"Look at this." She pointed to a line on the top page. "What do you mean, *the heated beetle pants?* Beetles don't pant. Basket [her white poodle] pants, don't you, Basket? But beetles don't. And here you've got purple clouds. It's all false."

"It was written without conscious intervention," I told her sententiously. "It's not my fault. I didn't know what I was writing."

"Yes, yes, but you knew *afterwards* what you'd written, and you should have known it was false. It was false, and you sent it off to *transition.* Yes, I know; they published it. Unfortunately. Because it's not poetry."

The remarks hurt terribly. Bowles, at twenty, was extraordinarily confident in his past achievements, proud of his publications in the leading literary magazines. Previous criticism of his poetry had always come from sources he could easily dismiss, but Stein, for him, represented the cutting edge of avant-garde poetics. She could not be written off as incompetent to judge his arcane *oeuvre.* He was delighted, therefore, when about a month later he got a letter from Stein informing him that not all of his poetry was as bad as she had first thought: "I take back the harsh things I said after reading the Morada one. Alright, only it's alright to learn to play Bach in poetry too, it's not so easy to see how to learn but not for that any the less interesting, advice to a musician who may be a poet, who knows. . . ." He wrote to her of his gratitude: "I am glad (gladder than that really) that you don't dislike all the poems as much as the first one. I was quite discouraged by the finality of: 'He's not a poet. No. He's not a poet' that evening. Things look up."

Copland arrived at the end of April. Bowles met him at the Gare St.-Lazare and immediately related to him his encounters with the famous, adding that Stein had invited them to dinner that night. Copland, Stein, and Toklas hit it off; the dinner was a great success, Stein inviting them to visit her in Bilignin, her country residence, in the summer. Although Bowles was quite content to remain in Paris, Copland was eager to get to Germany and back to work. After just a few days in Paris, Copland bought train tickets, and to Bowles's chagrin the two headed off for Berlin.

Copland had made advance arrangements to rent the Berlin apartment of the American poet Alfred Kreymborg; Bowles had to find a place to live. On the first day of his search he found through an agency a room in the house of a Baronin von Massenbach at 14 Guntzelstrasse. The room was pleasant enough; Bowles particularly liked its large balcony overlooking the street, but he did not care at all for Berlin. Partly it was the architecture, which Bowles found hideous, partly the discrepancy between rich and poor: "It was like a film of Fritz Lang's. The 'haves' were going hog-wild while the 'have-nots' seethed with hatred. There was a black cloud of hatred over the whole east end of the city."

Bowles had hoped to meet Roditi in Germany, but by then he had left for London. Nonetheless, Roditi sent him a few letters of introduction to some friends of his living in Berlin, among them Jean Ross, a young British woman who had grown up in Cairo, Sigismund von Braun, a young government official, and a sculptor, Renée Sintenis. Friendless in Berlin, and not able to speak German, Bowles decided to look them up. He wrote to Roditi about meeting Jean Ross: "When a few days ago I called on Miss Ross, she introduced me to Sherwood I believe he is called, and to a

Polish friend who was staying with her. Sherwood showed me a passport photo of you which makes you look slightly uncanny, or have you mad eyes?" Sherwood was, in fact, Christopher Isherwood, who in turn took him to meet Stephen Spender.

Bowles found Isherwood likable; Spender less so. "Together they were overwhelmingly British, two members of a secret society constantly making references to esoteric data not available to outsiders." He was also put off by Spender's attempt, through his dress, to draw attention to himself: "I noted with disapproval the Byronesque manner in which he wore his shirt, open down to his chest. It struck me as unheard of that he should want to announce his status as a poet rather than dissimulate it." For Bowles, it was far more important to be a poet than to be thought of as one. Indeed, having a true "civil status" meant that one was free from having to cultivate a presence.

Despite Bowles's mild aversion to Spender and his feeling of somehow not quite belonging, he began to have lunch with the English expatriates daily on the terrace of the Café des Westens. Bowles often brought Copland; Isherwood always brought Jean Ross. But Bowles remembers that at these lunches he felt that he was being treated with "good-humored condescension." "They accepted Aaron," he writes, "but they did not accept me because they considered me too young and inexperienced or perhaps merely uninteresting." The remark is curious in that Isherwood was only twenty-five at the time and Spender just twenty-one. But compared to either Englishman, Bowles certainly was inexperienced. Roditi comments that the two "did seem much older, as they were quite insular." In addition, he remarks that "they had never before known an American, and certainly not one like Paul." Isherwood, who found Bowles attractive but "aloof," would later immortalize his Berlin days, grafting Bowles's last name onto one of the most memorable characters in *Goodbye to Berlin* (subsequently adapted for the stage as *Cabaret*), Sally Bowles. The model for Sally was none other than Jean Ross.

With Sigismund von Braun, Bowles seems to have had a rather difficult relationship. The German made it clear at once that he had no use for the type of poetry that Bowles and Roditi were writing and continually expressed incredulity at Bowles's remarks. Bowles's main interest in Renée Sintenis seems to have been that she was a close friend of the French surrealist poet René Crevel, whom Bowles admired and to whom he hoped to be introduced through the sculptor.

Aside from socializing, Bowles was also studying composition daily with Copland. At the baronin's he had use of a grand piano on which to do his composing and practicing, but to his surprise, he found that the average German was no more sympathetic to contemporary music than the provincial Virginians had been. His daily work on a loud and dissonant piece for solo piano was met by cries from the neighbors who shouted, *"Fenster zu!"* [Shut the window!]. The more time Bowles spent in Berlin, in fact, the less he liked it. He wrote, in a letter to Burns that, "i have come to the decision that Berlin is the least amusing place i have ever seen. it is the synonym for stupidity. i should be happy if i never saw the city after today." But it wasn't just Berlin that bothered him, it was Germany and the Germans. Small incidents escalated in his mind to become large ones. For instance, on a weekend visit to Rheinsberg with Copland the proprietor at the hotel refused to allow Bowles to sign his occupation on the register as *Komponist* (composer). Although he and Copland argued with the man, the manager steadfastly clung to his position that a person as young as Bowles could not possibly be a composer. Finally, after some more discussion, he relented, rewriting Bowles's occupation as *Jazz-Komponist*. Although Copland found the whole affair amusing, Bowles took it seriously, as another indication of "typical German" mentality.

As a result of his dislike for Germany, Bowles began to think of an escape. Out of loyalty to Copland, and because he realized how important it was to take advantage of learning from the master, Bowles did not feel he could leave Berlin permanently. He reasoned, though, that a short trip to France, or somewhere, could satisfy him and not have a detrimental effect on his relationship with his teacher. To his delight, about a month or so after his arrival, an invitation came from Carlo Suarès to accompany him on a visit to the metaphysical philosopher Krishnamurti, then living in Holland. Suarès was at that time quite involved with theosophy, actively editing the Krishnamurti newsletter. While Bowles was not an adherent, he was grateful for the opportunity to get out of Berlin.

Although Krishnamurti seems to have impressed Bowles, the most memorable part of the visit was apparently Krishnamurti's castle and environs. In a letter to Burns, Bowles devoted only one phrase to the philosopher, but went on at length about the atmosphere:

> i found holland épatant and krishnamurti extraordinary. Philosophy par excellence. . . . the castle where krishnamurti lives is a lovely early eighteenth century place standing in the middle of a standing moat green with water green from standing years on years about the castle. one lone swan swam sulkily about hoping for crumbs which were often forthcoming when various extheosophists decided to feed the noisy pigeons that complained throatily all day. and then at night the peacocks would begin to scream insanely.

Back in Berlin he was chided by Copland, who took Bowles's spending so much time away from his work as a lack of seriousness. Bowles appeared unmoved by the rebuke, and wrote to Burns: "i have written not a poem since march. nor any music. nor drawn a picture. nor learned anything. but what of it?" Still, despite his apparent unconcern, the mere fact that he bothered to mention his inability to work indicates that the matter was not one he took lightly. At about the same time he wrote to Roditi: "Music is so difficult. One follows in the footsteps ten years behind, of Antheil, Copland, Blitzstein, twenty years behind Hindemith, thirty behind Stravinsky, who said: *'Les autres, ils sont encore romantiques. Moi, je suis déjà romantique.'* [The others are still Romantics. *I* am already a Romantic.]"

Possibly because he was searching for a creative milieu, Bowles took up again with Isherwood and Spender and frequently visited Jean Ross, who lived in the same rooming house as Isherwood. The young Englishmen were all enthusiastic about Berlin; to Bowles it was still a "strange, ugly, vaguely sinister city." Roditi posits that part of the reason Bowles did not enjoy Berlin was that, accustomed to standing out physically and being admired for it, he was dismayed to find that his blond hair and "Germanic" looks were suddenly common. "The place was crawling with pretty, young blond men—Paul was nothing special there." Given his dissatisfaction, Bowles was delighted when Copland suggested they go to Bad Pyrmont to a *Musikfest* at which Bartók was to perform. Not only was he interested in hearing Bartók, he also thought he might be able to visit the Dadaist artist Kurt Schwitters, who lived in nearby Hannover. While the concerts, the ostensible reason for the trip, left little impression on him, his excursion to Hannover to see Schwitters was another matter. In a letter to Burns, he doesn't even mention the festival, but describes at great length his visit to the artist:

In hannover i stayed at schwitter's [sic] house. he is amusing and pleasant. he and his wife kept insisting that i stay longer so that though i went to stay two hours i stayed fortyeight. heard his vocal sonata and then he asked me to translate it into pianomusic. so most of the time was spent working at that. we took a walk about the dumping grounds to hunt for material for his statues he has in his studio, and found half a tin spoon, a piece of mosquitonetting and part of a thermosbottle. he was very thankful. and he went along picking up small pieces of glass and china that could be broken into still smaller pieces, and dashing them with zest against stones then turning grinning toward me. once he found a whole vase, and was *very* thankful. we were bitten severely by mosquitoes who he claimed were angry with me because i had not been to norway and spitzbergen like he had. . . . he has six salamanders, seven guineapigs and five turtles, oh yes, and two lizards that run about on the floor when one is not looking. at night the guineapigs squealed sulkily on the balcony so i could not sleep. he had never heard of gertrude stein.

The vocal sonata mentioned in the letter was actually a syllable poem, which went like this:

> Lanke trr gll.
> Pe pe pe pe pe
> Ooka. Ooka. Ooka. Ooka.
> Lanke trr gll.
> Pi pi pi pi pi
> Tzuuka. Tzuuka. Tzuuka. Tzuuka.

It would find its way into the rondo movement of Bowles's *Sonata for Oboe and Clarinet,* the syllable sounds suggesting the tonality of the two instruments; the rhythm and vocal inflections, the form. It was probably good that Bowles managed to get some music out of the visit, for once back in Berlin, Copland again admonished him for not working hard enough. His annoyance was lessened, however, once Bowles began work on his new composition. Copland, in fact, was so pleased with the piece that he would later include it in a program that he would produce in London in December of that year.

By now summer had arrived, and with it the inevitable departure that Bowles had been longing for almost since his arrival in Berlin. He would first go to Paris, then to Bilignin to visit Stein and Toklas. Copland was off to England but would rejoin Bowles at Stein's. Preparations were quickly made and Bowles bade his own good-bye to Berlin.

Bowles arrived in the Rhône Valley in mid-July. Stein, Toklas, and Basket met him at the train station in Culoz and drove him to their house in the tiny village of Bilignin. Bowles was delighted by the house, "as charming a place as one could ask for. High on a hillside overlooking a lovely valley, built the middle of the seventeenth century, walls, parapets, gardens, summer houses, all." Stein and Toklas were excellent hosts, taking him on excursions through the region.

At home, Bowles was assigned the duty of giving Basket his daily run. The ritual, like the bath that preceded it (given to the dog by Toklas), had to be performed at a certain hour every morning. For some reason it required Bowles to don lederhosen. Once outfitted, Bowles would proceed to run about the garden with the dog trailing behind. The quick pace had to be maintained or else Basket would overtake his exerciser, scratching the back of Bowles's exposed legs. All of this was done to the accompaniment of Stein's commands of "Faster, Freddy, faster." Stein obviously greatly enjoyed the session, and Bowles, almost in spite of himself, did too, for it seemed to him "a sign of the most personal kind of relationship."

As delighted as Bowles was at getting to know Stein, he also found her extremely opinionated, and at times, perplexing. Despite her hospitality, it was clear that she was also taking the opportunity to sum Bowles up. Her first judgment, as related in *The Autobiography of Alice B. Toklas,* was that "he is delightful and sensible in summer but neither delightful nor sensible in winter." After a couple of weeks at Bilignin, Bowles himself was becoming aware that he "existed primarily for Gertrude Stein as a sociological exhibit." He commented further on this notion in the autobiography:

> For her I was the first example of my kind. I provided her initial encounter with a species then rare, now the commonest of contemporary phenomena, the American suburban child with its unrelenting spleen. . . . After a week or so, Gertrude Stein pronounced her verdict: I was the most spoiled, insensitive, and self-indulgent young man she had ever seen, and my colossal complacency in rejecting all values appalled her. But she said it beaming with pleasure, so that I did not take it as adverse criticism. "If you were typical, it would be the end of our civilization," she told me. "You're a manufactured savage."

In between excursions and exercise sessions, Bowles did a great deal of reading, particularly of Stein's work, spending considerable time discussing it with the author herself. From Bilignin he wrote to Burns:

> I am also getting a light on Miss Stein's own works, which become constantly more difficult. All my theories on her I discover to have been utterly vagrant. She has set me right, by much labor on her part, and now the fact emerges that there is nothing in her works save the sense. The sound, the sight, the soporific repetitions to which I had attached such great importance, are accidental, she insists, and the one aim of her writing is the superlative *sense*. "What is the use of writing," she will shout, "unless every word makes the utmost sense?" Naturally all that renders her 'opera' far more difficult, and after many hours of patient reading, I discover that she is telling the truth, and that she is wholly correct about the entire matter.

The importance of the discovery was what it said to him about his own writing. With this comment began his new awakening as to how the saying must be said. Bowles's work, including the few poems he would write after this point, are decidedly imbued with "sense." Words are no longer used simply for their sensorial effect, as in the early poems, but because they also communicate something important to the reader. If Bowles did not subsequently abandon the practice of allowing unconscious revelation to dictate the substance of a piece, he nonetheless learned from Stein that the conscious mind must reshape the outpouring of the unrestrained imagination.

In the summer of 1931, he wrote to Burns: "And what is even more painful is that all my poems are worth a large zero. That is the end of that. And unless I undergo a great metamorphosis, there will never be any more poems."

It was not just the rejection of his work from some months earlier that was haunting him, but a more recent encounter. Already stung by Stein's criticism, he was hurt furthermore that summer when Stein inquired of Bowles whether he had yet revised the poems she had commented on so unfavorably. Bowles replied that he didn't see the point, as the poems in question had already been published. "You see?" she cried. "I told you you were no poet. A real poet, after one conversation, would have gone upstairs and at least tried to recast them, but you haven't even looked at them." Bowles had to agree.

There were, in fact, very few poems forthcoming after that summer. For three years, Bowles didn't write any verse; when he did begin writing again in 1934, the few poems from that year were all in French. It is as if in another language he could assume another persona, another style. Indeed, the French poems are distinctly different; the phrasing is economical, the language precise, the observations of reality more convincing. Far more than the early poems, they "tell the truth." "Ed Djouf" is a good example. Written in French in 1934, it is an evocative poem, as spare as the desert it depicts:

> One arrives there
> in nine stops of seven days each.
> In the animated sketch of the horizon
> are crests, wildly broken, then mended.
> Here, the smell of gas, progress, agony.
> In nine stops of seven days each
> one arrives in the silence.

His despair over poetry pushed him further into music and back to fiction, but with writing, the shadow of Stein loomed over him. It would take until 1935 for Bowles finally to throw off Stein's influence. In a letter written in August of that year to Morrissette, he wrote: "Here is a proclamation: knowing G.S. was the most retarding influence I've ever had to face! I've decided all that in the past few weeks. She is not pernicious because, and only because no one is so profoundly affected by her as I was. Not the work, of course, but *knowing* her. . . . Now that I have that settled, I try to console myself with the compensating tricks I imagine I learned directly or otherwise from knowing her."

In despair over his poetry, he decided to turn again to fiction the summer of 1931, feeling, however, that Stein would probably not approve of that either. He wrote to Roditi: "I am starting again to write stories, and I think you would like them as well as my poems. They are certainly not what Gertrude Stein wants, and I think I shall later have to do what she wants because she knows what is good for me and everything else I dare say is easier and I am lazy. She knows."

Copland arrived toward the end of July for a brief visit. He too was taken about by Stein and Toklas to tour the countryside. In addition, Stein used the visit to ask questions of Copland about her curious young houseguest. "Why does he have so many clothes? He's got enough for six young men," she would remark. But chiefly the interrogations were about Bowles's talent. When Copland replied that yes, Bowles was talented, but that he didn't work terribly hard at it, Stein triumphantly seized on the remark. "That's what I thought," she said. "He's started his life of crime too young." Toklas further recorded that for Stein the most memorable remark of all was Copland's admonition to Bowles: "If you don't work now when you are twenty, nobody will love you when you are thirty."

For Stein, Americans represented a rather peculiar species, more concerned with morality than aesthetics, greatly taken with honorable action, imbued with a work ethic, a sense of family. Bowles stood in contrast to all of this. At twenty, he was far more interested in art than action, in idleness than in work, far more engaged with himself than with his family history. Nonreligious and amoral, he truly exemplified a new breed, but a breed that had sprung, nonetheless, from an America that Stein had once known. Indeed, her fascination came from the fact that America had produced such a phenomenon.

Despite his newly acquired civil status of composer, Bowles was not quite as inwardly confident of his status as he appeared to be. In some sense, he was still searching for a clear sense of artistic direction and for a way of being an artist in the world. His near-obsessive desire to visit the famous can be seen, at least in part, as a reflection of this quest to learn how to live as a creative person. Having decided to pursue an artistic career, at this point he was struggling with establishing his own identity as an artist and in doing so, was forced to confront the old duality. For in spite of the models he found in Stein, Copland, Pound, Cocteau, Schwitters, and others, he was unable to achieve their seemingly effortless adoption of their roles. As revealed in his reaction to Spender, of one thing he was sure: an artist is an artist by virtue of his art-making, not by his outward appearance or pronouncements. For Bowles the notion of the outer and inner selves still held sway. And as in childhood, the idea of revealing one's true self was completely repugnant to him. Bowles was in many ways still a product of his father's manufacturing.

"You don't want to go to Villefranche. Everybody's there. And St. Jean-de-Luz is empty and with an awful climate. The place you should go is Tangier. Alice and I've spent three summers there, and it's fine. Freddy'd like it because the sun shines every day." So said Gertrude Stein to Bowles and Copland one day over lunch when they were discussing where they should go to spend the rest of the summer. After some deliberation, and after Stein's promise to Copland that yes, they did have pianos there, it was decided. Tickets were bought on the *Imeréthie II,* sailing from Marseilles in late July, and almost before they knew what had happened to them, Bowles and Copland found themselves bound for Morocco. It would be "a rest, a lark, a one-summer stand," they reasoned, an exotic place, far from New York, that Bowles could write friends about having visited.

CHAPTER 8

A CHANGE IN destinations was announced, just as Bowles and Copland went on board the *Iméréthie II.* Instead of Tangier, the ship would make its last stop in Ceuta, the Spanish protectorate, northeast of Tangier. The first call would be in Oran, Algeria. On the second day of the journey, at dawn, the ragged mountains of the Algerian coast loomed on the horizon. Bowles became tremendously excited, "as if some interior mechanism had been set in motion by the sight of the approaching land. Always without formulating the concept, I had based my sense of being in the world partly on an unreasoned conviction that certain areas of the earth's surface contained more magic than others. . . . a secret connection between the world of nature and the consciousness of man, a hidden but direct passage which bypassed the mind."

A few hours later the ferry docked in Oran. To Bowles, the city seemed both "beautiful and terrible." As they had a one-day layover in the port, Bowles and Copland proceeded to explore the town. While working at Duttons, Bowles had spent a great deal of time studying the Baedekers. The name of a suburb, Eckmühl-Noiseux, stuck in his mind, and therefore, despite the heat and dust and cicadas screaming in the hot wind, he persuaded Copland to get on board a tramcar and ride out with him to visit the little suburb with the odd name. The place, deserted in the heat of the early afternoon, didn't amount to much.

Although his curiosity about Eckmühl-Noiseux was satisfied, Bowles was not quite content to go back into town but insisted on another brief side trip, this time to the fortress at Mers-el-Kebir. Approaching the fort, they were promptly met by a rifle-toting soldier who ordered them away from the premises. Once safely back on the road Copland expressed the sentiment that he was glad they were not staying in Algeria. "Morocco's much wilder," replied Bowles. The next morning they set out for the Moroccan coast, Copland apprehensive, Bowles delighted at the prospects of more encounters with the intensely exotic.

They arrived in Ceuta in the early afternoon and from there took the train to Tangier. Gertrude Stein had instructed them to stay at the Hotel Villa de France, but as it was full, they ended up at El Minzah, Tangier's newest deluxe hotel. The next ten days were spent exploring Tangier and looking for a house. Bowles immediately fell in love with the city:

> If I said that Tangier struck me as a dream city, I should mean it in the strict sense. Its topography was rich in prototypal dream scenes: covered streets like corridors with doors opening into rooms on each side, hidden terraces high above the sea, streets consisting only of steps, dark impasses, small squares built on sloping terrain so that they looked like ballet sets designed in false perspective, with alleys leading off in several directions; as well as the classical dream equipment of tunnels, ramparts, ruins, dungeons and cliffs. . . . The city was self-sufficient and clean, a doll's metropolis whose social and economic life long ago had been frozen in an enforced perpetual status quo by the international administration and its efficient police. There was no crime; no one yet thought of not respecting the European, whose presence was considered an asset to the community.

The Moroccans, with their passionate involvement in everyday matters, their love of argument, and their seemingly perpetual energy, greatly pleased Bowles. Copland was not so enthralled. "It's a madhouse, a madhouse!" he exclaimed. Bowles countered him: "It's a continuous performance, anyway." Thus it went and would go; although neither had ever encountered anything quite like Tangier, for Copland Morocco was a continual source of bewildering frustration, for Bowles a continual source of amazement.

About a week or so after their arrival Bowles made an excursion by bus to the foot of a forested mountain just outside of Tangier. Climbing up the narrow dirt road to the summit, he came upon a large, deserted old house in a rather rundown condition. Learning that it was for rent, he quickly made his way back to the hotel and excitedly described it to Copland, finally persuading him to take a look at it the next day. Copland was quite unsure about taking it—the house was isolated, large, unfurnished, and in a rather poor state of repair—but Bowles's enthusiasm finally won him over. That afternoon they began to buy furnishings. The major priority, though, at least for Copland, was to find a piano to rent. He was, unlike Bowles, eager to get back to work.

Despite Stein's assurances, they had considerable difficulty in locating a piano. They at last succeeded in finding an old black upright, made in Morocco, the only one in the shop available for rent. Their difficulties were not over, however. First, there was the problem of getting it up to the old house on the mountain. Second, it was horribly out of tune. But as the salesman assured them that neither obstacle was insurmountable, they arranged for a donkey and men to deliver it. A tuner, the shopkeeper informed them, would be sent out shortly.

At about the appointed time on the day of the delivery, Bowles and Copland saw the men and the donkey slowly coming up the dirt road. All went well until the donkey reached the gate leading into the villa and would not go through it. A struggle ensued between the delivery men and the donkey. The result, predictably enough, was that the piano fell to the ground "with an attractive, but unreproducible sound." Unconcerned, the two Moroccans simply righted the instrument and pushed and pulled it the rest of the way into the house. Surprisingly, the piano was no more out of tune than it had been in the shop. The tuner, promised them by the piano salesman, was not soon forthcoming. When he did finally arrive, he was drunk and obviously knew little about tuning pianos anyway. Finally, in desperation, Bowles and Copland did the tuning themselves: the "tuner" loosened and tightened the strings to the chorus of Bowles and Copland calling out "higher" or "lower." After a couple of hours, they finally managed to get the instrument tuned to a point where at least the notes were recognizable.

With the piano in place and with the acquisition of a few pieces of furniture, a stove and cooking utensils, Bowles and his teacher set up housekeeping. In early August Bowles wrote to Burns of Tangier and environs:

> The heat here is like that of a Turkish bath. It is utterly delightful, and it is permanent. There is never any objectionable let-up that

makes one so conscious of it all when it returns. Steady, hot, dry weather, with a sun that burns a white hole in the ultramarine sky, with a moon that is like the sun when it is full.

Sometimes there is music being sung from a distant part of the mountain, and often there are complicated drum rhythms that continue hours at a stretch. We live at the top of the cliffs over the Strait of Gibraltar, and Spain is always clearly visible for a stretch of 100 km. along its sandy bluffs, across the blue expanse. The countryside is blotched with cacti of all varieties, and the roads are narrow and fenced in by waving walls of a sort of bamboo that grows fifteen feet or so in height. Our villa is big enough for 10 people, with spacious gardens where palms, figs, flowers, grapes, huge eucalyptus trees and dozens of other things rush about madly in the wind. And the view down south to the Riffian Mountains is épatant.

In this setting, work erratically recommenced. Copland, however, could not get accustomed to Morocco, finding it difficult to work there. He also found it difficult to endorse Bowles's penchant for experiencing life in Tangier. Bowles wrote to Stein that "occasionally Aaron vociferates: 'Well, you'll be able to go exploring again soon, because I'm not going to stay here much longer.' He is unable to work, and it upsets him. . . . Up here on the mountain there are drums that beat a lot. That worries Aaron, as he cannot get it out of his head that the Arabs are grieved about something, and are all set to go on the warpath."

Finally, in an effort to curb Bowles's wanderlust and to be able to work himself, Copland imposed an order on the day. Each morning, just after breakfast, Bowles had his harmony lesson. Afterward, he would retreat to the garden where he would work on analyzing the Mozart piano sonatas while Copland composed at the piano. After lunch, prepared by an old cross-eyed servant named Mohammed, Copland would nap and Bowles would sit at the piano working on his *Sonata for Oboe and Clarinet*, inspired in part by Schwitters's syllable poem. In the evening the two would venture into Tangier for dinner. To Stein he wrote that "going into town is an event. Our estate is so secluded that it is rather easy to forget that one is in Morocco. . . . But when we are down at the Grand Socco, we are always pleasantly shocked."

On one of these evening visits into Tangier, Copland decided that they should look up a friend of Stein's, a Dutch painter named

Kristians Tonny. Bowles was not particularly interested in meeting Tonny, having decided in advance that it would be "a static evening with a square-headed Dutchman who would show us his canvases one by one." Copland, however, wanted someone else besides Bowles to talk to, and lacking Bowles's prejudices, proceeded to Tonny's house with Bowles in tow.

Contrary to his expectations, Bowles found Tonny and his American girlfriend, a black woman from New York named Anita Thompson, thoroughly charming. Tonny, for his part, also enjoyed meeting the two composers, but he regarded Bowles as being somewhat mad. On their second meeting he confided to Copland: "That young man with you is slightly off his head, isn't he? I noticed it the other night right away. I heard shutters banging in the wind in there somewhere." Bowles took the remark as a compliment. During their stay in Tangier, Copland and Bowles saw quite a lot of Tonny and Anita, Bowles becoming enthusiastic about Tonny's drawings of surreal Moroccan landscapes and busy scenes populated by a host of djellaba-wearing figures.

Autumn arrived, and with it the end of the idyll in Tangier. Copland needed to be back in Berlin; Bowles was to go to Paris to study with Boulanger. During the first week in October, they disbanded the house, returned the piano, this time without incident, and sold the furniture. But Bowles was in no hurry to leave Morocco. Finally, he persuaded Copland to go with him to Fez for a few days before the ultimate departure from North Africa. Tonny had given glowing reports of the city and in addition had provided them with an introduction to a Swiss gentleman named Charles Brown, who was in charge of the American Fondouk, an organization devoted to preventing cruelty to animals. Just before they were to leave Tangier, however, a wire arrived from Harry Dunham, who had spent the summer in Dresden, announcing that he was on his way to Morocco and wanted to meet up with Bowles. Bowles wired back that he would be delighted to see him in Fez. This fortuitous event now allowed Bowles to postpone his departure from Morocco, and to delay having to start serious lessons with Boulanger. Copland, feeling that Bowles was being a bit cavalier about postponing a real opportunity, was not so pleased with Bowles's decision. But used to Bowles's youthful penchant for travel and for probing the exotic, he accepted the young man's assurances that he would definitely proceed to Paris later in the fall.

Fez astonished Bowles, "where everything was ten-times stranger and bigger and brighter" than in Tangier. In a letter to Morrissette he proclaimed that "Fez I shall make my home some day!" To Stein he wrote: "Fez is full of flies and dust, and rats knock everything over on the tables at night. It is quite dirty and *very* beautiful." But Copland saw only the flies, rats, and dirt. Finding Fez even less to his liking than Tangier, he was obviously glad to be returning to "civilization" after this final concession to his young friend. His visit was short; less than a week. On October 8, he left Bowles alone in Fez to await Dunham's arrival. Dunham arrived a few days later, buoyant, curious, and excited to be in such a unique locale. In Germany he had taken up photography and spent much of his time taking hundreds of pictures of nearly everything that came before his lens. Bowles was frequently embarrassed by Dunham's total disregard of propriety, for in order to snap an unusual picture, he would think nothing of climbing over a garden wall or strolling into a private courtyard. These antics were often met by outraged cries from the property owners. Totally unmoved by their protests, Dunham would simply flash a smile, shoot a couple more frames, then beat a hasty retreat.

Despite their mutual enjoyment of adventure, and particularly Moroccan adventure, Bowles and Dunham were somewhat odd traveling companions. Dunham was fearless, willing to get engaged totally in any activity that interested him, while Bowles was more guarded. Virgil Thomson later defined the difference between the two: "Harry did things, Paul just talked about them. Paul scouted the town and picked up what he wanted. Harry took in everything." In addition to the differences in personality, they also had very contrasting attitudes regarding how one should behave in an alien environment. Dunham "expected his presence to change everything and in the direction which interested him." Bowles, on the other hand, had exactly opposite feelings: "I wanted to see whatever was happening continue exactly as if I were not there. . . . I believed we should strive for invisibility." To some extent Bowles's attitude was that of the ideal traveler who observes without intrusion, who enjoys new experiences without feeling the need to alter them through active participation. But it is also evident that such a stance also sprang from his desire to remain aloof, outside—a result, at least in part, of Bowles's deeply held fear of becoming vulnerable to others and of getting involved in situations in which he was not quite sure of himself. Acknowledging this, he wrote, "I was so used to hiding my intentions from everyone, that I sometimes hid them from myself as well."

In spite of Bowles's aversion to involvement, Morocco made it difficult for him to remain the anonymous spectator. "Even with my practice of pretending not to exist, I could not do it in Morocco. A stranger as blond as I was all too evident." Although Bowles insisted on keeping the matter superficial, the fact that he suddenly stood out in the crowd seemed to have contributed to his enchantment with the country. It is an interesting paradox: Because the Moroccans would not allow him to remain invisible, he did not feel as if he were betraying himself by becoming involved in what was actually going on. By being forced to relinquish his need for anonymity, he began to experience a new sense of freedom.

It was this attitude that propelled him forward to further adventure. Remembering Tonny's letter of introduction to Charles Brown, Bowles and Dunham one morning called on the Swiss gentleman, who invited them to lunch later that day. Several other guests were also present, including a young Moroccan aristocrat, Abdallah Drissi. Drissi invited them to tea that afternoon at his palace in the old quarter; the two readily accepted. Although many of the original Moroccan ruling class had lost their fortunes during colonialization, the Drissi family were as wealthy as ever. The opulence of the palace where Abdallah and his brother lived greatly amazed the two Americans. This was Bowles's first glimpse of Moroccan grandeur, reminding him of scenes from the *Thousand and One Nights*. Even Dunham, who had grown up in affluence, was impressed. Whenever Drissi wanted something, he simply clapped his hands and a servant (referred to by him as a slave) magically appeared to carry out the order. Even outside his palace, his power and riches commanded extraordinary respect; upon his approach, the local men would bow low to kiss the sleeve of his djellaba.

Although the enormous contrast between the Drissi wealth and the normal standard of Moroccan life must have been evident, Bowles did not apparently give much thought to the discrepancy.

His obvious awe of the Drissi fortune notwithstanding, he seems to have felt that it was as natural for them to be rich as for the majority of Moroccans to live in poverty. It was an attitude that he would always largely subscribe to, even when, a few years later, he would become an avowed communist. "Paul always liked people with money and had an instinct for finding them," recalls Virgil Thomson. Sympathy for the oppressed on Bowles's part seems to have been largely theoretical.

From Fez, Dunham and Bowles set out for Marrakech. They stayed in a tiny hotel there run by a French couple who took great pains to warn the young men about the rampant dishonesty and savagery of Moroccans. As if to prove their total disregard for the local populace, they made a point of openly mistreating their native employees. It particularly bothered Dunham that one boy, about fifteen years old, was assigned the duty, ostensibly to guard the hotel against interlopers, of sleeping across the threshold of the doorway at night without benefit of mat or blanket. When the proprietress was questioned about this practice, she replied scornfully that the boy didn't deserve better as he was no good. What was more, she went on, he owed her two months' wages for scorching one of her husband's shirts. Dunham, angered and upset by the woman's attitude, decided to take matters into his own hands. A few minutes later, Bowles found the boy, named Abdelkader, and Dunham talking. Abdelkader was beaming. When Bowles asked Dunham what was going on, he replied that he had invited the boy to go to Paris with him to be his valet. (Dunham had now decided to spend the winter in Paris, as he hoped to study with Man Ray.)

The news did not sit well with the owners. Madame kept insisting that Abdelkader couldn't leave as he owed her money. That evening, the argument still not settled, she warned Bowles that if his friend attempted to attack the Moroccan sexually, he'd fight back; then she concluded her harangue by announcing that she'd call the police if Dunham tried to remove Abdelkader. At precisely that moment Dunham entered the room, pulled out a revolver, and pointed it at the woman. Falling back, she screamed for her husband who came storming into the room. Dunham shifted his aim and pointed the pistol directly at the husband. Then, laughing, he laid the pistol down on a table. Further insults were exchanged; Bowles and Dunham moved to a new hotel.

The next morning they confronted their former hotel keepers at the police station, where Dunham and Bowles had gone to fill out forms for Abdelkader's exit from Morocco. Monsieur and Madame had to clear the boy before he could leave, and would not do so until paid the money they said was due them, which by now amounted to far more than the original amount. Dunham finally paid them, but that did not end the matter. Before Abdelkader could leave, his entire family had to sign consent documents as well. Owing to the considerable bureaucracy involved, the police informed them that it would take a while before everything could be arranged. Dunham did not have much time left in Morocco; his family still thought he was in Dresden and as his twenty-first birthday would be in a couple of weeks, he needed to be there to send them a wire. It was therefore decided that if Abdelkader's release had not been obtained by that time, Dunham would return to Europe and Bowles would stay on to bring the boy to Paris.

After a week, as Abdelkader had still not gotten his release, Dunham went on to Germany to finish up his business there, leaving money for Bowles's and Abdelkader's passage and with arrangements to meet them in Paris by December. Bowles remained in Marrakech for a few days to try and get the clearance. When it was obvious that no one was in a hurry to process the papers, he went back to Tangier, giving Abdelkader instructions to come when he could. A couple of weeks later, the boy arrived at Tonny and Anita's, where Bowles was staying. From the start, Abdelkader and Anita did not get along. The boy thought her to be a terrible housekeeper and an even worse cook. It was soon clear that they had worn out their welcome. On a mid-November morning, Bowles and Abdelkader left Morocco on board the ferry bound for Algeciras, Spain. Tonny left them at the docks, presenting Bowles with a drawing. On the launch going out to the ferry, however, the saltwater sprayed the motorboat, and much to Bowles's chagrin damaged the drawing.

Unlike other places Bowles had visited, Morocco had left a firm mark on his imagination. Even before arriving he sensed it would be that way:

> Like any Romantic, I had always been vaguely certain that sometime during my life I should come into a magic place which in disclosing

its secrets would give me wisdom and ecstasy—perhaps even death. And now, as I stood in the wind . . . I felt the stirring of the engine within, and it was as if I were drawing close to the solution of an as-yet unposed problem. I was incredibly happy . . . but I let the happiness wash over me and asked no questions.

Had he not been looking for a "magic place," it is unlikely that Bowles would have been so drawn to Morocco: to a certain degree, the quester was simply ready to end his quest. At the same time, however, Morocco affected him in a way unlike any other place he knew. In particular, he loved Tangier from the beginning, "loved it more than any place I'd ever seen in my life. . . . I'd never liked any place strongly, I realized, until I came [to Morocco]. I'd always felt negatively about places before. That is, I wanted to go here or there in order to get away from where I was at present." For Bowles, Tangier was "a pocket outside the mainstream," one totally lacking in the artifacts of Western culture:

> You couldn't get any books in those days. You couldn't even get any newspapers. There were no radios, of course. Very few automobiles. Never any theater, ballet, opera, exhibits—nothing. You didn't have to put up with all that nonsense.

For some, the very lack of these items would have proved to be a hardship, as they did for Copland. But for Bowles, the whole notion of Western "culture" was an alien idea. He had always attempted to divorce himself from the quintessential American values, and in Europe, particularly Germany, he also found that he did not want to fit into prescribed modes of European culture. Moreover, in Morocco, he could be regarded simply as who he was, rather than what he was supposed to represent—"a composer," for instance, or "a writer." In a sense different from any he'd ever known, he was free to be himself, not part of a particular community in which he needed to conform to the community strictures. Not being judged, he didn't judge either:

> When I was a very small child, I learned the difference between the family and the neighbors. It's always better to be with the neighbors, because you have an intrinsic value for them. They want to know all

about you. You are a person. But with the family you don't have any value at all, except as part of a group. I always hated that. Your family thinks it owns you. It expects certain things of you just because you are one of the family. . . . I suppose, really, that this passion for living away from the place where you are born is probably a childhood neurosis. If you speak to real expatriates . . . you will often find they had unsuccessful childhoods. In any case, if you live in a place where you are a person and have an intrinsic value, I think you have a much better idea of yourself.

In Spain, Bowles and Abdelkader went first to Seville, then to Madrid, where they visited the Prado. Transfixed by the Bosches, Abdelkader suddenly announced to Bowles that the paintings were beginning to move and that he and Bowles had to get out of there. Having never seen representational art, Abdelkader assumed that the paintings must be films. Outside, he warned Bowles that all the "cinemas" in that house were made by Satan.

From Spain they quickly made their way to Paris, arriving in late November. Copland was by then in England, arranging the final Copland-Sessions concert, which was to be held at Aeolian Hall in London. The program was to feature Bowles's *Sonata for Oboe and Clarinet*, Virgil Thomson's *Capital Capitals*, a cantata based on Stein's text, Copland's *Piano Variations*, Carlos Chávez's *Sonatina*, Roger Sessions's *Piano Sonata*, and Israel Citkowitz's settings of Blake's poems. Bowles had still not quite finished the *Sonata*. In response to a letter from Copland asking him for the work, he wrote:

I didn't receive your letter until ten days or more after you had written it. . . . I shall start making the parts, but God knows how right they'll be. I wish there were some way for your seeing them before I send them to London. Oh dear, oh dear! I insist on getting them done in time for the rehearsals. In fact, I should blow up and die immediately if it could not come off on account of lack of time.

Copland wrote back telling Bowles that he had faith that he'd finish, and finish with aplomb. Bowles, in fact, did complete the score in early December, sending it on to London. In the meantime, he called Stein, now back in Paris, who invited him and

Abdelkader to visit. Also present at the gathering was Joan Miró. The Spanish artist agreed with the Moroccan about the Bosches; he also took an immediate liking to Bowles, inviting him to visit him in Barcelona or Mallorca. Abdelkader, for his part, charmed everyone, regaling Stein and Toklas with tales of Anita's terrible housekeeping. As the two of them were opposed to her relationship with Tonny, they were delighted to hear their suspicions about her confirmed.

Dunham, meanwhile, arrived from Dresden, ready to set up housekeeping in Paris. He quickly found a furnished studio on the top floor of 17 Quai Voltaire, in the same building where Virgil Thomson lived. He and Bowles moved in and shortly thereafter called on their neighbor. Thomson recalls the visit:

> They were radiant. He [Bowles] was a dazzling blonde and so was Harry, and they were at the height of their beauty, which is around 19 or 20. And they had on yellow overcoats and yellow cashmere scarves and my place had yellow walls and the yellow sunlight was streaming in the northeast window, so they fitted right in. Paul and I became very good friends right away. Harry too. They were very companionable. At that time Paul purported to be a poet. Stein found him enchanting but didn't think much of the poetry and told him so. I couldn't find its quality either. But with the music it was different. He started playing me his music as soon as we got acquainted. It was absolutely charming, sweet, school of Ravel.

The ostensible reason for the visit was that Thomson too was going to the Copland-Sessions concert, and around December 7 the trio took off for London. Copland was already there rehearsing the orchestra. Bowles and Thomson were responsible, though, for guiding the performers through their own works. This was a first for Bowles, who was both anxious and excited at hearing his own work performed. He got a lot of support from both Copland and Thomson, but Thomson remembers Bowles being a bit embarrassed about receiving assistance in rehearsing the players.

He was not at all concerned, though, about accepting hospitality. While in London, he stayed first at Mary Oliver's house. Again quite generous, she put at Bowles's disposal a car, chauffeur, and footman. Bowles greatly enjoyed being treated to such extravagance and used the opportunity to travel about London. On one of his visits he went to see Edouard Roditi. Roditi struck Bowles as being "tall, suave and polyglot." And Bowles made a great impression on Roditi:

> When Paul and I finally met, I was dazzled, like Saint Gregory in the slave-market of ancient Rome, by his angelic Anglo-Saxon physical appearance, but also appalled by his apparent other-worldliness, helplessness and poverty, though perhaps unconsciously he played the part of the starry-eyed young genius in order to foist on others the responsibility of solving most of his material problems.

Roditi invited Bowles to stay with him for a few days. Not wanting to become too intrusive at the Olivers', and because he and Roditi had immediately taken a liking to each other, he accepted. After a few days, however, he moved back into the Olivers'. "Although we got on wonderfully well," Roditi later explained, "I had a very small apartment and we had to sleep in one bed. The first one or two nights Paul was absolutely terrified that I was going to rape him."

On December 16 the Copland-Sessions concert took place. Copland was in a frenzy. That same night, a symphony concert of British music was on as well, drawing away many prospective hearers. In addition, Citkowitz never came through with his "Blake" songs, substituting instead "Five Songs from James Joyce's *Chamber Music,*" written the previous year. But the concert went on as scheduled. It was hardly a success. One reviewer, Henry Boys, wrote that only Copland's piece was interesting, but it seemed as if Copland was "craving after originality for its own sake," and that "the composer wrote only for himself." Of Bowles's debut he wrote: "The *Sonata* for oboe and clarinet by Paul Bowles has . . . a sure sense of style, but the workmanship is not yet accomplished enough to deal with such a combination and rather matches the immature and superficial mode of thought." Another review was offered by Dunham's sister Amelia, who had arrived in London from Cincinnati to meet her brother. "If I had a little boy and he wrote a piece like that, I'd know what to do with him." "What would you do?" asked Bowles. "I'd see that he got hospital treatment," she answered.

But Bowles did not allow either piece of criticism to crush him. As all of the work featured was generally panned, he reasoned that if such greats as Copland and Thomson were treated badly by the reviewers, it had to be a problem with the reviewers, not with him or the others.

A few days after the concert, Copland went back to the United States, and Thomson, the two Dunhams, and Bowles returned to Paris to celebrate the new year. Bowles had much to celebrate. As 1931 had begun he was still looking for a direction and had just thrown a knife at his father. At its close he was not only back in Europe but had made the acquaintance of Stein, Thomson, Cocteau, and others; had discovered Morocco; and had seen his first piece being performed in public on the same bill as some of the most important contemporary composers.

CHAPTER 9

Back in Paris, Bowles first moved into the studio with Dunham, his sister, and Abdelkader, and prepared to enroll in counterpoint classes with Nadia Boulanger at the École Normale. But life at the Dunhams' was far from pleasant, mainly because of the extraordinarily jealous Amelia, who conspired to remove anyone who came close to her brother. Edouard Roditi remembers her as being about twenty years older than Harry and a "sourpuss old maid who didn't approve of anything in the world." This included Abdelkader, whom she positively loathed, and Bowles. Her animosity toward Bowles probably had something to do with an arrangement that her brother had made to provide him with an income. Says Thomson:

> Harry became very attached to Paul and Paul didn't mind people being attached to him as long as they helped him out with money and Harry certainly did. He paid all his bills, trips and so on, and from about that time, maybe before, Harry made a sort of tithing vow. He gave Paul ten percent of everything he ever earned—from inheritance or work. It continued until he died in the war.

Roditi also remembers Dunham as being quite dashing and generous, but also adds some information about another side of his character, namely that he was an extremely promiscuous homosexual. "Everyone went to bed with him or tried to, except Paul, I think." Despite Dunham's obvious predisposition toward frequent sexual encounters and love of a good time, all of this was apparently kept from Amelia, who "worshiped her younger brother, and could find absolutely nothing reproachful in his character." She decided that Bowles was a bad influence. But Thomson remembers it as clearly being the other way around. "Harry was charming, a star presence, and had nothing to do but have a social life.

He had some money and moved around fast and he took Paul with him. He could lead Paul into anything."

It was not Dunham, however, who led Bowles to Anne Miracle Manheim. "Charming, quite attractive, dainty and devoted," Anne Miracle was a French artist, separated from her husband who lived in Germany. Shortly after they met—in late 1931 or early January 1932—Bowles "became mad and ran away with Anne Manheim," as he wrote to Morrissette. Because Miracle was a ski enthusiast, the two had "run away" to Clavières, in the Italian Alps. By the time they had arrived in Turin, however, Bowles was quite ill. As a result, they aborted the trip there and Bowles was taken to a hospital. An Italian doctor checked him over. He concluded his examination by pronouncing the cause of Bowles's illness as syphilis, and prescribed a series of injections. Miracle wired Dunham with the news, and he boarded the next train for Italy; upon learning what was the matter, he became furious. Thomson remembers the incident, noting that from Dunham's reaction he assumed that he and Bowles must have, at one time at least, been lovers: "Harry attacked Paul; I think he started hitting him when he was in bed or something. He was concerned that Paul would have given it to him. . . . But they didn't permanently quarrel over the matter. . . . As Harry's father was a doctor he knew what to do and found out he didn't have it."

The quarrel greatly upset Bowles. On January 10, from Turin, he wrote Stein the following letter, perhaps in the hope that Stein would intercede on his behalf with Dunham:

> Harry left this morning saying he was on his way to America. So the whole ménage is over. Unfortunately this time we had a quarrel and he left me in a not too happy financial condition. I shall get on all right, as you say. But I think it would be better if I could find things like translations to do. . . . We had our bagarre only because my nerves were completely on edge and he refuses to realize it. I think it is all too bad but there is nothing to be done about it. . . . I am upset, as upset I suppose as I shall ever be, which is not so terribly, but enough to bother me and make me have occasional desperate exciting thoughts.

Stein apparently showed the letter to Dunham, who went to see her on his return. Having been to a doctor and pronounced healthy, Dunham immediately reconciled with Bowles, showing his forgiveness by giving Bowles a $240 watch: "My request. Why not?" Bowles wrote Morrissette on January 26. Dunham also waited in Paris until Bowles's return, deciding not to depart quite so precipitously after all.

Meanwhile, Bowles partially recovered and went on to Clavières with Miracle. The news of Bowles's "syphilis" had, in the interim, quickly spread through the small Paris community, partly because Bowles himself wrote to all of his acquaintances telling them that he had been taken ill, never failing to add a few sentences about his poverty; in his letters to Thomson, he went so far as to plead outright for money. Thomson sent him 500 francs, urging him, though, to return to Paris, not only because of his illness, but so that he could get on with his studies. Stein, too, advised him to return, writing him in Clavières:

> I did not answer sooner because being a little troubled about you I wanted to see Harry first. Now I have and as it seems you are really not well don't you think it would be best to come to Paris where you can be looked after, and then we all can decide what you ought to do.

A few years later Bowles set the letter to music, entitling the composition simply "Letter to Freddy."

Heeding Stein's and Thomson's advice, Bowles and Miracle came back to Paris, with many pictures of Bowles, "looking quite well," and Miracle on skis. Bowles was still worried about having syphilis, however, and asked Virgil Thomson for advice. Thomson sent him to his doctor, who continued the treatments but concluded from his knowledge of the symptoms that Bowles had probably not contracted syphilis. Once back in Paris, Bowles stayed with Miracle, who took care of him. "Paul loved being taken care of. He was a virtuoso at being taken care of," remembers Thomson.

Recovering quickly from his illness, and becoming concerned that Miracle's husband would return any day from Germany, Bowles moved back into the Dunham studio, effectively ending the relationship. He installed a rented Pleyel grand piano as well and began working again on composition. Dunham, meanwhile, did finally depart for the States, leaving Bowles his room. With Dunham gone, Amelia felt free to torment both her guests, Bowles and Abdelkader. "I'm going to get you into a hospital yet," she would tell Bowles, insisting that he undergo a spinal tap as a test for syphilis. Although most everyone else, including Bowles, had come to believe that he had not in fact contracted the disease, she was adamant about insisting that her brother's friend was a disgusting syphilitic.

As for her treatment of Abdelkader, it worsened. She now kept him confined to the kitchen and his adjacent living quarters and also began to starve him systematically. Her intense dislike of the Moroccan, however, seems to have been at least somewhat justified. Edouard Roditi recalls that "the moment Abdelkader found himself alone with any house guest, male or female, out, literally, popped his prick. Quite popular, he took a number of them to his bedroom and was making a roaring trade out of it until this got to the ears of Amelia Dunham." Although Bowles was sympathetic to the young Moroccan, as it was Dunham's apartment, and as Bowles was living there for free, he couldn't really do much about it except protest weakly to Amelia.

Carlo Suarès, convinced by Bowles that Amelia was mad, invited him to move back again to his apartment. Suarès's wife had just gone to California to be with Krishnamurti, and he felt he could use the company. Bowles still went daily to the studio to use the piano, but arranged his visits to coincide with Amelia's absence. Going one day to the studio, he discovered the place in a shambles. Abdelkader was gone and with him most of Bowles's and Dunham's clothes. On Amelia's return he countered her. Unmoved, she calmly replied, "If you have street Arabs in the house, you expect to lose things, don't you?" To Bowles's forceful protest that Abdelkader did not steal, she simply responded that as he had wanted to leave she had simply taken him to Vuitton's and bought him some luggage and invited him to fill the bags. Bowles was furious, but had no recourse: Abdelkader was by then bound once more for Morocco.

Despite the incident, Bowles still used the piano, as he was working rather hard on a series of songs. The reason for his diligence was that Copland had written to him in late January 1932, informing him that he would like to have some songs for a concert to be given at the end of April at Yaddo. Ada MacLeish, Archibald MacLeish's wife, was to sing them. The idea struck Bowles as intriguing, particularly after he decided that he would use his own texts as lyrics. If his poems were not really poems, as Stein had insisted, perhaps they could be songs.

In the end he produced six songs, occasionally cutting the texts, giving all but one new titles. The results were remarkable, the music fitting the words perfectly. Although this was his first serious attempt at writing songs, he had a superb sense of what to do with a text. Part of the success stemmed from knowing so well his own prosody, knowing how the words should behave in song. So while the poems may have been written "unconsciously," the rhythmic design was quite careful, with the timbre, stress, and cadence of the poem integrated into the musical illustration. From the despair about his poetry of six months earlier, he had come back, managing to transform his "failed verse" into music of true merit.

Despite his success at writing songs, neither Copland nor Thomson was terribly happy about Bowles's not studying formally. Urged from abroad by Copland to begin studies, he did finally attend two lessons with Boulanger, but found her not to his liking. Thomson decided that the problem was not with lessons per se, but with having the right teacher and felt Bowles would be better off with Paul Dukas, who "might be able to get a little more discipline out of him than Nadia." He wrote to Copland to tell him so:

> If he wants Nadia's particular and special merchandise; namely, a motherly guidance to overcome American timidity about self-expression, then he had better go and get it and take the trimmings with it. Otherwise he had better buy his trimmings where they are cheaper and better.

Copland responded:

> You certainly state the case *against* N.B. well enough and I'm not so blind as to be unaware that there is such a thing. In relation to Paul . . . there is no matter where or how a pupil learns his stuff just so that he learns it. Therefore it makes no difference whether he studies with N.B. or Dukas. . . . It is useless to be a pupil if you are unwilling to enter into a pupil-teacher relationship. . . . I'm all for the teacher

influencing the pupil—it doesn't matter what pet ideas the teacher happens to have or what means are employed to drive them home— the pupil should swallow it whole for a time and if he has any guts he'll throw them overboard soon enough. If not, it proves he's just a pupil and it doesn't matter whom he studies with.

The debate continued for most of that year. In the end, Bowles studied with neither. Thomson later realized that Bowles's reluctance to study with a teacher was less a matter of unconventionality than of economics: "He was too stingy to pay for lessons. He just couldn't bear to spend money on them. Paul, of course, didn't like to spend money on anything. He liked it better if he were invited and paid for." In fact, at this time Bowles was quite hard pressed for cash, although as Thomson points out, "Paul could probably have found someone to pay for lessons."

Meanwhile Roditi arrived back in Paris, as did Charles-Henri Ford, who had published both Bowles and Roditi in his little magazine, *Blues*. Ford had also gotten to know Bowles slightly during Bowles's brief stay in New York in 1930. When he arrived in Paris, Ford had just written with Parker Tyler a novel, *The Young and the Evil*, which was condemned upon publication as pornographic. According to Roditi, "To his new Paris friends, Charles needed to provide proof that he was indeed as evil as he was young, so that he decided to set about exploring the sinks of iniquity for which the French capital had long been famous."

Ford convinced Bowles and Roditi to accompany him on a visit to a Turkish bath. When they arrived in the middle of the afternoon, the place was deserted save for a few "pasty-faced young masseurs." Then a young Arab customer joined them, and took an immediate liking to Bowles; but as soon as the Arab pressed, Bowles "fled in a panic to the relative safety of the lounge." Ford had a similar reaction, while Roditi "came to an understanding" with the Arab.

What such episodes show is that, although Bowles appeared to be quite drawn toward homosexuals and homosexuality, his earlier conception of sex as being "a necessary evil" and a "vice" were still very much a central notion. Indeed, Bowles's sexual orientation at this time is rather curious. According to some accounts, Bowles invited speculation that he was gay. Some, for instance, assumed, given Copland's predilection for handsome young men, that the Bowles–Copland liaison was sexual as well as professional. It was certainly true that the two were enormously fond of each other and that Bowles relished the prominent position he held in his mentor's affections, even referring to himself as Copland's "pet." There is no real evidence to suggest, however, that there was a sexual component to the relationship, and, indeed, those closest to the two during this period claim this was not the case. They do admit, though, that Bowles was quite coy about the matter and did nothing to prevent suspicions of a homosexual affair. This sexual charade, played out in regard to Copland and perhaps others, was no doubt perceived by him as an advantage, since the American music scene at that time was largely dominated by gay men.

But the sexual act itself apparently still produced in him a considerable amount of anxiety, perhaps even revulsion. With the possible exception of Dunham, Bowles seems to have been a nonparticipant in homosexual affairs during this period. Virgil Thomson's feeling was that "Paul made like being queer, and he got money out of that and friendships. But he was really not interested in the physical side." Roditi remembers that though "Paul was a great success physically in Paris gay circles, he was always elusive. With him, it was all mental." According to Bruce Morrissette, "Paul, in his early twenties, professed to be quite antisexual. He used to get quite irritated with Virgil because he was always advising him to go out and have sex with anybody, so long as he enjoyed it." Bowles would firmly reply to Thomson "that he was not interested in that."

Although he seemed to find a heterosexual affair more acceptable than a homosexual one, his involvement with Anne Miracle only lasted a few months and "was imbued with more friendship than passion." William Burroughs, although he came to know Bowles much later, comments shrewdly that "there's a real New England streak in him and how much of that is put on I don't know. But he felt very definitely that there was such a thing as too much fun."

Clearly, Bowles was still very much influenced by a strong sense of codified morality. Whether a result of his New England heritage or, as Thomson thinks, a result of basic uninterest in the sexual act, he was not terribly keen on physical sexuality. Finding himself in a largely homosexual milieu, Bowles played the part, but stopped short of actual physical involvement.

Lacking funds and, to some extent, interest, Bowles began to seek relief in the spring of 1932 from the problem of studying. As before, escape came in the form of a trip. In March, a friend of Roditi's arrived in Paris. By this time Bowles was quite hard pressed for money and Roditi thought possibly that his friend, a literary agent named John Trounstine, might be willing to help Bowles out. At dinner one evening with Thomson and Bowles, Trounstine mentioned that he would like to see Spain. Bowles jumped at the idea, offering to be Trounstine's guide, and in the early spring the two set off. In Barcelona, Bowles tried to look up Miró, but learned that he was in Mallorca. When they got to Granada, however, he did succeed in meeting the composer Manuel de Falla. Although he arrived unexpectedly and without an introduction, he was warmly received.

Bowles found Spain enchanting: "In every town there was rejoicing; people were singing and dancing in each *plazuela.*" Part of the euphoria was due to the new Republican government that had just come into power. But although Bowles enjoyed the atmosphere, he began to long for Morocco. In Granada he convinced Trounstine to accompany him, promising that Morocco was even more delightful than Spain, and in April of 1932 the two took the ferry across the Strait of Gibraltar.

Arriving in Tangier, Bowles went first to look up Tonny and Anita, but found that they had moved. On the way to the new residence he met Anita, who informed him that Tonny had locked her out of the house as he had become jealous of her male friends. The particular target of his wrath was the West Indian writer Claude McKay, who was at that time living in Tangier. McKay had first met Anita in Paris in 1929, had fallen in love with her, and was now hoping to woo her back. Tonny refused entry to Bowles as well as Anita when they arrived at the house. Bowles shrugged it off and made his way back to the hotel. A few days later, Tonny and Anita reunited, and the four of them, Trounstine included, went to see McKay. "Plump and jolly, with a red fez on his head . . . he was living exactly like a Moroccan," as Bowles later described him. To entertain his guests he clapped his hands and his

Moroccan dancing girl, about twelve years old, performed. Trounstine, who didn't care much for Morocco anyway, was appalled at
the performance. He did, however, agree to become McKay's literary agent.

Meanwhile, a curious episode was unfolding. McKay had come
under suspicion by the local authorities of being a Trotskyite. His
passport was seized and he was brought into the commissariat for
questioning. As the one who had denounced him to the police
proved to be a Moroccan acquaintance of Bowles's, McKay decided that Bowles was responsible for the denunciation and went
to his hotel, cursing and screaming at his supposed antagonist. As
the proprietor refused to let McKay in, he eventually went away.
The case against McKay was finally dropped, and he remained in
Morocco, in seemingly pleasant exile, until 1934.

Shortly after the McKay episode, and following a violent falling-
out with Trounstine, Bowles headed for Fez, where he stayed with
the Drissi brothers. He later wrote of the visit:

> So that I should feel truly at home, I was given an entire wing of the
> establishment, a tiled patio with a room on either side and a fountain
> in the center. There were a great number of servants to bring me
> food and drink, and also to inquire, before my hosts came to call,
> whether I was disposed to receive them. When they came they often
> brought singers and musicians to entertain me. The only hitch was
> that they went to such great lengths to treat me as one of them that
> they also assumed I was not interested in going out into the city.
> During the entire fortnight I spent with them I never once found my
> way out of the house, or even out of my own section of it, since all
> the doors were kept locked and bolted, and only the guard, an old
> Sudanese slave, had the keys. For long hours I sat in the patio
> listening to the sounds of the city outside, sometimes hearing faint
> strains of music that I would have given anything really to hear.

After about two weeks of this life, Bowles moved out to a hotel.
Like a prisoner just released from confinement, he wandered the
city at will, on one excursion coming across an extraordinary pro-
cession inching through the narrow streets. The crowd, many in
a trance, many chanting to a drum accompaniment, were members
of a Muslim sect, generically known as the brotherhoods. Fanatically religious, such adherents, through dance or prolonged sleep-

lessness due to processions of several days, hoped to achieve a transcendental state of ecstasy in which normal consciousness was overtaken by a higher psychic level of being. Detached from the world around them, they typically exhibited rather extreme forms of behavior, including uncontrollable spastic motions and frothing at the mouth until collapsing in total oblivion. It was such a group that Bowles came upon; the impression was unforgettable, confounding: "Here for the first time I was made aware that a human being is not an entity and that his interpretation of exterior phenomena is meaningless unless it is shared by the other members of his cultural group." The comment is curious, particularly coming from Bowles, who consistently prided himself on standing apart from the group. And yet this discovery is perhaps central to understanding Bowles's labor over the years in interpreting non-Western culture for the West, for while he has always striven hard to maintain a personal distance, he has been extremely interested in explaining the observed reality of other groups of people so that such perceptions may find resonance and meaning in a culture alien to those values.

Running short on cash, Bowles found it necessary to end his Moroccan sojourn; he returned to Paris in early May of 1932. Settling down in a small furnished apartment in Montmartre, he began work on a sonata for flute and piano. But almost from his return he had not been feeling well. Now, toward the end of May, he began to feel progressively worse. One day at lunch with Carlo Suarès, the Egyptian took a good look at him. "I think you have typhoid," he said. "I've seen it so often in Egypt." Suarès was right. A few days later Bowles was admitted to the American Hospital in Neuilly. Morocco had left more than a mental impression upon him.

PART III

On the Map

CHAPTER 10

For two weeks Bowles lay nearly unconscious, fever alternating with chills. Packed in ice and sponged down with cold water, he was unable to comprehend fully what was happening to him. Visitors came, but in his delirium he was not even aware of their presence. Years later, he would describe the state in *The Sheltering Sky:*

> He was at the edge of a realm where each thought, each image, had an arbitrary existence, where the connection between each thing and the next had been cut. . . . He looked at the line made by the joining of the wall and the floor, endeavored to fix it in his mind, that he might have something to hang on to when his eyes should shut.

Finally the fever subsided and he was able to sit up again, but could still tolerate few well-wishers. Virgil Thomson came for a few minutes, remarking to Bowles that with his growth of red beard he looked "just like Jesus." After Thomson left, Bowles procured a razor and shaved. Amelia Dunham came too, exclaiming that she now had him where she wanted him—in a hospital. Bowles hurled a glass of water at her; she was not allowed in to visit him again. Bruce Morrissette, arriving at Bowles's bedside on his way to Grenoble, was distraught over his friend's deteriorated physical condition. As part of the typhoid treatment consisted of withholding food, Bowles had lost a considerable amount of weight, and being thin to begin with, now "looked positively skeletal." Morrissette decided to hold off on his trip to Grenoble until Bowles could go with him.

Toward the end of his stay in the hospital a surprise visitor arrived: Abdelkader. With one of Bowles's monogrammed handkerchiefs protruding from his pocket, he was all smiles, announcing that he was now back in Paris working for the Marquis de Villeneuve. Questioned about the theft of Bowles's clothes, he simply responded that Amelia had given them to him. Meanwhile, word came that Rena had booked passage to France with Daniel Burns to be with Bowles during his convalescence.

A letter also came from Copland, which probably did more to hasten Bowles's recovery than anything else. Reporting that Ada MacLeish had sung Bowles's songs at the First Festival of Contemporary American Music at Yaddo to great enthusiasm on the part of the crowd, Copland added: "You're on the map now, and don't you forget it."

The critics agreed with Copland's assessment of the songs. In the influential journal *Modern Music*, Alfred H. Meyer devoted considerable attention to Bowles's "exceedingly sensitive songs," ending with this comment: "One remembers particularly a few miraculous chords on the word 'clouds' in the second song ["Will You Allow Me to Lie in the Grass?"], in which the effect was so wondrously wrought that one actually seemed to be seeing color rather than hearing sound." It is important to point out that competing for attention were works by Charles Ives, Walter Piston, Copland, Thomson, Sessions, Israel Citkowitz, Marc Blitzstein, and ten others—a virtual who's who of contemporary American music.

Finally, in July, after more than a month in the hospital, the day of his discharge came. Morrissette booked Bowles a room at his hotel and went to bring him home. They spent a couple of weeks in Paris until Bowles had recovered sufficiently to travel, then made their way to La Tronche, a town outside Grenoble, where Morrissette had a teaching appointment. It wasn't long before Morrissette was taking Bowles on his motorcycle for excursions to the countryside. One weekend they decided to visit Gertrude Stein at Bilignin. She met them, arms outstretched, obviously delighted to see "Freddy." Morrissette was amazed at her tremendous warmth and goodwill: "It was clear that she was enormously fond of Paul, behaving very maternally towards him." The visit, though brief, was important to them both. It would become even more precious to Bowles later on, as it would turn out to be the last time he ever saw Stein.

At Morrissette's, spurred on by Copland's words and the rave notices from the Yaddo festival, Bowles began working on two new compositions. The first was a sonata for flute and piano; the second, a song sequence based on five sections of the long poem

Anabase by St.-John Perse, an author whom both he and his host were quite excited about at the time. Working very quickly, Bowles completed *Sonata No. 1 for Flute and Piano.* Reminiscent of some of Satie's chamber works in its fluidity, the sonata is thoroughly charming, the flute part lyrically balancing the delicate scoring for piano. In addition to the sonata, he finished the first part of *Scènes d'Anabase,* but before he could complete the song sequence, his work was temporarily interrupted by the arrival of his mother and Daniel Burns in early August.

After a short stay in La Tronche, Bowles and his mother set out for Monte Carlo, arranging to meet Morrissette and Burns in Mallorca in a few weeks. In Monaco, Bowles sunned, talked with Rena, and wrote the second section of *Scènes d'Anabase.* From there, the two went to Mallorca, where Bowles doggedly began to search the island (to no avail) for Robert Graves and Laura Riding, "absolutely intent on meeting them." In the evenings, Bowles, Rena, and friends would sit outside, taking in the scenes of summer. According to Morrissette, Bowles seemed at great ease with his mother and obviously enjoyed showing her his Europe. She seemed as delighted to be there as he was to have her once again in his proximity. "Not sophisticated, Rena would listen with great interest to Paul, taking in his words, making mental notes of his opinions. She had a constant look of surprise on her face at whatever we were discussing, a look that seemed to indicate she was about to interrupt the conversation at any moment with 'Oh, you don't say?' "

From Mallorca they all went to Barcelona where, still weakened from his bout with typhoid, Bowles quickly succumbed to sunstroke. "While I lay in bed with protracted fever and sloughing skin, Mother sat reading Richard Hughes' *A High Wind in Jamaica* to me. It was like being a child all over again," Bowles later remarked. After a few days, he and Rena went up into the Catalonian Pyrenees to continue his convalescence. As Rena's visit was quickly coming to an end, the two of them returned to Paris, where Bowles played tour guide, much to his mother's delight. Although it was clear that she was greatly enjoying her trip, she claimed, in response to Bowles's protests, that she could not really stay beyond her planned departure date as his father would "be getting most impatient."

For Bowles, Rena's visit served to sanction him and his European life. To some extent, it also allowed him to acquire, at long last, the attention from his mother that he had always craved. It is worth noting, though, that he gained her concern primarily through a very old, almost infantile mode: illness. While not feigned, his sunstroke was in some ways fortuitous, for it allowed him to replay gracefully one of the happiest memories from his childhood, having his mother read to him. His obvious joy in the situation ("It was like being a child all over again") is indicative of this feeling; it is also, in part, untrue, for while it is the case that his mother read to him nightly when he was young, Bowles never had the luxury of having his mother all to himself. As a result, the situation was far purer than any in childhood; Bowles could finally be the recipient of his mother's affection, and Rena could play the role of caring mother, without fear of interference or remonstrance from Claude.

After Rena's departure, Bowles did not linger in Paris but made his way south again to L'Ile de Porquerolles, where he had been invited to stay with Thomson and the painter Maurice Grosser, who were summering there. Again he came down with sunstroke; again he had to spend a week or so recovering, during which time Thomson consulted a local witch who assured him that Bowles would "either be dead or all right after sunset." During his recuperation he avidly read Lautréamont's *Les Chants de Maldoror* and reread *Anabase.*

But literature was not the only diversion on this visit. In a letter to Thomson, written some time after his stay, Bowles recounted the following:

> I never told you about Porquerolles. How finally I managed to get one of the two who held out for fifty francs. Not the *voyou,* but one of the two who came up to us on the quai. The next day he came to my house there and went away satisfied with a handshake. . . . I was encouraged by those tactics and used them perfectly everywhere later: Marseilles and points south.

It is difficult to know what to make of this anecdote, given Bowles's earlier reaction to the similar advances of a young Arab in the baths in Paris. Possibly, he was simply boasting in an attempt to convince Thomson that he was not really as sexually repressed as he was thought to have been, but it could be that Bowles, when faced with the opportunity for a sexual encounter with no lasting consequences, took it. If so, it is the first indication that he had relaxed somewhat vis-à-vis his own sexuality. Regardless of the account's veracity, in general, Bowles was still quite shy of any open homosexual involvement with anyone from his own milieu.

Returning to Monte Carlo in October, Bowles continued to work at his setting of the Perse poem, which he chose to score for piano, oboe, and tenor voice. Rather than attempt a direct translation of Perse's words into music, he conceived of the work as "more of an homage to the author of the text than anything else." The result, while not terribly sophisticated musically, nonetheless managed to be quite evocative of Perse's text. Only the fifth section, a bold experiment, is not wholly successful. By casting it into a "tempo di rag," Bowles failed to interpret accurately the rather solemn text. Instrumentally, though, it is the most interesting section of the entire sequence; it simply does not seem to fit the mood of the poem as well as did the other four parts. At the time, however, Bowles was quite pleased with it. To Morrissette he wrote: "The fifth [section] is a result of pure inspiration, one of those things that happens once a year; that is, a trick that is so good it holds even when obviously a trick."

Scènes d'Anabase was an important work in Bowles's musical formation, for it showed, even more convincingly than the songs made from his own poems, that he was inordinately gifted at putting words to music. Although his craft would improve dramatically within just a few years, in this early and quite ambitious undertaking, he was already working out for himself the fundamentals of the art song. He had achieved a remarkable ability to know precisely when to extend a vowel or collapse a consonant, thereby effecting a natural rhythm, creating a phrasing that seems, more often than not, exactly right.

It took Bowles from August to December 1932 to write *Scènes d'Anabase,* the last three sections being completed during his second stay in Monte Carlo. During this period, he made the acquaintance of the American composer George Antheil and his Hungarian wife, Boski, who lived up the road in Cagnes-sur-Mer, France.

Antheil was at this time a highly celebrated composer, having received considerable acclaim for his *Ballet Mécanique* of 1925–26. An intimate of the Stein circle, a close friend of Thomson's and Ezra Pound's (both of whom promoted him assiduously), it was natural that the composer would attract Bowles's special interest. He was not disappointed; Antheil turned out to be as dynamic as the advance notices had promised. A passionate talker, ardently opinionated, he and Bowles discussed music, debating the question of whether opera, as Antheil contended and Bowles disputed, was the musical form of the future. They also discussed North Africa, where Antheil had spent a considerable amount of time, mainly in Tunisia. The talks with Antheil, in combination with the dreary December weather, soon set Bowles to thinking about heading across to the African side of the Mediterranean. By mid-December, with *Scènes d'Anabase* completed, he left Monte Carlo and booked passage on the first boat to Algiers.

Antheil had regaled Bowles with tales of the Sahara. En route, he met some French soldiers recently returned from Algeria; one of them was enthusiastic about a town called Ghardaïa, an outpost in the northern Sahara. Located in a particularly barren region of the Sahara called the M'Zab, Ghardaïa was an old city with large palms and whitewashed mud houses. Bowles was fascinated by the town from the moment he arrived; deciding to spend the winter there, he began looking for a place to live. He contacted the French army's regional commander, a Lieutenant d'Armagnac, who quickly found Bowles a house near the army post, a short distance outside the town. He also sent him a servant, a one-eyed Algerian, to do the cooking.

The house was extremely cold, even though the ambient temperature during the day was quite warm, and Bowles procured a terra-cotta charcoal-burning brazier to use as a heater. One morning, to ward off the cold, he lighted it and went back to bed to read. A short while later he found himself feeling inexplicably groggy; soon he couldn't sit up. From the blackness into which he quickly descended, he heard a voice crying, "Monsieur!" then suddenly felt his servant's strong hands dragging him into the kitchen and out of the house. Once outside he began to revive. He then learned that he had nearly asphyxiated himself from carbon monoxide given off by the newly lighted brazier.

Taken to the lieutenant's house, Bowles remained in bed for two days, then set off for nearby Laghouat to stay in a hotel until the cold had passed. In Laghouat he managed to persuade the local curé to allow him to use the harmonium in the Catholic church in order to be able to continue his burst of composing. There in the church he began work on a cantata, using his own French text as the lyrics. Consisting of four parts, "Romance," "Chanson," "Valse," and "Finale," the cantata was written for soprano, four male voices, and harmonium. Entitled "Par le Détroit,"—the "detroit" being the Strait of Gibraltar—the piece, noted Bowles, might well have been called "Dream Cantata," as several sections of it actually appeared to him in a dream. Upon awakening, he simply wrote the parts down in exactly the form he had seen them in his dream, checking them later for accuracy: the music was in perfect form. This was the only time in his life that music would be "delivered" to him in this fashion, although he would be able to use his dreams as a source for several stories.

After a little more than a month in Laghouat, he decided to return to Ghardaïa. There he met another American, George Turner, who was around twenty-two or twenty-three years old. Turner had been traveling around North Africa for several months and was determined to go into the Sahara. He invited Bowles to accompany him; soon the two were on their way to Algiers, where they spent several days exploring the Casbah. From Algiers they took the bus to Bou-Saâda, a city southeast of the Algerian capital on the edge of the Sahara. Upon arriving there, a "guide" quickly came up to them, insisting on showing them the "sights"—the market, the dry riverbed, the sand dunes. Finally, he suggested taking them to see "Ouled Nail girls," who would dance naked for them. The Ouled Nail are a nomadic people from the Algerian Sahara, but throughout North Africa the Ouled Nail women are famed for their artful dancing; usually, however, the dances are performed in a brightly colored costume and feathered headdress. Although the dancers are often prostitutes as well, it is rare for them to dance naked. Arriving at what was obviously a brothel, the two young men soon picked out their "dancer," about sixteen years old. The madam set the price: it would cost 15 francs for each of them to sleep with her but 75 francs to see her dance naked, as she was not accustomed to baring herself. Turner was unwilling to pay for her dancing but Bowles insisted, saying he would fork over the money himself. Bowles thought that her dancing was "not very good, and it only lasted about five minutes. Nevertheless her beauty was such that nothing mattered. Whatever she did was esthetically satisfying." When she had finished dancing she asked which one was going to take her to bed. Neither accepted the offer, to her apparent chagrin. But after returning to the hotel, Turner thought better of it and quietly slipped out to take advantage of the Ouled Nail's availability.

After a few more peregrinations in the northern Sahara, they headed for Tunisia, finally arriving in the town of Qairouan. By now Bowles was nearly out of cash; to his dismay he was unable to cash a traveler's check. Proceeding to Tunis, he met with the same problem. According to the American Embassy officials in Tunis, the reason for the situation was that Roosevelt had temporarily halted transactions at American banks. They advised him to borrow some francs from friends until dollars could again be bought and sold. Bowles, of course, knew no one in Tunis and Turner was in nearly the same predicament. Bowles sent wires to friends in France. Only Morrissette responded, sending him 150 francs, enough to buy a third-class train ticket to Algiers. Turner went north, taking the ferry to Sicily; Bowles boarded the westbound train to Algeria.

On the train, passing through the corridor, he came upon a surprising scene taking place in one of the compartments: a young Algerian man giving an injection to his companion. Seeing that they had an onlooker, the man giving the injection came out into the passageway and began to explain to Bowles that his brother was ill with tuberculosis and that the doctor had ordered him to administer frequent morphine injections to him. He further told Bowles that he was taking his brother to a sanitarium just on the other side of the Tunisian border, but that he feared his brother would die anyway. They continued to talk for a while, Bowles finally informing the Algerian of his money problems. Responding, the young man told Bowles that he should come to his house in Constantine, but as the man would not arrive for another day, he wrote Bowles a note to take to a friend of his, a keeper of a *hammam,* who would put him up free of charge for the night.

Getting off the train in Constantine, Bowles made his way

through the snow to the address given to him. He was taken in cordially after presenting his note. He was unable to sleep, however, as one of the guests decided to entertain the others by playing the *guinbri*—a North African lute—to the delight of all, it seems, but Bowles. In the early evening of the next day he was met by his Algerian friend and taken to his house, where he was treated with extraordinary hospitality. From there, well-fed and rested, he went on to Algiers. The banks were once again accepting dollars. Bowles cashed some checks and set out for Tangier.

Although Bowles's sojourn in the North African desert lasted only a few months, it left enough of an impression to provide the background for his novel of death in the Sahara, *The Sheltering Sky,* written nearly fifteen years later. The three Americans in the novel, Port and Kit Moresby and George Tunner, wander through much of the same desert region; there they also meet a Lieutenant d'Armagnac, a sympathetic, helpful man who keeps several Ouled Nail mistresses; George Turner lends his name, a bit transposed, to the Moresbys' traveling companion. (Indeed, in an early draft of *The Sheltering Sky,* Tunner is called Turner.) Even the visit to the brothel is reconstituted in the early pages of the novel, where Port, accosted by a persistent "guide," is finally persuaded to venture to a makeshift encampment, where he goes to bed with an Ouled Nail dancing girl, sixteen or seventeen years old.

In Tangier, Bowles took a little house on the Marshan, slightly on the outskirts of the city, and went through the process of renting a piano. As the house had no running water or furniture, he slept in a hotel in the Medina, using the house only for work. By the time he had arrived in Tangier, in fact, he had already begun to compose a piano sonatina in his head and was rather desperate for a piano on which to try out his ideas. "The truth was that Aaron's little warning of two years before, 'If you don't work when you're twenty, nobody's going to love you when you're thirty,' although scarcely meant seriously, had remained with me and taken root," remembered Bowles.

Charles-Henri Ford had also arrived in Tangier about that time. When Bowles met up with him, Ford was staying with a Spanish couple awaiting the arrival of his friend Djuna Barnes from England. Learning that Bowles had a "free" house, he made arrangements to occupy it at night and in the morning. When Barnes arrived, they moved in together, vacating the premises each day by 1:30 in the afternoon, when Bowles arrived to work. After a few weeks, though, Barnes and Ford moved to more comfortable lodgings, despite the cost. In the evenings the three of them would often rendezvous, usually in the Medina, near where Bowles was staying, to sit for hours in the Café Central, watching the crowds, gathering various others at their table. It was a time of great productivity for them all: Barnes was completing *Nightwood* (then called *Bow Down*), Ford working on some poems, and Bowles on his sonatina. Bowles found Barnes engaging, if odd. Fond of wearing rather outlandish makeup—blue, purple, and green—she was an object of curiosity to the Moroccans. Although Bowles had rather strong feelings about ostentation, Barnes's manner of calling attention to herself did not bother him in the same way that it had in Spender. He gave her more ground, partly because she was a woman, partly because he was more convinced of her talent.

Although Tangier was an extremely cheap place to live, Bowles found himself quickly exhausting his money supply. He reluctantly decided to head back to the United States:

> Had I believed that my constantly changing life, which I considered the most pleasant of all possible lives (save perhaps the same one on a slightly more generous budget), would go on indefinitely, I should not have pursued it with such fanatical ardor. But I was aware that it could not be durable. Each day lived through on this side of the Atlantic was one more day spent outside prison. I was aware of the paranoia in my attitude and that with each suceeding month of absence from the United States I was augmenting it. Still, there is not much doubt that with sufficient funds I should have stayed indefinitely outside America.

At this point, Bowles had spent almost two years abroad, ingeniously managing to survive financially through a series of fortunate events, not the least of which was the generosity of newly made friends and acquaintances. Dunham provided him with small sums of cash and picked up travel expenses; when first in Paris, Carlo Suarès put him up; later in France that first summer Gertrude Stein gave him free room and board at Bilignin; in Tangier,

Copland paid the rent. Back in Paris, the Dunhams took care of him; in London he was able to take advantage of the hospitality offered to him by Mary Oliver and Edouard Roditi; and once in Paris again, Anne Miracle, Suarès, and the Dunhams provided both lodging and meals. Trounstine apparently paid his travel expenses to Spain and Morocco; Abdallah Drissi took care of him in Fez; and after his bout with typhoid, Morrissette and Thomson, in addition to loaning him money, also gave him places to stay. George Antheil supported a portion of his Sahara trip and fed him regularly while Bowles was in Monte Carlo. In Tunisia, he had no qualms about burdening, with his financial problems, a young man with a dying brother.

Nearly everyone was always good for a dinner or two. Rena apparently was also quite generous, picking up the tabs on her visit and leaving a small sum for her son to use after she left. In addition, Bowles had inherited money from his Aunt Adelaide at the end of December 1931, most of which he managed to hold on to for more than a year by pleading poverty at every turn. It should be pointed out, though, that costs were not great during the early thirties. "You can live comfortably here [in Paris] including entertainments and everything for at most one dollar fifty cents a day," Bowles informed Morrissette. North Africa was even cheaper; about half that amount was needed, particularly if one was willing to rely on "the kindness of strangers."

By the early spring of 1933, however, Bowles had run out of eager providers. He crossed the Strait of Gibraltar and went to Cádiz, where he bought a third-class ticket on board the *Juan Sebastian Elcano,* bound for San Juan, Puerto Rico. The trip took three weeks. After another week, spent exploring the interior of the island, he took a ship to New York.

CHAPTER 11

Back in Manhattan, Bowles wasted no time in getting in touch with Copland. He was eager to show him that despite all the traveling he had been doing, he had also been composing. Copland, in fact, had already seen the sonata for flute and piano, had even had it performed, himself playing the piano part, in late February 1933 at the Interpreters-Composers Party. The other music, particularly the *Sonatina for Piano,* greatly impressed him. Through a contact at WEVD radio in New York, he arranged for it to be performed on the air June 18. For assistance, he wrote to the pianist John Kirkpatrick on May 29, asking him if he would play it: "I can recommend [the *Sonatina*] as a highly amusing and successful piece . . . simple to play technically, except for a spot here and there in the last movement." Kirkpatrick responded affirmatively; in December he would play the piece again, this time at the League of Composers' Concert, also arranged by Copland.

Despite Copland's efforts, Bowles was feeling distinctly estranged, both from him and from his own country. On June 24, 1933, he wrote to Virgil Thomson:

Have been here three weeks and sick three weeks naturally. Certainly nobody hates New York as much as I do. Aaron of course has a new pet so there is no snuggling there. They leave soon for the country. Bref, I should not like to be here. Because of course it can never amount to anything. I have no piano to work at and nothing to say anyway. And feeling miserable keeps me from seeing, looking up anyone. Why the hell Aaron advised me to return is more than I know. He wrote "there are just as many people interested in what you have to offer in USA as there are in Europe. Quel mensonge!!

About a week later, he decided that if he had to remain in America, it would be better to be at least in the countryside. He arranged, therefore, to go up to Massachusetts to stay for a time with his Aunt Emma. A few years before, she had divorced Guy Ross and was now living in Westhampton, Massachusetts, married to a farmer named Orville Flint. Flint's former wife had killed herself with a shotgun one evening in the parlor of the farmhouse; Aunt Emma refused to go into the room where it had happened. The story so intrigued Bowles that he never forgot it. Nearly half a century later he wrote his own account of it, which was published in 1984 as "Massachusetts 1932."

But that summer Bowles was working on another piece of fiction in an attempt to come to terms with his feelings about returning home. The story, which was never published, was titled "A Proposition." It is the tale of a young man's homecoming after being away for several years. Walking from the train station to his house, he finds the town changed: suburban-style houses have sprung up; the weather is colder than he expected; even the "flat provincial accent" of the locals startles him. When he finally arrives home, his parents, "smaller, older, greyer, surrounded by the odor of cooking, but smiling," greet him undemonstratively. His mother almost immediately flees to the kitchen to attend to the dinner, his father settles down to listen to the news as it is "still too soon for father and son to trust themselves to be alone together." He panics: "Going back into the empty hall, he suddenly sees his situation as desperate, and glances longingly at the door into the street. Then he sighs and tells himself that he is too tired to think logically." Going upstairs to his room he catches a glimpse of his parents in the kitchen: "In front of the bright orchestra of simmering pots on the stove his parents are waltzing together. . . . It is a triumphal dance; they are celebrating his defeat." Once in his room he is surprised to find it exactly as he left it. Looking over the items scattered about, he ponders his return in which "the prospect of dinner tonight and breakfast tomorrow and all the days to come seems to him unbearable." As the story ends he goes down to dinner. "A Proposition," while less accomplished than most of his fiction, may be read as an accurate account of Bowles's difficulty in readjusting to being back in the States, where he felt himself curtailed in his freedom, dependent on his parents who are only too delighted to celebrate his defeat as an expatriate artist.

From Westhampton he went to visit his Aunt Mary at Holden

Hall. Although the country was more to his liking than the city, he still found himself terribly isolated. Again to Thomson, he wrote about his continued sense of estrangement:

> I am so completely alone here that sometimes I am at a loss to know what to do. And that for the first time in my life. I really do want to see people once in a while. Instead, I have to follow brooks to their sources and plan new four hour walks. Utter silence, utter country. Utter chastity, moreover! It gets on one's nerves, there's no doubt about that. And gets into one's music, but America is America.

Despite never feeling quite at home in his home, Bowles did manage by late in the summer to begin composing. He was, in fact, fairly productive, writing among other pieces a long song cycle based on texts by Georges Linze entitled *Danger de Mort.* He also reworked and completed a composition begun in Puerto Rico, *Suite for Small Orchestra,* consisting of three parts, "Pastorale," "Habanera," and "Divertissement." The *Suite* was his first piece for orchestra and also the first to incorporate Latin rhythms. Scored for flute, oboe, clarinet, fagotto, Trombe in C, trombone, piano, tambour de Provence, violin, viola, cello, and bass, the orchestral work is a spirited piece with rapid tempo changes, numerous glissando passages, and polyrhythms. Although clearly the product of a young composer, the *Suite* has some sophisticated and evocative passages; for Bowles it would also serve as an important exercise in musical quotation, for in this piece he is learning the art of transposing heard folk rhythms into a contemporary musical idiom, a major element in many of his later works.

This ability to reproduce aural patterns links his compositions with his writing, for both rely extensively on a finely attuned ear, capable of hearing and recording the most subtle aspects of speech or music. Although he improvises freely, both his prose and music have an unmistakable quality of being grounded in reality, as if Bowles were serving as a medium through which a tune or dialogue is delivered intact to the receiver; indeed, the seeming "artlessness" inherent in his music or fiction is itself the art. It is that quality of "artlessness" that Gertrude Stein called "telling the truth"; it was the aspect singularly lacking in most of his early poems, where pretense outstripped the expression of experience.

But in "A Proposition," and in his songs and other compositions, Bowles can be seen as nurturing what would become his hallmark: an ability to create products of the imagination that read or sound absolutely natural, without a false note, with an unwavering under-pinning of truth about them.

At the end of the summer of 1933 Bowles found himself back in New York, this time staying with Harry Dunham, who had taken an apartment on East 58th Street. The arrangement only lasted about two weeks, however, for once Dr. Dunham learned that Bowles was in residence he threatened to cut off his son's income. The elder Dunham apparently bought the family line that Bowles was a bad influence, a "corrosive element" that needed to be excised from Harry's life. Copland, as usual, came to the rescue, offering his protégé a place to live and work just a few blocks away at 52 West 58th Street. The apartment actually belonged to Harold and Stella Clurman, but had been passed on to Copland who now gave it to Bowles. Although the two split the rent, Copland only used the apartment occasionally to compose at the grand piano and to hold meetings of a newly formed association of composers that quickly came to be called the Young Composers Group, with an age limit of twenty-five (except, of course, for Copland). Its members in-cluded Arthur Berger, Henry Brant, Israel Citkowitz, Lehman Engel, Vivian Fine, Irwin Heilner, Bernard Herrmann, Jerome Moross, Elie Siegmeister, and occasionally Marc Blitzstein. Bowles was on the periphery, not really accepted into the group, for as Copland explains, "when Bowles and Virgil were visitors, the regulars were less than friendly toward the expatriates. The Young Composers were interested in the situation of the American com-poser."

Bowles was as disenchanted with the Young Composers as they were with him: "I would often ask myself what I was doing there, and I questioned the value of the venture." He further remembers being aggressively attacked, particularly by Bernard Herrmann (who apparently hated everyone's compositions); "he thought both my music and I were absurd and said so in no uncertain terms." After dutifully attending a few sessions, he decided the group was not for him. Bowles became further outcast when he announced that he found nothing to interest him in the harmony lessons with Roger Sessions that nearly all the Young Composers had decided to take.

Bowles's "expatriate" status also caused him problems with the "Stieglitz crowd," who, angered by expatriate American artists who had thrown their lot in with Europeans, formed a group called An American Place. The group gathered one evening at the apartment of Dorothy Norman, an acquaintance of Bowles's, who invited him to attend. When the talk turned to a denunciation by Stieglitz of Gertrude Stein, Bowles countered Stieglitz, incurring the wrath of those present, the photographer and his wife, Georgia O'Keeffe, most particularly. When the evening broke up, it was clear that neither Bowles nor his views were welcome any longer at meetings of An American Place.

Rather than attempt to become more "American," Bowles remained staunchly convinced that his European sensibility must be maintained at all costs. With a small amount of capital, probably acquired from Dunham, he launched a music publishing venture called Éditions de la Vipère. The name was apt, for at the time he truly thought himself to be the viper residing in the American nest. He first published, in an edition of one hundred copies, two compositions of his own, songs based on texts by Gertrude Stein. Entitled *Scenes from the Door*, the short songs were made from Stein's "Red Faces" and "The Ford," both taken from *Useful Knowledge*. The cover was printed in horizontal red, white, and blue stripes, a direct attempt to convey his sense that this too was American music on American texts. He later also had printed under the Vipère imprint two previously unpublished pieces by Erik Satie that he had somehow managed to acquire in manuscript form in Paris.

In December, John Kirkpatrick performed Bowles's *Sonatina for Piano* at the League of Composers' Concert. Given the rather stormy reception he had received from his peers in New York, Bowles was a bit anxious about how the work would be received. Luckily, the review for the journal *Modern Music* was assigned to Blitzstein, who was less insular than many of the other Young Composers. Still, Blitzstein felt compelled to comment on its European quality: "Paul Bowles' Sonatina: what is called 'damned clever.' The up-to-date facetious Parisian mood, whiter even than the White Russians who dispense it in Paris. A really striking first movement (the mood is possibly authentic in Bowles)."

At the end of the concert, "a strange little man" came up and introduced himself to Bowles, saying that he was a friend of Bruce Morrissette's. He told Bowles his name was Treville Latouche and that he was a poet from Richmond. Quite a bit younger than Bowles, he had been "discovered" by Morrissette through his submissions to *The Messenger* while still a high school student. He was, in fact, still in high school, at the Riverside Boarding School in New York. Precocious, determined to get to know everyone in New York, within a few months of his arrival he had changed his first name to John and had begun to frequent various Greenwich Village haunts noted for their bohemian personalities and atmosphere. Although Bowles didn't see much of him during that winter, by the next year they would become good friends.

Bowles also began writing his first film music late that autumn, for a movie edited by Harry Dunham called *Siva* (later *Bride of Samoa*). A loose documentary with a "leering commentary," the film had been shot in Samoa. It was, in Bowles's words, "atrocious"; nevertheless, as there was a small sum of money involved and as it provided an opportunity for a useful learning experience, Bowles assented to the project, spending long hours behind the movieola counting frames and timing his music to fit particular scenes.

Near the end of the year Virgil Thomson arrived back in New York to oversee the production of his opera *Four Saints in Three Acts,* based on Stein's libretto. It was no coincidence that Bowles began to gravitate more toward Thomson and away from Copland during this period. One reason had to do with Bowles's jealousy about Copland's "new pet." But the other, ultimately more important, reason was that Copland was becoming more and more involved with producing "American" music, while Thomson, undoubtedly the most important American expatriate composer of the time, was still fervently championing the cross-fertilization of American with European (particularly French) music. Bowles, therefore, naturally looked to Thomson for support, and got it. The composer took Bowles around, introducing him to others with like sensibilities and made sure that he had a prominent box in the theater on the opening night of *Four Saints.* In February 1934, Bowles wrote to Stein of the premiere and the reaction:

Here is the stub of my ticket for the opening night of *Four Saints.* I have collected some of the notices about it. . . . I am sending those I have in another large envelope. . . .

The smart thing among the younger artists is to be violently against it. Stieglitz decides also to side with them. Most of the defense must be taken for Virgil, against whom they allow themselves to rage for having the audacity to give Gertrude Stein in modern dress. That is all I make of their fury anyway. People walking on Broadway and sitting in automats talk of "the Saints Play" and usually sound doubtful as to whether it would be worth while trying to get tickets for it.

In the same letter he mentions to Stein that "I have made songs out of two short things from Useful Knowledge, but no one has seen them yet, because I want to do more." This was not, in fact, quite true, for Bowles had already published the pieces in his Éditions de la Vipère, and Thomson had been presented with a copy. But there were reasons for this deception: Bowles, first of all, had not asked Stein for permission to set the texts; second he was indeed hoping to write further songs. The letter continues:

But I should like some more short romantic poems to make a group out of. What I want is to write several lieder on your words, but I can't find the right words to use. Would you at any time be interested in writing four or five lieder? Perhaps you would prefer hearing my music first. Still I should like to have them all written when I return to Paris, and show them to you. I think you would like them very much.

Stein apparently never sent Bowles any further texts, nor did the composer ever show Stein the two songs he had written and published. Instead, he ended up writing to Cocteau for permission to compose a song cycle based on six of his texts. The cycle, for voice and solo piano, finally completed eighteen months later, was entitled *Memnon.*

Late that same winter, either Thomson or Antheil, now also in New York, introduced Bowles to Lincoln Kirstein and George Balanchine, who were in the process of forming the Ballet Caravan. The idea was that Bowles might be able to provide the new company with a ballet score. On February 23, 1934, Bowles wrote to Morrissette of his "audition" for Balanchine: "I have just come in from seeing Balanchine, who insisted that I play the piano to him. Fingers froze. I had not played in six weeks. Nor those pieces in months. He insisted on keeping everything with him. Kirstein was encouraging driving me home, but I'm still worried." A month later Bowles received Balanchine's verdict: "Kirstein told me this afternoon that Balanchine found my music not danceable. Antheil is going to learn some of them, and have Bal. up one night to his house, where he and I will play to him." Whether Antheil ever did try to persuade Balanchine further that year is not known, but no ballet was commissioned from Bowles that spring.

Despite the flurry of activity and his involvement in the New York musical world, Bowles was again becoming discontent, longing for a change of scene, preferably to the other side of the Atlantic. Without funds, it seemed unlikely that he would be able to journey to Europe or North Africa at any time in the near future; suddenly, however, he managed to secure a job in Morocco. It came about by calculated accident. In the early spring of 1934 he learned that Colonel Charles Williams was in New York for a visit. Williams was responsible for running a foundation in Morocco dedicated to ending the mistreatment of pack animals in that country. The American Fondouk, as the foundation was called, was managed locally in Fez by Charles Brown, whom Bowles and Dunham had visited several years before. Deciding that he had nothing to lose by introducing himself to the colonel, Bowles promptly proceeded to the hotel. During the next hour he learned from Williams that he was not at all pleased with the way Brown was running things in Fez and was scheming to oust him from the post. Bowles volunteered his services as a secretary, a position that naturally would involve going with the colonel to Morocco. After impressing Williams with his typing ability, and following a routine interview, Bowles was hired. The position, however, was contingent on Bowles paying his own passage to Morocco. Although he did not yet know how he could afford the fare, he arranged to meet Colonel Williams in Gibraltar in August.

Ever resourceful, Bowles had found work by early July, as a personal travel guide to a Wall Street stockbroker who wanted to vacation in Spain. A few weeks later he and the broker were on board the *Conte di Savoia,* bound for Cádiz. After a few weeks in southern Spain, he crossed to Tangier. There he met up with his old friend from Virginia days, John Widdicombe. Together they traveled down to Casablanca, where Bowles bought an old hand-cranked phonograph and a large collection of Moroccan folk recordings. From Casablanca they set off on the grand tour of Morocco, Bowles lugging several suitcases and the phonograph, until it was time for Bowles to report to Williams in Gibraltar.

Once in Fez with the colonel, Bowles found himself in a somewhat difficult situation, as it appeared that the only real objection Williams had to Brown's management was that he socialized with Moroccans. Bowles's sympathies were squarely with his former host, who had after all introduced him to the Drissi brothers, but as he was employed by the colonel he was forced to side with him. This meant working with Williams to discover some error of fiduciary wrongdoing on Brown's part, which proved to be quite difficult as Brown had been a careful and quite competent manager. Finally, the colonel found some small item in the books that had not been accounted for properly. He immediately dictated a letter for Bowles to type and send to New York, explaining that due to gross negligence Williams had been forced to sack the unfortunate manager. He then proceeded to replace him with a crony, a retired British army officer. Bowles continued to work for Williams, despite serious misgivings about the colonel's mission.

In understanding Bowles's behavior it is important to recall his ability to construct elaborate justifications for his actions, particularly those acts performed under duress (as in the knife-throwing incident). By creating an abstraction out of reality, he was able to place himself outside the realm of accountability. Further, he was quite adept at comforting himself during these early years with the notion that the end justified the means—the end here being to remain in Morocco, which required an income. On a somewhat lesser scale, this attitude is observable in his willingness to accept money, lodging, or meals from whoever was willing to provide these things in order to continue his own pursuits. Just as he shrugged off Amelia Dunham's mistreatment of Abdelkader, since he was benefiting from her "generosity," he now allowed himself to be used as a pawn in Colonel Williams's game. A similar problem faces the protagonist, Dyar, of Bowles's novel *Let It Come Down,* who finds himself doing a job that he also finds contrary to his principles. Reflecting on the dilemma, Dyar rationalizes it this way:

> At each moment his situation struck him as more absurd and untenable. He had no desire to do that kind of work, and he had no interest in helping Mme. Jouvenon or her cause.
>
> However, it was nice to have the money. . . . You had to make a choice. But the choice was already made, and he felt that it was not he who had made it. Because of that, it was hard for him to believe that he was morally involved.

Although it is perhaps a bit too easy to read Bowles's philosophy into Dyar's assessment of his predicament, there is clearly a good deal of correspondence between Dyar's outlook and Bowles's, at least at this stage in his life. Such a rationalization provided a general construct that allowed him to keep on working for the colonel, despite the odiousness of the task he was forced to perform.

Having successfully completed his mission in Morocco, the colonel had no desire to remain longer. As a result, in mid-October, less than three months after he had begun his employment, Bowles found himself without a job and with little cash. He returned to Tangier and from there to Cádiz. Spain, however, was at war, and Bowles needed to be escorted everywhere by the local police and the Guardia Civil. He wrote to Burns of the sad state of affairs: "What a plight to be in Spain now that's state of war [sic]. Police here and more there, and government and army papers to carry about without so much as a que guapo [how handsome]." As Spain was not conducive to a visit, he booked passage on the first westbound ship leaving Cádiz, the *Juan Sebastian Elcano,* the same ship he had taken the year before. This time, though, he decided to stay on board all the way to its final destination, Puerto Colombia. From the ship, on November 2, he wrote Burns about Morocco, and the music he had collected there, but did not mention anything regarding the Brown affair:

> I have some lovely records: from Fez, choral works of ancient origin, accompanied by strings and drum; from the Atlas, (Sous) Chleuh

songs and dances, from the desert, songs with flute and chalumeau accompaniment, from Andalucia, saetas, with drum and trumpets, songs by Marchena, with guitar, and solos by Montoya, Sabicas and Maravilla. And some extra, from Algeria and Egypt.

Bowles had developed a considerable interest in ethnomusicology. The results of this immersion in traditional indigenous music would eventually lead him to incorporate several of its rhythms and themes into his own compositions. In addition, although he could scarcely have known it at the time, this initial acquisition, the first of many, would ultimately become a consuming passion; twenty-five years later, in fact, Bowles would occupy a position as one of the world's leading authorities on North African music and play an extremely important role in its preservation. But in 1934 his primary motivation for collecting the records was simply his interest in the music for its own sake, as a way of keeping a link to cultures he was intent on penetrating.

When the ship docked in San Juan, a Puerto Rican woman and her teenage son boarded, bound for Venezuela. Bowles became friendly with the boy, who offered him some marijuana. "I could not imagine why the boy considered these homemade cigarettes more interesting than ordinary ones. The taste was unpleasant, and since I did not inhale, I got no effect," recalled Bowles. Later, however, he tried them again. "This time I did experience a strange sensation of being irretrievably *there* in that place. . . . Because I also had the impression that my heart was beating in a manner both more violent and more rapid, I classified the experience as unpleasant and thenceforth refused the cigarettes when they were offered." When the ship arrived in Venezuela, however, the young Puerto Rican became frightened that he would be caught with the marijuana, and gave all he had to Bowles. Bowles secreted the substance in his luggage; when he disembarked in Colombia, he passed through customs without a hitch.

Not one to pass up an opportunity to explore new terrain, Bowles decided to spend a few weeks in Colombia before heading back to the States. (Also, having begun to study Spanish in earnest while working for the colonel, he reasoned that this would provide him with an occasion to practice it.) In the town of Santa Marta he immediately became ill from drinking unpurified water, and lay sick in bed for four or five days. Finally the hotel proprietor mentioned to him that the place for him to recuperate was at the coffee plantation of an American named Flye, high up in the mountains rising behind Santa Marta. Reluctant to take him in, Flye finally agreed when Bowles told him he was sick. Although he only remained a week, the memory of the visit would remain long in Bowles's head. In 1946 he would set his story, "The Echo," on a plantation above Jamonocal, describing with extraordinary accuracy the wild primeval terrain glimpsed fleetingly twelve years earlier.

Back in Santa Marta he bought some medicine for amoebic dysentery, the malaise that was still afflicting him, and after a couple of days, he booked passage to San Pedro, California, mainly because it was the first destination he could get.

Due to a clerical error, he was placed in steerage class his first night out rather than in a cabin on the upper decks. In the dormitory he had two young Americans, ages sixteen and eighteen, for companions. As they sat up talking, the conversation turned to marijuana, of which the two had become quite fond. They had exhausted their supply, however, so Bowles offered to sell them his. He wrote to Burns:

> I have sold all I had, and profited thereby pleasantly (inasmuch as all I had was given me by a frightened person who was carrying pounds!). The only souvenir is the very strong odor in my luggage, which will probably intrigue customs officials who sniff it out. I shall say it is a variety of South American civet, one of them having discovered my luggage one evening in a prowl onto the verandah of the finca in the selva.

The next day he was able to get the cabin he had paid for, leaving the young men to smoke their *grifas* in peace.

In California, he went first to stay with his Uncle Shirley Bowles, his father's brother, who had moved to Santa Monica around the end of the First World War. In his uncle's house he took the opportunity, during the month he spent there, to write some new music, including a couple of piano preludes and "Letter to Freddy," using as text the letter he had received from Stein in Paris during his scare with syphilis. By now, a familiar pattern was emerging: travel followed by work followed again by travel. He commented on this mode in a letter to Burns: "When the exterior life palls, the interior starts working. If I moved always to new places, I should never work at all: no music, no nothing. If I were enclosed ill in a room, I should work prodigiously, be happy in the way at the antipodes."

From Santa Monica, he journeyed up the coast to San Francisco and visited Henry Cowell at Stanford. This time when he showed Cowell his new music, the older composer was visibly impressed. He was, in fact, so taken with the new compositions that he asked Bowles whether he could publish some of them in a magazine he was editing, *New Music, A Quarterly of Modern Compositions.* For publication he selected a short solo piano piece, "Café Sin Nombre," "Letter to Freddy," "Part III" from *Scènes d'Anabase,* and the last song from *Danger de Mort.* The publication of these compositions greatly delighted Bowles, as this was the first time any of his music had appeared in print, aside from the music he'd published himself. He was also quite pleased that he had earned Cowell's blessing.

Invigorated by his meetings with Cowell, Bowles decided to head back to New York to reimmerse himself in the music scene there. Typically, he did not hurry, but took the bus, stopping off in various places along the way, including two weeks in Chicago, where he stayed with George Turner, the fellow he had knocked about with in the Sahara. From there, he went to see Bruce Morrissette in Baltimore. Finally, in the early spring of 1935, he arrived back in New York, broke, unsure of how he would be able to support himself now that the Depression was in full swing across America.

CHAPTER 12

Iɴ Nᴇᴡ Yᴏʀᴋ, Bowles again faced the perennial problem of how to make a living as an artist. Getting a job, say in a bookstore or bank, would eat into his time for composing, and yet he had to have some means of support in order to write music. The Depression, with its devastating effect on the American economy, further complicated matters. By and large, however, it seems to have remained an abstraction for Bowles. His family and close friends were left untouched by layoffs; and as he was not really actively searching for a job, he did not experience firsthand the diminishing availability of employment. Only a few years later would the impact of the Depression become a reality for him, but even then he would not suffer the dire consequences felt by so many other Americans.

After a month or so of trying to find a way to survive and compose, he decided to accept an offer that had been made to him while he was visiting Morrissette. The job consisted of being a live-in companion to a wealthy bed-ridden Austrian named Fuhrman, who was suffering from epidemic encephalitis. The position was extremely attractive, as the duties consisted primarily of reading to Fuhrman each morning, leaving Bowles plenty of free time to compose on the Austrian's grand piano. In addition, Morrissette, who was then at Johns Hopkins, lived nearby, thus reassuring him that he would not be lacking for friendship.

Once Bowles had received written confirmation that he would be allowed use of the grand piano, he set out for Baltimore, carrying with him his collection of folk recordings. He also had a particular project in mind: the composition of a ballet, in collaboration with the Russian neo-Romantic painter Eugene Berman. He had first met Berman in Paris through Virgil Thomson, but had renewed his acquaintanceship with the artist after the latter had emigrated to New York. Berman was to do the story, costumes, and sets, Bowles the music. Although the plot line was sketchy, Bowles felt confi-

161

dent by the time he had left New York that he could provide a full score.

The situation in Baltimore proved to be quite conducive to work. His duties were minimal, and he actually enjoyed talking with the cosmopolitan and multi-lingual Austrian. Through Morrissette he met an eccentric etymology professor named Dyar, whose hobby consisted of excavating his basement. At the time Bowles met him, Dyar had already managed to create a trilevel series of tunnels under his house, all, as far as anyone could tell, for absolutely no purpose. In the backyard, a mound of dirt rose two stories, all hauled up from the cellar in buckets. (Some fifteen years later, Bowles gave his name to the protagonist of his novel, *Let It Come Down,* the only apparent similarity between the two.) There were also excursions to the Communist party headquarters, where Bowles bought pamphlets championing the Popular Front, whose slogan was "Communism is Twentieth-Century Americanism." Although he didn't join the party then, he did read the literature, giving it some token consideration.

Bowles had been interested in communism since his adolescence, when he faithfully read *The New Masses,* but this was his first serious attempt to learn more about the movement. Even at this stage in his life, however, his attraction to the party was still in some ways quite adolescent. He reports that he viewed communism largely as a "harassing instrument" rather than as a force for radical change. As a fundamentally antiestablishment cause, it represented a final step in his rebellion against his father, who held rather staunch conservative views, even to the point of regarding any sort of social program as a leftist plot.

Work also progressed on the ballet, but Bowles found himself distinctly isolated. It was not the sort of feeling he'd experienced in Morocco or even South America, for in those exotic geographies there was always the unknown to explore, something new to learn. Baltimore was merely provincial, and if he had to be in the United States, he reasoned, he might as well be in New York.

The sensation was heightened when Thomson wrote to him from New York requesting a copy of *Scènes d'Anabase* for a concert to be given at the Wadsworth Athenaeum in Hartford, Connecticut, under the auspices of The Friends and Enemies of Modern Music. Founded by Chick Austin, curator of the Athenaeum and an old friend and classmate of Thomson's from Harvard, The Friends and Enemies provided support for contemporary music and composers. Thomson was its musical director, with the performances generally taking place at the museum, often with elaborate decor created especially for the event by a variety of contemporary artists. Bowles, naturally, wanted to be present, particularly as he'd never heard *Scènes d'Anabase* performed. As it was impossible for him to get away, however, he copied the parts and sent them to Thomson.

By the summer Bowles was back in New York. Two events caused him to take leave of his job with Fuhrman: his Grandmother Bowles had died, requiring him to return for the funeral; and another Friends and Enemies Concert had been organized by Thomson, which Bowles was determined not to miss this time. Although the performance space was small, the concert being given in Chick Austin's drawing room, the composers, who also doubled as performers, were stellar. Copland played Thomson and his own *Piano Variations;* Thomson played portraits of those present, including one of Bowles; while Bowles countered with his own portraits and his *Piano Sonatina.* George Antheil, meanwhile, shared duets with Thomson and played a suite of his own.

Bowles's short portraits were gentle and melodic, each echoing (and in the case of Antheil's portrait, nearly parodying) the subjects' distinctive styles. Thomson's portrait of Bowles, on the other hand, was more of an attempt to capture the personality of the young composer. Charming, light, and lyrical, it was quite flattering.

That summer, Bowles quickly began to reenter his New York social circle as well as acquire new acquaintances, mainly through introductions provided by Virgil Thomson. His new friends included the director Joseph Losey and the jazz impresario John Hammond, who began to educate Bowles about jazz, playing him recordings of Teddy Wilson, Duke Ellington, and others. He renewed his friendship with George Antheil as well, who was now living in the city. He also saw a lot of Berman, but the two had by this time decided to abandon their ballet, as both were busy with other projects.

For Bowles, specifically, it was another ballet. Unlike the project with Berman, however, this one had a sponsor—none other, in fact, than the American Ballet Caravan under the direction of Lincoln Kirstein and George Balanchine, the same company that had rejected him the year before. On several occasions Bowles had gone to see Kirstein, who, urged on by Thomson, had decided to commission a new work for the company. From Thomson's glowing reports about Bowles's new compositions Kirstein felt that Balanchine might be able this time to find Bowles's work more "danceable." The Ballet Caravan office, however, was so "chaotic" that Bowles was quite wary about leaving behind any compositions that he really cared about. As a result, he kept bringing Balanchine pieces written as early as high school; naturally, the choreographer was as unimpressed as before. Finally, after explaining to Kirstein the problem, the matter was settled; Bowles played some new pieces for Balanchine. At their conclusion he was charged with producing a new ballet score, with Eugene Loring assigned to choreograph it.

Since Kirstein regarded Bowles as a consummate traveler, the theme, appropriately, was to be a trip around the world. The title given to it was *Yankee Clipper,* the scenario calling for dance music evocative of various ports of call, as well as some shipboard scenes. It was the perfect sort of plan for a composer like Bowles, who was already freely incorporating a variety of musical idioms into his own work; *Yankee Clipper,* with its emphasis on remote locales, gave Bowles what amounted to a musical mandate to fashion compositions along these lines. He set to work at once, and over the next few months nearly completed a long pianistic score. But being fairly ignorant of the demands required by orchestration, he simply wrote the ballet music as if the entire work would be performed as a piano solo. (When it did finally come to be orchestrated, nearly a year later, this would cause him considerable problems.)

Yankee Clipper was not the only work that engaged him that summer. He also got involved through Henry Cowell, who was now in New York teaching at the New School for Social Research, in having some of the North African Chleuh records mechanically reproduced as recordings for Béla Bartók, long a pioneer in reworking folk tunes, mainly Slavic melodies, into his compositions. Although the reproductions were not very good, they were apparently sufficient, as they would reappear, considerably transformed, in Bartók's *Concerto for Orchestra.*

Dunham, too, was back in town, recently arrived from Germany, and an avowed Nazi. Shocked by his newly acquired politics, Bowles and others began to work on him. Within a few months Dunham had swung 180 degrees to the left, joined the Communist party and put his talents and money toward making campaign films for Earl Browder, the Communist party's presidential candidate.

Not completely given over to politics, however, Dunham also made an "artistic" film that year, *Venus and Adonis,* a plodding, stylized version of the classical myth, for which Bowles furnished the music. It had its premiere on January 26, 1936, in conjunction with an all-Bowles concert at Midtown Center in New York, sponsored by the Federal Music Project. The program featured a number of Bowles's pieces, most of them written two or three years earlier. They included *Sonata No. 1 for Flute and Piano,* "La Femme de Dakar," "Guayanilla," "Café Sin Nombre," "Portrait of KMC" (Kay Cowen), and "Portrait of BAM" (Bruce Morrissette). But it was the film that caused the most uproar. Bowles remembered that "Harry had to hold his hand in front of the projector during the nude sequences; the accompanying music together with the blank screen made an effect that was far more suggestive than the images would have been."

The reaction of both the audience and critics was mixed. Colin McPhee, writing in *Modern Music,* commented: "In spite of the incredibly stupid film, both from the standpoint of photography and plot, the music carried it along in its allure and melodic individuality." McPhee also had high praise for the chamber and piano works, citing the *Sonata* as particularly beautiful. Cecil Beaton and Natalie Paley, "flamboyant members of Café Society," also took in the spectacle, much to their delight. Bowles's parents, however, were far less enthusiastic: "And this is where our tax money goes now. My God!" remarked Claude. Even Rena found it hard to dredge up an accolade: "At least they can't ungive the concert now that they've given it. If it were trees they'd been planting, they'd be digging them up again tomorrow." Bowles, however, was delighted. It was the first time he had heard most of his works publicly performed, not to mention that this was the first time an all-Bowles concert had ever been given, proof to all concerned that the young composer was indeed "on the map."

But it was not just the concert that demonstrated Bowles's increased recognition as a rising young composer. The publication in April 1935 of his work in Cowell's *New Music,* followed shortly by the inclusion of the last part of *Scènes d'Anabase* in a volume entitled *Ten Songs by American Composers* (published by Cos Cob Press, a music publishing venture largely directed by Copland), gave him far greater visibility. In addition, Copland wrote a long essay, published in *Modern Music* in May–June 1936, in which he singled out a few young composers to highlight as "young men of promise." The essay included the following observation on Bowles:

> There are those who refuse to see in Bowles anything more than a dilettante. Bowles himself persists in adopting a militantly non-professional air in relation to all music, including his own. If you take this attitude at its face value, you will lose sight of the considerable merit of a large amount of music Bowles has already written. It is music that comes from a fresh personality, music full of charm and melodic invention, at times surprisingly well made in an instinctive and non-academic fashion. Personally I much prefer an "amateur" like Bowles to your "well-trained" conservatory product.

Such recognition did much to bolster Bowles's status. Indeed, within a few months of being back in New York, he had made the transition from being best known as an expatriate composer of delicate art songs in the French tradition to a much-in-demand composer of theater and film music. Following *Venus and Adonis,* he produced scores for two short films by Rudolph Burckhardt, *Seeing the World* and *145 W. 21,* and incidental music for a play directed by Joseph Losey, *Who Fights This Battle?* The film *145 W. 21* (the title came from poet Edwin Denby's New York address) "starred" Copland, Denby, and John Latouche. For the film Bowles "was both composer and orchestra: I played piano, sang, whistled, clicked my tongue, and made percussive noises, all as part of the music." For the play, a propaganda effort to raise money for the Republicans in Spain, he donated a score for piano, chorus, trumpet, and organ, using as inspiration much of the music he had collected in Spain the year before.

Despite the flurry of recognition and activity, budding fame did not translate into dollars. Bowles received no compensation for any of the films nor for the Losey production. Instead, he supported himself, in part, by copying music for the composer known on Broadway as Vernon Duke, but whose real name was Vladimir Dukelsky. The pay was minuscule, but Duke's mother frequently provided Bowles with free meals. In addition, Bowles had inherited a small sum from his grandparents' estate, but in his usual fashion, he salted most of the money away to be used at a later time for travel. In spite of a chronic lack of funds, however, his social life was full. Along with Thomson and Dunham, there was John Latouche, who was living with Dunham at the time, and through them a whole circle of friends, including e. e. cummings, Thomas Mann's daughter Erika, Edwin Denby, and many others.

But economics continued to be a very real problem. Indeed, with the Depression now making itself felt in New York, many of the composers, musicians, artists, writers, and actors were signing up for work under the auspices of the WPA. Thomson had gone on the payroll of the Federal Theater Project the year before, working with John Houseman and his assistant, an eighteen-year-old wonder named Orson Welles. Together, under a WPA grant, they were staging a version of *Macbeth* with an all-black cast at the large Harlem playhouse, the Lafayette, with Thomson providing the music. Thomson took such a liking to it, and to the directors, that he urged Bowles to get on the federal payroll. Although the competition was keen, Thomson, always astute at turning up paying projects, kept an eye out for an opportunity for Bowles. When Houseman and Welles formed a new theater group, called Project 891, but still funded by the WPA, Thomson interceded on Bowles's behalf.

In the early spring of 1936 he informed Bowles that there was a job for him. As it turned out, it was a job that Thomson had largely created himself, through urging Welles and Houseman to stage a production of Eugène Labiche's nineteenth-century farce, *Un Chapeau de Paille d'Italie.* He argued so persuasively for the play that he even managed to get Welles to work on the translation, in the meantime also finagling a job for Edwin Denby as co-translator. The new title was *Horse Eats Hat,* and for it to be a success, he convinced everyone, "it would need a lot of music." Further, Paul Bowles was just the man to write it.

Moving quickly, Thomson introduced Bowles to Welles and

Houseman and got him signed up at the going rate of $23.86 a week on the payroll of the Federal Theater Project. Because a great many out-of-work musicians were also working under the Federal Theater Project, the orchestra was huge. Although accounts differ a bit on the actual number, there were apparently about thirty-five musicians in the pit, encompassing a full range of strings, woodwinds, brass, percussion, and two grand pianos. In addition, on stage, there were two dance bands (one playing turkey trots, the other gypsy waltzes), a pianola, and a lady trumpeter. Luckily, the stage bands played set period pieces, supplying mostly their own music.

Nonetheless, a tremendous volume of music had to be written; and as it had taken a while to pull Bowles into the play, it had to be written very rapidly, the rehearsals having already begun. In addition, there was a considerably greater obstacle: Bowles did not know how to orchestrate. But since it had been Thomson who had gotten Bowles into the project, it was naturally Thomson who would now have to help him out by taking on the orchestration of the parts for the ensemble. Given the time constraints, Thomson advised Bowles to gather up everything he had already written and "see how he could fit what into the play."

"Paul had a natural sense of the stage," Thomson later said, "and caught on quickly. And since the music was written to be used without the show, the pieces—marches, intermezzos, meditations, songs—are so much richer, and more elaborate than music written for a show ever is." Although according to Bowles a few compositions were written especially for *Horse Eats Hat*, the majority was put together in this manner, thus enabling him to produce a complete score, orchestrated by Thomson for two pianos and full orchestra, and rush it to the musicians in time for rehearsal.

The play opened on schedule. Welles not only directed it, but he also acted, and even sang a song. The other actors included Joseph Cotten, Arlene Francis, Hiram Sherman, Sarah Burton, and Paula Lawrence. Thomson remembers the play as being "a circus," made even more so by a chaotic occurrence on opening night: "When at the end of Act One, with guests waltzing and waiters coming in with champagne, our harassed hero, Joe Cotten, jumped to the chandelier, which swung with him, and the fountain below began to spout on him, and then in the pandemonium stagehands began to carry off the scenery and a blank curtain came down as if to end the disaster but itself fell clean to the floor, and as the house curtain finally descended, [the socialite] Muriel Draper was heard to cry, 'It's wonderful! They should keep this in the show.' "

Despite the opening night disaster, the reviews were, for the most part, laudatory. Frederick Jacobi, reviewing the play for *Modern Music,* likened the performance to "a riotous night in a mad house," adding that the "acting, costumes and scenery are excellent." Although he noted that "the music appears to be hastily made," he acknowledged that it was "amusing too and fits well the spirit of the production. It comes in at precisely the right moments and our composer has given us just the kind of music we want at the time we want it." Thomson further recalls that Joseph Cotten's wife became so enamored of the incidental pieces that "for years after that [she] used to play them for us on the piano."

Although *Horse Eats Hat* was a rousing success, Bowles was not thoroughly satisfied with it, feeling "so ashamed of himself for not being able to orchestrate." He vowed to learn orchestration so as not to have to rely on anyone again to do what he thought of as his job. Almost as soon as he had completed *Horse Eats Hat* he got his chance: another Welles project fell into his hands, again through Thomson, who had originally been signed up to write the music, but who decided to go to Paris for six weeks instead. This time, the play, of a very different stripe, was Marlowe's *Dr. Faustus.* With a bit more lead time, Bowles was able to create and ably orchestrate most of the music specifically for the production, which opened in early January of 1937. Both the play and its music were a success. Thomson, arriving back in New York for the opening, remarked to Bowles: "Well, baby, I see you got your name on the front of the theater all by yourself this time."

Impressed by the score, Thomson took on the job of reviewing it for *Modern Music.* Although it might seem as if Thomson could hardly have been nonpartisan, he consistently distinguished himself as an objective reviewer. His report is worth quoting at length for not only does it describe Bowles's triumph, it also prescribes what theater music should be like:

> Paul Bowles's music for *Dr. Faustus* is excellent. There isn't enough of it to interfere with the main business of the production, which is the recitation of Marlowe's "mighty" lines. What there is is of a rare

musical richness and of great precision. It is conceived, as is the whole production, in the "modernistic" manner and in the "functional" convention. The most excruciatingly musical should be able to listen to the orchestral interludes with pleasure, while the tone-deaf will not be dependent on them for a comprehension of the play. More nearly average people will probably find them expressive and pointed. They have also the historical interest of marking both by the professional workmanship of their texture and by their impeccable cut and placement Mr. Bowles's definite entry into musical big-time.

Thomson's assessment that Bowles had now entered the "musical big-time" was accurate: within a few weeks the young composer had another commission, this one for a full-length documentary film by Louis Hacker profiling the condition of sharecroppers in the South. Called *America's Disinherited,* the film was sponsored by the Southern Tenant Farmers' Union, and like *Who Fights This Battle?* was largely a propaganda piece. To help Bowles with the music, Hacker brought a number of Kentucky farmers to New York. They sang him traditional songs, which he then worked into the final score consisting of both instrumental and sung portions. He later described it as "militant-sounding music," appropriate, it seems, for the subject.

The major event for Bowles in early 1937, however, was not the writing or performance of music, but a meeting that would literally change his life. It took place in February on a rainy night in the lobby of the Plaza Hotel in New York. He had gone there to meet John Latouche and Erika Mann. With them was "an attractive red-haired girl with a pointed nose. . . . [Her] name was Jane, and she was not communicative." Bowles had already heard about the redhead from Latouche, who had met her the year before in a bar and kept insisting that Bowles had to meet her. But her total disinterest in him that evening did little to endear her to him. Indeed, he wrote her off as just another character that Latouche, well known for his collection of characters, had somehow managed to hook up with. Of the outwardly suave and charming Mr. Bowles, she later wrote the following: "He wrote music and was mysterious and sinister. The first time I saw him I said to a friend: He's my enemy."

The following week he met her again, this time at e. e. cummings's, where he had gone with Kristians Tonny and his new wife, Marie-Claire Ivanoff, just arrived from Paris. Again Jane was with Latouche, but this time was more talkative. The conversation turned to Mexico, with Bowles recounting stories he had heard from Copland, who had recently returned from his second visit. Tonny suddenly decided that he wanted to go there; Bowles, remembering that he had hardly touched the inheritance left him by his grandparents, said that he would accompany them. Then, to his surprise, Jane announced that she too was interested in making the trip. She then left the room to make a phone call. A couple of minutes later, she called Bowles to come to the telephone, saying that her mother wanted to speak to him. Startled, Bowles picked up the receiver and heard a voice at the other end tell him: "If my daughter's going to Mexico with you, I think I should meet you first, don't you think?" She suggested that he accompany Jane home after they had left the afternoon party.

On that February day in 1937, Jane Auer had just turned twenty. The only daughter of Sidney and Claire Stajer Auer, both second-generation Austro-Hungarian Jews, she had spent most of her childhood in comparative affluence, living in Manhattan, until the age of ten, and then in Woodmere, on Long Island, for a few years after that. When she was thirteen her father died, and she and her mother moved back to Manhattan. The following year she was sent to Stoneleigh, a girls' school in Greenfield, Massachusetts, but after less than six months there she fell from a horse and broke her leg. Although the leg was set immediately, it didn't heal; several further operations were required but soon tuberculosis of the knee set in. In 1932 her mother decided to place her in a sanitarium in Leysin, Switzerland, where she remained until the spring of 1934. In Leysin she mastered French and studied French literature, becoming, to some extent at least, "Europeanized." Cured of the tuberculosis but still suffering from knee trouble, she returned to the States. Finally, later that year, or early in 1935, when she was seventeen, it was decided that the only way to repair the knee that refused to heal was to perform a further operation, one that would permanently fuse the joint. Although she would be unable to bend her knee, she would no longer suffer from the continual pain she had endured since the accident. The operation was successful, the convalescence long; the ultimate result: a permanent limp.

But the above sketch does little to describe who Jane Auer really was. Indulged by her mother, particularly after her accident and father's death, she had matured without really maturing. At the age of eighteen she still relied on her mother to dress her and provide her with money and clothes and whatever other whims came into her head. That she was spoiled, petulant, witty, charming, and bright was a given. So, too, the fact that she was a lesbian. Attracted to torch singers from about the age of eleven or twelve, she had become homosexually active about the time she returned from Europe and became a habitué of New York's lesbian bars. By the time Bowles met her she had already had a string of female lovers, a fact that she did not bother to keep secret. She was also a budding writer, having decided to become one upon her return from Switzerland. During her recuperation, in fact, she began a novel, in French, entitled *Le Phaeton Hypocrite* (now apparently lost).

Edouard Roditi remembers her as being quite striking: "The natural curls of her dark hair were tinted with henna, so that they had copper-colored highlights and were fairly close cropped in an almost boyish style above her childlike face, in which her small and slightly tilted nose contrasted surprisingly with her rather full lips." Thomson remembers her large dark eyes, "full of mischief." Maurice Grosser painted her portrait in the late 1940s. He too chose to focus on the eyes, bright and expressive, at once dreamy and knowing.

It was this young, enigmatic, and impulsive woman who asserted herself into Bowles's life on that Sunday in February. Captivated by her and somewhat amused at her precipitousness, he proceeded to take her home to the Hotel Meurice on West 58th Street, where the Auers were living, in order to meet her mother. The interview went well and to Bowles's surprise, Mrs. Auer seemed to accept the idea of her daughter running off to Mexico with a man she'd just met. What Bowles probably didn't realize at the time was that Jane's mother was, in fact, delighted that her daughter had finally brought home a marriageable young man. For years she had been trying to interest Jane in various men, but Jane had steadfastly refused even to go out on a date with one of her mother's prospects. Apparently Claire was also aware of at least a few of Jane's lesbian relationships, and while she at first considered it "just a phase," she had by this point become worried about her daughter's future.

Years later, Jane wrote:

> My mother was very nervous about me because I was not looking for a husband. She would try to frighten me with threats of being taken to live at the poor farm. . . . Like all mothers she hoped I would marry a man who would take care of me. By the time I was twenty she had become extremely nervous.

Thus, when Jane appeared at the hotel with her new friend, an exceedingly handsome, unmarried, well-mannered, cosmopolitan up-and-coming young composer, it must have seemed to Claire a most marvelous turning point for her daughter. After she met the Tonnys at a dinner the following week, permission for the trip was wholeheartedly granted.

During the next couple of weeks the four of them hastily made preparations. Bowles resigned from the Federal Theater Project, much to the delight of his parents, who were totally opposed to their son being employed by an obviously left-wing "welfare" organization. Bowles, however, was hardly resigning because of its left-leaning affiliation. Indeed, although not yet a member of the party, he was so indoctrinated by the Stalinists, who dominated the American Communist party, that in a fit of zealotry he went to a printer and ordered 15,000 stickers printed in Spanish denouncing Trotsky. The stickers bore messages like *"El Peligro Inmediato: Trotzky"* [The Immediate Danger: Trotsky] and *"Muera Trotzky"* [Death to Trotsky]; the idea was to distribute them to various groups in Mexico who were opposed to the Russian exile's presence there. This project, along with the usual preparations, including getting letters of introduction from Copland to composers in Mexico, took up so much of Bowles's time that he saw little of his new traveling companion, and never was with her when she was not in the company of others. He therefore knew little more about her when in early March, they boarded a Greyhound bus, southbound on yet another adventure.

CHAPTER 13

THE FIRST stop on the trip was in Baltimore, where Bowles, concerned about Tonny's finances, managed to sell several of his drawings to the curator of the Baltimore Museum. Now satisfied that Tonny had enough cash for the trip, Bowles was ready to continue south. After a few days each in several other cities, including New Orleans and Houston, they crossed the border at Laredo and into Mexico. They had thus far been gone more than two weeks, during which time Bowles had spent the many hours on the bus conversing with Jane, getting to know her well, or so he thought.

She clearly intrigued him; and he, her. Their conversations ranged from French literature and European travel to their respective biographies and their attitudes toward sex. Bowles remembers that Jane told him quite forthrightly that she was a virgin and was determined to remain so until married. He also recalls that for all of her sophistication, she was quite uncultured; aside from "Swing" she knew little about music. Her awareness of contemporary literature extended only to French fiction writers, mainly Céline, Proust, and Gide. And, despite her international travel, she was fairly ignorant of events in Europe, and seemed to desire to stay that way.

Jane was also unprepared for the realities of travel south of the border. Their first night in Mexico was spent in the relatively modern city of Monterrey, but as soon as they left it, her enthusiasm dropped sharply. The buses, far more primitive than in the United States, appalled her, and the road, largely unpaved and snaking through the rugged sierra, absolutely terrified her. "For two days going through the mountains," recalls Bowles, "she crouched, frightened and sick, at the back of the bus, unmindful of Tonny's scornful remarks." At night, when they stopped in various little towns along the way, she was still malcontent, unwill-

174

ing to be with them or do anything that the other three were interested in doing.

By the time they reached Mexico City, a week or so later, Jane strode off the bus and announced that she was putting up at the Ritz. Bowles tried to prevent her from going off by herself, but the Tonnys, by now fairly tired of her "babyish" behavior, insisted that Bowles let her have it her way. The three of them then proceeded to find a small, cheap hotel, deciding that they would simply fetch Jane the next day. When in the morning they went to the Ritz, however, Jane was not there, nor had she ever been. They began a search of the hotels in the city; three days later they found her, sick with dysentery in bed at the Hotel Guardiola. They stayed with her a while, telling her of the bullfight they'd been to, of the food, of the music, of the loveliness of the city, but she continued to be disagreeable, insisting that as soon as she was well she was going to leave Mexico. Nonetheless, plans were made to pick her up the next day for lunch. When they arrived, the hotel desk clerk told them she had checked out that morning and had flown to the United States. Of her departure, Bowles wrote to Morrissette: "The fourth among us was horrified at the voyage in the bus over the mountains, and fled by plane from Mexico D.F. back to San Antonio without notifying us. We weren't sorry to lose her."

Initially, however, an argument ensued between Tonny and Marie-Claire, when she accused her husband of driving Jane away with all of his nasty comments. (Part of the reason for Tonny's rather constant abuse since they crossed the border was that he had failed to convince Jane to go to bed with him.) Despite Marie-Claire's brief moment of sympathy, the three quickly decided that as far as they were concerned, Jane had proved to be neither a very able nor desirable traveling companion.

With Jane now gone, Bowles began to act on the introduction provided him by Copland. Shortly after his arrival in the capital, he looked up the Mexican composer Silvestre Revueltas, then in his late thirties, who was teaching at the Conservatorio Nacional de México. Bowles remembers that the Mexican composer was one of the warmest men he had ever met, "his arms always outstretched." After a brief conversation, Revueltas suddenly asked Bowles if he had read García Lorca and Guillén. Without waiting for an answer, he took Bowles in tow and proceeded to the conservatory where "he conjured up an impromptu orchestra in less than an hour, and conducted a magnificent performance of *Homenaje a García Lorca.*" The piece, recalls Bowles, was "violently moving" and filled with a "luminous texture." Afterward, Revueltas invited Bowles to go have a few drinks with him so that they could talk music and get to know each other better.

A few days later he invited Bowles to his home, in a slum quarter of Mexico City. The deplorable poverty, unlike anything Bowles had ever seen, even in North Africa, deeply shocked him. There was no running water, no sanitation, no electricity, the streets unpaved. He was further appalled at Revueltas's own living conditions: "There were no walls, properly speaking, between one apartment and another. Partitions went up eight feet or so and stopped. The hubbub of voices, radios, dogs, and babies was infernal." The only furniture Bowles remembers was an old upright piano. Nonetheless, Revueltas was as hospitable as if he'd lived in a palace. But for the young American, it seemed inexplicable that a composer of such stature should have to live in such horrible conditions. (At that time Revueltas's only rival for the title of leading Mexican composer was Carlos Chávez.)

The visit to Revueltas's house gave Bowles much to think about. Revueltas was the embodiment of the quintessential artist, sacrificing life for art. Extraordinarily passionate about music, poetry, life and politics, he was the consummate creator, seeing in existence itself the inspiration for the creative act, or as Bowles would write of Revueltas a few years later, "one had the sense of an organism attaining complete expression in the creation of music which was an accurate and very personal version of the life that went on around him in his country."

Bowles, while also eager to embrace a variety of experiences as much as he could, was at the same time teetering between a desire to live comfortably and a desire to make art, not believing that the two were, or need be, mutually exclusive. But he would take away from Revueltas a sense, already nascent, of the need not only to open himself to a myriad of encounters, but also the importance of transforming that lived experience into art. Although not prone to the hedonism that affected Revueltas, Bowles was learning at the time a way of using the energy from events around him to create. Revueltas's legacy is paramount in Bowles. The compositions from

Mexico are infused with the reality of place, as if transcribed directly from actual encounter. In the obituary Bowles wrote for Revueltas in 1941, he described this talent; the words could apply to much of Bowles's Mexican-inspired music as well:

> [Revueltas] knew what music was for and what it was about. . . . He represented . . . the true revolutionary composer who in his work went straight toward the thing to be said, paying as little attention as possible to the means of saying it. Because he was musically a romantic, that thing to be said was usually an effect to be made rather than anything else. There is none of the preoccupation with form or conscious establishment of individual style that makes Chávez's music an intellectual product. With the instinct of the orator he made his effects, barbaric and sentimental, after which he might have remarked with quiet pride: *He dicho.*

It was a fertile period for Bowles. Caught up in the local music scene, he quickly began to write several compositions directly inspired by the various folk melodies and rhythms he was hearing on the streets and in the bars. The form that seems to have captured his imagination the most was the folkloric dance commonly known in Mexico as *el son.* Usually danced by couples, *el son* is characterized by rapid rhythm, usually based on a pattern of six beats per measure, with long sections executed by the dancers in what is known as a *zapateado,* or a kind of rhythmic and very fast drumming of the feet on either the ground or on a raised wooden platform, the dancers' feet thereby creating a very effective percussion instrument. The stock in trade of *mariachi* bands, *sones* are usually played on a variety of instruments, but always include a violin or two, a *vihuela* (small guitar), a *jarana* (large guitar), a *guitarrón* (very large guitar played pizzicato style), and occasionally a trumpet, drums, harp, and string bass. The lyrics, which abruptly cease during *zapateado* sections, are almost always sentimental tales of beautiful women and love lost or found.

Bowles's reworking of this rhythmically complicated form is both faithful to the original, and at the same time, just plain original. The most striking appropriations are the rhythms and liveliness of the melody line. On first hearing, in fact, they seem to be fairly pure transcriptions of Mexican tunes. But with a bit more analysis a number of other elements emerge. Most importantly, Bowles's compositions such as "Huapango No. 1" and "El Sol" ("Huapango No. 2")—the *huapango* being a type of *son*—are not scored for orchestral instruments, only for solo piano, an instrument rarely used in traditional Mexican music. As a result, Bowles has had to use the piano to convey the sense of several instruments being played simultaneously. He does this both beautifully and effectively by allowing the bass line to mimic the guitars, playing harmony, while the treble line takes the part of the violin. Normally, such a sophisticated counterpoint technique of playing off of one hand against the other could easily result in a very dense structure, but in these pieces the overwhelming impression is of lightness, even gaiety. The two pieces are also interesting in that the first *huapango* is far closer to the indigenous folk melody than the second, which is almost an abstraction of the form, and yet both compositions present a very sophisticated awareness of the folkloric roots. In short, Bowles's intuitive, not intellectual sense is operating here, allowing him to transform so successfully the "humble" folk idiom into a highly accomplished piece of modern music. It was a direction in which he was clearly heading before meeting Revueltas, but by the year of these compositions, under the older composer's indirect tutelage, it had become a pronounced method of giving a new, unique voice to "found" creations.

After spending about a month in Mexico City, Bowles and the Tonnys decided to head south to Tehuantepec, a region fabled for its long-standing matriarchy and hauntingly beautiful terrain. Bowles had been advised to go there by the artist Miguel Covarrubias, whom he had consulted about Mexico shortly before leaving New York. The area lived up to Covarrubias's account. The women did indeed control the society, and while they also did bathe naked in the river, as Covarrubias had informed him, the artist had neglected to mention that their morning ritual was not open to the public. In fact, as Bowles quickly discovered, female guards were posted at stream-edge to throw rocks at any male intruders.

The landscape of the region also fascinated him. Although he expected it to be a cross between Spain and North Africa, it was unique: "Tehuantepec was unforgettable. . . . There were indeed oases (the *labores*) of coconut palms towering above the mangos, zapotes and bananas. A highly spiced hot wind blew incessantly across the countryside, which was not really desert, but an impass-able wilderness of bare thorny trees and cacti."

Before leaving New York, Bowles had bought an accordion. Now, in Tehuantepec, he hauled it out and began to entertain the locals, mostly Zapotec Indians, who quickly named Bowles "Don Pablito." He also got involved in helping the town of Tehuantepec prepare for the annual May Day Festival by cutting, sewing, and printing banners with slogans such as "A Society Without Classes" and "Death to Trotsky," the latter, Bowles's addition. With the festival over, the Tonnys and Bowles decided to head to the border where they hoped to cross into Guatemala. At the crossing, though, they were turned back, according to Bowles because on the visa application form where it asked for religion, he had written "none." He was told that the group would have to get letters testifying to their character from six businessmen in the nearby town of Tapachula. After two days of trying unsuccessfully to ob-tain the necessary documents, they went to the Communist-domi-nated local trade union office, where the officials were more than helpful, even sending a representative with them to the border to expedite their entry. The trio wandered about Guatemala for three weeks before returning to Mexico City.

By the time they reached the capital Tonny informed Bowles that he was out of money, but was expecting to receive some cash soon from the States. He asked for a short-term loan. Bowles gave him $100 and looked about for a cheap place to stay, soon finding rooms at a dollar a day outside the city in a palace formerly occu-pied by Cortés and his Indian mistress. Tonny began to paint prodigiously; Bowles composed. But Bowles's stay was soon cut short by a wire from Lincoln Kirstein. *Yankee Clipper* was due to be performed in Philadelphia and he needed Bowles back in New York to do the orchestration of the piano score he had written the previous year. Before leaving he gave Tonny another $100, as the artist's money had not yet arrived. At the gulf port of Veracruz, Bowles booked passage to New York via Havana, leaving the Ton-nys behind.

Arriving in New York, Bowles quickly discovered that Copland was due to go to California. Naturally, that meant a free place to stay, a place that also had a piano. He moved into Copland's loft and set immediately to work, but as he had only a few weeks to finish *Yankee Clipper*, Kirstein assigned the young composer Henry Brant to do the shipboard scenes, while Bowles did the ports of call. Working rapidly, albeit with difficulty, the two successfully managed to turn Bowles's extremely pianistic score into well-orchestrated ballet music. Bowles admits, though, that he always preferred the piano version.

The ballet's story line is essentially that of a young farmer who leaves his home and true love to seek his fortune on the high seas. He meets the crew of the *Yankee Clipper*, which provides an opportunity for a couple of sailor's dances. The next scene at the first port of call, Argentina, naturally calls for a tango. This is followed successively by stops in Tahiti, Japan, Java, and West Africa, each with a distinctive dance setting evocative of the exotic locale. There is also a wonderful meeting with a mermaid followed by a lyrical pas de deux. The finale consists of a "General Dance," in which the entire cast participates.

Opening in Philadelphia, with subsequent performances in Hartford, Boston, and then New York, both the ballet and Bowles's music were hailed in the press. Elliott Carter wrote in *Modern Music* that "it is the Caravan's most deeply felt work. . . . The dancing and music are at times boisterous and at times tender. Bowles has written some of his best music in the tuneful sailor dances. He manages to retain his own personality while making pastiches of the exotica." The work also delighted the eminent critic Paul Rosenfeld: "It is music of a kind that no civilized community can do without. It is hard of edge and light in content, music in kid gloves, the music of a dandy; but it has artistic value, liveliness, color and a classical contour. . . . The sailor dances, tangos and other characteristic folk dances which compose it, satisfactorily work out their musical material, and form a bright little suite."

One afternoon in mid-July, while Bowles was working on *Yankee Clipper*, the phone rang in Copland's loft. It was Jane Auer. Without apologies or explanations for her abrupt departure from Mexico, she proceeded to invite Bowles to spend the weekend at a summer house her mother had rented in Deal Beach, New Jersey. She added that Thomson would be coming down, as would others. Although a bit startled, having decided that he would probably never see Jane again, he accepted. The visit went well; at one point Jane and Bowles made an excursion into Asbury Park and bought some marijuana. They smoked and talked, really alone for the first time. In the course of the conversation, although Jane was quite reticent about providing details or explanations regarding her adventures after leaving him and the Tonnys in Mexico, he did learn that she had stayed for a time in Arizona and then had gone to California to visit an old friend, Genevieve Phillips.

After that weekend, he continued to see her off and on; she even stayed with him for a while at his parents' house in Jamaica, where he was living temporarily while they were away on vacation. There he apparently tried to seduce her, but she was adamantly opposed to the idea. He didn't press it, nor did the incident interfere with the burgeoning friendship. By the time of the *Yankee Clipper* premiere she had become a special invited guest. For the event, the Bowles entourage, consisting of John Latouche, Marian Chase (a friend of Latouche's and Harry Dunham's fiancée), Rena, and Jane, made the trip by train to Philadelphia. As the drinks flowed one after another on the short trip, the laughter and general merriment increased. It was then, reasons Bowles, that his mother first got the impression that Jane was "wild."

Throughout that fall and the early winter of 1938, Bowles and Jane continued to see each other frequently, but also maintained their separate lives. In September, with Copland back from Hollywood, Bowles moved from Copland's loft to Edwin Denby's, where he began work on a new composition, an opera based on a libretto by Charles-Henri Ford. The story was of an unsuccessful slave rebellion led by a freed slave named Denmark Vesey. The Juanita Hall Choir was interested in performing the work at a benefit for *The New Masses.* Ford was opposed, calling it "a Stalinist trap." It took a while for the matter to be settled—almost a year, in fact— but Bowles, without any other commissions at that moment, kept working on the score anyway.

On November 14, Aaron Copland gave a birthday party for himself. Attending were most of New York's musical luminaries as well as a young student from Harvard, a devoted Copland fan named Leonard Bernstein. When Bernstein mentioned to Copland that he had learned the *Piano Variations,* Copland was astonished and dared him to play them. Bernstein told Copland, "It will ruin your party, but . . ." Copland responded, "Not this party." Bernstein played them, "and they were all—he [Copland] particularly—drop-jawed." He followed the *Variations* with a part of a Ravel concerto. "I remember distinctly Paul Bowles," recalled Bernstein, "sprawled out on some sort of studio-bed that everybody was sitting on, saying in that rather perfumed voice of his, 'Oh, Lenny, ne Ravelons plus.' "

The comment reveals how far musically Bowles had come in just a few years. His early pieces had all been "School of Ravel." Now, however, with his musical horizons broadened by North Africa and Mexico, and with his recent string of successes, he was almost contemptuous of Bernstein's regard for the French composer. It is also noticeable that Bowles, unlike his two great mentors, Thomson and Copland, was not nearly so charitable to young composers as he might have been. Although it is easy to read too much into a comment that was said at least partly in jest, it should be noted that there lingered in Bowles a definite niggardliness and competitiveness; not until much later, in fact, would he be willing to lend his support to the younger generation. By that time, however, he and Bernstein had become friends.

Bowles's financial charity also had strict limits. Now that the Tonnys were back in New York, Bowles expected to be repaid the money he had lent them in Mexico. He was not. Bowles was furious at Tonny, and equally incensed by Thomson, feeling that Thomson had encouraged Tonny not to repay him. Throughout the summer the rift between Bowles and Thomson widened; by winter, it had become what Thomson termed the "Bowles-Thomson War." When Tonny and Marie-Claire returned to Europe without repaying Bowles, Bowles immediately fired off an angry letter to Thomson; Thomson wired back; Bowles responded to Thomson's wire:

> There would be no reason in my trying to minimize to you the magnitude of my wrath, past and present, at the thought of you. . . . I am convinced that without your help Tonny would have paid me before he left for Europe. . . . Tonny has no friendship whatever

for me, and I can't believe that you have either, or you wouldn't have sabotaged the program of sympathy I was trying to build up. I never told Tonny I had any money in the bank, having kept him deliberately under the impression that I was destitute, simply because I know his character at least that well. And then you came along and deliberately ruined everything with your friendly advice, and enjoyed ruining it, I'm sure.

Thomson answered:

> I have never been involved either to your detriment or to your advantage except once on the eve of the Tonny departure (in the presence of Marie-Claire) I used every device I knew of argument and bullying for one hour to induce Tonny to pay you the money he owed you. . . . Your policy of nagging and humiliating both of them about the debt over a long period, made it difficult for him to repay you . . . in a humanly dignified way. . . . I've heard too much about Paul's poverty. You could hardly have less cash in hand than I. . . . As far as the Tonny debt, he has owed me exactly the same amount for almost exactly the same period of time. Do you wonder I get bored with you playing the martyr? . . . Already you have paid for your bad blood and your hateful thoughts by a considerable stoppage in your musical inspiration.

There is an irony about Bowles's anger over not being repaid—an irony, of course, of which Thomson was only too aware, namely, that Bowles was financially indebted to nearly everyone. Bowles, however, had rationalized his dependency on others by believing that he was rarely loaned money; instead, he had long ago decided that those to whom he was indebted had freely parted with their money as "gifts." At any rate, the "Bowles-Thomson War" never had any lasting consequences. Indeed, other matters quickly became far more important to Bowles in the next few weeks.

"Jane and I used to spin fancies about how amusing it would be to get married and horrify everyone, above all, our respective families. From fantasy to actuality is often a much shorter distance than one imagines," Bowles later wrote in *Without Stopping.* It was indeed. Sometime in late January or early February, they suddenly became engaged. To their surprise, neither family was "horrified," although Bowles does recall that his parents had some reservations. His mother was still a bit convinced from the Philadelphia trip that Jane was wild, and both Claude and Rena expressed concern about his "marrying a cripple." That Jane was Jewish did not seem to be among Claude and Rena's objections, or at least was not mentioned to Bowles as an objection to his marrying Jane.

As for her family, her mother and aunts seemed delighted. Presents, mainly clothes, began to pour in for Jane in large quantities. But the marriage itself was simple and small. It took place on February 21, 1938, the day before Jane's twenty-first birthday, at a Dutch Reformed church in Manhattan. The only invited guests were Bowles's parents and Jane's mother. The ceremony was short and traditional; their honeymoon was to be an extended voyage to Central America, for which they had already booked passage to Panama on board a Japanese freighter, the *Kano Maru.* They were to sail on March 1.

Why Jane Auer and Paul Bowles actually decided to marry is fairly unclear. Bowles has said only that he felt that it was simply something one did, as if it were an inevitable consequence of existence. As for Jane, she was said to have told composer David Diamond that she was doing so because she was lonely, this despite her having a wide circle of friends and ongoing relationships at the time, many of whom were quite close to her. Jane was also under considerable pressure from her mother, who wanted to get married herself, but felt that she could only do so after her daughter had. In addition, there seems to have been a feeling on her mother's part that once Jane had become the spouse of Paul Bowles she would cease to be a lesbian—or at least have a respectable cover for it. There was also possibly a matter of money: Jane was to inherit a tidy sum once she had married. The latter reason, however, seems less likely an explanation, more of a side benefit derived from her acquiescence. Perhaps more than anything else, though, there was a recognition on her part that Bowles was as uninterested in a traditional relationship as was she, and therefore represented the ideal mate.

It should also be remembered that Jane Auer was marrying a man whom a year earlier she had designated as her "enemy." Bowles claims that he never understood what she had meant. When years later he asked her, she replied, "I had never met anyone so inimical to me as you." Bowles says that it simply "wasn't true." And yet there were considerable differences between them, aside from the obvious one of sexual orientation. Where Bowles was reserved in expressing emotion or affection, Jane was demonstrative. In matters of self-judgment, Bowles was not self-critical, generally able to rationalize his actions with little difficulty; Jane, on the other hand, was constantly torn by self-doubt. Bowles was enormously fond of the exotic, while Jane was far more comfortable on familiar terrain. Although both were only children, Jane had grown up in a tolerant atmosphere and was indeed quite spoiled by her mother. The list could go on, but in some ways it is pointless to enumerate all the differences between them; suffice it to say that the dissimilarities in their personalities far outnumbered the similarities.

Not surprisingly, much speculation arose also on the part of their respective and mutual friends as to why they had decided to get married. Thomson remarks that "Paul was very attached to her and she was very attached to him and that was that. But I don't think that they ever slept together because she wouldn't have him. Jane was set up as a lesbian and that was her way of life." Others, like Edouard Roditi, conclude that it was largely a marriage of convenience. "It was the thing to do, and many at that time were doing it." He too feels that it was never a sexual relationship. However, Jane's biographer, Millicent Dillon, maintains that the Bowleses did initially have sexual relations, although she notes that they were short-lived. Whatever the case, it is clear that sex played a small role in the marriage and certainly sexual attraction was never a major factor in the relationship. And while the emotional commitment was great, it was evident to both of them that it would not interfere with their respective lives. Both Bowles and Jane had already established themselves as independent individuals and both intended to continue as free agents. With this understanding, they reasoned, they could have the best of both worlds: companionship and freedom to be themselves.

On February 23 a concert featuring some of Bowles's Mexican music was performed under the auspices of the High-Low Concerts, inaugurated by Vernon Duke, for whom Bowles had worked eighteen months before as a copyist. The idea behind the programs was that there would be a mix of "high" and "low" music. At the recital, which took place on the roof of the St. Regis Hotel, Bowles's dance suite *Mediodía, Grupo de Danzas Mexicanas* was performed. Although scored only for flute, clarinet, trumpet, piano, and string septet, a drum accompaniment was added at the concert with Bowles himself playing the drums. This was the "high" part of the program; the "low" was Duke Ellington and his band performing a number of original jazz compositions.

On March 1, 1938, lugging two steamer trunks, eighteen large valises, and a gramophone, the Bowleses boarded the *Kano Maru* and, "for better and for worse," set sail in search of a new life together.

PART IV

Entrances and Exits

CHAPTER 14

O N THE trip south, both Bowles and Jane were ebullient, spending the week on board the *Kano Maru* getting to know each other better, each taking delight in the other's company. They disembarked in Colón, Panama's bustling Caribbean port. The city intrigued them both; Bowles, despite having never been there before, felt as if he were on familiar terrain, the tropics having always appealed to him. For Jane, it was her first taste of a truly exotic locale and she marveled at the sight of the palms, the trains loaded with bananas, the swarm of people in the streets. Although they stayed only ten days in Colón, it was enough time for Jane to internalize the city to a point where she could use it as a major setting for her novel *Two Serious Ladies,* which she would begin working on that year. Other aspects of the trip also managed to work themselves into her novel—Virgil Thomson even claims that *Two Serious Ladies* is really the thinly disguised story of their honeymoon. This is both true and not true, for while there are indeed many similarities, much of the psychological tension is derived from later events in their marriage.

Two Serious Ladies is actually two stories of two ladies. Although the two are acquaintances, their tales are barely, almost artificially intertwined. Only at the beginning and at the end of the novel do their paths intersect. The first story is that of Mrs. Copperfield, who journeys to Panama with her husband. The trip is obviously Mr. Copperfield's idea, although his wife is footing most of the bill. He is immediately enthralled with the exoticism, the sinister aspects of the place, even the heat and the tawdriness. In order to save herself, Mrs. Copperfield takes refuge in the arms of Pacifica, a prostitute who occupies a room in the same hotel. As the story progresses, the Copperfields become more and more estranged from each other, Mrs. Copperfield clearly prefers the company of Pacifica, while her husband is more captivated with place than

189

people, including his own wife. Finally, Mr. Copperfield goes off by himself while Mrs. Copperfield remains behind with Pacifica.

The second story is that of Christina Goering. An eccentric woman of means, she decides to sell off the family estate and move to a rundown house on an island off Manhattan (Staten Island, in reality). She lives there with her companion, Miss Gamelon, and a slothful hanger-on, Arnold. Tiring of their company, she begins to make trips to "the mainland," where she meets a sardonic, low-life character named Andy, lives with him for a while, then takes up with a gangster named Ben, who finally deserts her also.

At the end of the novel Miss Goering and Mrs. Copperfield, who has brought Pacifica back with her from Panama, meet up again. Bound together by their mutual dependencies on others, they recount to each other the recent events in their lives. But they are too different, too self-absorbed to offer each other solace. Mrs. Copperfield leaves with Pacifica; Miss Goering, alone, reflects on their respective degrees of sin. These words conclude the novel: "'Certainly I am nearer to becoming a saint . . . but is it possible that a part of me hidden from my sight is piling sin upon sin as fast as Mrs. Copperfield?' This latter possibility Miss Goering thought to be of considerable interest but of no great importance."

It is not the plot that makes the novel interesting, but the language, the ruminations, the wit, the mélange of sexuality, sin, religion, and bewildering neuroses that form the substance of what really amounts to a chronicle of despair. At times baffling, the novel leaves more questions unanswered than answered, above all regarding the characters' motivation. But so it was with Jane Bowles herself, who was continually struggling to understand her own motivations. While in life this dilemma caused Jane considerable anguish, this same quality in *Two Serious Ladies* serves only to enhance the narrative, to draw the reader in to the novelistic web so adroitly spun by the author.

Although Bowles has asserted that *Two Serious Ladies* is "wholly non-autobiographical," this clearly does not seem to be the case. Just as it was Mr. Copperfield's idea to go to Panama, in life it was Bowles's; and, as in the novel, it was largely on Jane's money that they traveled. The Hotel de las Palmas where the Copperfields stay is modeled on the hotel in which the Bowleses stayed, and like Mr. Copperfield, it was Bowles who insisted on staying there over his wife's initial objections. Later, however, Jane, as was the case with Mrs. Copperfield, took a greater liking to the hotel, indeed found it far more interesting than did her husband, who shared Mr. Copperfield's feeling that "a room is really only a place in which to sleep and dress. If it is quiet and the bed is comfortable, nothing more is necessary." Bowles also admits that some of Mr. Copperfield's other character traits and attitudes are modeled on his own, while Mrs. Copperfield possesses many of Jane's characteristics.

Certainly, not all of the similarities linking the novel to real life emerged during the ten days in Panama. Between the time of the honeymoon and the writing of *Two Serious Ladies*, however, the major themes, many of the incidents, and particularly the attitudes, psychologies, and traits of the characters proved to be an accurate reflection of lived experience. Both Bowles and Mr. Copperfield, for instance, are enthralled with the "primitive," but far less enthusiastic about social encounters with others of their own ilk. Both are also quite self-contained and stubborn, and while they feel themselves to be in charge of the trip—indeed, desire to impose their itineraries on their respective wives—they are, in fact, unwilling to demand that things go as they have planned, opting to pursue their individual interests alone if they cannot convince their mates to accede to their wishes. Mrs. Copperfield and Jane also have much in common: both share a fear and a desire to be out of control, to let their impulses rule, and resort to alcohol, first as a catalyst and then as an excuse to indulge themselves in their passion for unconventional actions. This impulsiveness leads them to collect characters, to enjoy particularly the type of people of whom their respective spouses disapprove. Partly, this obsession with others is related to a fear of being alone, but it also springs from a desire to assert independence within the marriage. Both, of course, also become attached to women, substituting the lesbian relationship for the conventional heterosexual one.

Bowles, too, would write several pieces of fiction in which he charts the disintegration of a marriage, but one story, "Call at Corazón," owes at least part of its genesis to the honeymoon. As Jane did with *Two Serious Ladies*, he would mix lived events and imagined ones, take psychological details from later in the marriage and place them alongside many of the physical elements of location and landscape encountered on this trip.

Written eight years after the fact, "Call at Corazón" is a narrative of a couple also on a honeymoon in Central America. As the story opens, the man, over his wife's objections, has acquired a monkey, which he insists on taking with him on board the boat, tramp-steaming up the Central American coast. It quickly becomes obvious that the monkey is not the only source of difficulty: "I don't mind him," says the wife. "What I mind is you. *He* can't help being a little horror, but he keeps reminding me that you could if you wanted." The tensions between them continue to build until one night the husband awakens to find his wife gone. He searches for her, finally finding her drunk and asleep in the arms of a sailor: "He went upstairs, his heart beating violently. In the cabin, he closed her two valises, packed his own, set them all together by the door and laid the raincoats on top of them." When they dock, the husband disembarks alone and boards a train. The story concludes:

> On the crowded, waiting train, with the luggage finally in the rack, his heart beat harder than ever, and he kept his eyes painfully on the long dusty street that led back to the dock. At the far end, as the whistle blew, he thought he saw a figure in white running among the dogs and children toward the station, but the train started up as he watched, and the street was lost to view. He took out his notebook, and sat with it on his lap, smiling at the shining green landscape that moved with increasing speed past the window.

While this is fiction, Bowles drew more than just the incidental location from reality. The familiar theme of marital tension in which the reluctant wife turns the tables on her husband was not pure invention. Although the Central American trip, according to Bowles's account, went smoothly, the similarity between both Paul's and Jane's fictional renderings is too close to discount the possibility that a major dissolution had already begun to occur.

From Colón the Bowleses journeyed across the narrow isthmus to Balboa, on the Pacific, where they booked passage to Puntarenas, in Costa Rica, on a yacht that had once belonged to Kaiser Wilhelm but was now used as an intercoastal ferry; from Puntarenas, they traveled by train to San José, the capital. After a week or so in San

José, they met some people who had a vast cattle ranch deep in the tropical forest. Intrigued by the possibility of spending some time in a remote region of Central America, Bowles arranged a stay on the estate.

Just as Panama had inspired Jane, Costa Rica left its mark on Bowles. In Bowles's case, however, the particular impression of place would take more than twenty years to emerge from the recesses of memory into fiction, in the form of his novel *Up Above the World.* Set in a generic Central American country, the book's geography is an amalgam of both Costa Rica and Guatemala. From Costa Rica, Bowles drew many of the details for his descriptions of the ranch owned by Vero Soto, while the "capital" described in the novel is a fusion of both San José and Guatemala City. And while Dr. Slade and his wife, Day, the principal characters in the book, in many ways do not resemble Jane or Bowles, there are elements, as in *Two Serious Ladies,* that are drawn from their respective characters: Dr. Slade is aloof, somewhat distrustful of others, but clearly enjoys the natural exoticism of place, while Day is quite open to others but not nearly so interested in the landscape.

As with Day, the jungle in which the ranch was situated frightened Jane. At first unwilling to accompany Bowles on trips that he delighted in making on horseback, she finally relented when he assured her that the excursions could be made in the company of a group of ten or fifteen *vaqueros,* as well as the estate manager. After a couple of rides, she began to enjoy herself, but never would be as enthralled by the primitive as was Bowles. In a postcard written to Gertrude Stein during the honeymoon, Bowles seemed to take an almost sadistic pride in dragging Jane through the jungles: "I am married to a girl who hates nature, and so we are here with volcanoes, earthquakes and monkeys."

During the stay at the ranch Bowles made mental notes of the terrain; the pages of *Up Above the World* testify to the acuteness of his memory, for they read as if the book were written on location. Indeed, the success of the novel, in large part, is derived from the extraordinarily accurate descriptions of the jungle. Remarkably detailed, down to the sound of the wind and the scream of the night armies of insects, the evocation of a realm ruled by vegetation and myriad predators is responsible for some of the book's most powerful passages.

Another result of their stay at the ranch was that Bowles became, as he put it, "parrot-conscious." Returning one day from a ride, they stopped at a gatehouse between properties. Inside the house seven baby parrots were perched on a stick. They were offered one, but Jane declined, explaining to her husband that "she couldn't bear to break up the family." A week later, while waiting for the boat to take them back to Puntarenas, they were forced to spend the night in the tiny town of Bebedero. The owner of the hotel suddenly appeared with a full-grown parrot, which he left with them. They quickly discovered, as the proprietor had assured them, that the parrot spoke, but that its vocabulary was all its own: "Its favorite word, which it pronounced with the utmost tenderness, was 'Budupple.' When it had said that several times with increasing feeling, it would turn its head downward at an eighty-degree angle, add wistfully: 'Budupple mah?' and then be quiet for a while. Of course we bought it."

In the course of picking up parrot lore from the locals, Bowles learned that the Indians felt that parrots, due to their ability to mimic human speech, were actually capable of providing a temporary abode for the human spirit. "Our own rational system of thought unhappily forbids such extravagances; nevertheless the atavism is still there, felt rather than believed," explained Bowles. This notion seems to have inspired Bowles and Jane to the point that they created a game in which Bowles played the part of Bupple Hergesheimer, a man-parrot, Jane the role of Teresa Brawn, alternately Bupple's governess, aunt, and mother. Bupple's vocabulary, like that of all parrots, was limited to a few words: "bupple," for indicating pleasure, "rop" for disagreement. The play, which they indulged in for many years, consisted of Teresa taking care of the obstreperous Bupple. Often disgruntled, Bupple required a great deal of reassurance, which Teresa would provide, soothing the creature by pointing out to him how lucky he was to have such a fine cage, such good food to eat, such a nice provider as she. But if Bupple continued with his "rops," which he usually did, Teresa would take to scolding him severely for his unruly behavior, ordering him to get back into his cage.

Although a game, the roles were, in no small part, similar to those played out in reality, particularly in the early years of their relationship. (Later, it would largely reverse, Bowles being the one to alternately praise and cajole.) During this time, Bowles was often perceived by his wife as being disagreeable, standoffish, unwilling to go along with her whims. Often, with the same charm employed by Teresa, she would convince him, at least temporarily, to accede to her view of the world. But just as Bupple would eventually retort with a "rop," so too would Bowles often ultimately hold his ground, unswayed by Jane's attempts at persuasion.

The Bowleses remained a month in Costa Rica, returning to San José after the interval on the ranch. Much of their time in the Costa Rican capital was occupied with Budupple, who managed during the course of their stay to eat Jane's lorgnette, a tube of toothpaste, and most of the pages from a Russian novel. Concerned that the glass from the lorgnette lens would certainly cause Budupple's death, the Bowleses watched the parrot with anxiety, but to their relief, there was no visible change in its condition.

From San José they journeyed to the Caribbean coast where they stayed for a few days in the town of Limón, waiting for a ship to take them to Puerto Barrios, in Guatemala. Also while in Limón they had a tin cage made for the parrot, but as with the two previous cages, he managed to chew through it during the two-day boat trip, the consequence being that Budupple liberated himself while they were going through customs in Puerto Barrios. The parrot decided it would be quite amusing to climb up the fleshy calf of one of their traveling companions, described by Bowles as "a very stout French lady." He added wryly, "The incident provided an engrossing intermission for the other voyagers."

It was not just Budupple, though, who was intrigued by the French woman. She also provided Bowles with the character for Mrs. Rainmantle in *Up Above the World.* The woman, Lady Edme Owen, had originally been a Paris dance hall chorine, but somehow had managed to marry an English lord who took her to live on his manor. After his death, she had returned to France and was now on her way to British Honduras as a mail-order bride. As she had become something of a society lady, news items about her had appeared in various British tabloids capturing the attention of a transplanted Scot named Macall who owned a coffee plantation in the wilds of Central America. He had fallen in love with her through the mail and had sent her money to come join him. Bowles later recounted the events of the journey, details of which worked themselves into his late novel:

[We first] saw her on ship between Puerto Limón in Costa Rica and Puerto Barrios in Guatemala, and she got off the ship with us and she shared our room in this hotel—the Gran Hotel de la Independencia, which was a real shambles. And that's where I got the idea [for using her as a fictional character], she was such a mysterious woman. She was traveling *de luxe* in an enormous cabin on the *Caribia* . . . and she had trunks all over the cabin. Everything she owned was with her. . . . She was fascinating. We were only with her for three days. We saw her all the time. Jane thought she was marvelous. She was *filthy*. Her clothes were all spotted, she was drinking heavily. . . . She looked very strange, too. She wasn't old but she had let herself go, and she had dyed hair and it was all frizzy and it wasn't right. . . . When she came to get off the ship they wouldn't let her off because she had a bar bill and she had to go and get the British consul to go out and pay it. . . . (All this is in *Up Above the World*. . . .)

She came to the hotel and she spent an afternoon, taking a siesta in our room. There were two beds, with a space in between, and they had mosquito nets over them. And she and Jane had the siesta in one, and I had siesta in the other. I think it was later the same day (she didn't spend the night with us—she had no money, of course, not a penny, which was why we let her in, invited her—at least she could take a siesta . . .). She was waiting for a little launch to come over from a place called Livingstone . . . to take her off to a place called Punta Gorda, where [the Scot] would pick her up and drive her into the jungle.

At the time, however, writing a novel was far from Bowles's mind. He thought of himself then as a composer, with literary interests to be sure, but in 1938 music was his métier, and also his bread and butter.

After a short stay in Guatemala City the Bowleses made their way to Chichicastenango, the parrot still in tow. The primary motivation for going there was to take in the Holy Week festivities, a mixture of Catholic and Mayan rituals. Bowles also wanted to speak with a Father Rossbach, an authority on the ancient Mayan *Popol Vuh,* who was at that time something of a local legend as he allowed, even encouraged, the Quiché Maya to continue their "pagan" practices alongside those of Christianity. They stayed about two weeks in the Mayan town, enough time for Bowles not only to talk with the priest, but also to observe the Easter morning services in which the Indians dug up a life-sized Christ from behind the church altar that they had buried there on Good Friday. To Morrissette he wrote: "At last I got to the birthplace of the POPUL BUJ I have been reading for the last four years. Magnificent." From Chichicastenango they made their way south to the town of Antigua. It was in Antigua at the pension of a Señora Espinosa (the model for the pension in Jane's story "A Guatemalan Idyll") that they managed to get rid of Budupple. It wasn't really that they lost the bird, it simply happened to find a convenient avocado tree in the back of the pension where it decided to take up residence, firmly refusing to come down. After a few days in Antigua, they returned birdless to the capital.

In Guatemala City, Jane, for the first time on the trip, decided to strike out on her own. During the afternoon the Bowleses had met a group of students with whom they began discussing literature. That evening they all went to a café together, but as the evening wore on Bowles became tired and around 10:30 decided that it was time to return to the Hotel Astoria. Jane refused to go. After pressing her for a bit, Bowles decided to go on without her.

At the café, the talk turned from literature to brothels. Somehow the students, possibly at her urging, decided to take Jane to see one in action. After a short time at the whorehouse, a presidential bodyguard arrived in full uniform, a pistol at his side. Seeing Jane, he decided that it was with her that he wanted to go to bed. The students and prostitutes protested, telling him that she was a tourist, but he became insistent. Finally the prostitutes managed to help Jane escape through a window in a back room. Realizing he'd been tricked, the official set off in a rage to look for her. Driving through the streets, shining his spotlight into doorways, he searched for her for some time, but she eluded him by hiding behind a pile of garbage in a nearby alley. Terribly shaken, she finally arrived back at the hotel in the early hours of the morning. Bowles, awakening upon her arrival, could see that she was visibly upset; despite his attempts to get her to tell him what had happened, she said nothing of the escapade. Only years later did he finally learn what had occurred that night.

A day or so later they left the capital for Puerto Barrios in order to pick up a ship bound for Europe. The train ride down to the port was made even more unpleasant than usual as the cars were filled with hundreds of swastika-bearing Germans, all making their way to Puerto Barrios in order to vote on a referendum sent to them by Hitler. The voting was to take place on board the very ship, a German passenger vessel called the *Cordillera,* on which the Bowleses had booked passage to Le Havre. They both felt that it was an inauspicious beginning to a European sojourn.

Their misgivings were confirmed when once on board they became aware that the ship was overrun with Nazis, their numbers growing at each Caribbean stop. It wasn't just their swaggering pro-Hitler talk, however, that interfered with the trip; there was physical interference as well. Returning from a brief shopping trip in Port-of-Spain with a large sampling of calypso records, Bowles proceeded to play the records on deck. "The Germans could not bear to hear such music, even pianissimo," related Bowles. "They came up to us and gave us a serious lecture on the insidious spread of degenerate forms of music. After that we played the phonograph only in our cabin."

Arriving in Le Havre in early May 1938, the Bowleses immediately headed for Paris. In many respects it was a homecoming for them both as they each knew the city well, had friends there, and were on equal footing with the language. As a result, Bowles soon found himself at odds with Jane, who, freed from the need for security in his companionship, went very much her own way. The short interval of closeness, of sharing days and adventures, had come to an abrupt end. The honeymoon was clearly over.

During the day Jane frequented the Left Bank cafés, where she began to work on the story that would eventually become *Two Serious Ladies.* She began writing it in French, the language in which she had written her adolescent novel *Le Phaeton Hypocrite,* but soon changed to English. Perhaps because Bowles had never indicated much interest in her writing, apparently having never read her first novel, or possibly because she was rather secretive about her own work (and life), she did not show her new work in progress to her husband, or discuss it with him. He did not press her about it either, indeed does not remember even being aware at the time that she was writing. At night, Jane met up with friends or went by herself to various lesbian bars.

Bowles occupied himself with looking up old acquaintances, including Henri Cartier-Bresson, whom he had met a few years earlier in New York. He also tried to interest Jane in meeting some of his friends, or in making mutual friendships. He very much wanted to present his new wife to Gertrude Stein, but when he rang her up she was in the process of leaving Paris for Bilignin and could not spare the time to see them. The couple did go to visit Max Ernst, whose work Bowles had admired for years. Bowles's recollection is that, at the time, Ernst was living with both British painter Leonora Carrington and Gala Eluard.* Although Bowles does not remember much about the visit, he vividly recalls Jane's response: "We wandered around his [Ernst's] big flat in Paris and were given something mad to drink like cider or beer. . . . We left finally. I was interested in Jane's reactions. She thought Ernst and the rest of them were mad. For one thing, there were two women living with one man, and she wondered if they all slept together and so on. She always considered Surrealists to be mad; she thought the whole movement was very fake. I thought it was interesting." After that, he made visits to the surrealists alone.

On other, rather rare occasions, it was Jane who introduced Bowles to people whom she thought might interest him. One of them was a fresh-faced young man about Jane's age named Brion Gysin, whom Jane met one day at a Left Bank café. Although just twenty-two at the time, Gysin was already quite accomplished. Having graduated from an English boarding school at the age of fifteen, after spending his younger years in the United States and Canada, he was now studying literature at the Sorbonne and earnestly learning on his own how to paint. By 1938, when the Bowleses met him, he had already exhibited with the surrealists and was preparing a one-man show for the following year. Self-

---

*Despite Bowles's impression, it is unlikely that Gala was living with Ernst and Carrington. She had indeed had an affair with the painter, and had earlier lived in a ménage à trois with him and her then husband, poet Paul Eluard. By 1938, however, Gala had left both of them to marry Salvador Dalí.

assured, suave, and cosmopolitan, Gysin immediately charmed them both.

At his first meeting with Bowles, Gysin was with a man named Denham Fouts, later immortalized by Gore Vidal, Christopher Isherwood, and Truman Capote. He had just returned from Tibet. The four of them had dinner together, going afterward to the premiere of Stravinsky's *Dumbarton Oaks Concerto.* Later, Fouts decided to demonstrate his prowess in Tibetan archery by shooting flaming arrows from his hotel window onto the busy Champs Élysées below. Bowles initially was aghast, but as the others were so obviously delighted with the outrage, he did not interfere. "Fortunately," he remembers, "there were no repercussions." Although Bowles had little opportunity to talk with Gysin that evening, they took a liking to each other. Over the years, in New York, Paris and especially Tangier, their paths would cross; eventually a close friendship would form.

Apart from these brief moments of enjoying Paris and people together, the Bowleses saw little of each other, a situation that greatly bothered Bowles. "It was painful for me to go back to the hotel room at dinnertime," he later said, "and find that she had not yet come in, finally to have dinner alone and rush back to find the room still empty." When Jane did finally return, often in the early hours of the morning, the two quarreled. Although Bowles had always prided himself on his independence and had a decided love for the unconventional, he was not prepared to accept that he and his wife would lead largely separate lives.

After about six weeks in Paris, during which the relationship seemed to Bowles to deteriorate further each day, the situation reached the boiling point. One night upon Jane's return to the hotel, Bowles, as usual, set about interrogating her regarding where she had been and with whom. Unlike on previous occasions, however, Jane began to respond to his questions, flaunting her life-style. In the midst of her account of how much she had been enjoying herself at a lesbian bar, Le Monocle, and of the encounters she had had there, Bowles became enraged. The argument continued, Bowles insisting that she go with him to the south of France and away from the useless life of drink and debauchery that she had been leading. Jane ignored his remonstrances, taunting him, heedless of his anger. Finally it was too much for Bowles; the inner anguish overcame his outer pretense of calm, and he slapped her. Later, guilt driving them both, they reconciled, but within a few days Bowles, like the husband in "Call at Corazón," boarded a train, leaving his wife behind.

As soon as he arrived in St. Tropez, however, Bowles realized that escape was not a solution: "Once I got there, I found that I was completely miserable. I wired and urged Jane to come to Cannes." She too, apparently, was sufficiently distressed by the separation that this time she complied with his entreaty. A few days later he met her at the train station. They did not stay long in Cannes, but instead proceeded to Èze-Village, a small town nearby on the Côte d'Azur. There, through an acquaintance, the composer S. L. M. Barlow, they found a little house to rent. With fewer distractions of the big city sort, their life together became more harmonious; from a distance, it could almost have been construed as domestic. Jane divided her time between writing, learning how to cook under the tutelage of Jacqueline, their hired French servant, and visiting friends with her husband. Bowles, for his part, finally resumed work as well, writing a piece for chamber orchestra entitled *Romantic Suite,* "romantic" connoting the type of music, not romance. Indeed, romance, despite the restored relations, was not part of their life, even on the Côte d'Azur.

They did, however, begin to work out some of the knots in their relationship, talking with each other of events in the recent and distant past, reavowing to respect each other's freedom. To some extent this meant capitulation on Bowles's part, but to view it only in these terms is far too narrow an interpretation. In fact, the recognition of mutual independence must also be seen as a private statement of care and concern, one for the other, a confirmation of a true, deep friendship. Upon marrying they had sworn to accept the other for who he or she was, but the implications of the agreement had obviously not been fully realized by Bowles until it became clear that Jane intended to hold him to it. At this juncture, then, he had two choices: he could either renege on his earlier promise, which in his solo journey south he had tried to do, or go along with it. Having concluded that it was more desirable to be with Jane than without her, he in essence made his decision. By joining him, she affirmed as well the importance to her of the relationship. But there was still much to work out. In some ways, they would spend the rest of their married life together attempting to understand the meaning of what they had committed themselves to during the summer of 1938.

The quiet interlude in Èze-Village was broken in early September when a telegram arrived from Harry Dunham. He asked Bowles to return to New York as John Houseman and Orson Welles wanted him to write the music for their upcoming production of *Too Much Johnson,* the William Gillette farce. The music was needed, Dunham explained, to accompany a series of short film sequences that he had already begun shooting. Although Bowles's original plan had been to spend another six months or so on the Côte d'Azur, the offer seemed too rewarding to pass up. Not only did the prospect of working with Dunham and Welles appeal to him, he was also beginning to worry about finances. The money Jane had received as a result of her marriage was dwindling rapidly, with no immediate prospects of replenishment. Bowles cabled an affirmative response to Dunham. Within a few weeks he and Jane were westbound from France to New York.

CHAPTER 15

In THE FALL of 1938 the Bowleses moved into the Hotel Chelsea, renting a room with a bath for $15 a week, a price compatible with their budget. As temporary lodging the Chelsea was fine, but as Bowles had no piano, it was hardly a suitable place to work, and he quickly began to search for a free room in which to compose. Using his well-established network of friends, he managed, in short order, to obtain the loan of a penthouse studio on 57th Street, owned by the Austrian architect and stage designer Friedrich Kiesler. Each day, in the tranquillity of Kiesler's studio, Bowles worked on the score. Progress was rapid. Dunham's rather absurdist and amusing film sequences (reminiscent of The Keystone Kops), which were to be used between scenes to advance the action, immediately inspired Bowles. An additional source of inspiration was the promise of payment for the music; having spent most of what remained of Jane's money to buy their passages over from Europe, the Bowleses were nearly broke.

By mid-October the music was finished. Scored for a small ensemble consisting only of piano, trumpet, clarinet, and percussion, the piece is a delightfully madcap composition, as if Erik Satie had met vaudeville. Four fast-paced sections open the work, scored respectively "Allegro risoluto," "Presto (Tempo di Tarantella)," "Allegretto (Tempo di Quickstep)," and "Allegro." Each is unique, easily identifiable, the Tarantella and Quickstep splendid send-ups of the dance forms. The middle section consists of a schmaltzy waltz followed by three more rapid sequences, "Allegro (Tempo di Marcia)," "Presto," and finally "Allegretto (Molto staccato)." This is clearly Bowles at his most vivacious, witty, and charming, music calculated to do nothing other than bring delight to the listener, the ideal accompaniment to a series of slapstick images.

Pleased with the music, Bowles took it to Welles, but to his great surprise was told that the Mercury Theater had decided not to produce *Too Much Johnson* next, but instead to put on a tragedy, *Danton's Death.* Bowles was considerably upset, having counted on an initial payment for the music in order to get him and Jane through the next few months. Welles advised him to go see Houseman, who was the Mercury's producer and controlled the financial arrangements. By the time Bowles arrived at Houseman's office, the producer had apparently been warned of Bowles's anger over the postponement and had prepared his part in advance. Houseman was sitting at his desk, slumped in a chair; when he looked up to greet Bowles, tears were in his eyes. Handing over a check for $100, he expressed his dismay at the events but told Bowles that he hoped the check would help to soothe his annoyance. Still extraordinarily angry—the boat ride alone had cost far more than $100—Bowles stormed out of the office.

With no immediate prospect of the play being produced, Bowles was in a considerable dilemma. He decided on two courses of action. The first was to turn the composition into a piece that could stand alone. Cutting a bit here and there, he produced a "new" work, which he called *Music for a Farce.* A few months later the suite had its premiere at the League of Composers' Concert in New York, receiving enthusiastic reviews. While this had managed to salvage the music from oblivion, it did little to ease the financial crisis.

As a result, Bowles decided to find less expensive accommodations. He quickly came up with a place in a conveniently located but ramshackle building on Seventh Avenue and 18th Street, and he and Jane moved in. The building was run by an eccentric alcoholic named "Lady" Saunders, who "divided her time between building fireplaces and bookshelves for her lodgers and drinking wine with odd characters from the neighborhood." Apparently, however, she was not terribly adept at fireplace construction, for soon after the Bowleses moved into the building a fire in their fireplace set the floor ablaze, requiring a call to the fire department. Totally unfazed, she simply laughed and set about (slowly) rebuilding it. During the construction, the winter winds blew through the house, chilling it so thoroughly that the Bowleses moved in temporarily with their friend John Becker, who had an apartment on Sutton Place.

Even with the reduced expenses, it was clear that a regular

source of income was needed. Bowles got in touch with the director of the Federal Music Project, hoping to be able to get back on the government payroll. He was told that in order to become enrolled in the project, he would have to be on general relief. Seeking advice as to how to proceed, Bowles then went to the local Communist party headquarters. At the party office he learned that he must first establish residence in a blighted portion of the city, then declare himself unemployed at the nearest Worker's Alliance hall. With nothing to lose, Bowles immediately installed himself in Brooklyn, in the room he had taken as a studio the year before on Water Street. It had the proper location and was small and sparsely furnished; in short, it had the right appearance. As he had to spend the days there, he rented a piano and began work on the second act of *Denmark Vesey,* the opera he had begun writing, and whose first act had premiered the year before.

The investigator arrived sooner than Bowles had expected. Telling her his tale of how he had returned from France especially to write music for the Mercury Theater and had then been left destitute by the play's cancellation, he managed to convince her of his dire predicament. Within a few days he was on general relief and now eligible for the Federal Music Project, at the going rate of $23.86 a week. In exchange, he was given various assignments, including writing some first-grade piano music, a variety of choral pieces, and arranging traditional American folk songs for voice and piano. To Morrissette he wrote: "At last I'm on relief! We gave a champagne party to celebrate the day I got on! (Not we who paid, however.)"

For a number of reasons—mainly gratitude for their quick action in getting him on the relief rolls, because of events in Europe, and "to a certain extent . . . to shock [his] father"—Bowles decided to join the Communist party. Although Jane was not terribly political, she followed Bowles's lead. Many of their friends, including John Latouche and Harry Dunham, were already members; at the time there was no stigma attached to membership. Unlike many who were more cautious, however, they joined under their real names. In the early 1960s Bowles would greatly regret this, as he was turned down for several teaching jobs in American universities because of his previous Communist affiliation; but in 1939 it seemed the thing to do.

The decision was perhaps less indicative of a firm political stance on Bowles's part than simply a rather shrewd act of opportunism. The theater in New York at that time had a large left-leaning contingent. As Virgil Thomson noted, "If you wanted to work in the theater in those days, and Paul did, it was very beneficial to you if you were a member because the union [which was dominated by Communists] would squeeze you out if you weren't. Not only that, you had to be a Stalinist, because [the] New York [branch of the party] was Stalinist."

As new members, the Bowleses were sent to workers classes in Marxism-Leninism in order to become acquainted with party doctrine. The theories were too arcane for Jane: "I don't know what I'm reading," she confessed to her husband. Bowles did understand the dogma, which, he said, actually "made it worse." Theory aside, Bowles was sympathetic to the general aims of the party and was rapidly becoming increasingly upset at the terrifying rise of fascism in Europe. Republican Spain, too, was teetering on the brink; by late March 1939 it would fall to Franco.

As Bowles viewed being a member of the Communist party as an opportunity rather than a sociopolitical statement, he saw no reason why this should preclude hobnobbing with the rich or social elite, and the Bowleses continued to do a fair amount of it. They frequently went to the Askews', where they socialized with the "arts crowd," among them Alfred Barr, director of the Museum of Modern Art; the painters Pavel Tchelitchew, Buffie Johnson, and Eugene Berman; poets and writers such as e. e. cummings, Charles-Henri Ford, and Parker Tyler; a wide variety of theater and ballet people such as Houseman, Joseph Losey, George Balanchine, and Lincoln Kirstein; and, of course, composers, chief among them Thomson and Copland. According to Buffie Johnson, Jane, in particular, loved the atmosphere at the Askews': "Jane once said to me, which rather shocked me, 'I think I might die if I wasn't asked to the Askew salon.'" They also saw, on an almost daily basis, though often individually, their intimate friends: Dunham and his fiancée, Marian Chase; Latouche and his girlfriend, Teddy Griffis.

But Jane had her own set of friends as well, and once again began to lead an independent life, coming and going as she pleased; often, as she had in Paris, she stayed out most of the night, frequently arriving home in a stupor. While not pleased with the situation, Bowles put up with it. Having realized in Èze-Village that he preferred to be with Jane than without her, if even on her terms, he made only weak protests. It was a complex situation. The qualities he loved in her, her spontaneity, charm, and wit, were also the very qualities that led her not to comply with his own desires. To bring her under his control would amount to stifling the person and personality in whom he took so much delight, in short, reenacting the role his father had played in his own life. Indeed, he had married her, in large part, precisely because of these qualities. The solution, he understood, was to be found in exercising a similar degree of freedom, but it would take him a few more years to become as truly independent of her as she now was of him.

At the same time, it was easier for Bowles to handle the situation with Jane in New York than in Paris. For one thing, he was far more occupied with his own work than he had been earlier; he also had a large circle of friends with whom he could spend his days. New acquaintances were being added to the list all the time, among them a young playwright and short-story writer from California named William Saroyan. Saroyan's first play, *My Heart's in the Highlands,* was about to be produced by the Group Theater, and the director, Robert Lewis, asked Bowles to write the music. As this meant real money and real work, Bowles immediately agreed, though he kept his federal job as well. In six weeks, using as a composing studio the vacated apartment of playwright Clifford Odets, he wrote the entire score.

Bowles made the decision to use the fee received from *My Heart's in the Highlands* to secure a more permanent place to live. Deciding on an isolated farmhouse at 1116 Woodrow Road on Staten Island, he paid five months' rent in advance in order to have that concern out of the way, at least for the interim. With the security derived from having a fixed residence, he and Jane became reengaged in their own creative projects. Jane resumed writing *Two Serious Ladies;* Bowles divided his time between the Federal Music Project assignments and working on the second act of *Denmark Vesey.*

Living on Staten Island provided Jane material for her novel. Miss Goering's farmhouse, described in the book, is actually a description of their own house and surroundings:

Behind the house was a dirt bank and some bushes, and if one walked over the bank and followed a narrow path through some more bushes, one soon came to the woods. To the right of the house was a field that was filled with daisies in the summertime. This field might have been quite pleasant to look at had there not been lying right in the middle of it the rusted engine of an old car. There was very little place to sit out of doors, since the front porch had rotted away, so they had . . . got into the habit of sitting close by the kitchen door, where the house protected them from the wind. . . . there was no central heating in the house: only a few little oil stoves.

The farmhouse and environs were not the only sources of inspiration, for like Miss Goering, Jane too made frequent trips to the "mainland." The unnamed town that Miss Goering visits in the novel was actually modeled on Perth Amboy, at the end of the ferry ride from Tottenville. Like Miss Goering, Jane was attracted to the rather seedy side of the town, particularly the local dives where she frequently wiled away the evening hours. Unlike the character in her novel, however, she rarely made the trip alone, but usually found someone to go with her. As their house was frequently filled with visitors, it was fairly easy to persuade one of the guests to make the excursion. Those who visited most frequently were the "little friends," as Virgil Thomson dubbed them: Dunham, Latouche, Marian Chase, and Teddy Griffis. They were something of an odd group in that Dunham and Latouche were predominantly gay, Griffis a lesbian; only Chase was fully heterosexual.

Many others came too, including the composer and critic Colin McPhee, the Brazilian folk singer Elsie Houston (who actually took up residence for a while), and on at least one weekend, Leonard Bernstein. Bernstein, however, had an allergy to cats, and though Bowles sequestered their Siamese in a shed behind the house, it was apparently not far enough away. After one miserable night spent sneezing, Bernstein declined to stay on.

Despite a host of friends and acquaintances and a relatively good living situation, Bowles found himself becoming increasingly restless. The music for the Saroyan play had given him a small amount of financial security and (owing to generally favorable reviews) a good deal of personal satisfaction, but he couldn't help wondering what he was really doing in New York. It was hardly the first time he had felt distinctly alien in his own country, however it was now a bit different. As a married man, he no longer was making decisions only for himself; his freedom of movement, while not curtailed entirely, was constrained in a way it had not been earlier, for he also had to consider Jane. And Jane was not particularly interested in leaving New York, even if they had had the means to do so.

Physically unable to relocate, Bowles nonetheless found that he could do so mentally. With his mind on North Africa, he suddenly found himself doing something he had not done in years: writing. As a child, his imagination had always rescued him from the mundane, allowed him an exit into a world far beyond the day-to-day reality of his situation. But having been able for years to actualize his desire for travel, for exotic locales, he had not felt such a need to create an escape for himself through the written word. Now, in 1939, he returned to an invented cosmos. The result: a short story called "Tea on the Mountain," a wistful tale of a brief encounter between an American woman writer and a young Moroccan. Although only a few pages long, the writing of it provided him with a way to get back to Tangier.

Reality, however, except for a few moments here and there, was inescapable. With no more lucrative theater projects, and the prospects looming again of having to pay rent, the Bowleses began to feel a financial crunch. Bowles appealed to Harry Dunham to pay half of the rent on the house, in exchange for the right to stay there at any time. This usually amounted to the weekends only, when he and Marian Chase would descend, often with others, for a bang-up time. Dunham usually provided the drink, and if necessary, some food.

Toward the end of the summer another complication arose. Bowles received a letter from his former benefactress, Mary Oliver, informing him that she and her German maid would be arriving in New York soon and requesting a place to stay for an indefinite period of time. She was now a widow, her husband having died the year before, and also in financial straits herself. In her letter to Bowles she informed him that although a bit down on her luck she had enough money for "beer and champagne" if he had enough money for food. While he sensed at the time that a prolonged stay could lead to complications, he wrote back saying that she was indeed welcome. She had been so generous to him when he was penniless in Paris that he felt he had little choice in the matter.

Jane, despite having never met her, also wrote inviting her to stay, but Bowles never mailed the letter, apparently finding her straightforwardness objectionable. The letter read, in part:

> First I shall explain about money and then I shall go on. Paul earns at the moment twenty-two dollars a week on W.P.A. (music project) and that is what we live on. I'm perfectly willing to take a chance on our all eating on that if you are. . . . Two people or rather four people are not twice as expensive to feed as two, strangely enough. Paul will probably stop getting his checks suddenly anyway and then we will all be in the soup, which doesn't frighten me. The only people who must eat are Paul and the cats. Paul is extremely desperate and neurotic if he doesn't. I have explained all this to you because I want you to know what you are getting into. . . . As for room during the week there are two extra beds. On many weekends Harry Dunham comes down with his fiancée, therefore one bed is occupied. I have two very fine mattresses which we bought in Nice and three thick sofa cushions all of which could be made into an adequate bed which I would be glad to sleep on when there were extras. . . . I myself have a huge inner spring mattress on a straw mat which sleeps at least three and many extra ladies have slept with me on weekends. Paul has one too but he refuses to share it with anyone.

Soon after receiving Oliver's letter, Bowles got a call from her. Despite her lack of money, she was staying at the Waldorf Towers with her German maid. She insisted that Bowles and Jane join her for dinner and stay over as her guests at the hotel. Over dinner she explained her circumstances to them, recounting a tale of how she had lent $50,000 left to her by her husband to an actress who had never paid her back. She had just recently managed to get a small lien on the woman's wages, from which she derived her sole income. She reassured them, though, that her moving in with them would not present a problem, as she repeated her offer to pay for all the booze.

The next day the four of them made the trek to Staten Island, and the liquor, as Mary Oliver had promised, almost immediately began to flow, its quantity seeming to increase daily. Realizing that the local liquor store would allow her to purchase large quantities on credit, and even deliver it to the house, Mary did not see any reason to make good on her promise to pay for it; she had soon run up a rather gigantic bill that far exceeded her meager income.

Jane eagerly joined in the drinking bouts, which continued late into the night, often until one or both of them passed out. Bowles found the whole situation distressing. He was, in fact, so bothered by what he perceived as the obvious effects of excessive drinking that he suddenly abstained entirely. This new stance further contributed to the tension in the house, for as Bowles noted, "from the drinker's point of view there is nothing so unpleasant as having a nagging ex-drinker at his side." As the weeks of continual drunkenness and mounting bills continued, Bowles became more and more concerned. But the more upset he became, the more Jane and Mary Oliver seemed to delight in it. In fact, Jane had grown extremely close to her drinking companion, constantly defending her from Bowles's criticisms. By mid-October he decided he could endure the situation no longer and moved out.

His new room was again in Brooklyn, this time in Columbia Heights. Once he had rented it, he again tried to persuade Jane to move in with him, but she steadfastly refused, saying that Mary needed her more than he did. Bowles now became a visitor to the farmhouse, but each visit left him feeling more and more disquieted. Whatever semblance of a conventional marriage there had been was now utterly destroyed.

About a month after Bowles had taken up a separate residence, he discovered on one of his periodic visits that Mary Oliver had rented, again on credit, an apartment in the Village and was to move out around November 15. He was temporarily delighted with this new turn of events, but his elation soon turned to anger when he learned that Jane had decided not to move in with him, but rather to continue living with Oliver, in her new apartment on West 13th Street. He soundly denounced the plan, telling Jane that the amount she was drinking, and what he envisioned she would drink if she remained with Oliver, would ruin her health. Jane was characteristically firm in her decision, accusing Bowles of being a killjoy.

Jane's relationship with Mary Oliver, though one of great affection, was apparently not sexual. It was, however, as Bowles well knew, destructive, based in large part on mutual weakness. This pattern would be a recurring one in Jane's life, and despite Bowles's efforts to persuade her of the potential for harm, on this occasion and on others, he would never really be able to help her.

Indeed, the more he disapproved of her relationships and actions, the stauncher she often became in her desire to embrace them.

Whether Jane deliberately sought self-destruction or was unknowingly killing herself through her hedonism is impossible to decipher, but one thing is clear: she was driven by a desire to usurp authority and conventionality. For her, Bowles often seemed to represent these aspects of society, and so her unrelenting refusal to give in to his demands was in some ways a refusal to respect an outer authority. The people to whom she was drawn were often chaotic, amoral, as bent on self-destruction as she was. Consequently, they were incapable of seeing how she was frequently a victim, albeit willingly, of her own impulses. And although Bowles was hardly the conventional moralist, there was a bit of old-fashioned Yankee about him.

As far as Jane was concerned, Bowles frequently seemed to be erecting some a priori value structure that too often, for her liking, coincided with conventional standards. His reproach, therefore, was taken not as a sign of his obvious concern for her well-being but as a sermon. By the time she had moved in with Mary Oliver an impasse had been reached in their relationship, battle lines drawn. She would continue to please herself; Bowles could either join her or go his own way.

Although Bowles and Jane lived separately for the next five months, they saw each other frequently, often meeting friends, having dinner, or going to parties. The main event of January 1940 was the lavish Dunham-Chase wedding, which brought together at the reception virtually all of New York's "interesting people." At the wedding, Bowles and Jane played the part of the happily married couple, but after the reception Bowles went back to Brooklyn, Jane to Mary Oliver's.

Oddly enough, both found (perhaps more to Bowles's surprise than Jane's) that the distance in their private lives was actually beneficial to their mental health, and for Bowles at least, a boon to his creative work. Living apart, they could enjoy each other's company, and as Bowles was not a daily witness to Jane's disorder and drinking bouts, he did not feel compelled to play the role of critic. As a result, their friendship flourished.

Toward the end of March, Mary Oliver's situation collapsed: her furniture, bought on credit, was repossessed, and the landlord was threatening her with eviction. Reduced to eating Broadcast hash at nine cents a can, she buoyed herself with liquor and levitation, a practice she had taken up some years before. Although no one was ever an actual witness to her physical rising in the air, she continually claimed that she was quite capable of leaving her body. Bowles concluded that the sensation was more a result of the enormous quantities of gin that she consumed than a manifestation of psychic power. Because of the deteriorating circumstances, Jane decided it was time to move out. Bowles too was becoming weary of living in Brooklyn, and so they moved back together to the Chelsea, a move made possible financially by another theater project.

Again, it was for Saroyan, this time for his new play, *Love's Old Sweet Song,* which was being produced by Lawrence Langner at the Theatre Guild. Unlike *My Heart's in the Highlands, Love's Old Sweet Song* called for a great deal of music, including setting Saroyan's lyrics for three songs: "Of All the Things I Love," "The Years," and "A Little Closer Please." None of this was seen as an obstacle; what did bother Bowles, though, was Saroyan's constant rewriting of the play, which he continued to do well into the final rehearsals. Each time a scene was changed or cut or added, the music had to be refitted and sometimes reworked to correspond to the new situation or atmosphere.

The play was performed on April 6 in Princeton, New Jersey, then moved to the Forrest Theater in Philadelphia for further trial runs. Bowles, Jane, and Bowles's young cousin, Oliver Smith, now twenty-two, went down with Saroyan, the cast, and crew for the Philadelphia run, which was enthusiastically received. As to the music, Saroyan commented, "the music and two songs . . . contributed so much to the play, but were so integrated in the material, that I am afraid critics and theatergoers alike were not sufficiently aware of their importance. I must say, however, that I am aware." On May 2, *Love's Old Sweet Song* opened at the Plymouth Theater in New York. It was an immediate success, delighting the audience and critics. Bowles too was pleased with the outcome, amazed that the play had finally come together so well.

He was also glad for the income received from the production, as his meager relief allotment had suddenly been cut off by the local assistance bureau. When his case had come up for review, an investigator was sent not only to his house, but to the home of his parents as well. The investigator was black; when he arrived at Dr. Bowles's house in Jamaica he was shown the servant's entrance. Furious, he filed a report that stated unequivocably, "not in present need."

Given this turn of events, Bowles decided that he had nothing to lose by applying for a Guggenheim Fellowship. He had applied once before to record North African music but had been turned down. Now, however, with his recent string of accomplishments, he thought he might have better luck, and so again stated the same project. The Guggenheim Committee called him into the office and told him that while no funds were available for such an extensive proposal as the one he had envisioned, they would entertain an application for a "creative project" and that he should fill out the forms before leaving the office. Without thinking too much about it, he wrote down that he wished to be funded for an opera.

Bowles had already discussed with William Saroyan the possibility of doing an opera together; with a potential fellowship now on the horizon, he approached the playwright again, this time in all seriousness. Saroyan replied that though he had never even been to an opera, he would be willing to supply Bowles with some sort of libretto. Bowles didn't give much more thought to the matter— the awards would not be announced until March 1941 anyway— and turned his mind to other ways of getting work, hopefully work that would take him out of New York, realizing that the small sum he had saved from *Love's Old Sweet Song* would not last him much longer.

As it turned out, Bowles did not really have to rely much on his reserve to pay for his living expenses, for almost simultaneous with his dismissal from the relief rolls, he was offered another job. This one came from the Department of Agriculture, which wanted him to write music for a film it was producing. The title was *Roots in the Soil,* its subject being soil conservation in the Rio Grande valley of New Mexico. While the subject matter may not have seemed terribly inspiring, Bowles was not about to turn it down. When he learned that the department wanted him to write the music on location in Albuquerque, New Mexico, the job suddenly seemed far more interesting than he had first imagined. In the end, it would also prove to be an excellent vehicle for his own composing skills, as he was able to incorporate into the soundtrack much of what he loved about Mexican folkloric music.

The only question remaining was whether Jane would accompany him to New Mexico. Once they had resumed living together, the old quarrels had begun again. Jane was enjoying life in New York; Bowles, characteristically, was eager to get away. For a while it seemed that he would go alone, then suddenly Jane made a proposition to him: she would go if she could bring a friend of hers, Bob Faulkner. Bowles remembers being "so eager to get away from New York that I did not much care who came along with us." He gave his consent, realizing it was probably poor judgment on his part. "I knew Bob was a heavy drinker, just as I knew that was the reason why Jane wanted his presence." In discussing the issue with Jane, it became clear, though, that it was not just a drinking companion she desired. She also wanted to have another person along in order to create a buffer between herself and Bowles:

> She had finally told me that my "view of life" depressed her so deeply that when she was with me, everything seemed hopeless. The result was, she said, that she could be with me alone only for short periods, and then she had to escape the overwhelming gloom I created. (Much later she confided that she was frightened of being alone with me, particularly away from New York.) In Bob, who liked to laugh more or less continuously, she hoped to find a counterbalance to me. For my part, I imagined that I could control events and see to it that she did not drink too much.

It was in these circumstances, with this knowledge, that Bowles, Jane, and Faulkner set out by train for Albuquerque. As Bowles had predicted, Jane spent much of her time in the club car drinking with Faulkner. Contrary to what he had imagined, however, he could control neither events nor Jane.

CHAPTER 16

Bowles took an immediate liking to Albuquerque. The strong presence of indigenous Mexican and Indian cultures pervaded the town, giving it a foreign feeling, an atmosphere quite different from other places Bowles had visited in the United States. Upon arrival he went to see Richard Boke, the film's director, who helped him find a house about a mile outside of the city. He rented a piano and began to work on the score. Jane and Faulkner busied themselves exploring the local bars, in the process getting to know the locals, many transplanted big-city Americans who were living in Albuquerque in order to soak up the last remnants of vanishing Indian culture.

Bowles, as usual, was more taken with the countryside than with his neighbors; he spent a great deal of time walking in the desert, where "there was nothing but the complex sinewy pattern of rocks, sand, driftwood and pebbles." But there was more to these walks than just observation; it was, in fact, a way of working. While walking through the vast open spaces he would carry with him the written sequence of scenes and a stopwatch. When a melody line came into his head he would consult the script, then time it so that it would fit into the minutes allotted for its duration. Returning to the house he would write it out and play it on the piano.

Scored only for piano, percussion, double bass, and wind instruments, the music, while fresh, also made good use of popular Mexican material. Unfortunately, in the final film, the dubbed-over commentary often obscured Bowles's strains, but when the music was allowed to emerge, it came through in a finely tuned manner. This was clearly a project that allowed Bowles to exercise his extraordinary ear for "popular" song patterns, but given its rather unusual scoring, it had a delicacy that was lacking in much of the original material that it echoed.

* * *

Despite his desire for solitude, social encounters were inescapable. The Bokes, being hospitable, invited the Bowleses to dinner on several occasions. Although Bowles realized that courtesy demanded a reciprocal invitation, he was quite wary of having them come to his apartment, as he did not want to have to explain Faulkner's presence. Jane, however, insisted, saying that she would simply pass Faulkner off as her brother. She also invited a local character named Desert Rose, who frequented one of their favorite bars. It was a plan destined to backfire. Almost immediately the Bokes were disconcerted by the crudeness of the other dinner guest, for Desert Rose, in her best barroom manner, drunkenly dominated the conversation. The brother-sister charade also collapsed when Jane and Faulkner began to talk about their individual families, clearly distinct one from the other. By the end of the evening Bowles was mortified; Jane, Faulkner, and Desert Rose, who seemed to feel it was enormously entertaining, were as fully amused by Bowles's consternation as by that of the Bokes.

Fortunately the score was almost finished, and after the dinner disaster Bowles worked even harder to bring it to completion. He was also hurrying it for another reason: he wanted to get to Mexico before the 1940 presidential elections there during the first week in July, as he was afraid that if the fascist candidate won, the border would be closed. Around mid-June he presented Boke with the completed score, and a week afterward he, Jane, and Faulkner set out by train for El Paso, Texas, where they crossed the border into Ciudad Juárez. Ten days later, after spending a week in the north-central town of Zacatecas, they arrived in Mexico City.

Just before leaving for Mexico Bowles received the promised opera text from Saroyan, called *Opera, Opera!,* and now, on the trip south, he read it over, trying to envision what he might do with it. To Bowles's mind, it "was not a libretto any more than Gertrude Stein's text for *Four Saints in Three Acts* was a libretto." After studying it for some time, he decided that it was totally unusable. He wrote Saroyan a brief note which said, "Well, I've been thinking about it, but there just doesn't seem to be enough in the idea for an opera," on which Saroyan later commented, "Too bad. He wrote a one-line letter, and I lost a whole opera."

On this trip to Mexico, unlike on the previous journey with the Tonnys, Jane was in good spirits. Part of this, of course, was due to her spending most of her time making merry with Faulkner. Also, in contrast to the earlier trip, Jane did not have to fend off sexual advances from Faulkner, who was homosexual.

Arriving in the capital, they were shocked by the political chaos that gripped the city. It was not just the usual sloganeering and demonstrations on behalf of one candidate or another, but a hectic, random violence. On July 7, election day, the disturbances escalated. While strolling through the stately pathways of the Alameda they suddenly found themselves dodging hails of bullets fired into the crowds from passing cars. The city, as Bowles had feared, was clearly on the brink of civil war. His earlier concern of not being able to get into Mexico was now superseded by a rising fear of being caught literally in the crossfire. But as quickly as the violence had arisen, it dissipated. With the victory of the moderate candidate, the situation returned to normal within a few days.

The trio did not remain long in Mexico City. Remembering his brief but pleasant stay at Malinche's palace with the Tonnys, Bowles wanted to get out into the countryside again. After a short search, they managed to lease a large hacienda complete with eighty-five cows and hundreds of sheep, about fifty miles outside the city near the town of Jajalpa. Situated in the mountains about 10,000 feet above sea level, and with a breathtaking view of the volcano of Toluca, the hacienda at first seemed to be the perfect location in which to work. But Bowles soon discovered that "the vastness of the landscape had a paralyzing effect," to the point where he could not work at all. There were other problems as well. The remoteness of the village made it difficult to acquire servants to assist with the upkeep of the huge place. In addition, once hired, it was hard to retain the help, for being superstitious, the locals quickly decided that the hacienda was haunted. Bowles remembers that there was indeed a sinister quality to the house: "It was a melancholy place; the fact that it was so beautiful made the melancholy more insidious, more corrosive."

One day while in Mexico City, Bowles paid a visit to the local Communist party office to offer his services. When they found out that he was living in a hacienda, they quickly decided that he could be most useful to the party by giving Sunday tours of the capitalist premises to groups of sightseers. Soon the tour buses began to arrive. Thrown into the bargain excursion was lunch, which naturally the Bowleses had to provide. Jane was "stoical" about it; Bowles, on the other hand, welcomed the diversion, feeling somewhat satisfied that he was contributing to the welfare of the party.

As it turned out, the tour groups descended on them only twice, for within a few weeks after taking the place Bowles decided that he was suffering from what he believed to be altitude sickness. The symptoms were constant fatigue, nausea, and a consequent loss of appetite. As a result, he decided to take up an invitation to go to Acapulco that had been extended to him by friends now in Mexico, Lewis and Peggy Riley (now Rosamond Bernier), whom he had known previously in New York. Jane and Faulkner stayed behind, saying that they would join Bowles in a couple of weeks. Once at sea level, Bowles's appetite returned and within a short time he was feeling quite well.

Jane and Faulkner soon arrived in Acapulco with two servants in tow, and even though Faulkner stayed only a few days, the Rileys quickly discovered that having the Bowleses in their house was more than they could hospitably bear. Concluding that it was far easier to enjoy their company as neighbors rather than as houseguests, they set about finding them a home nearby. The new accommodations consisted of a large house with a huge tree-filled patio strung with hammocks.

Once settled in, the Bowleses realized that given the large garden and expansiveness of the patio, the place was well suited to collecting a variety of animals. Over the next month the menagerie expanded to include a parrot, a cat, a duck, an armadillo, and two coatimundis, a small tropical American mammal. Jane was particularly fond of the armadillo, which she named Mary Shuster, and the coatis. One of the coatis was apparently quite attached to her, as well, as each night it refused to sleep anywhere else but in her bed, frequently nestling in her hair.

As at the hacienda, Jane and Bowles had individual bedrooms. Although Jane thought nothing of intruding at night into the rooms of their houseguests, she would never disturb Bowles in his room. If sex had ever been an aspect of their relationship, it was by now clearly not.

Shortly after they moved into the house a young man arrived at the door one morning and asked to see Bowles. Going to the entranceway Bowles encountered a very sunburned fellow in a floppy straw hat and striped sailor shirt. Although he was not particularly interested in receiving unexpected visitors, being always the gentleman he decided to see what the man wanted: "I went to the door and he announced himself. He said, 'I'm Tennessee Williams and I have a note for you from Lawrence Langner.'" As they were about to depart for the beach, Jane demanded that Bowles "get rid of him." When Bowles persisted in inviting the young man in, Jane announced firmly, "Well he's just got to stay here then because he can't go with us." Bowles placed two servants at Williams's disposal and took him out to the patio, telling him to choose a hammock. "He was still there when we came back. We saw him after that a few times."

Despite the frequency of American visitors such as Williams, Morris Golde, Gordon Sager, and the Rileys, Jane quickly began to feel that Acapulco did not have enough to offer by way of social life. Therefore, when Golde and Sager announced that they were planning to go up to Taxco, a town with a large expatriate community, she decided to drive up with them. She took an instant liking to the town and its transplanted colony of Americans, mostly bohemians (or aspirers to being that). Within a few days she wired Bowles that she had rented a house there. Bowles was furious, as that was the one town in Mexico in which he did not want to live. As far as he was concerned, it had lost all of its native charm and was overrun with pretentious foreigners, most of whom seemed dedicated to living above the culture while pretending to indulge themselves in it. Bowles again found himself in a familiar predicament. He could either remain in Acapulco by himself or join Jane in Taxco. He finally relented, packed up, and moved, hauling the menagerie with him.

As Bowles had foreseen, he did not like living in Taxco. It became even worse when Faulkner arrived on the scene and was invited by Jane to move in with them. She and Faulkner again began to spend a lot of their time in a local bar; it was possibly there that Jane met Helvetia Perkins. Like many, Perkins was in Mexico because, with the war on in Europe, it was impossible to follow through on her earlier plan to go there. Like Jane, she enjoyed the milieu of Taxco, its expatriate characters, the artists and pseudo-artists. Whether Jane fell in love at that first meeting in the summer of 1940 is not known. What is a matter of record is that the affair would have enormous consequences for them both. It would also have an extraordinary impact on Bowles, altering permanently his relationship with Jane.

The romance began as nothing more than a flirtation, one of many that Jane was having that summer and had had before. But with Helvetia Perkins it quickly proceeded to become something far more than that. Perkins was to some extent an unlikely candidate for Jane's attention. In 1940 she was forty-four years old, divorced, accompanied by her only daughter, then twenty-one, much closer in age to Jane than was Perkins. Accounts differ as to whether she had had lesbian affairs before, but this did not seem to bother Jane; if anything, it intrigued her even more. Photographs show Perkins to be a rather handsome though plain-looking woman. In the photos she always seems serious, a bit dour, a fact confirmed by many who knew her. Most everyone also remembers her as possessing a piercing gaze. The poet Kenward Elmslie, however, claims that she wasn't nearly as serious as she may have seemed to others: "She was quite charming," notes Elmslie, "and could have a very merry personality."

For all the differences, however, there were also similarities. She had grown up in relative wealth in Evanston, Illinois; like Jane, her father had died when she was a child; also like her lover-to-be she had early on asserted her independence, but unlike Jane had become something of a political radical. Worldly and cosmopolitan, she had spent most of her adult life, subsequent to her divorce after five years of marriage, rambling from one place to another—New York, Paris, Chicago, now Taxco. Determined to be a writer, she was apparently living in Mexico in order to work on a novel.

At first they met by chance, but after a few encounters, by design. Jane, in fact, was in hot pursuit, and though Perkins did not invite Jane's attention, she apparently did nothing to discourage it either, as she found Jane wonderfully unconventional, charming, and witty. Bowles did not react much, at least at first, to Jane's desire for Perkins. There had been flirtations before and he seemed to feel that it would pass quickly, like the others. Indeed, at that time he was far more concerned about her excessive drinking than with a possible love affair.

In September Bowles received a wire from the Theatre Guild in New York, asking him if he could return to New York immediately to write the music for an upcoming production of Shakespeare's *Twelfth Night.* As he was finding life in Taxco unpalatable, he readily accepted, catching a plane the same week for New York. Jane, caught up in her new romance and with the expatriate social scene, remained behind. Unlike on other occasions, Bowles did not attempt to persuade her to accompany him. Both of them, it seems, felt that they could use a little separation.

Back in New York, Bowles moved into the Chelsea and set to work at once on the score for *Twelfth Night.* Although he was by now quite accomplished at writing theater music, *Twelfth Night* presented him with a special challenge: the difficulty of writing Elizabethan-sounding music in a contemporary age. There was also the usual difficulty of having to compose quickly, for the show was to open in early November.

Bowles's success was indisputable. Virgil Thomson, then chief music critic of the New York *Herald Tribune,* was so enchanted by the music that he devoted an entire column in the paper to it, in the process breaking with an established tradition which relegated theater music to second-class status, not worthy of comment by classical music critics. S. L. M. Barlow, writing in *Modern Music,* praised Thomson for what was seen then as a courageous move, and in turn heaped accolades on Bowles: "As with everything he has done for Broadway, it is skillfully scored, fresh and apt. His theater-music always has enough profile to make one want to listen to it and yet enough discretion not to make one have to listen to it. In this case, he has taken Elizabethan songs and made them his own without robbing Shakespeare."

Twelfth Night opened at the St. James Theater in New York on November 19, 1940, starring Helen Hayes and Maurice Evans. Almost simultaneous with the opening, Bowles received another commission, again from the Theatre Guild. The play this time was *Liberty Jones* by Philip Barry, with John Houseman—who had broken with Welles the year before—directing. As the production required a tremendous amount of music (there were 158 musical cues), Bowles sent a wire to Jane urging her to return to New York since it was clear he was going to have to be there for quite a while. Although apparently somewhat hesitant to leave her incipient romance with Perkins, she eventually agreed when Bob Faulkner said he would accompany her. Perkins also assured her that she too would come to New York within a month or so.

Jane and Faulkner arrived in New York on Christmas day. Taking a separate room at the Chelsea, Jane quickly renewed old friendships and began once more to lead an active social life, sometimes going with Bowles to the houses of various mutual friends or to the Askews' salon; more frequently, she went with her own crowd to nightclubs and parties. Bowles, caught up in his work and with his own life, did not attempt to restrain her nightly bar-hopping, even though he was aware that it culminated occasionally in casual sex. Virgil Thomson, also living at the Chelsea at the time, recalls that during this period Jane was quite active in her pursuit of sexual adventures: "I think all her life Jane was promiscuous. She didn't really care too much who she slept with, as long as they were female. . . . She'd go out regularly when they were staying [at the Chelsea] and pick up women. She called them her 'drugstore cowboys.' It was just for a good time; there was no drama in these affairs."

She was also writing and by now was far enough along with *Two Serious Ladies* to read parts of it at private gatherings. Usually present were John Latouche, Edwin Denby, Thomson, and from time to time, Bowles. Latouche found the book wonderfully comic and would often break into laughter during the reading. The others were often a bit mystified by Latouche's amusement; Jane, however, appeared to enjoy his outbursts and good-natured gibes at her expense. It made the undertaking seem less serious, less at odds with her personality.

Perkins arrived in early January and moved in with Jane at the Chelsea. Jane took her around to meet her friends, including Thomson, who found Perkins serious, somewhat elegant, and much more mature than Jane. Bowles, in the final stages of writing *Liberty Jones*, immersed himself in his work, more or less ignoring Perkins's presence. He did insist, though, that Jane accompany him to Philadelphia for the tryout of the play at the end of January. As Perkins was planning to return to Taxco about this time anyway, Jane accepted Bowles's offer.

Liberty Jones opened on Broadway on February 5, 1941. The reviews were not good, of either the play or the music. S. L. M.

Barlow, normally a champion of Bowles's, wrote: "On hearing this really long score, an unhappy suspicion arises that Bowles isn't aware that mere contrivance or invention aren't enough. The rhythms are there but no waltz, the clever satire is there but no gusto, the heat is there but no love."

The poor reception, however, hardly influenced theater producers, for while the play was still in production, Bowles received another commission, this time for Lillian Hellman's *Watch on the Rhine*. As usual, Bowles had little time—only a month or so—to write the score. As usual, he came through, on this occasion with considerably more success. Indeed, the theme song from the play, reechoed in various other scenes, is a beautiful, haunting melody. Delicate and wistful, it ably mirrors the fragile yet determined hopes of the anti-Nazi movement. When in 1943 the play was made into a film, it also featured Bowles's theme song, but did not credit him. Bowles hired a lawyer and eventually received a settlement, but the film still does not acknowledge his contribution.

For several reasons—his general disenchantment with the totalitarian aspect of the Communist party, the diminution of communist domination in the theater, and a string of well-paying successes behind him—Bowles decided at about this time to quit the party. When he went to resign, however, he was told that he could not; he could only be expelled. When Bowles suggested that this be done, he was informed that although they had decided to do exactly that with Jane, the party officials had concluded that it served their purposes to keep him on the roster. As a result, despite his attempt to sever his affiliation, Bowles remained, and possibly still remains, a member of the party.

Having written scores for three plays in six months, Bowles was looking forward to a much-needed rest. He was also toying with the idea of returning to Mexico, but suddenly another opportunity came his way: Lincoln Kirstein asked him to write another ballet. Pleased to have a more "serious" musical project, he accepted, quickly deciding on a Mexican theme—that of the traditional Christmas *posadas,* processions made by villagers from house to house in reenactment of the search by Mary and Joseph for a room at an inn. It was a bold idea, particularly as Bowles conceived of the work as being something of an opera-ballet, having in addition to the normal orchestral score a number of vocal sequences. Kirstein apparently welcomed the idea, possibly because, as American Ballet Caravan was being sent to tour South America in the fall, he felt it appropriate to have a "Latin" ballet on the program. The work was entitled *Pastorela*.

Kirstein, perhaps concerned that Bowles would disappear on him again (as he had during the writing of *Yankee Clipper*), decided to introduce him to George Davis, fiction editor of *Harper's Bazaar*, who in the fall of 1940 had established an "artists' residence" in Brooklyn. The old brownstone on Middagh Street in Brooklyn Heights had a vacancy, and Kirstein thought that Bowles and Jane would find the atmosphere both convivial and conducive to work. In addition, it was cheap—about $25 a month. Bowles and Jane met with Davis and the other Middagh Street residents and were immediately accepted into the household, which at that time included Davis, who lived on the first floor; W. H. Auden, tenor Peter Pears, and Benjamin Britten on the third floor; and Golo Mann, Thomas Mann's younger son, who occupied the attic. Two rooms on the second floor were for Bowles and Jane. Shortly thereafter, Bowles's cousin, Oliver Smith, now a successful stage designer, took the remaining room on that floor.

As Kirstein had expected, Bowles and Jane fit well into the somewhat quirky household. "It was an experiment, and I think a largely successful one, in communal living," said Bowles. "It worked largely because Auden ran it; he was exceptionally adept at getting the necessary money out of us when it was due." Although each of the residents had separate quarters, meals were taken together, again with Auden presiding. "He would preface a meal by announcing: 'We've got a roast and two veg, salad and savory, and there will be no political discussion.' He had enough of the don about him to keep us all in order."

Despite the intriguing household, they did not remain long in Brooklyn Heights. Shortly after moving in, Bowles was informed, on March 23, 1941, that he had been awarded a Guggenheim Fellowship with a stipend of $2,500 to be used for writing an opera. Suddenly, he found himself rather well off. In addition to the Guggenheim money, he had received slightly over $5,000 in advances and royalties from the theater productions. With *Pastorela* nearly finished, and the Mexican composer Blas Galindo set to orchestrate it, Bowles realized that there was no real reason to stay in New York. Characteristically, he began to plot an escape. As Europe and North Africa were convulsed in war, Mexico again loomed as the most likely foreign soil on which to alight. Jane, too, was all in favor of returning to Taxco and to Helvetia Perkins. By early June they were there.

They moved back into their former house, in which Bob Faulkner was still living, and tried to reestablish themselves in Taxco. Jane quickly resumed her affair with Perkins, in the process reimmersing herself in the expatriate social life. She also began working on her novel again, torturously writing a few paragraphs each day. For relief, she began spending her evenings drinking—at home, at Perkins's house, or in one of the local bars that catered to a foreign clientele. Bowles found the scene as disagreeable as he had previously. He and Faulkner immediately quarreled about Faulkner's noise, drinking, and late hours; within a few weeks Faulkner moved to his own house nearby. But Faulkner was not the only objectionable character in Taxco. In a letter to Virgil Thomson, Bowles described the foreign community this way:

> The foreign colony is made up still of about the same proportion of dopes, drunks and nice individuals. Then there are the hordes of Californian, Middle Western and Texas tourists who come afresh each day with guides from Mexico [City], have lunch and go back again. And a certain number of wealthier New York and Connecticut people who stop on their way to Acapulco in their cars. But unless you seek them out, all these people, you never see them.

Bowles, in fact, did not seek them out. Indeed, in order to escape from Taxco he rented a little adobe house outside of the town. "I have a mud hut and a jungle down in a valley some thousand feet below Taxco," he wrote Thomson. "Plus a Paul et Virginie waterfall that looks like Yosemite. And no one else in the valley as far as one can see, save the guardian of a ruined hacienda another five hundred feet directly beneath me." It was not just the tourists, though, that he was shunning; his retreat, ostensibly taken in order to have solitude in which to work, also allowed him to avoid what was happening to his marriage. It was the same pattern he had used all his life. As a child and adolescent he had retreated to his room in order to make the household reality disappear. Now, at thirty, he employed the same tactic, still firmly believing that involvement was a curse to be avoided, that it could lead only to bad feeling. Isolation was a well-learned mode for preventing confrontation.

There was also pretense, an art at which Bowles was equally accomplished, having learned early on as well to hide his feelings. It was this Bowles, "glamorous, swathed in thick fumes of homemade patchouli," that young composer Ned Rorem, just sixteen years old, saw that summer. In Taxco with his father, Rorem already knew of Bowles as a composer (*Twelfth Night* had recently played in Rorem's hometown of Chicago) but it never occurred to him that they would soon meet in person. The opportunity came at a tea party, "over tea and a yellow cake with chocolate frosting chez two European women, Magda and Gilberte," whom Rorem had been told to look up. The other guests were Bowles and Jane. Rorem remembers that at some point during the evening, Jane came up to Bowles and began stroking his back. Bowles looked pained, then reproached Jane by saying softly, but firmly, "Such intimacy!" Knowing nothing about their life together, the comment struck Rorem as odd: "Married people didn't say things like that to each other." A day or so later, he went around to see Bowles in order to show him some of his scores. "Paul was kind about my music, perceptive too, a touch condescending perhaps." He saw the Bowleses once more before he left Taxco, again at a party, but this time Jane was with Helvetia Perkins. According to Rorem, the Bowleses "seemed close, but separate—platonic pals."

If Bowles impressed Rorem, Rorem also apparently intrigued Bowles. According to some, the central figure, Racky, in Bowles's celebrated story "Pages from Cold Point," written in 1947, is based on Rorem. Although Bowles claims this is not the case, there are similarities between the young Rorem and Racky. Both are precocious and independent, both already sexually aware. In the story, Mr. Norton, a recent widower, and his sixteen-year-old son, Racky, leave the United States to settle on a Caribbean island. The reason for leaving is obscure, but apparently Racky has already made his predilections known, and possibly he has even been involved sexually with his father. If Mr. Norton was hoping that removal from "civilization" would also remove his son from homosexual encounters, he was wrong, for once there, Racky immediately begins to seduce the local boys. Although fully cognizant of Racky's seductions, Mr. Norton feigns ignorance, indeed takes great pains not to reproach his son. The story culminates with Racky entering into an ambiguous sexual liaison with his father and ultimately being set up in his own apartment in Havana, supported handsomely from afar by Mr. Norton.

The circumstances of Rorem's visit also have parallels with the story. Although in Taxco with his father, Rorem, like Racky, was clearly in charge of himself, acting quite independently. Many, in fact, were not even aware that there was an elder Rorem. Also like Racky, Rorem was brought by his father to Mexico because of "post-adolescent psychological upheavals back in Chicago."

Whether Bowles really had Rorem in mind as a model for Racky is impossible to determine, particularly as Bowles does not acknowledge the debt, but it should also be noted that there is more than a bit of Bowles in Mr. Norton. His response, for instance, to Racky's homosexual promiscuity—feigning ignorance or indifference—is very much the response that Bowles was making to Jane's liaisons. Similar, too, are Mr. Norton's pronouncements on "civilization":

> Our civilization is doomed to a short life: its component parts are too heterogeneous. I personally am content to see everything in the process of decay. The bigger the bombs, the quicker it will be done. Life is visually too hideous for one to make the attempt to preserve it. Let it go. Perhaps some day another form of life will come along. Either way, it is of no consequence. At the same time, I am still a part of life, and I am bound by this to protect myself to whatever extent I am able. And so I am here. Here in the Islands vegetation still has the upper hand, and man has to fight even to make his presence seen at all.

Although these statements are those of a fictional character, and are written six years after Bowles's stay in Mexico, they echo the sense of despair that was already gnawing at his consciousness during this time. His earlier attempts to cope with his present, through isolating himself by physical removal or by pretending involvement, had collapsed by mid-July. Feeling the need to put even more distance between himself and Jane, he went down to the capital, using as an excuse for leaving Taxco the visit of his cousin Oliver Smith. But even with the diversions of the city and good company from abroad, Bowles could not shake a persistent feeling of disquietude. To Thomson, he wrote:

> The old, accustomed paralysis takes hold of one's consciousness here. The place in itself is nonexistent, and some days are so completely empty, the hours of events and the air of any suggestion of an idea, that one is tempted to look down at one's toes and think of life and death. Which is a very bad sign, as you know. At any rate, I can truthfully say that nothing has happened, because no matter what did happen, nothing would really have happened at all.

Part of Bowles's malaise had to do with his domestic situation, but he was also upset because of Kirstein's reception of his ballet. Bowles had delivered *Pastorela* before leaving New York, but Kirstein was not pleased with the results, writing him that it was "lousy, terrible." Kirstein, in fact, was demanding that Bowles rewrite a good portion of it. To Thomson, Bowles complained: "Lincoln has been quite a louse about Pastorelas. I wouldn't mind his gossip and intrigue if he'd pay me for the music. But he seems determined to get it for nothing." Bowles became ever further aggravated when Kirstein asked him to work with another composer in order to put the ballet in shape:

> He insisted I listen to the squeakings of his friend Martinez, and use what I could. I used as little of the material as I could get by with, and made up most of it myself because I liked my own inventions better. Then L. decided that since Galindo orchestrated the work (for which I paid), and Martinez squeaked at me that I had done nothing at all. But there'll be a suit in the fall if he doesn't come across! Or has he made promises to all the others of deferred settlements?

Bowles and Kirstein finally did come to an agreement. Bowles was paid around $1,000 and the ballet went on tour with the company to South America. It would not receive an American premiere, however, until January 1947, and then the reviews would be less than favorable, although most of the criticism would not be aimed at Bowles's music, but at Lew Christiansen's choreography.

* * *

In August, Bowles went with Oliver Smith, Smith's stepfather and mother, Bob Faulkner, the Mexican painter Antonio Álvarez (a Smith discovery), Jane, and Perkins to Acapulco. Bowles found the visit helpful in restoring his spirits. The hot, tropical climate suited him, the food was good, and there was enough natural distraction to keep him occupied. He also became quite friendly with Álvarez during the visit, spending a lot of his time there engrossed in conversation with the young painter. When the rest of the party returned to Taxco in late August, Bowles stayed on by himself for a few weeks, enjoying the peace that accompanied solitude.

Returning to Taxco in September, he had pretty well decided that he had had enough of Mexico and that the best thing to do was to return to New York. His plans were suddenly altered, however, when he became quite sick. At first, thinking it was simply the usual case of dysentery, he did not take the symptoms seriously; but after a week or so, it was clear that he was extremely ill. Transported to the capital, apparently in Perkins's station wagon, he was immediately admitted to the British hospital. The diagnosis: jaundice.

While Bowles was recuperating in the hospital, Copland arrived in Mexico City for a performance of his *Short Symphony* but spent most of his week there visiting Bowles, bringing him the latest New York "news and gossip." Bowles greatly enjoyed the visits of his former mentor, and wished more than ever that he could be back in New York. Jane, however, in the final stages of writing *Two Serious Ladies* and fully involved with Perkins, did not want to leave Mexico at all. Realizing as well that it would be a while before he was fit enough to travel, he decided to spend the fall in Mexico City, and persuaded Jane to join him. By November Bowles suffered a relapse of the jaundice and was sent to the sanitarium of a Dr. Wurzburger in Cuernavaca, a mountain resort midway between the capital and Taxco. It was there that he began working on his opera. It was also there that he first read Jane's novel.

Bowles's initial reaction to it was far from kind: "I found great fault with it for its orthography, grammar, and rhetoric. 'You can't let anyone see such an abject manuscript!' I shouted. She was very calm about it. 'If there's a publisher, he'll take care of those things,' she assured me." Later, Bowles regretted his initial eruption. "I doubt that I told her how much I admired it, but perhaps I did. I hope so."

If Bowles did not tell Jane this at the time, he did show her that he cared tremendously about the book through his careful reading of it. Indeed, it was his suggestion that prompted Jane to alter her novel substantially, cutting around a hundred pages from the manuscript. Originally the novel was about three serious ladies, and even had that working title. Bowles, however, felt that the novel would be much tighter if a long section set in Guatemala, featuring the third lady, Señora Ramirez, were excised. Jane went along with the suggestion, later turning the Guatemalan narratives into two stories, "A Guatemalan Idyll" and "A Day in the Open." A third section, about a Señorita Cordoba, was never published.

During December and into January 1942, Jane worked on revising the novel, deciding that she would head back to New York in the early spring to look for a publisher, but feeling doubtful that she would succeed. In the interim, Bowles, Jane, Perkins, and Antonio Álvarez, with whom Bowles had become quite close, decided to do some traveling around Mexico. Álvarez and Bowles went first to Veracruz on the Gulf of Mexico, then met Jane and Perkins in Tehuantepec. The trip seemed to do Bowles a great deal of good. By March, however, he was feeling the need to get back to work, and Jane, now that the novel was finished, decided to try her luck in New York. Bowles would remain a bit longer in Mexico, then join her back in the States.

CHAPTER 17

With Jane off to the States, Bowles began seriously to turn his attention to his opera. Having abandoned the idea of using Saroyan's text, the idea came to him of using García Lorca's surrealist tragicomedy *Así que pasen cinco años* as a basis. This was hardly the simplest choice, as the play is an often absurdist and highly psychological drama, not necessarily the best stuff for an opera.

Realizing that it would be impossible to use the entire text, Bowles decided to create a libretto by carefully selecting a few short passages from the second half of the play that he could then set to music. The result is that *The Wind Remains,* while using García Lorca's words, is all but unrelated to the original. While García Lorca's play is an intense and ultimately tragic drama, populated by no fewer than twenty-two characters, Bowles's opera is basically a burlesque and has but two characters, and these, composites of several of the play's personages. As a consequence, the plot of *The Wind Remains* is quite different as well, becoming essentially a story of courtship: a harlequin attempts to woo a lady who alternately welcomes and spurns his attention. Unlike most conventional operatic works, however, there is no definitive resolution in the end, unless one takes the soaring final duet as an indication that the harlequin has finally been successful in his pursuit of the fair damsel.

Although critics have persisted in calling *The Wind Remains* an opera, it really is not. Bowles, in fact, has always insisted that it is a *zarzuela,* the Spanish version of light opera, and indeed this is the case, for it perfectly follows the conventions of the *zarzuela,* in which songs alternate with spoken dialogue and dance. In addition, the limited cast, one soprano and one tenor, and the use of a variety of musical styles, including Spanish folkloric material and even American jazz, immediately set it apart from more traditional operas.

Despite his immersion in the creation of *The Wind Remains,* and the brilliance of its final execution, Bowles was suffering physically and emotionally. In April 1942, he wrote to Thomson:

> I have been ill so often lately that I am completely fed-up with this republic. I suppose that means I am returning as soon as possible, which isn't immediately because I have a mess to clear up regarding my getting permission from the American Consulate to get out of Mexico. . . . This is a charming country if one is full of vigor. Otherwise it easily turns into an almost perpetual nightmare. If I hadn't had previous years of Morocco and other hostile spots to prepare me more or less, by this time I think I should be completely mad. The way of staying sane is simply that of accepting, accepting, one horror after another, and being thankful to be still alive.

Bowles did finally get out of Mexico in late June, but not before he had been twice more in the hospital, once with jaundice again, and once in order to have a tumor extracted from his jaw. His own troubles, though, were superseded by those of his friend Antonio Álvarez, who in May, suffering from acute depression, took an overdose of Nembutal. He survived, but his arm became partially paralyzed as a result; Bowles decided to take him to New York for medical treatment, thinking also that it would do Álvarez good to have a change of scene. On arrival, they stayed for a few days at the Chelsea, then went on to Watkins Glen, New York, where Jane and Perkins had taken up residence in the house of Bowles's recently deceased Aunt Mary.

Jane had just received good news: Knopf had accepted *Two Serious Ladies* for publication. There was other news too; some she told him about, some she didn't. Omitted from her accounts of what had transpired since leaving Mexico was the fact that she had attempted suicide by slashing her wrists. The irony inherent in Bowles's concern over Álvarez's attempt to kill himself, while never once suspecting that his own wife had been in as dire a predicament, must have been evident, possibly even amusing to her. Her reason for withholding this information, though, was quite different: she did not want Bowles to know that her relationship with Perkins was far from trouble-free. When she finally did tell him years later, she dismissed the incident as an act resulting from anger at Perkins. Knowing at the time that Bowles was far from happy about her situation, Jane no doubt felt that her precipitous, self-destructive action was best left unmentioned.

She did tell him, however, that she had been recently questioned by the FBI about his activities, following its interception of what it believed to be a suspicious telegram sent by Bowles from Mexico to Jane at Holden Hall. The message read: "PLEASE WIRE WHEREABOUTS OF DRUM STOP SCHWAB CLAIMS NOT IN BODEGA." What Bowles was asking about was a drum that he had purchased in Ixtepec and that had been stored at the Hotel Carlton in Mexico City, run by a gentleman named Schwab. In the minds of the FBI, overly zealous about ferreting out spies now that the war had broken out, the wire could only be a coded message. A General Drum, it seems, was at that time in Mexico.

While Perkins hid in an upstairs room, afraid that the FBI was there to question her, Jane tried to explain the telegram's innocent meaning. Absurdity led to further absurdity, culminating in the agents asking her who Friedrich von Winewitz was: the name had surfaced in a conversation she had had with Latouche some days earlier, which they had wiretapped. Friedrich von Winewitz, in fact, was a name that Latouche used to call Bowles in jest, as he liked to assert playfully that Bowles's mother was really Jewish. Although apparently still suspicious, the agents, after several more rounds of questioning, finally left.

Curiously, they never returned to question Bowles himself. He did, however, have his run-ins with the local police, chiefly because of his association with Álvarez, who, being pure Indian, from a distance looked sufficiently Japanese for the neighbors to call the police. Twice, in fact, Bowles and Álvarez were arrested and held at the police station. The reason, according to Bowles, was that "Antonio couldn't say anything. He didn't speak a word of English. . . . Since we were speaking Spanish . . . the police thought he was a Japanese spy and they thought I was German!" On one occasion, the police had to telephone Bowles's uncle in Glenora to come down and vouch for the pair before they could be released.

At Holden Hall, in the music room, Bowles completed the piano score for *The Wind Remains.* In the fall, while Jane and Perkins were in Vermont looking for property for Perkins to purchase, Bowles moved back to New York, installing himself in the Chelsea. He finished the orchestration for the opera in October and set about getting someone to produce it. He found an eager sponsor in the Marquise de Casa Fuerte, who had founded and produced La Sérénade concerts in Paris before the war. She avidly began to raise money for the production and by the end of the year had arranged for the opera to be performed at the Museum of Modern Art in March 1943.

Although Perkins was also successful in her search, upon returning from Vermont she and Jane decided to take an apartment together on Waverly Place in Manhattan. Bowles, still at the Chelsea, soon came up with more permanent lodgings as well, moving into a small penthouse apartment owned by Friedrich Kiesler at the corner of 14th Street and Seventh Avenue. Its previous occupant had been Marcel Duchamp, with whom Bowles now became acquainted, and who occasionally suggested that he and the composer have lunch together. "God knows what we discussed!" said Bowles, on whom the lunchtime conversations left little impression. "He was like any educated Frenchman as far as I could see. I wasn't listening to find out how brilliant he was; I liked him."

The Bowleses were living separately, and it was an arrangement that seemed to suit them well. As before, it was in many ways easier for Bowles to have this sort of contact with Jane than to be with her on a day-to-day basis. They would have lunch or dinner together several times a week, but were quite engaged in their independent lives. In public, however, they strove to maintain an illusion of being married. Edouard Roditi, who saw them that fall at a dinner party they hosted jointly, came away with the impression that the two of them were role-playing marriage:

> Marriage had considerably changed Paul's way of life, if not his whole personality too. In Europe, I had seen him lead a very marginal and unstable existence. . . . In New York, I now found him occupying a pleasant penthouse apartment in a good neighborhood. . . . Paul's physical appearance had not changed much . . . but his manner seemed less youthfully exuberant or prone to depression . . . while Jane gave me the impression of scarcely being an adult. On this occasion, a number of other guests were in the apartment and Jane, although obviously an experienced hostess and quite at ease with me whom she'd never met, was behaving rather like a child playing the game of being a "married lady" with a real sense of

comedy. . . . Although Paul and Jane both appeared to be well matched and happy as a harmonious couple, it never occurred to me that their marriage could in other respects be quite as normal as they seemed to want the world to believe. They were behaving too much like actors playing the parts of a married couple in a comedy of manners.

It was at about this time that they became financially independent of each other as well, Bowles refusing to share any of his income with Jane. Already notorious among his friends as a penny-pincher, Bowles was always quite careful to separate his bills from Jane's. This extended even to dinners, where if the Bowleses happened to be dining with others, the check would always be split individually, "down to the last nickel." According to Virgil Thomson, "it was Paul's way of getting back at Jane for her refusing to live or sleep with him." The arrangement would continue, more or less, for the rest of Jane's life.

Whether for vindictive purposes or not, the separation of finances also served as an expedient for Bowles, who was again beginning to run low on cash. He began to look for theater productions for which he could furnish music, but in the interim Thomson again came to Bowles's rescue, offering him a job as assistant music critic at the New York *Herald Tribune*, where Thomson himself had become chief music critic after his return from France in 1940. Although Bowles had been writing occasional music criticism for several years for *Modern Music*, he had never had tight deadlines. When he learned that the average amount of lead time for these reviews was less than forty-five minutes, Bowles, although quite interested in the position, became concerned about his ability to produce anything coherent in such a short amount of time. After Thomson's reassurances that it was quite feasible to write a review in the allotted time, he agreed to give it a try.

He made his debut on Friday, November 20, 1942, with a review of a Spanish orchestral work by Soutullo y Vert; the Monday edition contained two reviews, one of a piano recital of eighteenth-century pieces, the other of a WPA concert; the Tuesday paper had still another. The "trial run" rapidly became a regular assignment, and over the next few weeks Bowles's byline appeared on more than twenty reviews. Although he sweated over the first couple of pieces, he quickly realized that Thomson had been right; he was soon completing most reviews in half an hour or less.

That winter, Bowles's career as a reviewer, and his entire way of life, was put in jeopardy when he was called by selective service to report for a pre-induction examination. The physical part of the examination proceeded without a hitch, despite Bowles's long history of ailments, but when he went in to see the psychiatrist the situation rapidly changed. When asked how he thought he'd like the army, he explained that his one concern was that he would be unable to sleep because of noise, which being a composer he constantly endeavored to avoid. "The doctor looked at me with a suddenly aroused interest," Bowles wrote in his autobiography. "He reached out quietly and pulled a pair of scissors toward him across the surface of the desk—out of my reach, I noted. Then he said something very strange, with an inflection which made him sound as though he were reasoning with a small child: 'No one's going to hurt you.' . . . he went ahead questioning me, finally getting me to admit that I felt hostility toward him. Cheered by this confession, he went on from there. In the end he wrote: *Not acceptable. Psychoneurotic Personality.*" Bowles went home, "had a whiskey and continued my work."

With the concern over being drafted now ended, Bowles turned his attention to what would be the major event for him that spring—the production of *The Wind Remains,* which premiered on March 30, 1943, at the Museum of Modern Art. Yvonne de Casa Fuerte, working closely with Bowles, had recruited an all-star group. The work was produced and directed by Schuyler Watts, the orchestra conducted by Leonard Bernstein, and the rather extraordinary and fanciful set, worthy of being displayed by itself in the museum, was designed by Oliver Smith. Merce Cunningham did the choreography and danced the part of the clown. The singers were Jeanne Stephens, soprano, and Romolo de Spirito, tenor. But despite the stellar support, the opera did not receive rave reviews. The main reason seems to have been, as Bowles himself acknowledges, that "its text was an excerpt from a Surrealist play. It meant nothing and went nowhere."

Another major event also took place that spring, when on April 19 *Two Serious Ladies* was published. The immediate euphoria of seeing it in print, felt by Jane and some of those around her, was quickly dissipated by the reviews, both printed and spoken. Most of the "official" critics seemed baffled by it. "To attempt to unravel the plot . . . would be to risk, I feel sure, one's own sanity," wrote Edith Walton in the *New York Times Book Review*. Despite praise from Bowles, who went around giving out copies of the novel to anyone he thought might like it, and from Thomson and Latouche, others were less kind. Perkins thought the book too openly lesbian. Neither Jane's family nor Bowles's had a good word for it. Not surprisingly, it didn't make much money either, less than $150 in its first year of publication.

Jane, although keenly disappointed by the novel's reception, remained outwardly stoic. She told Bowles that she had always suspected the book wasn't any good anyway. While this response was undoubtedly a pose, she seemed somehow to be able to use this position to shrug off the negative criticism. She relied, as well, on her traditional remedies: socializing and drinking to excess. She also apparently began to have occasional brief affairs. All of these were simply distractions from the reality of the book's poor reception, from the daily quandary of existence itself.

Bowles, while aware of Jane's infidelities, did nothing to interfere, choosing instead to concentrate on his own pursuits. Indeed, he was riding rather high. Chick Austin, who years before had been an early supporter of Bowles's music through his Friends and Enemies of Modern Music concerts in Hartford, was now directing a revival of John Ford's Jacobean tragedy *'Tis Pity She's a Whore*. Bowles was signed to do the music. Although the production was small and only ran in Hartford, it marked his return to writing theater music. A few months later he was signed to do the incidental music for *South Pacific*, which before it became a well-known musical was presented as a play.

In addition, through his *View* and Kiesler connections, he was introduced to Peggy Guggenheim. They took a liking to each other. Soon, Guggenheim decided that she wanted to issue a series of recordings of contemporary music to complement the art she was showing in her Kiesler-designed gallery, Art of This Century. She decided on Bowles's work for her first recording. Five sides of the 78-rpm recording were devoted to his 1932 *Sonata for Flute and Piano* performed by René Le Roy, a highly regarded French flautist, and George Reeves on piano. Side six contained two lively

Mexican pieces, "El Bejuco" and "Sayula," with the young duo Arthur Gold and Robert Fizdale on twin pianos. The latter performers would later become virtuosos at performing Bowles, contributing much to his reputation in the late 1940s and early 1950s through their commissions and superb renditions of his work. The cover of the album was done by Guggenheim's husband at the time, Max Ernst.

Bowles was soon able to return the favor. As the summer approached, Guggenheim decided that she wanted to rent a vacation home in Connecticut, but learned from friends that the lakefront community excluded Jews. Determined, nonetheless, to take the house, she persuaded Bowles to rent the property in his name, a scheme to which he readily agreed.

During that year, Bowles and Jane also became friendly with a number of other composers, including Samuel Barber, Gian-Carlo Menotti, David Diamond, and John Cage. It was a period of parties, hard work, and frivolity. Despite the news of Harry Dunham's death in a bombing raid over Borneo in 1943, the war seemed to touch them little. Bowles felt no guilt, only relief at being 4F; and Jane, although Jewish, did not identify with, or (publicly, at least) express strong sentiments about, the annihilation of European Jews. Even when a childhood friend, Miriam Levy, came to see Jane in the late 1930s and described the Jewish refugee work that she was doing, Jane was relatively unmoved. "I had a feeling the whole thing didn't exist for Jane," said Levy. Caught up in their own lives and in their own social whirls, the Bowleses gave the impression of being indifferent to the entire situation. Part of their lack of concern may have been simply that, with the exception of Dunham, most of their close friends were not directly involved in the war. As a result, life went on more or less as it always had; indeed, the droves of European exiles only added to the cosmopolitan flavor of New York. With such a rich array of talented and intriguing people around them, the daily headlines could be easily ignored.

Besides, there was work to do. For Bowles, as 1943 ended, this meant composing the music for *South Pacific* and writing several reviews each week for the *Herald Tribune.* Jane, meanwhile, turned two of the excised sections from *Two Serious Ladies* into self-contained short stories.

In October, Bowles took a vacation from the paper: he wanted to visit Canada. Picking Jane up in Vermont, where she was staying with Perkins, they proceeded to Montreal by train. This was the first time since their honeymoon trip of 1938 that they had traveled alone together, and Jane was visibly nervous. To quell her anxiety, she drank one whiskey after another on the trip north. Upon arrival in Montreal, she suddenly passed out at the foot of the escalator leading to the main lobby. Bowles, with the help of others, stretched her out on a bench, and then got her into a taxi and to the hotel, where she quickly revived. After a brief rest, she was completely restored—although lacking any memory of what had happened—but it was clear that excessive alcohol consumption was beginning to have rather dramatic effects on her. Also clear was the insecurity that Jane felt when alone in Bowles's company, and the relative inability on his part to put his wife at ease. It took something as dramatic as losing consciousness for her to allow Bowles to demonstrate his concern and for Bowles to reach out to her.

Although Bowles did not know it at the time, there was another reason for Jane's fear on the ride up to Canada, which had to do with the transportation itself. In Mexico Jane and Perkins had been involved in a train wreck in which Jane had ended up with the arm of a dead man draped over her. Since the accident, she had developed a phobia about taking trains, which only contributed to her anxiety.

Apparently, after the initial incident in the railway station, the trip improved and both of them managed to enjoy themselves. Indeed, Bowles remembered that, "Although Montreal was dull, Quebec still looked French. . . . Absurdly, when I returned to New York, the city seemed a little less sinister and virulent because I knew that Quebec was nearby."

As 1944 began, in addition to the relentless schedule of reviewing, Bowles had some new projects lined up to keep him gainfully occupied. The first order of business was to provide a score for the Theatre Guild production of *Jacobowsky and the Colonel,* under the direction of Elia Kazan and Louis Calhern. Bowles, deciding on music that would be "full of nostalgia for prewar Paris," came up with what was by all accounts a delightful score, but the producers for some reason decided to have it reorchestrated. The result was bashed by reviewers: S. L. M. Barlow, for instance, grumbled that this "undeserved trick . . . ruined his ingenious *bal-musette* score." The show was nonetheless a success, paying Bowles's rent for a good many months.

His next project was a far cry from Broadway. In 1943, John Latouche had gotten involved with Belgian filmmaker André Cauvin, who was making a film on the Congo for the Belgian government in exile. Now that the film was finished, Latouche wanted Bowles to provide the music. Although initially hesitant about contributing to what he saw as essentially a propaganda film advocating colonialism, Bowles decided to do the music when he learned that they had enlisted Paul Robeson to narrate Latouche's script. Once he'd accepted the lucrative job, Bowles remembers that he thought it would be best to try to compose a score that would reflect the indigenous music. From Cauvin, who was by then back in the Congo, he received several records of native music. After listening to the recordings, he was struck by the way in which the Pygmy instrumentalists assigned one note to each man, but as part of a recurrent rhythmic pattern. It was this mode that he decided to imitate in several sections. The result, when played on Western instruments, is thoroughly unique and surely one of Bowles's most interesting, if not wholly successful, musical efforts. From the perspective of more than forty years, much of it seems a bit too contrived. Possibly if the original native instruments had been used it would have had a greater degree of authenticity. But Bowles is to be commended, if not for evoking the magic, at least for preserving much of the sonority and plaintiveness inherent in the original material.

The music that Bowles was called upon to write in 1944 was extraordinarily diverse. His next two commissions that year couldn't, in fact, have been more different from each other: The first was for another ballet, with sets by Salvador Dalí; the second, theater music for *The Glass Menagerie*.

The ballet came about, indirectly, through Oliver Smith. For some time he had been insisting that Bowles meet the Marqués de Cuevas, a wealthy supporter of the arts who had decided to found a ballet company in New York. One night at a party given by the marqués, he and Bowles began talking. The conversation soon turned to doing a ballet with Dalí as set designer. The idea appealed to Bowles and over the next few weeks the nobleman and Bowles talked about it some more. Finally, the marqués announced that he had decided that the ballet was to be based on a poem by Verlaine, "Colloque Sentimental," and that Dalí had already provided sketches. Bowles signed a contract and proceeded to compose the music, not with an eye to Dalí's possible design, but with an ear to Verlaine.

Having written and orchestrated the music in a hurry, Bowles decided a vacation was in order and promptly booked a flight to Mexico. He spent a month there by himself, most of the time near Manzanillo, on the Pacific coast. Returning to New York, he began writing reviews again and rehearsing his *Colloque Sentimental* score with the orchestra, under the direction of Alexander Smallens, who had conducted *Yankee Clipper* years earlier. Because of his reviewing commitments, he was unable to attend dance rehearsals, and therefore was largely unaware of how the production was shaping up. When he did finally manage to attend the dress rehearsal prior to the ballet's opening, he was shocked at how the production was staged:

> My heart sank as I saw the stage and what was happening on it. Eglevsky and Marie-Jeanne came on sporting underarm hair, great hanks of it that reached to the floor. There were men with yard-long beards riding bicycles at random across the stage, and there was a large mechanical tortoise encrusted with colored lights. . . . The *marqués* had assured me repeatedly that this ballet would have none of the usual Dalí capers; it was to be the essence of Verlaine, nothing more. I had been royally duped. . . . He [Dalí] was sitting directly in front of me with Gala, watching the rehearsal. All at once he swung around and said: *"Vous auriez dû être ici hier soir. Merde, c'était beau! J'ai pleuré."* [You should have been here last night. Jesus, it was beautiful! I cried.] I wanted to reply: *"Ce soir c'est mon tour."* [Tonight it's my turn.] Instead, I smiled vacuously and said: *"Vraiment?"* [Really?]

The reviewers generally agreed with Bowles. "Paul Bowles' beautiful score was wrecked by Dalí's usual outlandish weirdness," wrote *Newsweek*. S. L. M. Barlow, in *Modern Music*, while reporting that Bowles "wrote an excellent score, full of grace and mood," went on to denounce Dalí's set, "resplendent with . . . decomposing cadavers, huge eyes, stray fish, more and moribundia."

Although the general public might be expected to respond negatively to Dalí's sets, Bowles's own reaction is rather curious. How had the budding surrealist, whose credo was *épater le bourgeois,* become such an aesthetic conservative? Undoubtedly, part of the problem had to do with the fact that he had created music with Verlaine's symbolist poem in mind and felt that Dalí's surrealistic appropriation of it was antithetical to the score's sentiment or tone. Dalí himself seems also to have rubbed Bowles the wrong way. They had met at least twice before, once at the Askews' and once on Middagh Street. On the first occasion, Bowles had found Dalí excessive, domineering, and egoistic, but it was their meeting in Brooklyn that truly soured him. The source of the difficulty was a remark that Dalí made upon seeing a stray cat that Bowles was attempting to nurse back to health. Turning to Bowles, the painter informed him that he hated cats, above all, ones with sores. "This would not have been an endearing remark, even if made to an ailurophobe," comments Bowles. A battle line, if only in Bowles's mind, was apparently drawn that evening. At the very least, the ultra-reserved Bowles was hardly sympathetic to Dalí's flamboyant excesses, feeling that they were largely indulged in simply because they were excessive. Given Bowles's attitude, the collaboration was no doubt doomed from the start.

While still recovering from the blow dealt to *Colloque Sentimental,* Bowles was suddenly presented with another opportunity. It came in the form of a visit from the young man that had once knocked on Bowles's door in Acapulco, Tennessee Williams:

> He suddenly appeared one night at my New York flat with Donald Windham and Margo Jones and the script which he called *The Glass Menagerie.* He left it with me and said, "we have a production lined up and you'll only have the weekend. If you can write the music for it over the weekend it will be fine." And I had no contract. I had nothing. But . . . I wrote the music over the weekend. . . . and then . . . flew out to Chicago, arrived in a terrible blizzard. Laurette Taylor [the principal actress] was on the bottle, unfortunately. . . . The night of the dress rehearsal she was . . . found, unconscious, down by the furnace, by the janitor. And there was gloom, I can tell you, all over the theater because no one thought she was going to be able to go on the next night. She pulled herself together, as you know, and gave an historic performance the next night, and from then on. It was marvelous.

Even though written in a weekend, *The Glass Menagerie* is clearly one of Bowles's best theater scores. Lyrical, melodious, and often haunting, it is extraordinarily accomplished, fitting the mood of the play at seemingly every juncture. As in Chicago, the reviews of the play and music, after it moved to Broadway in March of 1945, were all raves. "Paul Bowles has added a score which has every desirable quality of discretion and salience combined," wrote S. L. M. Barlow. "It has character and profile, also the peculiar timbres and combinations for which Bowles has so felicitous an aptitude; yet the music stays where it belongs, emphasizing the nostalgic moods of the nocturne on stage." When a remake of the movie was produced in 1987, Henry Mancini was so taken with Bowles's original score that he retained "Jonquils" (the *Glass Menagerie* theme), and indeed, based his own treatment on the foundation laid by Bowles.

While *The Glass Menagerie* initially only provided Bowles with a powerful vehicle to write some of his most sensitive music, the long-term consequences were even greater, for through this collaboration a close friendship with Williams was formed that would endure until the latter's death.

From the time Bowles returned from Mexico he scarcely had a moment to think of much else but the next reviewing assignment or musical commission. Although during this period he had written some of his best music, displaying in each composition an inordinate degree of versatility and mastery, he was open to a new direction as 1945 began. With the financial success of plays such as *Watch on the Rhine* and *The Glass Menagerie,* he was also in a position to become a bit more choosy about assignments. He did not think at the time, though, that words would begin to overtake music within the next few years, that the new direction in his life would come from tapping into a creative fount that had largely lain dormant inside him since his adolescent experimentations. Although there would be more music, including some of his best serious works, a chapter was slowly beginning to close on the life of Paul Bowles, composer. As the final pages turned, it was not just a chapter, but a new volume that was unfolding, a volume entitled: Paul Bowles, writer.

CHAPTER 18

Bowles's transition from a man of music to a man of letters came about very gradually. Indeed, if one looks at his artistic production for the years 1945 and 1946, music still dominates. In those two years alone Bowles wrote the music for six major theater productions, two little theater puppet plays (one for Jane's puppet play, *A Quarreling Pair*), the *Concerto for Two Pianos*, and the four *Blue Mountain Ballads* on lyrics by Tennessee Williams. In addition, there are more than half a dozen songs and several short classical pieces.

But there is another record of production from those years, a verbal one, regarded then by most as simply a sideline that the polymath Mr. Bowles also engaged himself in from time to time. For Bowles, though, writing was becoming an increasingly compelling activity. It was at first through translation that he found himself working his way back into literature, in part through his association with *View* magazine. Edited by Charles-Henri Ford and Parker Tyler, the magazine was one of the most avant-garde periodicals of its time. Although Bowles's first piece for *View* in 1943 had been, not surprisingly, an article on jazz, by 1944 he had begun doing translations from French and Spanish for them. They also had published his "Bluey: Pages from an Imaginary Diary," his childhood piece from late 1919–early 1920.

At the beginning of 1945 Bowles was given the task of putting together, in the capacity of guest editor, an issue devoted to tropical America. John Meyers, who was managing editor of the magazine at the time, remembers that "Bowles was the perfect person to edit a whole issue of *View* devoted to tropical America. He had been collecting all sorts of material during his travels through South and Central America and the Caribbean."

But the material he had been collecting was, to be sure, not a tourist's view of Latin America. The issue, Myers wrote, "demon-

245

strated to what extent Bowles was drawn to the magical and supernatural, and the strangeness to be found among other peoples,
other ways of life. . . . Bowles presents a dazzling array of words
and images, texts both ancient and primitive. There are stories,
votary collages, a suffusion of pagan and Christian incantations,
rituals, horseplay." Not only was Bowles the editor of the issue, he
was also the main translator, collage artist, and in one case, an
original contributor.

Bowles did not take credit for his own contribution, however,
pretending instead that he simply was the translator, and that the
story was a factual account of an incident culled from the pages of
a contemporary Mexican magazine. It was printed alongside another supposedly real event under the heading of "documents."
Both of the "documents," recounted in a straightforward, journal-
istic style, are stories of possession and murder. The first, Bowles's
invention, tells the tale of a woman who, guided by an "angel,"
proceeds to eat the hearts of young children. Four years later,
Bowles would rework and expand it, using it as the basis for his
story "Doña Faustina." The second "document," actually a passage from a short story by the Mexican writer Juan de la Cabada,
relates a story of witchcraft, in which a man who discovers that his
child has had a spell cast upon him, kills his mother, the supposed
perpetrator of the possession.

While Bowles's hoax can be looked at as simply a tongue-in-
cheek exercise, it can also be seen as an attempt on his part to get
back into fiction, a sort of trial run without the consequences that
always accompany personal authorship. How important his imaginary document really was in his return to writing fiction is impossible to say, but working with the native Mexican materials and
mythologies certainly played a major role in initially inspiring him.
Indeed, the first story from that period that he put his name to was
"The Scorpion," which with its mythic elements could also easily
have appeared in *View* as an example of local Mexican storytelling.
He recounted its genesis in his autobiography:

I had been reading some ethnographic books with texts from the
Arapesh or from the Tarahumara given in word-for-word transla-
tion. [One of these, "John Very Bad," appeared in the *View* that
Bowles edited.] Little by little the desire came to me to invent my

own myths, adopting the point of view of the primitive mind. The only way I could devise for simulating that state was the old Surrealist method of abandoning conscious control and writing whatever words came from the pen. First, animal legends resulted from the experiments and then tales of animals disguised as "basic human" beings. One rainy Sunday I awoke late, put a thermos of coffee by my bedside, and began to write another of these myths. No one disturbed me, and I wrote on until I had finished it. I read it over, called it "The Scorpion," and decided that it could be shown to others. . . . The subject matter of the myths soon turned from "primitive" to contemporary, but the objectives and behavior of the protagonists remained the same as in the beast legends. It was through this unexpected little gate that I crept back into the land of fiction writing.

It is interesting to note that Bowles found his way back into fiction in very much the same manner that he had originally been led to it. As in childhood, animal stories provided the necessary conduit for the imagination. And the method, automatic writing, was the way in which he had first freed himself to write poetry and prose. But now, in addition to these older modes, Bowles's heavy immersion in myth and primitive narrative had a paramount influence on shaping this story and several others from these years. It was this additional force that powered his imagination, allowing him to become his own mythologist. In many ways, this particular method of creation is not terribly different from the technique he had been using so successfully over the years with musical composition. In pieces such as the "Huapangos," or even *The Wind Remains,* Bowles borrowed heavily from native rhythms. Now, although creating verbally, he took "found" elements, textures, and themes gathered from less sophisticated cultures in order to create his new, often deracinated narratives. It is a way of working that he has continued to use throughout his writing career.

"The Scorpion," one of Bowles's most mythic stories, tells of an old woman who lives alone in a scorpion-infested cave. She has no visitors, although an old man often stops on his way from the village to the valley and sits on a rock outside the entrance. One day her son comes to get her. She at first refuses to go, then finally tells him that she will leave the following day. That night she dreams she swallows, or possibly really swallows, a scorpion.

Awakening, she cries out, and her son, who has been waiting outside, takes this as a sign she is ready to leave. She does not disabuse him of the notion, but goes on her way. As she is leaving, the old man is sitting on the rock. He bids her good-bye. It is the first time that he has ever spoken to her, although he has known of her existence. Her son demands to know who he is. She says she does not know, whereupon the son angrily accuses her of lying.

It is a strange story, one that defies easy interpretation. Bowles himself has acknowledged that he has no idea what it means: "It's an enigma, even to me. It came right out of the unconscious. It wasn't made, it was formed. . . . That often produces the best things, to start before you know what you're going to write. As you build, sentence by sentence and inference by inference, you make a story."

He gave "The Scorpion" to *View*. It was well received, and Bowles went on inventing myths. Later that year he also published in *View* another of his "mythic" stories, "By the Water," a terrifying tale of a young Arab, Amar, who is pursued by a deformed, crablike human creature called Lazrag. Commenting on its origins, Bowles noted that "it was an experiment in automatic writing. . . . I sat down with no previous idea in my head, wrote the thing without 'knowing' what I was writing, and at a certain point stopped, probably because I was physically tired, and called that the end."

Toward the end of 1945, after completing "The Scorpion" and "By the Water," Bowles began work on another piece of short fiction: "A Distant Episode." Although this story has many hallucinatory elements, it is not so obviously indebted to a mythic consciousness. One of Bowles's most powerful stories, the plot, as in much of his short fiction, is fairly simple: a French professor of linguistics goes to North Africa to study the Maghrebi dialect. Deep in the desert, he is seized by some local Reguibat nomads, has his tongue cut out and becomes enslaved to them. Tin cans are tied to his body and he is forced to perform preposterous dances for the amusement of his captors. Over the course of a year, living in a kind of delirium, he gradually begins to assume his new identity. When he finally is able to escape, he goes not to the police, but into the desert. The terror, inherent in the story line itself, is further accentuated by Bowles's detached narrative style, as precise, cold, and delicate as cut crystal.

"A Distant Episode" is also the first enunciation of what would become a major theme in Bowles's work, that of the interloping Westerner who confronts an alien culture and inevitably comes up short, realizing too late that his "civilization" cannot protect him. All of the novels and a good many of the short stories revolve around this central concern. Sometimes the consequences are not so dire as in "A Distant Episode," but even in the less obviously dark tales, there is an underlying sense of the impossibility for those of us in the West to understand, let alone penetrate, a "less civilized" culture. At the time, Bowles claims, he did not think of the fiction as having any consistent unifying principle. Nonetheless, "A Distant Episode" can be seen as a first and crucial step in Bowles's development of this central preoccupation. Two years later, when he was beginning to conceptualize his novel *The Sheltering Sky,* he began his thinking by evoking for himself "A Distant Episode." "I knew it was going to take place in the desert, and that it was going to be basically the story of the Professor."

But a novel was still not in the forefront of his mind in those days, occupied as he was with reviewing, writing music, and doing a considerable number of literary translations—from French or Spanish, mostly surrealist or fantastic, all on assignment for *View.* Nor was he only engaged in pursuits of the artistic imagination. Day-to-day existence still had to be lived and Bowles was as involved in it as ever. There were, in fact, two major changes in his life that year. The first involved moving from Kiesler's penthouse to an apartment at 28 West 10th Street; the second was that he decided at the end of 1945 to leave his post as regular reviewer for the *Herald Tribune,* accepting only to do reviews for the Sunday edition.

The move was more than just a change of locales; it was also a change of life-styles, as it reunited under the same roof, if not in the same apartment, Bowles and Jane. It was instigated by Oliver Smith who, fondly remembering the Middagh Street days, decided to try to set up a new household reminiscent of the one in Brooklyn Heights. Finding that the top three floors of an old brownstone were available, he talked Bowles, Jane, and Helvetia Perkins into taking the place with him. Bowles signed a lease for the top floor, Smith took the third, and Perkins and Jane, the second.

Although Jane was still greatly involved with Perkins, their life together was not all bliss. One aspect of their relationship was

presented by Jane in a very curious little puppet play written that
year for John Meyers, who in addition to managing *View* also was
engaged in putting on what he called "bizarreries." The playlet,
called *A Quarreling Pair,* is ostensibly a conversation between two
sisters, Harriet and Rhoda. Harriet is the older, "stronger looking" puppet, more concerned with appearance and pretension.
Rhoda, by contrast, is more tortured, less able to conform. The
dialogue is biting, obsessional, absurd in a Beckettian way. It is also
filled with Jane's concerns at the time:

RHODA   I suppose it's wicked to squeeze love from a small heart. I
         suppose it's a sin. I suppose God meant for small hearts to
         be busy with other things.

HARRIET Possibly. Let's have our milk in my room. It's so much more
         agreeable to sit in here. Partly because I'm a neater woman
         than you are.

RHODA   Even though you have a small heart, I wish there were no
         one but you and me in the world. Then I would never feel
         that I had to go among the others.

Going "among the others" was in fact what Jane was doing at
the time, apparently having rather frequent affairs—one of them,
with a woman from Boston, of some consequence. In love with
Perkins, loving Bowles, she nonetheless could not feel that either
of them had hearts large enough to encompass her.

Despite the turbulence in Jane's personal life, the period was a
productive one for her. In addition to *A Quarreling Pair,* she completed her story "Plain Pleasures" and began work on a long play,
In the Summer House. Writing was still not easy, but she was able,
at least, to put down a few words each day on paper. Bowles
recalled just how difficult this was for Jane:

It cost her blood to write. Everything had to be transmuted into
fiction before she could accept it. Sometimes it took her a week to
write a page. This exaggerated slowness seemed to me a terrible
waste of time, but any mention of it to her was likely to make her stop
writing entirely for several days or even weeks. She would say, "All
right. It's easy for you, but it's hell for me, and you know it. I'm not
you. I know you wish I were, but I'm not. So stop it."

Despite her anxiety over Bowles's judgment, she still sought his approval; likewise, he regarded her as his "literary confidante." "We showed each other every page we wrote. I never thought of sending a story off without discussing it with her first," he said.

Reading and criticizing Jane's work also helped spur Bowles to embark on writing fiction himself. He had gone over *Two Serious Ladies* with her "again and again, until each detail was as we both thought it should be. Not that I put anything into what she had written. We simply analyzed sentences and rhetoric. It was this being present at the making of a novel that excited me and made me want to write my own fiction." When Bowles did begin to write several years later, he was encouraged by Jane. Although she was clearly envious of the apparent ease with which he could write, she did not seem to regard him as a rival, nor he her.

During this period, however, he was quite reticent about proclaiming himself a writer in her presence; indeed, he often insisted that he was really a composer. This finally provoked a response from Jane, as it was becoming quite clear that he was in fact changing his art. In a letter she told him, "I don't mind how much better or worse you write than I do as long as you don't insist that I'm the writer and not you. We can both be, after all, and it's silly for you to go on this way just because you are afraid to discourage me."

There were other jealousies, though. During this same period Bowles began to develop a very close relationship with an Australian composer, Peggy Glanville-Hicks, who was residing in New York with her husband, an Englishman named Stanley Bate, also a composer. Her marriage, however, was also considerably troubled, as Bate frequently abused her physically. In Bowles, she found a true kindred spirit, and perhaps more. Virgil Thomson noted that "Peggy was wildly in love with Paul, and Paul was just as charming as he could be to her. I doubt if they had a physical relationship. But they were very, very close." In return for Bowles's friendship, "she did all sorts of things to get his music published and recorded."

During the time Bowles lived on 10th Street, Glanville-Hicks was his "almost constant companion." They frequently had lunch or dinner together and often accompanied each other to concerts or the theater. Inevitably there was a certain amount of gossip as to the nature of their relationship. This naturally reached Jane, and even though she was physically detached from Bowles, she became jealous of his relationship with his fellow composer. Bowles's response was to ignore Jane's fits of jealousy, steadfastly refusing to give in to her desire that he limit his association with Glanville-Hicks.

A curious document—a reading of Bowles's fortune—survives from 1945, which could easily be discounted save for its accuracy in pinpointing certain aspects of his character—and strangely enough, in predicting his eventual success:

Talent and personal circumstances (7)

Destiny (8)

Contradiction and conflict involved: introvert character, extrovert expression indicated. No talent for making money or for personal success or ambition yet success, money, power on a large scale quite possible either through commercialization of ideas or by endowment or bequest. (This could be determined by a horoscope no doubt.)

Slow to develop: feels a kind of world-idea or cosmic soul and has no time-sense. Marked affinity for numerals and metals. Has a sense of having to work out a destiny either consciously or unconsciously and acts as if impelled to do unconventional things. Not really as unconventional as he thinks he is—except in being totally unable to settle down. A born nomad he feels the natural state of man is to wander. Possesses all the necessary faculties for research or invention of an important kind except concentration on a single object and a sense of time.

Philosopher, inventor, mechanically and mathematically endowed. Much more intellectual than emotional, finds it almost impossible to establish personal relationships. Very poor correspondent. Extremely obstinate and hard to change in any way except through logic.

This year 1945 a (7) year for him corresponding to his own talent number so all personal characteristics intensified to highest point. *Next year* (1946) his *destiny* year (money success power) so if possible should *unify* efforts in some way so as to benefit to the highest degree from the atmosphere of power which will surround him.

While it is folly to try to make a great deal out of this reading, it is impossible not to note certain uncanny correspondences between Bowles's actual character and life, and those noted by the fortune-teller. Of the character assessment, the notions of Bowles being consciously or unconsciously driven to work out a destiny and the emphasis on his inability to express his emotions particularly ring true. His penchant for peripateticism was, of course, also a major trait. As for the reader's predictions, Bowles largely fulfilled them as well, achieving within the next few years "money, success and power." Although during this period he consulted a fortune-teller on more than just this occasion, it is uncertain how much credence Bowles gave to the readings. It is the case, however, that he never destroyed the document, whereas letters, manuscripts, and other memorabilia disappeared with frequency.

In early July, Bowles and Oliver Smith took a month-long trip together to the Caribbean and Central America. "I'm such a masochist when it comes to the tropics and their curses that I enjoy everything as soon as the first horror has worn off or become a habit," Bowles wrote to Marian Chase from El Salvador.

It was also through Smith that Bowles took on another project that year, an adaptation (as Bowles preferred to call it) of Sartre's *Huis Clos.* He had first become aware of the play in late January 1945, while convalescing from a tonsillectomy. Reading *Horizon* magazine, he came across a review of the English production, which had been called *Vicious Circle.* When Smith came to visit, he told him about it. Smith was immediately enthralled and decided to try to acquire the American performance rights; Bowles, naturally, would provide the dramatic translation. As Sartre was then currently in America as part of a contingent of French journalists, they quickly tracked him down and arranged to meet him at the Statler Hotel in Washington. The contract was signed over lunch.

Once the rights were acquired, Smith did not rush to produce it. Indeed, Bowles would not begin work on the adaptation for nearly a year, as it would take Smith time to raise capital and to find actors, a director, a theater, and a set designer. When the production did finally come together, John Huston directed and Kiesler designed the set; the actors were Claude Dauphin and Annabella, both imported from France, along with Ruth Ford and Peter Kass. Bowles's translation is smooth and idiomatic, but not particularly elegant. While faithful to the original in most respects, there are a number of minor changes, the most significant being that the leading character, Garcin, a pacifist Brazilian, becomes in Bowles's version, Cradeau, a French collaborator. These changes, however, were not Bowles's doing.

> There were difficulties connected with *Huis Clos.* John wanted to particularize the references made to his past life by the male character upon his arrival in hell; by substituting political for metaphysical motivations he hoped to enliven the argument for the American public, which he considered generally incapable of appreciating the play's existentialist basis. I was against any changes being made in the script, but my secondary status in the venture was made clear to me at a succession of meetings called for the purpose of making a series of just such textual alterations with an eye to "Americanizing" the material. . . . Sartre got wind of what was afoot and sent me a cable of protest from Paris. John's opinion, however, was that Sartre was surrounded by busybodies who hoped to sabotage the American production. He believed that he was clarifying the play rather than weakening it. Very likely the drama was made more immediately interesting to a great portion of the New York public by being presented in this way, but since it was done by injecting political concepts into a primarily philosophical argument, it seemed not only unethical but self-defeating. However, I had agreed to "adapt" *Huis Clos* to the satisfaction of the producers.

Although the translation was not particularly difficult, it was not so easy to come up with an English equivalent for the title. Months went by; lists, with allusions to literature and the Bible, were drawn up in a search for a concise but provocative name for the play. Finally, in the subway one day, the title appeared to Bowles as he was attempting to go out the "in" turnstile. Unable to proceed, he noticed before him the printed words NO EXIT. Both Smith and Huston immediately accepted this solution, and every subsequent English translation of the work has used Bowles's title.

While from an artistic standpoint Bowles may have been right about not wanting changes in the *No Exit* script, Huston apparently knew his public. When the play opened on November 26, 1946, Brooks Atkinson, writing in the *New York Times,* gave it a rave review, crediting Bowles with conveying in his "excellent" and "idiomatic" translation the "knife-edge dexterity" of Sartre's writing. The public and other critics agreed; the play was a great success in New York and went on to receive the Drama Critics' Award for best foreign play that year. Only Thornton Wilder disagreed with the general attitude. Taking Bowles aside on opening night he informed him that his translation was totally unsatisfactory: "You stick to your music and you'll be better off."

While Bowles acknowledged that Wilder was correct in his assessment of the translation, he did not heed his advice about sticking to music. Continuing to work on his stories during this period, he managed to publish "The Echo" in *Harper's Bazaar* in September 1946, and in January 1947 *Partisan Review* printed "A Distant Episode." Bowles felt that with this latter publication he had truly become launched as a writer, as *Partisan Review* was one of the more discriminating and important literary magazines of the period. Taken seriously by the literati, Bowles now felt himself on firm ground as a writer of fiction. Where this would lead him, however, he didn't know, but he was resolved to pursue it as a profession rather than as a sideline to his activities as a composer or translator.

There has always been much conjecture among Bowles's friends and critics as to why Bowles decided to change artistic directions. In 1952 Bowles told an interviewer that he had "always felt extremely circumscribed in music. It seemed to me there were a great many things I wanted to say that were too precise to express in musical terms. Writing music was not enough of a cathartic." Some years ago he claimed that what happened was that he became increasingly dissatisfied with doing theater work: "I always seemed to find myself doing what someone else had done. I furnished music which would embellish or interpret the ideas of others; this is taken for granted, of course, in the writing of functional music. . . . To my way of thinking I was only marking time. . . . I was made aware of a slowly increasing desire to step outside the dance in which inadvertently I had become involved." More recently, he has said simply that he "didn't want to live in New York any longer."

Virgil Thomson has a slightly different theory: "Why did Paul do anything? He found out quite simply that he could make more money writing." Thomson also feels that Bowles's lack of formal musical education began to hinder his ability to create the more serious classical compositions expected of a composer in middle age: "Anybody without a musical education copies what's around, and Paul's music was always sweet and charming but the most advanced thing he knew or could handle was Ravel." Ned Rorem for his part, feels that Bowles really only left music behind when he discovered that his writing brought him far more accolades in one year than his music had in all the years he had been composing.

No doubt a combination of factors were ultimately responsible for his "cutting the composing chord," but they all seemed to coalesce toward the spring of 1947. His first step on this road was a decision to try to collect the various stories he'd been writing over the last couple of years into a book. Dial Press invited him to come around to their offices and discuss the prospects. Once there, however, Bowles was told that no publisher would buy a collection of stories by someone who had not already published a novel, and that furthermore, he needed an agent. They then offered to hook him up with one and on the spot telephoned the William Morris agency. A week or so later, Bowles had lunch with a young woman from the agency, Helen Strauss. As they parted, he handed her his "collected stories" to read. She said she'd look them over and get back in touch with him soon.

Another important event in this direction took place at about this time: he dreamed of Tangier. "This dream was distinctive," Bowles later wrote, "because although short and with no anecdotal content beyond that of a changing succession of streets, after I awoke, it had left its essence with me in a state of enameled precision: a residue of ineffable sweetness and calm." Through the whole day, Bowles continued to feel the presence of the "magic city." "It did not take me long to come to the conclusion that Tangier must be the place I wanted to be more than anywhere else."

Suddenly dream and reality converged. Helen Strauss called Bowles with the news that Doubleday had offered him a contract and an advance on a novel. "Once I had signed the contract I began to make plans for my trip to Tangier." Shortly afterward, the outline of the novel came to him:

> I got the idea for *The Sheltering Sky* riding on a Fifth Avenue bus one day going uptown from Tenth Street. I decided just which point of view I would take. It would be a work in which the narrator was omniscient. I would write it consciously up to a certain point, and after that let it take its own course. You remember there's a little Kafka quote at the beginning of the third section: "From a certain point onward, there is no turning back; that is the point that must be reached." This seemed important to me.

On that same bus ride, he devised the title:

> Before the First World War there had been a popular song called "Down Among the Sheltering Palms"; a record of it was at the Boat House in Glenora, and upon my arrival there each summer from the age of four onward, I had sought it out and played it before any of the others. It was not the banal melody which fascinated me, but the strange word "sheltering." What did the palm trees shelter people from, and how sure could they be of such protection? . . .
>
> The book was going to take place in the Sahara, where there was only the sky, and so it would be *The Sheltering Sky*.

The Bowles family around 1913. Claude is in the middle row on the far left; Rena is in the front row, second to the right. Henrietta Winnewisser holds Paul on her lap while August, seated next to them, stares proudly into the camera.

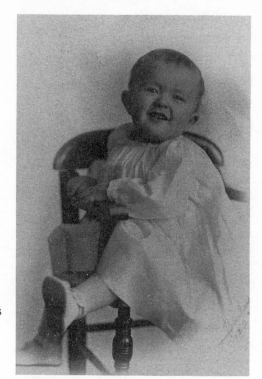

Paul, about a year after the attack on his life by Claude.

Self-portrait of the artist at a very young age.

The young author of "Bluey."

Photo-booth picture with Bowles's inked embellishment, sent to Bruce Morrissette from Paris in 1930. The French phrase translates as "and who sees the mystery."

The young dandy in North Africa, in the early 1930s. Gertrude Stein disapproved of Bowles's wardrobe, remarking that he had "enough [clothes] for six young men."

Bowles in the Sahara, in the winter of 1932.

Colonel Williams flanked by Bowles and John Widdicombe. The photo was taken in Fez, in 1934, during Bowles's brief employment as Williams's secretary at the American Fendouk.

John Latouche, Paula Miller Strasberg, Aaron Copland, and Edwin Denby in a scene from the 1936 Rudolf Burckhardt film *145 W. 21*. Bowles supplied the music.

Another scene from *145 W. 21:* Virgil Thomson, Bowles, and Edwin Denby burlesquing at a burlesque show.

Virgil Thomson in 1936,
at about the time he was
helping Bowles with *Horse
Eats Hat.*

Man of music and letters, and rising star, taken by Carl Van Vechten.

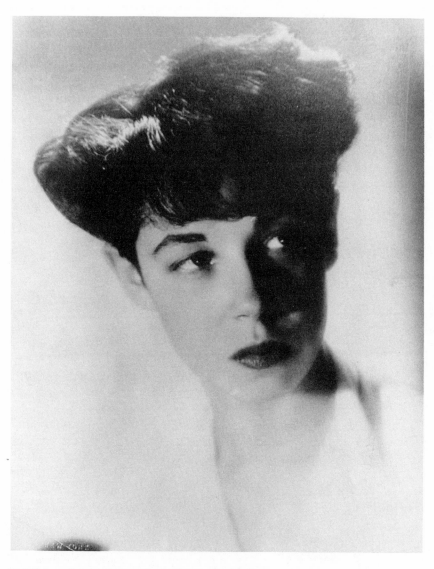

Publicity photo of Jane from the early 1940s.

The Bowleses with Oliver Smith, as captured by Irving Penn in May 1947.

Southern Mexico, early
1940s: "an impassable
wilderness of bare, thorny
trees and cacti."

The author of *The Sheltering
Sky* in a writerly pose.

"Not a very good picture of me, I'll admit, but very recent," Bowles wrote. "Taken in the new part of town. Janie and I were on our way to the beach for lunch." The Jaguar was bought with the proceeds from *The Sheltering Sky.*

Surveying Hong Kong harbor in 1955.

Bowles with Rena in Tangier, 1956.

In Rome, working on the screenplay for Lucchino Visconti's film *Senso*. From left to right are Ahmed Yacoubi, Tennessee Williams, Frank Merlo, Mohammed Temsamany, and Bowles.

Ahmed Yacoubi.

Even in the tropics, Bowles always managed to dress impeccably.

In the summer of 1961, the Beats descended on Tangier. From left to right: Bowles, Allen Ginsberg, William Burroughs, Gregory Corso, and Michael Portman pose in the garden of the Villa Muniriya, Burroughs's hotel. Ginsberg recalled that the group spent the day taking pictures of one another.

Jane on the terrace in the early 1960s, with Tangier in the background.

The Inmueble Itesa,
Bowles's apartment house
in Tangier. His three-and-
a-half room flat is on the
top floor.

Bowles and Mohammed Mrabet take tea at a café in Tangier.

Bowles on his terrace in Tangier, at the age of 76.

PART V

"... And Morocco Took Over"

CHAPTER 19

W<small>HEN THE</small> SS *Ferncape* sailed out of Brooklyn harbor on July 1, 1947, bound for Casablanca, it carried among its passengers Bowles and a friend the Bowleses had known in Mexico, Gordon Sager. Jane remained behind in New York, telling Bowles that she would probably follow within six months. Bowles considered himself fortunate to be on board, for he had nearly missed the boat. On the morning of his departure his passport, which he had seen the night before, could not be found. After an extensive search it was located hidden in the back of Jane's drawer. At the time she claimed not to have any remembrance of putting it there, but after his arrival in Morocco she wrote him: "As for packing your passport away—I thought it was mine—I looked to see whose picture was in it—and I dimly remember my own face and not yours." On board the *Ferncape,* Bowles spent most of his time writing a new story, "Pages from Cold Point." He "finished it the day before we got to Casablanca. . . . Then we landed and Morocco took over."

It did indeed take over. Going up to Fez, exhilarated with being back in Morocco, he lived "in a state of perpetual excitement." It was there that he began working on the novel. As he had imagined, the writing came easily:

> I had already chosen my method regarding the selection of descriptive detail. The structure and character of the landscape would be supplied by imagination (that is, by memory). I would reinforce each such scene with details reported from life during the day of writing, regardless of whether the resulting juxtaposition was apposite or not. I never knew what I was going to write on the following day because I had not yet lived through the day.

Over the next several months, the book gradually began to take shape in this fashion. It was not so much daily events that found their way into the novel, as the amplification of memory along with the newly reexperienced textures, sights, and smells of Morocco. Bowles recalled that he really had no sense of what was going to happen to his characters as they made their way deeper into the desert. "I thought whatever would happen, would happen." Only the Lyles, the mother and son duo who make a number of brief but important appearances in the novel, were drawn from his daily experience. They were modeled on a strange couple named the Perrins, whom Bowles kept bumping into seemingly everywhere he went in the first few months after his arrival. Precisely because they are drawn from immediate experience, Bowles later came to regard their inclusion as the novel's "biggest flaw." Although they "gave the book a sense of reality," he explained, "they are painted with a different set of paints," not in keeping with the predominant tone of the novel.

Just as the novel is constructed around a journey, Bowles was himself quite peripatetic during the period in which he was writing it. Fez was, in fact, only an initial stop; over the next few months he went up to Tangier, then over to Spain. By the fall, though, he was back in Tangier, ensconced in a two-room cottage at the Hotel El Farhar, directly opposite the place on the mountain where he had spent the summer of 1931 with Aaron Copland.

For company, he bought an Amazon parrot; for diversion, he wandered the streets of Tangier, particularly in the Medina and Casbah. It was on one of these meandering walks that he began to ponder the idea of purchasing one of the empty houses that he seemed to keep coming across fairly frequently. Inquiring about their cost, he was told that they ranged from $250, for a small one, to $2,000 for a villa. Even in 1947, these prices were astonishingly low, and Bowles quickly decided to buy a little house. He settled on one for about $500, but as he was running short on cash, he wired Oliver Smith, asking him if he were interested in going in with him. Smith cabled him on October 18, saying that if Bowles truly wanted it he would send him some money, at the same time letting him know that he questioned the practicality of the purchase.

Bowles responded that he indeed was keen on it; Smith wired him the money and the house was bought. This greatly annoyed Jane. In a letter to him in late October of that year, she wrote:

Everyone seems to know about your buying a house in Africa except myself. . . . I just *happened* to be in town when Oliver got your wire and I of course advised him to send the $500. I knew you were getting a kick out of the house and I cannot help but want your pleasure. I was hurt though that you had written to Oliver and Bob Faulkner about it and yet no word to me. In your letter to Oliver you don't sound at all as though you expected us *both* to come over but only he. He refuses however to go without me and perhaps you didn't expect that he would. I know that you asked me over in a letter to me but that was before this house came on the scene, and possibly now you feel instinctively that it is all wrong for me.

Bowles, in fact, had been urging Jane to come in more than one letter, but she had continually found one excuse after another to stay in New York. The hurt expressed in the October letter was transformed by December into annoyance about him pressing her to come. She chided him for making assumptions about her arrival before Christmas: "I think it is rather mean of you not to be more careful of what you say when you know how easily upset I am and how quickly guilty even when I know I'm not in the wrong. I don't know where on earth you got the idea that I would arrive suddenly in Tangier." This vacillation on Jane's part continued for another six months. She concluded one letter from this period by acknowledging and attempting to explain her inability to move: "I miss you very much indeed and want to see you naturally. If ever you are troubled or puzzled about my inertia just imagine everything you feel about 'setting out' in reverse!! Of course I vacillate but I have come a long way nonetheless. I can now actually imagine the trip alone without exactly shuddering."

Making the trip alone was, in fact, a major obstacle for Jane. She was also apprehensive about whether she would like Morocco, and whether she would be able to find any romance among the local women. To Bowles she wrote: "I am . . . all the time marvelling more and more over at American womanhood. It is nice to find as many miracles as I do but perhaps it is time I rested my overblown heart and looked at some Arab houses. Heaven knows I shall be made nervous over there by the absence of any charming possibilities, whereas for you and Ollie [Smith] it will be just the opposite."

In addition to these concerns, she was quite busy finishing her play *In the Summer House,* working on a story and on a novel, *Out in the World* (never finished), while also trying to end gracefully her long affair with Helvetia Perkins. At the same time she was becoming quite involved romantically with a woman from Massachusetts named Jody, whom she was trying to persuade to accompany her to North Africa. Her friendship with Libby Holman was also deepening. Although she had actually met Holman with Bowles in 1945 through John Latouche, by the summer of 1947, with Bowles in North Africa, she began to see more and more of her, spending weeks at a time at her house in Connecticut.

The other major task for her that autumn was dealing with Bowles's apartment on West 10th Street, first by sorting out his belongings, and then trying to sublet it. Indeed, cleaning up after Bowles was apparently a major task, as he had made no attempt to put any of his things in order before he left for Morocco. Jane, in fact, was furious at "the havoc of your clothes and pure junk left around the apt. . . . The number of filthy articles that were simply stuffed into the closets is unbelievable. It was like cleaning out an old Vermont farmhouse—the dirt left by two generations of maniacs." For several hundred more words she continued, finally telling him that "you do not live in an apartment but in a *storeroom* with a little space in the middle!" With order finally restored, though, she did manage to sublet it, much to Bowles's relief, as he was finding his cash supply steadily dwindling and did not need the expense of keeping up a vacant apartment.

While Jane fretted, cleaned, wrote, and attempted to extricate herself from Perkins, Bowles was working steadily on the novel. Although he had not planned it in advance, he finally reached the point in *The Sheltering Sky* where he knew that his protagonist, Port, was going to die. "Very consciously I had always avoided writing about death because I saw it as a difficult subject to treat with anything approaching the proper style; it seemed reasonable, therefore, to hand the job over to the subconscious," recalled Bowles. But even with this conscious decision, he was having considerable difficulty. Finally, he hit upon a stratagem that he hoped would sufficiently provoke the subconscious into producing the necessary state of being that could in turn induce the "proper style": a local drug, made from cannabis, called *majoun.* Although he had smoked kif (a mixture of cannabis and tobacco) on several occasions, as he didn't inhale, he had never felt much of an effect;

as *majoun,* however, was a cannabis jam and taken internally, he felt it might have more profound effects. He got the address of a house in the Medina where *majoun* could be purchased, then went back up the hillside to a point on a rock high above his cottage to consume it.

> The effect came upon me suddenly, and I lay absolutely still, feeling myself being lifted, rising to meet the sun. For a long time I did not open my eyes. Then I felt that I had risen so far above the rock that I was afraid to open them. In another hour my mind was behaving in a fashion I should never have imagined possible. I wanted to get off the boulders, down the mountainside, and back home as fast as I could. When I returned to the Farhar, the sun was low. I could see its pink light fading on the villas that edged the cliffs across the valley. There were cypresses outside the cottage; they stood unprotected, high above the sea, directly in the blast of the *cherqi,* which roared through them with a sound louder than that of the waves against the rocks. . . . Later that night I noted a good many details, and the next day wrote out much of the scene. . . . It is certain that the *majoun* provided a solution totally unlike whatever I should have found without it.

While the *majoun* no doubt freed Bowles's mind enough to imagine Port's death, the details themselves were largely derived from his memory of the typhoid delirium he had experienced years earlier in the American Hospital in Paris.

Relieved that he had finally managed to write what he regarded as the most difficult section of the book so far, he quickly came to realize that this was not the novel's end. He remembers thinking at the time that "the death of the main character does not make the book satisfactory. The book has to go on." But knowing that and knowing how to maintain the momentum were not the same. As he was still using the same technique of unplanned composition, he did not really know how to finish it, only that he had to find some way to "keep the book going." It was then that he came up with what he terms "Kit's madness." "It was the only way . . . of making it satisfactory."

In December Bowles went back to Fez. Acquiring more *majoun,* he continued to experiment with it, becoming better acquainted with its properties and the ideal conditions under which to ingest it; as before, it provided him with further ability to visualize events that could be worked into the novel. But the drug was no substitute for lived experience. To revive his memory of the desert and to escape the winter, he decided at the end of 1947 to leave Fez and head into the Sahara. He went first to Oujda, on the Algerian border, then crossed into Algeria itself, the setting for much of the novel. On the train from Oujda to Colomb-Béchar he wandered into the fourth-class coach. The scene of human chaos is described vividly in *The Sheltering Sky:*

> As she entered the car, her first impression was that she was not on the train at all. It was merely an oblong area, crowded to bursting with men in dun-colored burnouses, squatting, sleeping, reclining, standing, and moving about through a welter of amorphous bundles. . . . Stumbling over the crouched figures, she worked her way to one side of the windowless wall and leaned against it. . . . her fingers struck a small, soft object on the nape of her neck. She looked: it was a yellow louse. She had partly crushed it. With disgust she wiped her finger against the wall. Men were looking at her, but with neither sympathy nor antipathy. Nor even with curiosity, she thought. They had the absorbed and vacant expression of the man who looks into his handkerchief after blowing his nose.

It was not just physical elements that Bowles was appropriating for fictionalization. A great deal of the psychological tension that is centered on the relationship between Port, Kit, and Tunner has a genesis in reality, as well. The fact that there are three travelers, rather than just the two, is reflective of the Bowleses' way of traveling, as is the way in which Tunner is "invited" by Port to join them on the trip: "It was only at the last minute that Tunner had been asked to come along, and perhaps that, too, had been subconsciously motivated, but out of fear; for much as he desired the rapprochement, he knew that also he dreaded the emotional responsibilities it would entail." Once in the Sahara, however, Port realizes, as had Bowles, that "the longing for closer ties with [Kit] was proving stronger than the fear. To forge such a bond required that they be alone together." Tunner, however, at least in Port's mind, seems determined to frustrate any attempt for him to get close with his wife, a situation familiar to Bowles, whether it involved Bob Faulkner, Helvetia Perkins, or others. "He had been present with them all day and half the night, ceaselessly talking, and apparently without a wish in the world save that of sitting with them, eating with them, taking walks with them, and even going with them to Kit's room at night, when of all times Port wanted to be alone with her."

Like the Bowleses, Port and Kit have also reached a sexual impasse and turn to others for sexual gratification. Naturally, they also occupy separate rooms at each successive hotel. Although obviously loving each other, they are not in love, nor have they been for some time. Each attempts to act independently and each attempt fails. And yet publicly they seek to maintain the facade of marriage; defend each other against the outside, while internally feeling disquietude, vast uncertainty as to their actual mutuality. These are the elements that form the underpinning of the novel; and while Bowles will push the situation much further than it existed in actuality, it is as much these appropriations from psychological reality, as that from the physical experience of place, from his previous travels in the desert, that truly produce what Bowles has called "a novel from memory."

From Colomb-Béchar he continued by produce truck, the same sort upon which Port and Kit hitch a ride, to Taghit. There at the hotel he met a Swiss schoolteacher on holiday named Fräulein Wendling. In 1962, thinking back on this woman and her involvement and love for the pre-independent Sahara, he would write a poignant story, "The Time of Friendship," in which he imagines how independence would have affected both her relationship with a young Algerian and the Algerian's relationship with her. After a week or so in Taghit ("probably the most intensely poetic spot I've ever seen"), he continued deeper into the Sahara, first to Béni-Abbès and then to Timimoun. It was in Timimoun that he heard a tale from the local military commander that would stick in his imagination, ultimately being transformed the following year into surely one of his most terrifying and haunting stories, "The Delicate Prey." Open completely to ideas, to inspiration from his surroundings, he now gathered up material for stories and for the novel in the way he had previously unearthed indigenous melodies to rework as original compositions.

While still in the Sahara, in the town of Adrar, he received a cable from Jane. She announced her arrival in Gibraltar on January 30. In a vain attempt to meet her he flew from Adrar to Algiers in a small plane. As the pilot was "flying blind," they had to stop when the sun went down. Kit, at the end of the novel, makes a similar trip, sitting like Bowles in the copilot's seat. The next day Bowles arrived in Algiers to discover that Jane was already in Tangier with her new lover, Jody. On the third of February he finally managed to get himself to Tangier via Fez.

Although he had not seen Jane in seven months, and had been urging her in one letter after another to come, he apparently accorded her a rather diffident reception. "I can't believe that after ten years [of marriage] you would have secretly been expecting someone like yourself (or Edwin Denby) to arrive from Gibraltar," Jane wrote Paul some months later, after witnessing his eager anticipation at the arrival of Oliver Smith. In fact, the difficulties attendant upon her arrival were compounded by three main factors: first, she was with a new lover; in addition, having never been to Morocco before, she was undoubtedly experiencing a good degree of culture shock; finally, Edwin Denby arrived from New York just a few days later, thus putting Bowles in the position of being host to yet another visitor.

Once Denby arrived the four of them went to Fez, where Bowles looked up a young man he had met during the summer, a painter named Ahmed Yacoubi. Through Yacoubi he acquired some *majoun* prepared by Yacoubi's mother, in order to introduce the recently arrived Americans to what he regarded as a wonder drug. Jane, never one to consume anything in moderation, ignored Bowles's warning not to ingest too much. The results were disastrous for her. She spent the night hallucinating madly. At one point she became convinced that Bowles was in mortal danger; but this soon changed to fear that he was about to come in and murder her. This dual paranoia, to some extent, can be seen as a reflection of her own state of ambivalence about their relationship: she was at once worried about him and afraid of him.

Jane's fear of Bowles operated on several levels, centering on his disapproval—as she saw it—of her writing and her life-style, and on her own feelings of anxiety, guilt, and unworthiness. In the case of writing, she felt a mixture of envy and admiration at the ease with which he achieved artistic success, while she had to struggle so hard for it. Moreover, she could not help comparing herself to her husband, and now that he too was writing, she began to fear that she would seem somehow unworthy of his attention. In a letter written to Bowles prior to her arrival, she laid out this concern: "The plans are to come in Feb. I hope maybe to have done enough writing by then so as not to be completely ashamed and jealous when confronted with your novel. At the moment I can't even think of it without feeling hot all over. And yet if you had *not* been able to do it I would have wrung my hands in grief—I say this sincerely. If by Feb. I *haven't* done enough maybe I shouldn't come because you'll view me with such disgust."

There were other factors, as well. Jane sensed that in Morocco they were on unequal footing. Bowles was on familiar terrain, able to use it for inspiration; she, however, was less sure of what she could find in Morocco to inspire her and yet yearned to feel as he did. This concern resulted in her fearing that she would not fit into his world; that, in fact, as Bowles had exactly the sort of life he desired, he might feel that he had no use for her. As a result she continually expressed concern about him, hoping that by demonstrating how worried she was for his physical safety, for the progress of the novel, she would somehow be able to link herself to him. It is as if she felt that through this concern she could demonstrate her usefulness to him. The essence of this, of course, is fear of rejection.

In a letter written in July 1948, she directly expressed this notion:

> I was peculiarly disturbed by the fact that you lingered on in Fez with Edwin instead of rushing to the Farhar to see me. I felt very jealous and left out; I sensed that you were really better off with Edwin and that there would be an unfortunate comparison made at some future date. Alas! it came much sooner than I had expected it would and I have not ceased brooding about it yet; also I have never tried harder to be in your world—to see it the way you did which probably is why I was in such a foul temper the whole time. I wanted to be companionable and pleasant—a source of mild pleasure at meal times and otherwise calm and self-effacing. I am really and truly sorry that it turned out so differently.

While the emotion is genuine, the circumstances were, in fact, a bit different. What had happened was that after a few days in Fez,

Jane and Jody went off on their own to Marrakech, then to Spain for a few weeks until Jody returned to the United States. During this period, Jane was obviously quite engaged with her lover; however, she expected that once she was by herself in Tangier, Bowles would naturally return to be with her. When he did not, she began to feel the rejection she writes about in the letter.

The puzzle of their relationship, therefore, was considerably complex. While Jane was extremely desirous of independence—and when independent, not jealous of Bowles's similar assertion of his own need for free action—when alone she immediately began to feel unwanted, unworthy, and unloved. Bowles was often hard pressed to know when he needed to be responsive and when to leave her to her own devices. While in the first years of their marriage it was often Bowles who felt rejected, once in Morocco the situation was reversed. Here, Bowles was clearly in less need of her than she of him. That she sensed it was obvious, and this knowledge only contributed to her anguish. With the familiarity of surroundings stripped from her, and with no friend or lover to bolster her, she felt, perhaps more than ever in the past, the need to understand the true nature of her relationship with Bowles. "I am not attached to you simply because I'm married to you, as you certainly must know," she wrote to him. "Oliver thinks that I'm 'hanging on to you.' I hope you don't think that or that it isn't the actual truth even without your thinking it."

Bowles apparently did little to allay her fears, and in June of that year this state of anxiety produced a physical response. It happened, perhaps not so coincidentally, during Oliver Smith's visit. When he arrived in late May, the trio went up to Fez, Bowles's favorite Moroccan city at the time. There, Smith became quite ill and for a couple of weeks was in bed with a fever, Bowles serving all the while as nursemaid. During this same period, Jane suffered what appeared to be a heart attack. Consulting a local doctor, she was told that something was organically wrong with her heart, although later tests never showed any physical problems. Bowles, apparently, did not take her "heart attack" seriously (and claims to remember nothing about it today). He seems to have dismissed it at the time as a ploy to get attention. In the same July letter, she tried to explain again that this was not the case:

I hope that you did not really *think* I would *"pull* a heart attack" on the trip. . . . I can find only two explanations for such statements— either you never believed for a minute there was anything wrong at all or else you were really worried and therefore mean. . . . Sometimes I find nice explanations like the above for your attitude and sometimes I feel that you saw the whole thing, I mean the state of my health, as nothing but a threat to your trip, which mattered to you more than anything.

Despite these ups and downs in his relationship, Bowles managed to keep working on *The Sheltering Sky*. On May 10, 1948, he wrote to Peggy Glanville-Hicks that the book was finished, describing it as "a novel just like any other novel: a triangle laid in the Sahara." In fact, it is far more than that, as Bowles knew, though the basic plot can be described in just a few sentences: an American couple, Port and Kit Moresby, and their friend George Tunner set out into the Sahara. Port and Kit, married for twelve years, have reached an impasse in their sexual relations. Kit has a brief sexual encounter with Tunner; Port with an Arab prostitute. Tunner eventually goes off on his own while Port and Kit continue deeper into the Sahara, where Port contracts typhoid fever and dies. Kit wanders off into the desert and is picked up by a traveling caravan. She winds up deep in the desert, secretly married and sexually enslaved in the harem of Belqassim, the nomad who had rescued her. When her identity is discovered by the other wives, though, she is driven out of the house. After her "escape," she is brought back to Oran, but by now has descended into madness. The novel ends with her wandering off again to an unknown fate.

This plot summary, however, really gives nothing of the flavor of the novel, nor is it simply a "triangle set in the Sahara." In a surviving draft of a letter to James Laughlin, who eventually would become the book's American publisher, Bowles described *The Sheltering Sky* like this:

Really it is an adventure story in which the adventures take place on two planes simultaneously: in the actual desert, and in the inner desert of the spirit. . . . The occasional oasis provides relief from the natural desert, but the . . . sexual adventures fail to provide relief.

The shade is insufficient, the glare is always brighter as the journey continues. And the journey must continue—there is no oasis in which one can remain.

This is probably the best description of the book's "argument," as Bowles likes to call it, for it admirably captures the dual planes on which the novel is constructed; it demonstrates, as well, the relentlessness Bowles builds into the metaphysical and actual journey of his characters. While intertwined, the physical journey can be described easily; the metaphysical one is far more complex. Although Port and Kit are questers, there is no holy grail luring them onward. Their quest, in fact, is poorly defined in their own minds. More concerned with leaving behind the "mechanized age" than with actually going to something in particular, their journey is as much of an escape as it is a quest. Port prides himself on being a traveler rather than a tourist, defining the difference this way: "The [tourist] accepts his own civilization without question; not so the traveler, who compares it with the others, and rejects those elements he finds not to his liking. And the war was one facet of the mechanized age he wanted to forget."

From this premise, that of leaving industrial society behind, the book commences, but the journey also has other dimensions. For Port, a true traveler, the sense of deracination is not alienating, as it often is to the tourist, but comforting. On alien territory, he feels he can think better: "Whenever he was en route from one place to another, he was able to look at his life with a little more objectivity than usual. It was often on trips that he thought most clearly, and made the decisions that he could not reach when he was stationary." The decisions, however, are often of a less than profound nature. More often they simply involve conceiving of somewhere else to go; in exotic surroundings the pain of existence itself is alleviated by new distractions.

There is also, however, another aspect to the trip that cannot be overlooked, for in Port's mind he sees it as an attempt to rebuild his marriage which has been gradually disintegrating over twelve years: "He had felt a definite desire to strengthen the sentimental bonds between them. Slowly it was assuming an enormous importance to him. At times he said to himself that subconsciously he had had that in mind when he had conceived this expedition with Kit . . . into the unknown."

With these notions forming the psychological framework of the novel, ideas shared by Bowles himself, the quest away from nothingness into a possible something begins. But just as Sartre's characters found no exit in Hell, Bowles's find no exit, save madness or death, from the malaise of being in life. As the journey progresses, despite the characters' respective expectations, it is clear that Port and Kit will find only sand, sky, and rock in the Sahara, not the abstract enlightenment that they were seeking.

Although the philosophical outlook is clearly Bowles's own, and while many of the details are drawn from life and from his relationship with Jane, it is dangerous to assume, as many have, that Port is Bowles and Kit, Jane. While Bowles indeed derived many of the incidents and much of the tension from experience, many of the observations are memories. This is particularly the case with the theme of frustrated sexuality and failed attempts to strengthen the "sentimental bonds." Clearly Bowles drew his knowledge of this psychological situation from his own marriage, but at the time he was writing the novel he had reconciled himself—at least outwardly—to the marriage as it was. Indeed, the character traits of both protagonists, when they do reflect those of the Bowleses, are grossly exaggerated, pushed beyond the "point," as Bowles refers to it. In some ways *The Sheltering Sky* can be viewed as Bowles's exercising his imagination on his own life and relationship, positing a "what if?" construct onto his quotidian existence. Bowles later acknowledged this permutative element: "I think one is always writing about oneself. But you are writing about transformations of experience. In good writing, the works come out as something very different from the experience itself." By way of additional comment, he added: "Writing is, I suppose, a superstitious way of keeping the horror at bay, of keeping the evil outside."

CHAPTER 20

Wɪᴛʜ *The Sheltering Sky* finished, Bowles sent it off to his agent, Helen Strauss, figuring that that was the end of the matter, Doubleday having already contracted for it. But the relief and satisfaction of actually completing the book was short-lived, for Doubleday "unhesitatingly rejected it." In their letter to Bowles they explained that "they had contracted for a novel and [he] had produced something else." They did not attempt to explain what it was that he had given them, but did ask for a return of their advance. For several months, the book sat at William Morris while Helen Strauss attempted to find a publisher. James Laughlin of New Directions expressed interest, but did not commit himself.

Then the English publisher John Lehmann arrived in New York and met with his agent, Mike Watkins, who mentioned that he had been sent a first novel he thought Lehmann ought to read. Watkins told Lehmann, "It's a pretty strange book, and I'm not going to say anything more than that. Except that I don't see it on anyone's list in England except yours!" That rather odd endorsement piqued his interest and he asked to see it. When the manuscript arrived, Lehmann read it in one night, with "mounting enthusiasm." "[I] knew I had got hold of something of the utmost originality. I just couldn't understand why no publisher on either side of the Atlantic (for I was offered world rights) had seen what I saw in it." Lehmann immediately contracted for the book; James Laughlin followed suit a while later, agreeing to bring out the American edition a few months after Lehmann's.

While all of this was going on, Bowles, nearly broke, was meanwhile turning again to music to ensure his livelihood. That summer two projects presented themselves to him, both of which he accepted. The first was to write the music for a new Tennessee Williams play, *Summer and Smoke;* the second, to write another opera, this one for Libby Holman.

Although the play had first been performed in Dallas in 1945, it had not been accompanied by music. Now, however, with the Broadway production planned, Williams felt that music was needed and that Bowles was the man to furnish it. The director, Margo Jones, was initially reluctant to commission music from a man who was on the other side of the Atlantic; in fact, it took from February until late April for Williams to convince her that Bowles should and could do the job. Finally, on April 24 she cabled Bowles, inquiring whether he could furnish the music and how much it would cost. He wired her back at once, asking for a fee (mainly for his transatlantic passage) plus a percentage of the gross. Satisfied with his offer, she cabled Bowles again; he agreed to come to New York to write the score. Jane would stay in Tangier, as he thought at the time that he would be gone only a couple of months.

Arriving back in New York in early July, Bowles moved into Libby Holman's townhouse on 61st Street, and in a matter of weeks came up with a truly splendid score. Once it was completed, however, he did not rush back to Tangier, as he needed to go on the road with the show as well as be present at the New York opening. Even after the play opened on Broadway on October 6, 1948, following trial runs in Buffalo, Cleveland and Detroit in September, he remained in New York. There were several reasons for this: Gold and Fizdale were premiering his *Concerto for Two Pianos,* which they had commissioned from him in 1946, at Town Hall in November; in addition, Bowles was attempting to settle the arrangements for *The Sheltering Sky.* As he was now a visitor and not a resident of New York, he was able to enjoy what he could about the city, although he continued to grumble about it in letters to Jane and in remarks to friends with whom he socialized. He particularly saw a lot of Williams, Gore Vidal, Truman Capote, and Oliver Smith. In fact, during this trip he began to form real friendships with both Vidal and Capote, although he had to see them separately, as the two rival writers detested each other.

Jane, meanwhile, was involved in trying to secure the house that Smith and Bowles had bought in Tangier, a process that turned out to be enormously complicated. (It would, in fact, take another year and considerably more bureaucratic hurdles to overcome before Bowles would acquire the legal deed.) Jane spent her time attempting to get possession of the house and writing long letters to Bowles about the difficulties, along with numerous suggestions for renovative improvements.

She was also becoming emotionally preoccupied with an Arab woman named Cherifa, whom she had met through Bowles earlier that year. A handsome young woman of about nineteen or twenty, with wild, flowing jet-black hair and vivid, black eyes, Cherifa was a grain seller in the market in Tangier. Illiterate, monolingual in the Maghrebi dialect, she was rumored to be both a descendant of Tangier's patron saint and a lesbian. From the moment Jane met her, she was fascinated. By the summer the fascination had turned to obsession. Although Jane was also in pursuit of two other Arab women, it was Cherifa whom she most desired, finding her, not coincidentally, also the most elusive.

Over the summer and into the fall, in a number of letters to Bowles, she chronicled the nuances, the little successes and failures, the frustrations inherent in her attempts at seduction. Despite the myriad details, the message is basically the same from letter to letter: "Our relationship is completely static; just as I think that at least it is going backwards (on the days when she sneaks behind a stall) I find that it is right back where it was the next day. Nothing seems to move." One major obstacle, of course, was Jane's ignorance of Arabic. "I still have a dim hope that if I learned to speak Arabic she would be friendly *maybe* and I could sit in the *hanootz* [market stall] with her when I chose to."

Despite the stasis, and her inability to communicate in the language, she wrote Bowles that she truly loved being in Tangier, although she was bothered by the culture's very evident double standard: "I'm obliged to fight . . . a whole social structure, so different from the one you know—for certainly there are two distinct worlds here (the men's world and the women's). . . . I can understand how if one . . . were admired, courted, and feted, that one would *never, never* leave. Even so—without all that—and you've had it—I have never felt so strongly about a place in my life, and it is just maddening not to be able to get *more* of it."

The frustration she encountered with Cherifa was no less present with the other women she was courting. "I am crazy mad about Tetum," she wrote Bowles, "a hopeless, hopeless situation." In December she wrote Libby Holman that she had finally given up on her new pursuit, partly because of Cherifa's disapproval. "I have never understood why, but I am terrified of going against [Cherifa's] orders, and have therefore made an enemy of Tetum." This statement is extraordinarily prophetic, the terrible proof of it borne out as from year to year Jane would fall increasingly under Cherifa's control, become less and less able to contradict an "order." Among the other orders that Cherifa was giving Jane during this time was an escalating series of "requests" for money and objects that Jane felt powerless to deny her. "Between her and Tetum they have all my scarves, most of my money, my watch, and I am now taking Cherifa to the doctor's twice a week. . . . I feel that I have done everything, absolutely everything wrong, but perhaps something nice will happen anyway. I *would* love to have some fun again some day."

In addition to the obvious obsession with Cherifa, there was another, less evident one present in these letters: the need to confess, particularly to Bowles, her anxiety and her failure in love. One of the reasons for her long agonizing letters regarding Cherifa and others was that she felt Bowles was, in part, responsible for getting her mixed up with the Arab women to begin with: "Surely I would not have begun it—got the idea without you, I mean."

Beyond that, though, there was a profound sense of isolation. Never one to remain comfortably alone, in Tangier Jane was cut off not only from familiar people and surroundings, but also from the one person who was instrumental in her being there, from the confidant who might be able to help her make sense of the place and of herself in it. In some sense her letters must be read as an attempt to get some perspective on her situation from Bowles, some reassurance as to whether she can truly be said to "exist" on her own terms. In one, after telling Bowles that without him she would probably not bother to write, she goes on to ruminate on what this means. "It is awful not to know what one would do if one were utterly alone in the world. You would do just what you've always done and so would Helvetia but I don't exist independently."

Bowles's replies to these letters have been lost, but it seems from the one-way correspondence that he was not able to offer her sufficient reassurance. His characteristic detachment and fear of expressing emotion were apparently as evident as ever, despite the mounting hysteria in Jane's letters (and numerous wires) to him. The only extant glimpse of the sort of reply Bowles gave her comes from a complaint she made to Libby Holman: "Your letter was one of the sweetest and most inclusive I have ever received, in great contrast to Paul who must have entered the secret service he's been so mute about everything."

Finally, by November she was contemplating returning to New York, as Bowles seemed unable to say exactly when he would return. Finances, though, were a problem. Although Bowles had left her a small sum, with the admonition to allow herself only 100 pesetas a day (a little over $3), by October she was overdrawn at the bank. Both Oliver Smith and Holman sent her some money, but she did not really have enough to pay boat fare. She had been promised "at least $350" for her long story "Camp Cataract," which *Harper's Bazaar* had accepted, but not yet paid for, nor even decided on the exact amount. As a result, she began writing madly to Helvetia Perkins, to Jody, and to Holman, urging them to come. Holman, in fact, had visited briefly during that summer with her adolescent son, much to both Bowleses' delight, but was not contemplating a return soon.

Jane finally learned that Jody was planning to visit, but this also set her on edge regarding Bowles. "You may very well not want to be with me this winter because of Jody and would *prefer* me to come back in the spring. I had hoped you would express yourself on that in a letter but you didn't." The news of Jody's arrival, despite Jane's continued anxiety about finances, loneliness, and Cherifa, helped her feel less abandoned. Finally, in early December, Bowles informed her that he too was on his way back, traveling with Williams and Williams's lover, Frank Merlo.

Once on board the SS *Saturnia* that December, Bowles suddenly was moved to write a fictional version of the story he had heard while in the Sahara a year earlier. The story Bowles heard was this:

> The previous year three Moslem merchants had been murdered on their way south across the desert. The killer had appropriated their caravan and gone on with it to the murdered men's destination, where their colleagues had recognized the merchandise. They re-

ported their suspicions to the French military authorities, who surprisingly gave them carte blanche in the matter. Accordingly they carried the man far out into the desert and buried him up to his neck in the sand; then they left him to die.

This account of the original tale is also the synopsis of Bowles's story, but as always, a plot summary hardly gives the impact of the mastery with which Bowles reworked his source material. "The Delicate Prey," in fact, is one of Bowles's most menacing, terrifyingly memorable, and well-crafted works. Again, as in "A Distant Episode," the horror builds through attention to detail, through the powerfully vivid ability on Bowles's part to make us feel each moment as if we ourselves were experiencing it. Again as in his earlier macabre tale of the professor, he is a master of conjuring up pure terror through narrative detachment. This becomes most evident in scenes of utter violence:

The man moved and surveyed the young body lying on the stones. He ran his finger along the razor's blade; a pleasant excitement took possession of him. He stepped over, looked down, and saw the sex that sprouted from the base of the belly. Not entirely conscious of what he was doing, he took it in one hand and brought his other arm down with the motion of a reaper wielding a sickle. It was swiftly severed. A round, dark hole was left, flush with the skin; he stared a moment, blankly. Driss was screaming. The muscles all over his body stood out, moved.

Slowly the Mougari smiled, showing his teeth. He put his hand on the hard belly and smoothed the skin. Then he made a small vertical incision there, and using both hands, studiously stuffed the loose organ in until it disappeared.

Unlike many writers of horror, including Poe and Machen, two of Bowles's favorites, he rarely indulges in sensational description nor attempts to demonstrate through a plethora of adjectives how horrible a torture is. Instead, in almost clinical terms, he simply relates the facts, as if he were describing the most mundane matter, thus immeasurably increasing the impact. It is this ice-cold narrative technique that has won Bowles both admirers and detractors. Even Tennessee Williams found the story hard to take. When Bowles showed Williams the story the day after he'd written it, the playwright told him: "It's a wonderful story but if you publish it, you're mad. . . . Everyone is going to think you are some sort of horrible monster when they read it. . . . You'll give people the wrong idea." Bowles did not heed Williams's advice. "I think if you write something, you should publish it," he replied.

The story, in fact, also had a similar impact on others. When John Lehmann, who admired the story immensely, wanted to include it in the first collection of Bowles's stories that he published, Cyril Connolly and Somerset Maugham advised against it, as well as "Pages from Cold Point," telling him that if those stories got by the censors, which was unlikely, they would offend readers and hurt sales. Neither story was actually published in England until 1968, although both of them were included in the American edition of 1950.

When the SS *Saturnia* arrived in Gibraltar, Jane was there to meet them. As Williams had brought his car, a new Buick Roadster, they did not go directly to Tangier but first to Spain. They stayed there only a few days, crossing the straits to Tangier because of torrential rains. Tangier was not much better. Williams wrote Donald Windham a description:

> We arrived at just the beginning of the rainy season and for reasons of economy (the Bowles') [sic] we put up at a perfectly ghastly hotel called the El Far-Har (rhymes with horror) at the top of a very steep hill over the ocean. Spectacular view: every possible discomfort! The meals were about 25¢ each but were not worth it. I got ill there. A dreadful cold, still coughing from it, and I developed a peculiar affliction—vibrations whenever I lowered my head, running up and down my whole body like an electric vibrator!

After two weeks in Tangier, Bowles, Williams, and Frank Merlo headed for Fez. The trip gave Williams ample opportunity to see Morocco at its worst. The problem arose when they got to the border of the Spanish zone (in 1948 Morocco was still divided between French and Spanish zones, with Tangier international). In pouring rain they approached the customs shed so that the Spanish soldiers could examine their luggage. "They took out Tennessee's suits, his underwear, his shirts, his typewriter, manuscript paper, razor, and they confiscated it all," remembered Bowles. The soldiers then began vying for who got what items. But the adventure had just begun. Williams wrote Windham some additional details: "In the middle of this a scream from outside. The Buick had slipped its moorings and had started sliding backwards downhill. Frank rushes out, races it neck and neck down the hill, finally executes a flying leap into it just in time to prevent a serious crash." Finally they managed to clear customs, get their stuff back, including all of the belongings from Bowles's fifteen suitcases, only to discover that they had somehow lost the car keys.

It took them several more days and another series of misadventures before they could reach Fez, at which point Williams decided he'd had enough of Morocco. He booked passage on a ship to Marseilles, put the car aboard, and proceeded with Merlo, eventually to Italy. From Rome he wrote Windham, "I believe Paul was quite cross with us for leaving. He has not answered our letters. But can you seriously blame a girl for pulling out, under those circumstances? One can take just so much: then no more!"

Bowles stayed on in Fez as Jody was now in Tangier with Jane. In February the two women went together to Marseilles for a few days so that Jody could catch a ship back to the States. When Jane returned to Tangier, Bowles had come down from Fez and proposed a trip together into the Sahara. Jane readily accepted and for the next month they traveled together, following much the same itinerary as the one Bowles had taken the year before. Jane found the desert enormously appealing. "It is not like anything else anywhere in the world, not the sand or the oasis," she wrote friends in New York, noting also that, "of course, I'm not neurotic anymore." Indeed, the trip seemed to be just what she needed for reestablishing her perspective on life and love. In the oasis of Taghit she even managed to write "A Stick of Green Candy," a coming-of-age story, if that theme can be defined as an inability to believe any longer in childhood fantasies. Although the story is of a young girl, the loss of belief in one's own creations was a central concern for Jane. In some ways the story can be read as Jane Bowles's testimony on the difficulty of maintaining the life of the imagination while living in the world. It was, in fact, her last fictional testimony; she would never again complete another work of fiction.

* * *

Returning to Tangier, the Bowleses moved back into the Farhar Hotel, but decided to commission work on the house Bowles had acquired in the Medina. In May Bowles went to Paris, where his *Concerto for Two Pianos,* which he had orchestrated that year to become *Concerto for Two Pianos and Orchestra,* was to be performed at the Salle Pleyel. The city, with the war over, was again full of expatriate and visiting Americans: Gore Vidal, Truman Capote, Ned Rorem, James Baldwin, Aaron Copland. The reunion with Copland was important for Bowles, and probably for Copland as well, as they had not seen each other in years. There had never been a falling out; they had just gone their separate ways, but now in Paris they caught up with each other, reminisced. In the intervening years Copland had become the "dean of American composers"; his young protégé, no longer so young, had not only just completed a novel, but could still point with pride to his involvement in writing serious music despite a decade of being a Broadway composer. Copland, of course, could not understand why Bowles was actually choosing to live in Tangier, but had long ago come to realize that Morocco was a source of endless fascination for his former student.

During that visit, Capote decided that he wanted to summer in Tangier. When Vidal found out about this, he decided also to go there—according to Bowles, just to annoy Capote. A few days after Bowles returned, Vidal arrived. On the day Bowles went to the docks to meet Capote, Vidal insisted on going with him. "As the ferry pulled in, Truman leaned out over the railing, grinning widely and waving a very long silk scarf. When he saw Gore standing beside me, he did a little comic-strip routine. His face fell like a soufflé placed in the ice compartment, and he disappeared entirely below the level of the railing for several seconds." Vidal stayed only long enough to make Capote think he would be there all summer as well; then he slipped out of town unobtrusively.

That summer of 1949 was a period of intense socializing, as Bowles and Jane became integrated into Tangier society. Their entrée was facilitated by the city's "unofficial social arbiter," David Herbert, second son of the Earl of Pembroke, who had taken up residence in Tangier in 1947. At the time he was living with the photographer Cecil Beaton in a house that belonged to the Guinness family, the Villa Mektoub. The summer passed in a flurry of parties, dinners, and lunches. Just as Bowles had been gathering material for *The Sheltering Sky* before he even knew he was writing the book, a similar phenomenon happened that summer. His next novel would be, more than anything else, a portrayal of Tangier society, its parties, its people, its eccentricities. At the time, however, he was less an observer than simply a participant in the action, one who welcomed the diversion.

Indeed, that summer it was not a novel of Tangier society that he was planning but, rather, a book to which he gave the working title "Almost All the Apples Are Gone." A notebook surviving from those years contains the outline of the novel. It was to be the story of an American schoolteacher who quickly becomes "bored, bored, bored" and enters into correspondence with a wealthy Latin American landowner who eventually proposes marriage to her. Delighted with the offer, she decides to take a sabbatical and go visit him and his country. Arriving in Central America, she notes the "disparity between imagined tropics and first taste of them. (But at end she says: 'But it is real, and that is saying a lot.') In nearest large town to village where Mr. x lives she goes to hotel. Has decided not to go to village, to give up the venture." He, however, sends his servant for her and they end up eventually getting married.

The next part of the book was to contain a "series of short scenes wherein incompatibility of husband and wife is shown increasing. Show native servant becoming a character, gardener slowly emerging from his anonymity." She soon has an affair with the gardener and becomes pregnant but her husband has no realization that he is not the father. Before the child's birth he dies; subsequently the gardener tries to assume control over the plantation, but she has him framed for murder and imprisoned. As the years go by, the estate falls into near ruin. Protective of her son, Johnny, she does not allow him to play with other children and "always tells son he is white (the only white)." As he matures, he becomes a focus of the local girls' attention. "Mother pleased secretly. . . . By time boy is adolescent, mother (living as fortune-teller) conceives idea of selling son's services to women of town, both for themselves & their daughters. He remains ignorant of maneuver. Women & girls happen to be there, let themselves be seduced." The book was to conclude with the son going off to town and with this final twist:

> . . . mother, needing money, comes looking for him, tries to get him to go back. Refusal. (Finds white halfwit to take back with her in his place.) Son gives mother some money. She buys brass bed. (Final scene in room with broken ceiling, canvas stretched across like tent, bed beneath.) She spins fantasy. Gardener returns, innocent of her maneuver. Halfwit in garden hut with native woman. Gardener thinks he is her son. Puts woman out. Halfwit furious. Gardener announces intention of remaining. She suggests to halfwit to kill him. He does.

From even these cryptic notes it is easy to see Bowles's familiar preoccupations with the tropics, incompatible marriage, sexual power, evil, violence, and of course, the way in which Westerners fall apart on alien terrain or else become reduced to their lowest instincts. It is also possible to see here Bowles's first attempt to envision the possible consequences for the French mail-order bride that he had encountered more than ten years before while on his honeymoon in Guatemala.

In September, as Beaton had to go to England, David Herbert invited the Bowleses to move into the Villa Mektoub with him. They readily accepted, but stayed only six weeks. *The Sheltering Sky* had just been brought out in England to great acclaim and Lehmann wanted Bowles present. As Herbert was also planning to go to England at that time, he suggested they all go together. In October, the three of them set out, first by boat to Marseilles, then in Herbert's Jaguar through France. The journey was a leisurely one; Herbert and Jane, both great gourmands, turned the trip through the Rhône Valley into what amounted to a "*tournée gastronomique*," according to Bowles. For Bowles, the richness of the food was too much; having had a weak liver since suffering repeated jaundice attacks in Mexico in the early 1940s, he suddenly became quite ill in Lyons with liver problems. Jane and Herbert showed no sympathy, but instead would return to the hotel after a night spent gorging and relate in detail all they had consumed. "The lingering descriptions and discussion of the food's texture constituted a kind of torture," recalled Bowles.

Arriving in England in November, they stayed at Herbert's country estate. From there, Bowles traveled into London a couple of times a week, where Lehmann made sure he met "everybody." Jane wrote Libby Holman from Wilton, Herbert's estate, that "Paul is a great success here. . . . I don't think he's ever had such a success before in his life. . . . Parties were given for him every second in London, and though he was very tired after a week of it I know it has done him an enormous amount of good."

John Lehmann, who had never met Bowles, was "struck at once by his quiet charm and intelligence, his shrewdness about the ways of the world, and—when the reserve melted—a sharp wit that did not spare his contemporaries, of some of whom he could give very funny imitations." Lehmann also remembered that Bowles "seemed at first a little at sea in the literary world of London, and was a listener rather than a talker." This soon changed, however, and he charmed others, such as Cyril Connolly and Elizabeth Bowen, as much as he had Lehmann.

The book was also a success. Selected by the British Book-of-the-Month Club, it sold well and received accolades in the press. In the words of Ned Rorem: "In 1949, with the publication of *The Sheltering Sky* at the age of forty, Paul Bowles became the author-who-also-writes-music, after having long been the composer-who-also-writes-words."

CHAPTER 21

THE SUCCESS in England of *The Sheltering Sky* was minor compared to what it achieved in the United States. Published in New York on October 14, 1949, in an edition of only 3,596 copies, it had sold out well before Christmas. Laughlin, however, failed to reprint the book until late in the year. According to Bowles, the reason for this was that "Laughlin was tight. If he had made too much money on the book that year, he would have had to redo his income tax on which he'd already taken a loss." As a result, despite the immediate popular success of the novel, it took until the new year and a second printing of 45,000 copies for it really to take off.

On January 1, 1950, however, it entered the *New York Times* best-seller list at number 15. It stayed on the list for ten weeks until March 12, rising to ninth position on January 15. Among the competition were such notable achievements as Nelson Algren's *Man with the Golden Arm,* Alan Paton's *Cry the Beloved Country,* John O'Hara's *A Rage to Live,* Alberto Moravia's *The Woman of Rome,* and Joyce Cary's *The Horse's Mouth.*

The popularity of the book was no doubt helped out by Tennessee Williams's critique in the *New York Times Book Review,* which read, in part:

It brings the reader into sudden, startling communion with a talent of true maturity and sophistication of a sort that I had begun to fear was to be found nowadays only among the insurgent novelists of France, such as Jean Genet and Albert Camus and Jean-Paul Sartre.

With the hesitant exception of one or two war books by returned soldiers, "The Sheltering Sky" alone of the books that I have recently read by American authors appears to bear the spiritual imprint of recent history in the western world. . . . In its interior aspect, "The Sheltering Sky" is an allegory of the spiritual adventure of the fully conscious person into modern experience. . . . Actually this superior motive does not intrude in explicit form upon the story, certainly not in any form that will need to distract you from the great pleasure of being told a first-rate story of adventure by a really first-rate writer.

In addition to Williams's rave review, William Carlos Williams, also writing in the *Times Book Review,* placed it at the top of his list of "The Best Books I've Read This Year." The popular press liked it as well. Under the headline "Sex and Sand," the *Time* reviewer, after giving a basic plot summary, wrote: "All this may be taken straight as simply a lurid, supersexy Sahara adventure story completely outfitted with camel trains, handsome Arabs, French officers, and a harem. Nonetheless, *The Sheltering Sky* is a remarkable job of writing." *Life* magazine heralded Bowles under the heading "Our New Writers," printing a quarter-page, foppish photo of him while noting that the novel had "hit a financial jackpot." Indeed, by the time *The Sheltering Sky* slipped off the best-seller list, it had sold nearly 40,000 copies. Bowles was not only critically acclaimed in the press, but had also earned himself a fair amount of money. This latter aspect of his success even caused Claude to acknowledge that his son had finally done something right.

Bowles, however, was not a party to the hoopla in New York during December. Instead, he was on a freighter bound for Colombo, Ceylon (now Sri Lanka). While in London he had looked into sailings from England either to Thailand or Ceylon; discovering that the most immediate departure was to Colombo, he booked passage. He was glad to get a Colombo sailing as he had become intrigued by Ceylon after looking through a picture album at David Herbert's house. Herbert, who had spent a fair amount of time there in the 1930s and during the war, added effusive commentary about each picture.

Bowles became particularly captivated by pictures of a tiny island called Taprobane, in Weligama Bay, just off the southern tip of Ceylon. Herbert had stayed on it with his parents fifteen years before and gave glowing reports about it. The photos showed "a tiny dome-shaped island with a strange looking house at its top, and, spread out along its flanks, terraces that lost themselves in the shade of giant trees." Once his sailing was set, Bowles decided on Taprobane as an ultimate destination.

Bowles had at least a few reasons for wanting to go there. No doubt the most important was that he simply wanted to visit a place he'd never been before and now had the money to do so, but in addition, he wanted to work in peace on the opera Libby Holman had commissioned. He had already decided to create a libretto from García Lorca's play *Yerma* and had begun the translation, but was now at a point where he needed to get to a piano. Although he had thought of going to the Sahara again for the winter, as he found the rest of Morocco too cold or rainy, he knew that there was no likelihood of finding a piano there and rejected the idea in favor of Asia, where he had been assured pianos did exist. There was also another impetus: Jane had decided to spend the winter in Paris with Jody, who was coming over from the United States. Realizing that Jane would be occupied, and as he clearly did not want to be in Paris, nor become a spectator of Jane's affair, he felt it prudent to head off to the unknown.

As a result, he and Jane left England at the beginning of December; Bowles went to Antwerp, the port from which his ship was sailing, Jane to Paris to meet Jody. Before leaving England, however, he had given Lehmann a manuscript of his stories, at the same time sending another copy to Helen Strauss to peddle for him in the United States. Lehmann immediately accepted the collection, although as noted earlier, he excised "The Delicate Prey" and "Pages from Cold Point" for fear of censorship difficulties. Strauss soon informed him that Random House had agreed to publish the stories, but suggested he change the collection's title from simply *The Delicate Prey* to *The Delicate Prey and Other Stories,* as she felt buyers of the book would feel they were getting a novel rather than a collection of short stories. Bowles reluctantly agreed. (In England, when Lehmann brought out the stories, the book was entitled *A Little Stone.*)

At first the sea was rough and Bowles spent most of the time in his cabin working on the Lorca translation. But when the ship rounded the tip of Spain to head into the Mediterranean, he went up on board, staring out into the dark, watching for the lights of Tangier to appear off the starboard bow. Suddenly, they came into sight. This was followed by what can only be described as an intense visionary experience: "I started by imagining that I was standing on the cliff looking out at the place where I was on the ship. I transported myself from the ship straight over to the cliffs and began there." Once transported, he conjured up two characters, an American man and a Moroccan woman.

It was this vision that started Bowles off on what would become his next novel. Returning to his cabin, he wrote out the scene at length, beginning in mid-sentence: "strides, threw himself on the crackling leaves and twigs, and reached up to pull her face down to his." This, however, would not be the beginning of the novel. From this point he would work "backward and forward in time," establish a cause, then work forward to effect. He began writing this entry in the same notebook in which he had sketched the cryptic outline for *Almost All the Apples Are Gone,* working from back to front. His new inspiration caused him temporarily to abandon the previous idea for a novel and continue with his new work, which he entitled *Let It Come Down.* As it happened, he never returned to complete *Almost All the Apples Are Gone,* explaining years later that he simply "began to find it too melodramatic to go on with it."

By the time the *General Walter* had sailed into the Indian Ocean, Bowles had written several chapters of the new novel and had worked out an elaborate plan for it, complete with several pages of diagrams charting the relationships between characters. There are, in addition, a number of notes to himself. Often the entries are cryptic:

Intensity of vision
Inner physical pressure
Something's got to happen
Elation and apprehensiveness
Waves
Never told < this
Spillway of the sky

at other times, fairly extended:

At some crucial moment in later section, Dyar is put in contact with his early life—not reliving it, far too distant for that—like looking through telescope wrong way around—but very intimate, as if each gesture were now explained, completed, given its excuse, meaning. (Gesture, scene, situation) or seen in its final and true light & perspective.

But the result of all this is that everything is merely a repetition and was already complete, definite, unalterable. meaning having been implicit of its having occurred or existed. Feeling of content-ment (fulfillment) comes, however, with explanation of new under-standing which, changing nothing changes everything.

This way of working, so different from the method he used with *The Sheltering Sky,* was necessary, according to Bowles, to get the novel firmly fixed in his mind. In addition, he felt that a sufficient amount of progress on the actual writing of it was necessary in order to ensure that he could go on with it:

Notes are useless to me unless there is a portion of the finished text to which they can be applied; I knew I must write enough of that text to serve as an umbilical cord between me and the novel before I landed in an unfamiliar place, otherwise I should lose it all. As the ship drew nearer to Ceylon I found myself recalling Kafka's well-known aphorism: *From a certain point onward there is no longer any turning back. That is the point that must be reached.* I doubt that he meant it to be applied to the writing of a book, nevertheless it seemed relevant to the situation. I strained to pass that crucial point; only then could I be sure of not having to turn back and abandon the book when I tried to continue work on it later.

As Bowles had expected, once he arrived in Ceylon in early January, he was so overwhelmed by the place itself that he was unable to write much more of the novel. Indeed, there was such an array of details to take in that when he went to record his first impressions in his journal, the observations formed a catalog of sight, cultural notes, and poetic reflection:

variety of skin-color, variety of costumes, cleanliness of people and streets, the high degree of Europeanization (perhaps because of the lack of indigenous architecture) general courtesy of the people, ef-ficiency of servants, notable lack of parasitical elements waiting to prey on the tourist (there are of course some individuals around the harbor eager to act as guide if they think one is a sailor on a passing cargo ship, but even these are not offensive or persistent), the signs in Sinhalese and Tamil script (the former looks like spaghetti and the latter something like Hebrew) and the everpresent triumphant vegetation of the coast, like a joyous song in the air.

In Colombo, Bowles stayed first in a hotel on the beach, but after a week or so, through a chance encounter in an English bookstore, managed to get himself invited to stay on a tea plantation owned by an Englishman named Trimmer, born in Ceylon, and his Ceylonese wife. Bowles later described the estate, Maldeniya, in a travel article: "The landscape is restless—a sea of disorderly hills rising steeply. In all directions it looks the same. The hills are sharp bumps with a thin, hairy vegetation that scarcely covers them. Most of this is rubber, and the rubber is wintering. . . . Where the rubber stops the tea begins. There the earth looks raw. The rocks show between the low bushes; here and there a mulberry tree with lopped branches, planted for shade."

Bowles spent two weeks there as a guest of the Trimmers, learning from them about Ceylon, soaking up tales of rapidly vanishing colonial life, absorbing the atmosphere, recoiling continually from the oppressive heat. On their old upright piano he worked a bit on *Yerma*, adding two or three new sections to the opera. But eager to get on with traveling and concerned about wearing out his welcome, at the end of February he crossed over to South India, entering the country through Dhanushkodi. "An analogous procedure in America would be for a foreigner to get his first glimpse of the United States by parachuting into Death Valley," recalled Bowles. "It was God-forsaken, uncomfortable, and a little frightening."

By May he was back in Ceylon at the Maldeniya estate, taking advantage of the piano in order to write a few more sections of *Yerma*. As with most activities, composing in the tropics had its share of difficulties. Not only did the humidity cause the piano to be constantly out of tune, but there were other perils as well. One afternoon, as Bowles sat down at the instrument, he discovered that something was wrong with the action. Suddenly, from the back of the piano, a ten-foot-long snake rose into the air, wriggling its tongue at Bowles, who jumped back in fright. As Bowles watched from across the room, the snake disappeared into the space between the ceiling and the roof. When informed of the event, the Trimmers expressed little astonishment, choosing instead merely to speculate on why the snake had gotten into the piano in the first place.

Curiously enough, although one of the great attractions for Bowles in going to Ceylon was to visit the island of Taprobane, he had so far only caught a glimpse of it from the train. And while he kept thinking he'd get a chance to visit, the trip never seemed to materialize. When in late May Bowles decided it was time to head to Europe and Tangier again, he left without visiting it.

Jane was still in Paris, living at the Hôtel de l'Université. During that winter she and Jody had had a falling out; on the rebound, Jane had fallen in love with a New York woman now also living in Paris. Despite the emotional upheavals, the Paris period had been reasonably productive. Inspired by news from the States about a possible production of her play that year, she had been steadily revising the last act of *In the Summer House.* In addition, she had filled several notebooks with pages from a new novel. By the time Bowles arrived in Paris in early June, however, Jane was again in a great state of anxiety, owing to acute lack of finances, uncertainty about her own future, and most of all the off-and-on situation with her play.

Indeed, the play was causing both her and Bowles a fair amount of trouble in setting their immediate plans. Promised by Oliver Smith a production in August, Jane was geared to leave Paris for New York during the summer in order to attend rehearsals. Bowles too had agreed to come to the States and write the music. But everyone—Bowles, Jane, and Smith—felt that without a definite commitment from a Broadway theater to put the play on after a trial run, there was no point in mounting a small repertory production. And as there had so far been no interest in New York, both Bowles and Jane were reluctant about returning without assurance that the play would indeed go on beyond Westport.

Finally they decided to proceed anyway, Bowles feeling that he could at least work with Libby Holman on *Yerma.* But no sooner had this been settled than word was received from Holman that she was planning to come over to Spain in late July. Bowles canceled his passage to New York and went back to Tangier to await Holman's arrival, but with the proviso that if a production of *In the Summer House* should materialize he would return immediately to the United States to write the music. Jane, meanwhile, having had enough of waiting for things to happen on the other side of the Atlantic, decided to go to New York on July 7, taking a chance on the play actually being produced.

Before leaving Paris, Bowles had again met up with Brion Gysin, who was completing a Fulbright year and as Bowles recalled it, "seemed to be at loose ends." Bowles invited Gysin to come to Tangier, telling him he could stay with him in the house in the Medina on which reparations had just been completed. Gysin accepted wholeheartedly, following Bowles to Tangier about a week later. Reflecting years afterward on this initial invitation, Gysin remarked that, "I owe him [Bowles] my years in Morocco really because I wouldn't've gone there if he hadn't suggested it at that particular time."

Bowles was back in Morocco only for a month when he got a wire from Libby Holman announcing her arrival in Málaga. He met her; then they went motoring around Spain in her car, talking constantly about *Yerma,* working on it whenever they could get to a piano. In mid-August they went to Tangier, where Holman remained for a few weeks. But her Mediterranean idyll was broken when, on her way back to New York, she received a wire: her son Christopher had been killed in an attempt to ascend Mt. Whitney. When Holman arrived in New York, Jane stayed with her in Connecticut for the next several months, doing what she could to get her through the difficult aftermath.

The play, meanwhile, did not go on in Westport, nor would it be produced for another year. Jane, however, stayed on in the United States for the next six months, as she was working through her agent, Audrey Wood, and through Oliver Smith to have the play presented the following year. Now that it was obvious that Bowles would not have to rush back to New York to write music, he and Gysin went up to Fez, where he got back to work on *Let It Come Down.* Still, the most important progress for Bowles that summer was not literary, but, rather, the development of a close relationship with the young Moroccan artist Ahmed Yacoubi. Although they had known each other since Bowles first arrived in Morocco in 1947, they had not seen each other regularly or formed a particularly close bond. That summer, however, things began to change.

Struck by his quick intelligence, wit, talent, and, no doubt, physical beauty, Bowles was quite drawn to the young Moroccan, enjoying his company, his conversation, and ability to embrace life with joy and openness. His tales of magic also greatly intrigued Bowles, would in fact fuel Bowles's already considerable interest in the supernatural. In short, this was just the companion for whom Bowles had been searching, probably without even knowing it. From this summer in Fez until Yacoubi eventually left Morocco in the mid-1970s, they would remain friends, mutually teaching and nurturing each other. From Yacoubi, Bowles would learn about the intimate workings of a certain segment of Moroccan society; from Bowles, Yacoubi would develop the ability to know the West and be greatly aided in ultimately making a life there as an artist.

In the introduction to the catalog that accompanied an exhibition of Yacoubi's works, Bowles provided this information about the young painter:

> Ahmed Yacoubi was born in 1931 in el Keddane, one of the most ancient quarters of Fez. He is a Cherif on both his father's and mother's side; that is to say, his parents are both direct descendants of the Prophet Mohammed. His paternal grandfather and his father exercised the profession of f'qih, which means that they healed by laying on of hands, by the manipulation of fire, by collecting herbs and brewing concoctions of them, and most important, by the writing of sacred formulas at propitious moments. The office of f'qih was destined to be assumed by Ahmed; his education consisted solely of learning how to treat the sick, of learning the legends, songs and dances of his region, and paraphrasing the Koran.

Along with the talents of a *f'qih,* Yacoubi was also a totally self-taught painter. By the time Bowles met him again in Fez during the summer of 1950, he was, in fact, producing remarkably fine and unique canvases. In a journal, Bowles recorded these observations of how he perceived Yacoubi's work: "His conception of the world is not primarily visual; he paints what he knows rather than what he sees. . . . Lack of any artistic tradition in his society. Only drawings in his town are on walls of brothels, which is why he has kept fact of his paintings from his family."

The exact nature of their association was for most not a matter of speculation; almost everyone who knew Bowles and Yacoubi in the early days of their relationship—Tennessee Williams, Maurice Grosser, Edouard Roditi, William Burroughs, Allen Ginsberg, and various other members of Tangier society—assumed that there was a sexual component to their involvement, at least in the early 1950s. Both Yacoubi and Bowles, however, have denied this. What is curious about the denials is that they seem to have surfaced only after several years, and appear tied to an event that took place in late 1957, when Yacoubi was arrested on a morals charge involving a fifteen-year-old German boy. At that time, his relationship with Bowles was called into question by the local authorities, and although no harm came to Bowles (or Yacoubi), after this incident Bowles became increasingly wary of being accused of engaging in homosexual affairs. As David Herbert later pointed out, "Paul is scared of any form of authority. He can even be nervous of a second-rate junior consulate official for fear that he may be doing or is thought to be doing something."

But in 1950, this fear of authority was not, as yet, terribly pronounced. It developed gradually, and for a number of reasons. At this point, foreigners still enjoyed a rather free, if not exalted position within Moroccan society. While not above the law, or beyond reproach, the colonial structure of society certainly afforded them a great deal more license than was available to the Moroccan subjects or to the foreigners themselves in their respective countries. "It was one of the charms of the International Zone that you could get anything you wanted if you paid for it. Do anything too, for that matter," Bowles wrote in *Let It Come Down*. Clearly, though, this was the end of an era; colonialism was beginning to be challenged in Morocco, and the situation of any Westerner was no longer so secure, as the first anti-French rumblings began to surface within the country. By the winter, in fact, tensions would mount considerably between the Moroccans and their colonizers. Looking back on that summer spent with Gysin in Fez, Bowles realized that they "were living through the last two or three months of the old, easygoing, colonial life in Morocco."

While Bowles was still in Fez, *A Little Stone*, his collection of stories, was published in London by Lehmann. In November, Random House brought out an expanded collection, *The Delicate Prey and Other Stories*. The reviews, as with *The Sheltering Sky*, were generally quite good. Tennessee Williams again led the charge, this time in the pages of the *Saturday Review of Literature:*

> These seventeen stories are the exploration of a cavern of individual sensibilities, and fortunately the cavern is a deep one containing a great deal that is worth exploring.
>
> Nowhere in any writing that I can think of has the separateness of the one human psyche been depicted more vividly and shockingly. If one feels that life achieves its highest value and significance in those rare moments—they are scarcely longer than that—when two lives are confluent, when the walls of isolation momentarily collapse between two persons, and if one is willing to acknowledge the possibility of such intervals, however rare and brief and difficult they may be, the intensely isolated spirit evoked by Paul Bowles may have an austerity which is frightening at least. But don't make the mistake of assuming that what is frightening is necessarily inhuman. It is curious to note that the spirit evoked by Bowles in so many of these stories does *not* seem inhuman, nor does it strike me as being antipathetic. . . .
>
> The volume contains among several fine stories at least one that is a true masterpiece of short fiction—"A Distant Episode."

A somewhat dissenting note about the stories was sounded privately, however, by Alice Toklas. Although she had earlier written Bowles about *The Sheltering Sky* that "no novel since *The Great Gatsby* has impressed me as having the force—precision—delicacy that the best of Fitzgerald has until yours," she found *The Delicate Prey* less to her liking. In a letter to Bowles on December 7, 1950, she wrote: "Your delicacy is perfect—precise and poignant—but the macabre fate—though inevitable that overtakes most of your prey is not to my taste."

In the late autumn of 1950, Bowles and Gysin returned to Tangier; Jane was still in New York, having decided to stay on indefinitely. Dreading winter in the little unheated house in the Medina, Bowles chose to move into a hotel to work on *Let It Come Down,* leaving Gysin to occupy the Medina residence.

Perhaps it was just the slow progress he was making on the book or perhaps the terrible rainy winter in Tangier, but by February Bowles was experiencing what can only be described as a kind of psychic malaise. In February he wrote about it to Peggy Glanville-Hicks:

> Inside I am waiting to escape to somewhere else. I don't quite know where. Naturally one always wants to escape if one has no reason for being anywhere. And I have no reason for being anywhere, that is certain. If I work, I don't think of that, and feel the escape urge less, so that the work is largely therapeutic. But when one feels that the only reason for working is in order to be able to forget one's life, one is sometimes tempted to consider the work slightly absurd, like the pills one takes to make one's digestion easier. There should be something else in between, but what it is is anyone's guess.

There is also a fragment written on a single sheet of blue paper that can be connected to this same period, as it also contains a small portion from *Let It Come Down.* This meditation might too have been intended for the novel, but seems to be far more a reflection of Bowles's personal situation at the time:

> The only effort worth making is the one it takes to learn the geography of one's own nature. But there is seldom enough energy for that.
>
> One must accept one's own limitations as one accepts life and death, pain and pleasure. Only then can these natural defects be utilized to their fullest extent. Resistance cripples.
>
> Life is [what] I want, which in turn is beautiful and good. The less complex the desires, the more likely they are of attainment. The act of dying must be longed for as the ultimate attainment. Any philosophical or religious system which can instill this longing is justified, but not if doing so involves any sort of rejection.
>
> By striving with every facet of the imagination to conceive of chaos, one manages only to explore a little more carefully the terrain of order.
>
> To develop one's sensual characteristics, no matter how subtly, leaves one at the mercy of the physical world and its increasingly destructive onslaught. It takes an exceedingly insensitive person today to be able to continue being an artist.

While these two statements reflect the intense alienation from society and from himself that Bowles, to some extent, had always felt, they still do not explain why he was being overtaken by such darkness. All the more so since, on the surface, things couldn't have been better. His two major forays into literature had been extremely well received, both critically and popularly; his bank account had swollen considerably; he was living in the Morocco he loved, and was involved in a satisfying relationship with Yacoubi. But the superficial trappings of his existence were not enough to compensate for the inner anguish he was feeling at simply being alive. It is, of course, these feelings that pervade, indeed create the fiction. But the fiction may also have been creating Paul Bowles. The more he dwelt on the fictional isolation of his characters, the more he began to feel isolated himself, became increasingly unable to separate himself from his creations. To some degree, such identification with his delicate prey was necessary in order to chart so consistently and so well the themes of the disintegration of the individual. But in doing so, his own sense of self also began to be put fully into question.

In a letter written to his mother that summer he commented on the need to become one with what he was writing:

> With a novel the work is a good deal more than just consecrating so many hours of the day to sitting at a desk writing words;—it is living in the midst of the artificial world one is creating, and letting no detail of everyday life enter sufficiently into one's mind to become more real than or take precedence over what one is inventing. That is, living in the atmosphere of the novel has to become and stay more real than one's own life. Which is why it is almost impossible to work in a city, or with people around. At least, for me. Under the latter conditions I write more words, staying outside what I am doing, and anyone knows that is not the way to write a novel—at least, not a novel that people are going to become engrossed in.

There is also another component related to Bowles's identification with his characters, with the necessity of living within the creative process itself, namely, the need to withdraw from society, which goes deeper than simply wanting to be temporarily isolated from the exigencies of daily life in order to create. Tennessee Williams perceptively noted that Bowles "experienced an unmistakable revulsion from the act of social participation. One may surmise in him the social experience of two decades. Then the withdrawal is logical."

No doubt such a withdrawal was felt by Bowles to be a necessary condition for making art. But the retreat into himself and hence into his fiction had left him, in some ways, even more isolated. In rejecting society, particularly New York society, he also rejected the balance that such a society had once provided him. Williams, again, described such a retreat as Bowles's way of surviving as an artist: "The artist is not a man who will advance against a bayonet pressed to his abdomen unless another bayonet is pressed to his back, and even then he is not likely to move forward. He will, if possible, stand still. But Mr. Bowles has discovered that the bayonet is pointed at the man moving forward in our times, and that a retreat is still accessible. He has done the sensible thing under these circumstances. He has gone back into the cavern of himself."

Out of this "cavern of himself" sprang the fiction and, not coincidentally, a similarly bleak feeling about his own existence. But despite the difficulty of the position in which he found himself, for Bowles it seemed the only way of going about living or creating. It was this realization that he discovered in coming to terms with the "geography of his own nature." Therefore, instead of trying to overcome his malaise, he decided to use it, in the process creating a philosophical stance out of unhappiness. As he remarked in 1952, "I believe unhappiness should be studied very carefully; this is certainly no time for anyone to pretend to be happy, or to put his unhappiness away in the dark. (And anyone who is not unhappy now must be a monster, a saint or an idiot.) You must watch your universe as it cracks above your head."

Life, however, went on. Despite the nihilism of Bowles's outlook, he was still very much a participant in day-to-day living, actively socializing. Early that spring, in fact, after his return from the Sahara, he developed a very material longing—for a car. When he mentioned the idea to Gysin, the painter simply advised him to go ahead and buy one, telling Bowles, "You can afford it." Bowles could indeed afford it. Although the collection of stories was a best-seller neither in England nor in the United States, sales were nonetheless substantial, and with royalties still coming in from the novel, Bowles was in quite a good financial position. Despite his extended trips to Ceylon and through Morocco that summer, he had by no means exhausted even a small portion of his assets. Within a couple of weeks he bought a Jaguar convertible.

When Bowles appeared at the hotel with his new car, the English proprietress immediately informed him that it wouldn't do for him to drive it himself, that he needed a chauffeur for such an automobile. Although Bowles scoffed at the idea, she proceeded with her idea of acquiring a driver for Bowles. A few days later, Bowles discovered upon returning to the hotel that a young Moroccan, named Mohammed Temsamany, was waiting to be put into his service as a chauffeur.

Shortly afterward, Bowles and Gysin, with Temsamany at the wheel dressed in a military-looking chauffeur's coat, headed for Fez in order to try out the car on the open road. While there, he received a wire from Jane, who was now in Paris with Libby Holman. Jane thought it would be nice if Bowles drove to the French border to pick her up and take her back to Tangier. Bowles cabled back that he would be delighted to meet her. After picking up Ahmed Yacoubi, they headed back to Tangier, where he left Gysin; Bowles and the two Moroccans then made their way slowly through Spain until they reached San Sebastián in early June.

CHAPTER 22

Bᴀᴄᴋ ɪɴ Tangier, Bowles and Jane moved into the house in the Medina. Although they had not actually lived together for nearly two years, the arrangement did not last long. Within six weeks Bowles decided to head up to the town of Xauen, in the mountains above Tangier, in order to work in peace. As it had by now been nearly two years since he had begun the novel, he felt an overwhelming urge to complete it. He had also reached a point at which his well-worked-out plans, notes, and diagrams had been exhausted. This, in fact, had always been his aim, as he had decided early on to use the technique he had employed so successfully in *The Sheltering Sky,* letting the final section "write itself." In Xauen, he later wrote in an introduction to the novel, "in the absolute silence of the mountain nights, I accomplished what I had hoped to be able to do when I reached this point in the book. I shut off the controls and let 'Another Kind of Silence' [the last section of the novel] guide itself, without supplying any conscious direction."

The summer over, Bowles returned to Tangier, moving back in with Jane. It was there that he finished the novel, still employing the same method of "unconscious control." Bowles commented that "it went as far as it could go, then stopped, and that was the end of the book."

Let It Come Down, while also a book about expatriates in North Africa, is a very different novel from *The Sheltering Sky.* Whereas the earlier book was sparse in terms of both plot and characters, *Let It Come Down* is fully populated. And if the desert in *The Sheltering Sky* can be thought of as a protagonist, in the second novel, Tangier certainly must be accorded such a status.

The novel's plot concerns a young American, Nelson Dyar, who after ten years of working in a New York bank, decides to alter his life radically, to do something about the "progressive paralysis" that has, over the empty years, "gained on him constantly." He takes a job in Tangier with an old friend of his father's, Jack Wilcox, who runs a travel agency there. Although he must provide his own passage over, and while the pay is low and there is little certainty of it being anything more than a way out of his teller's cage, Dyar is eager for a change, having come to the conclusion that "any life would be better" than the one he was leading in New York.

Arriving in Tangier, he quickly realizes that his job is really not much of a job at all, that in fact Wilcox only seems to want to use him in a black market money-changing scheme. Meanwhile, and before he even catches on to what is happening, he finds himself caught up in the whirl of Tangier's International Zone, a microcosmos of intrigue, seduction, double-dealing, gossip, and dissolution. Adrift in this society he becomes a welcome victim for a great many who are keen on using him for their own ends. For Daisy de Valverde, gossipmonger, social arbiter, bored wife of a Spanish nobleman, he becomes both a new toy to manipulate and an object of her sexual desires; Madame Jouvenon, apparently a Russian spy, sees him as an informant for hire; for Wilcox, he is a patsy to be used for implementing his nefarious enterprise. Against this backdrop of schemers there is Thami Bedaoui, a small-time smuggler and the black sheep of a prominent Moroccan family, who befriends Dyar for no apparent reason; and for good measure, a love or lust interest for Dyar is introduced in the form of a young Moroccan prostitute, Hadija, patronized and protected by an older, corpulent American lesbian writer, Eunice Goode.

As Dyar makes his way through the novel, his role of victim becomes increasingly pronounced. Having taken $500 from Mme. Jouvenon for unspecified services, he suddenly finds himself pursued by the American Legation. Not knowing how to proceed or where to turn, he continues to bumble along, in the manner foreseen earlier in the novel when Daisy reads his palm, only to tell him that his life is "empty," containing "no pattern. And nothing . . . to give you any purpose." Finally, in an attempt to "discover the way out of the fly-trap, to strike the chord inside himself which would liberate those qualities capable of transforming him from a victim into a winner," he puts into motion a series of events that ultimately culminate in disaster.

It begins, despite his longing to change his status, not through his own volition, as he is incapable of making any real decisions, but by accident: he finds himself in possession of about $25,000, acquired through an illegal currency exchange, that he cannot deposit in the bank for his employer's client. It is only then that he thinks, "Legally the money belongs to whoever has it. And I've got it." Running into Thami by chance, and feeling more than ever the need to escape, he enlists the Moroccan's help in getting him out of Tangier and into Spanish Morocco. Using a boat Thami has just purchased, the two make their way into the rugged Spanish zone, holing up in a cabin belonging to the Moroccan's relatives.

It is there, in a kif daze, that Dyar finally commits his fatal *acte gratuit,* his only real act of the novel. Bowles's writing has rarely been stronger:

> "Melly diddle din," he said, quite loud, putting the point of the nail as far into Thami's ear as he could. He raised his right arm and hit the head of the nail with all his might. The object relaxed imperceptibly, as if someone had said to it: "It's all right." He laid the hammer down, and felt of the nail-head, level with the soft lobe of the ear. It had two little ridges on it; he rubbed his thumbnail across the imperfections in the steel. The nail was as firmly embedded as if it had been driven into a coconut. "Merry Mabel dune."

There is no central thesis in *Let It Come Down,* save perhaps the idea, as Bowles later put it, that "security is a false concept." Rather, it is a portrait of a certain aspect of life in Tangier. As Bowles himself has noted, "a town, like a person, almost ceases to have a face once you know it intimately . . . the character is what interests you. In the case of a town, the character is determined largely by its inhabitants." To some extent, it is this character of the city that really forms the nexus of the novel, from which all action, plot, and subplots radiate. Indeed, it is nearly impossible to conceive of another setting for the novel, so linked is it to the machinations of a peculiar set of people living in a particular place at a particular time.

Bowles acknowledged that he expended a great deal of effort on conveying details of Tangier and life in the International Zone in order to lend the novel greater depth and to prepare the reader for the "impossible" conclusion: "It [*Let It Come Down*] was completely surface-built, down to the details of the decor, choice of symbolic materials on the walls, and so on. The whole thing was planned. It had to be. It was an adventure story, after all, in which the details had to be realistic. It's a completely unreal story, and the entire book is constructed in order to lead to this impossible situation at the end."

Part of the reason for the novel's emphasis on Tangier itself may have to do with the fact that Nelson Dyar is not a particularly interesting or compelling character. As Bowles notes: "He wasn't terribly bright. . . . He expects to be a victim and then he is a victim; he's his own victim." But Dyar's moral and intellectual poverty ultimately cannot sustain the reader's interest. It is, in fact, only when Dyar is in a kif delirium at the end of the novel that the reader becomes totally engaged with him, but even this does not serve to make him more real; it is simply that Bowles's writing in this section is so expressive in a refined, but decidedly hallucinatory manner, that he vividly draws in the reader, feeds the raw, spectatorial imagination.

Despite the superb quality of the writing, it was the moral emptiness of the novel, as personified in Dyar's resolute unwillingness to be anything but a victim, that bothered many of the critics. Leonard Amster commented: "Bowles is one of a group of writers who communicate atmosphere and insidious rot and who delineate their characters by offering effects and leaving it to the imagination of readers to discover the sources from which they sprang. . . . The result is . . . a record rather than a revelation, for 'emotion is essential to a work of art.' " Of the major reviews, only one could be considered a rave. Robert Gorham Davis, writing on the front page of the *New York Times Book Review*, lavishly praised the novel, writing that *Let It Come Down* "is more continuously exciting than its predecessor and has more shape and style as a novel. It drives its central character relentlessly toward doom, toward the final orgiastic shudder, with the nightmare clarity, the hallucinative exoticism, of the best of Bowles's short stories."

Published in the United States by Random House and in England by John Lehmann in late February 1952, *Let It Come Down* sold well, on average 3,500 copies per month during the first year of publication, but was by no means the success that *The Sheltering Sky* had been. *The Sheltering Sky*, in fact, continued to make Bowles money, as it had been reprinted in paperback in the United States by Signet Books in June 1951 and had sold over 200,000 copies in its first year of publication. In January 1952, the New American Library issued a paperback edition of *The Delicate Prey* with a first printing of 244,000 copies. Despite the slower sales of *Let It Come Down,* therefore, Bowles, who was still not in the habit of having or spending a lot of money, was doing very well financially.

Characteristically, when the book was published Bowles was not on hand to be feted at the numerous publication parties in both London and New York. Instead he was in India, this time with Ahmed Yacoubi as a traveling companion. Although Bowles has said that his reason for bringing along Yacoubi was simply that he wanted to see what the Moroccan's reaction would be when suddenly dropped from the Medina into South India, the fact is that by this point Bowles and Yacoubi were nearly inseparable. Earlier that year they had stayed at the same hotel for a couple of months in Tetuan, and in Tangier, Bowles had arranged for Yacoubi's first show at the foreign bookstore. Clearly, the young Moroccan had become Bowles's protégé, as Bowles had himself been for others in his own youth. And just as others had paid Bowles's expenses, now Bowles provided for Yacoubi.

After criss-crossing South India for a couple of months, Bowles and Yacoubi decided to head for Ceylon, as Bowles was determined on this trip to get more than a glimpse of Taprobane. Before they could leave India, however, they were stopped by the authorities and held in a "screening camp" or, as Bowles called it, a "concentration camp," run by the Ceylonese government on Indian soil. When Bowles inquired as to why they had been detained he was simply told: "Spying for international." Once in the camp, which held around 20,000 people, some of whom had languished there for years, he became quite concerned about how and when he would get out. They were suddenly released forty-eight hours later, with no explanation as to why they had been originally detained. Although Bowles seemed to take his brief imprisonment in stride, he never returned to India.

Once in Ceylon, after a few days in Colombo, Bowles and Yacoubi stayed with the Trimmers, who were living not on their estate but in the town of Gintota. From there, after two weeks of mandatory daily cholera checks, all of which came back negative,

they finally headed for Weligama Bay and Taprobane. They spent
the night at the Weligama Rest House, which faced the island, and
early the next morning went over from the mainland.

"It was far better than I had expected," wrote Bowles, "an embodiment of the innumerable fantasies and day-dreams that had
been flitting through my mind and getting caught there during all
the years since childhood."

Enchanted, Bowles decided to make inquiries about whether it
was possible to buy the island. In Colombo he learned, however,
that it was not for sale and that the owner had previously refused
several higher offers. He told the Trimmers about his desire to
own the island, mentioning how much he was willing to pay for it
and asking them to wire him immediately if and when the owner
should ever decide to sell. Part of Bowles's desire to own the island
had to do with a sense he had at the time that nothing really
"belonged" to him. Years later he commented that he thought
buying Taprobane would enable him to say, "This island is mine."
In fact, it did not work out that way: "I couldn't. It was meaningless."

With the purchase still not settled, Bowles and Yacoubi left
Ceylon, bound for Genoa. In Italy they stayed first with Albert
Rothschild, where Brion Gysin was also staying. Rothschild's
brother, the filmmaker Hans Richter, was also there and enlisted
Bowles and Yacoubi to act in his new film, *8 × 8*. Richter and
Bowles had known each other since the late 1940s, when they were
both in New York, Bowles having supplied music for two sequences of an earlier film, *Dreams That Money Can Buy.* Now at
Rothschild's villa on the shore of Lago di Orta, over the course of
several weeks they renewed their acquaintanceship; before they
left, Bowles reluctantly, and Yacoubi enthusiastically, had signed
up as actors.

A few weeks later, after a side trip to Venice, Bowles and Yacoubi
headed for Madrid, where Bowles had a gallery contact who was
interested in mounting a show of Yacoubi's work. The exhibition
was a great success and Yacoubi earned a small amount of money;
more importantly he began to develop greater self-confidence as
an artist. While also in Madrid a wire suddenly arrived for Bowles.
It was from Trimmer and read: "OWNER TAPROBANE WILLING SELL
STOP IF INTERESTED WIRE MONEY IMMEDIATELY." Bowles recalls that

he didn't hesitate a moment in deciding what to do: "I was suddenly downstairs at the desk, the telegram still in my hand, and I wrote out two cables, one to New York and the other to Ceylon. The trees, the cliffs, the strange house with its Empire furniture, were all mine." But although the purchase of the island was now secure, it did not mean that Bowles could immediately head back to Ceylon. Instead, he needed to go to New York. Jane had returned there early in 1952. During the months in which Bowles and Yacoubi had wandered in southern Asia and in Europe, she had been completing *In the Summer House,* a task that continued to be enormously difficult for her. According to the poet Kenward Elmslie, Oliver Smith became so concerned with Jane's inability to finish the play that he sequestered her in a hotel room, hoping that the isolation might enable her to concentrate on reworking the last act. Although Jane dutifully remained in her room, the seclusion apparently did not help. When Smith came by after several days to check on her progress, he found, to his chagrin, only page after page of neatly typed picnic recipes.

Jane, though, did finally manage to finish the play early that year, and Smith arranged for it to be performed in repertory in several American cities, then in New York. Bowles was needed to write the music. Again with Yacoubi, Bowles sailed for New York in March 1953.

After spending a day or so in Manhattan, they went up to Treetops, Libby Holman's house in Connecticut, where Jane was also staying. Jane was quite involved with the play, with alcohol, with a new and difficult love affair, and now that Yacoubi and Bowles were there, with them. Bowles's fondness for Yacoubi, the intensity of their relationship, was a sore spot for Jane. She saw Bowles's avid support of the painter as diminishing his concern for her creative work.

. The period at Treetops was tense. In addition to Jane's jealousy, it was evident that Holman was attracted to Yacoubi. Without fully realizing it, she was quickly edging out Bowles by arranging several shows for Yacoubi and generally taking charge of his interests. In late April, to no one's real surprise, she announced that she was in love with Yacoubi and wanted him to stay with her. What made it worse was that Yacoubi agreed. Feeling jilted, Bowles decided by early May to return to Tangier, alone. The stay had been so

chaotic that he left without finishing the music; no doubt his not
coming through on furnishing a score further contributed to Jane's
feeling of abandonment.

Back in Tangier, Bowles spent the next month writing music, not
for *In the Summer House* but for a new commission from Gold and
Fizdale, a setting of James Schuyler's text, *A Picnic Cantata*. Meanwhile, by June, Yacoubi had gotten himself into considerable difficulties at Holman's and was once more on his way back to
Morocco. There are two versions of what happened, but both
center on a single incident: Yacoubi was accused by Holman of
trying to drown her seven-year-old son in the swimming pool.
According to Yacoubi it was simply an accident, and the real reason
for the accusation was that he had informed Holman that he no
longer wanted to be "kept" by her. The swimming pool incident
thus enabled Holman to dismiss him, rather than be left by him. She
threatened to call the police, but finally, apparently on Jane's advice, did not. Instead, after keeping Yacoubi locked in an upstairs
bedroom in her Manhattan townhouse for several days, she dis-
patched him (first-class) on the next ship crossing the Atlantic.

Learning what had happened and that Yacoubi was back in Morocco, Bowles went up to Fez to find him, but the Moroccan was
not there. When Bowles got back to Tangier, however, Yacoubi
was waiting for him. Bowles concluded that the whole business had
been a mistake on Holman's part, that Yacoubi was as innocent as
he proclaimed—was, in fact, something of a victim of riches. If
there had been no love lost between Yacoubi and Jane before, this
incident, and Bowles's willingness to believe him, served to fuel
her animosity.

Shortly thereafter Tennessee Williams cabled Bowles, asking if
he'd be willing to come to Rome to work on the English adaptation
of a Lucchino Visconti screenplay, *Senso*. Bowles readily accepted,
loaded up the Jaguar, and with Temsamany driving and Yacoubi
along as a companion, set off for Italy. Williams, meanwhile, had
gone from Rome to Barcelona for a short visit, arranging for a ride
back to Italy with Bowles and company. But in Barcelona, when
Yacoubi went to apply for a French visa at the consulate, he was
refused. Bowles put him on a plane for Rome, and he, Williams,
and Temsamany continued by car, arriving in Rome themselves in
mid-July. In a letter to Donald Windham, Williams wrote of Bowles
and his entourage:

He [Bowles] has two Arabs with him, his lover (stolen but now relinquished by Libby Holman) and a chauffeur and we all live on the same floor of this apartment building, a top floor which has only a trickle of water for us to divide among us. The Arabs smoke kif and eat "majum," which is some sort of drug that tastes like date-preserves, and Paul sweats and fumes over constant anxieties and discomforts which I find rather endearing as I do the same thing. He has some liver trouble and is down to 115 pounds. . . . [Yacoubi] is torturing Paul by not sleeping with him. It seems that Libby [said] that such relations were very evil and the opinions of a lady with thirty million dollars cannot be taken lightly by a young Arab whose family live in one room. Paul looks haggard and is almost too disturbed to do a good job on the film.

Indeed, when at the end of six weeks Bowles showed the screenplay to Visconti, the director was not satisfied, particularly with the love scenes. "He thought the love scenes cold, and Tenn agreed to work a week on them, which he did," Bowles recalled in 1966. Williams, who had originally been Visconti's choice to do the adaptation, managed to put just the right words on paper to please the director. In the end, both Williams and Bowles were credited with the English version, which was called *The Wanton Countess* on its release in England, although the original Italian title has since been restored.

Toward the end of September, Bowles decided to book passage to Istanbul in order to write an article that *Holiday* magazine had commissioned from him earlier that year. He had begun writing for the magazine in 1950, when he contributed an article on Fez; another on the Sahara and one on Paris had followed early in 1953. Now, however, he entered into a slightly new phase in his relationship with the magazine. Not only would he receive a fairly handsome fee for each article, but they would also assume his travel expenses.

On September 25, 1953, he and Yacoubi set sail for Istanbul. He began the piece with a description of why he chose to bring along Yacoubi:

When I announced my intention of bringing Abdeslam [Yacoubi] along to Istanbul, the general opinion of my friends was that there were a good many more intelligent things to do in the world than carry a Moroccan Moslem along with one to Turkey. I don't know.

He may end up as dead weight, but my hope is that he will turn out instead to be a kind of passkey to the place. He knows how to deal with Moslems, and he has the Moslem sense of seemliness and protocol. He also has an intuitive gift for the immediate understanding of a situation and at the same time is completely lacking in reticence or inhibitions. He can lie so well that he convinces himself straightaway, and he is a master at bargaining.

This passage completely ignores the personal nature of Bowles's relationship with Yacoubi, which was no doubt the real and overriding reason for bringing him along. While Bowles could scarcely be expected to bring this into a travel essay, to some extent the elaborate rationale seems almost an attempt on Bowles's part to try to erect for himself reasons other than the purely personal—to "lie so well that he convinces himself."

But even taking the passage at face value, it also reveals much about Bowles's current assessment of reality. Of particular interest, coming as it does on the heels of the Libby Holman incident, is his description of Yacoubi's ability to believe his own lies. In addition, the passage demonstrates as well Bowles's view of Muslim societies as enigmas, requiring a special passkey by which to enter. Despite his years in North Africa, Bowles still felt that he could not really get inside the Muslim mind or culture, save perhaps in the company of a Muslim. Although this inability to understand Arabic culture was certainly a major theme in his writing, it is somewhat surprising to see Bowles confess his own lack of comprehension. In fact, this was by no means the first time Bowles had expressed the idea. "I don't think we're likely to get to know the Moslems very well," he said in 1952, "and I suspect that if we should we'd find them less sympathetic than we do at present. And I believe the same applies to their getting to know us."

There is in this statement a rather profound acceptance of estrangement, a recognition on his part that he does not really want to penetrate beyond the surface for fear of what he will find. Yacoubi can be seen as functioning in the dual role of protecting Bowles from direct encounter with Muslim society, while at the same time serving to protect them from him. Gradually, Bowles was becoming increasingly dependent on Moroccans whom he knew well to serve as both entrées into society and buffers between him and elements of the society he did not wish to encounter. The pattern of dependency would, indeed, become even greater as the years went by; eventually Bowles would not even stray from his house in Tangier, save in the company of a trusted Moroccan.

By late October Bowles and Yacoubi were back in Italy, met at the dock in Naples by Temsamany. The three of them went briefly to Rome, then with Williams to Portofino to visit Truman Capote. From there they drove to Tangier, where riots had already broken out against the French, a result of the deposition of the sultan on August 20. The rest of Morocco had also been engulfed in sporadic violence. Bowles, having monitored the reports carefully while in Europe, was anxious about whether Tangier would still be safe for foreigners. As he suspected, the atmosphere in Tangier was less than friendly; although he did not feel physically threatened, it was distinctly not the carefree place it had been even three months earlier.

Williams left after a short visit; Bowles did too, not because of the tensions, but because *In the Summer House,* after a trial run in Ann Arbor in May, was about to open in various other cities in the fall: Hartford, Washington, Boston, and then at the end of the year, in New York. This time Bowles sailed alone, firmly committed to producing a score by the November openings.

From the beginning, the play's production had been surrounded by difficulty and confusion. By the time Bowles arrived, one of the original stars, Miriam Hopkins, who played the part of Gertrude, had pulled out and was replaced by Judith Anderson. But even before this major change, the Ann Arbor performance was beset with problems: the director, John Stix, found it hard to get what he wanted out of the actors; everyone seemed to be advising Jane on how to change the script, contributing even more to her already intense anxieties.

Once the play did finally go on, the reviews were almost uniformly negative, if not hostile. "All the efforts of a splendid cast and lively direction failed . . . to keep *In the Summer House* from degenerating into a verbose plea for understanding on the part of the playwright and into a pointlessly morbid study of the psychic difficulties of as useless a bunch of characters as we've ever seen assembled on a stage," wrote the reviewer for the Detroit *Times.*

While her friends and supporters—particularly Tennessee Williams, John Latouche, and Oliver Smith—did not hold back their admiration, the negative public reception and continuing difficulties with cast and director held sway.

By November, with a partially new cast and a rewritten play, the drama was once again set to be performed, but without much optimism. By the time it opened in Hartford, it was clear that Stix had to be replaced. Smith brought in José Quintero for the Boston opening on November 29. Finally, things were beginning to go right, but with a new director, the actors were put under tremendous pressure to rework their parts. Furthermore, Judith Anderson proved as difficult to work with as had Hopkins; she also kept insisting that Jane rewrite her part. When the play opened in Washington on December 14, Bowles had finished the score. Although the music appears to be now lost, by most accounts, Bowles succeeded marvelously in fitting the music to the tone of the play.

The play itself also had come together beautifully, or at least had been brought into a form that could please some critics. When it opened on Broadway on December 29, Brooks Atkinson, writing the next day in the *New York Times,* said: "Scene by scene her play is original, exotic and adventuresome, but very little of it survives the final curtain. From the literary point of view it is distinguished: it introduces us to a perceptive writer who composes drama in a poetic style."

After a run of just six weeks, *In the Summer House* closed in New York, but not without protests from a small group of admirers. On the night of the last performance, February 12, 1954, a full audience uproariously cheered the final curtain. Truman Capote, who claimed that he could not sit through most plays even once, saw it three times during the Broadway run, "not out of loyalty to the author, but because it had a thorny wit, the flavor of a newly tasted, refreshingly bitter beverage." His enjoyment and assessment were typical of a small coterie of enthusiasts, but they could not keep the play alive. Shortly after its closing, Jane, with two friends, Katharine Hamill and Natasha von Hoershelman, returned to Tangier. As a parting remark, Jane told a *Vogue* interviewer, "There's no point in writing a play for your five hundred goony friends. You have to reach more people."

The comment, made offhandedly, was picked up by Walter Kerr

of the New York *Herald Tribune,* who extolled the idea, in a back-handed way, in an article entitled "Writing Plays for Goons": "The hack may say what he means and say it flatly. The talented man may say what he means and say it richly. But the talented man who insists upon his right not to say it all, to hug his meaning like a secret close to his breast, to serve his goony friends rather than the gaping audience, is better off out of the theater. All hail to Jane Bowles for her happy pronouncement."

CHAPTER 23

Jane's return to Tangier, after more than two years in New York, was made easier by the presence of her two friends. She escorted them around the town, introducing them to life in the International Zone and to Cherifa, Tetum, and other Moroccan women. Neither Bowles nor Jane lived in their house in the Medina; Jane stayed at the Rembrandt Hotel, Bowles at the Massilia with Yacoubi. Although they lived separately, they resumed an old pattern of lunching together daily, talking on the phone for half an hour beforehand in order to arrange where and when to meet. Jane, who had always been indecisive, was becoming even more so. Bowles patiently indulged her, making a suggestion, then waiting for her finally to act. Once the restaurant and time had been agreed upon, they would each dress for each other as much as for the occasion.

After a month or so of being back in Tangier, Jane was again madly in pursuit of Cherifa, who held out as before, always with the idea of extracting money or objects from her ardent suitor. Bowles watched; although he advised, he could not interfere. It was as if they had signed an invisible pact, a pact which had as its sole provision that neither would get in the way of the other's personal life. Bowles would not reproach Jane about Cherifa; Jane would not remonstrate with Bowles about Yacoubi. "I wish to Christ you were here," Jane wrote Hamill and von Hoershelman after their departure. "I can talk to Paul and he is interested but not that interested because we are all women."

During the spring, Bowles felt terribly ill. Within a few days, he recognized the symptoms: paratyphoid. He had let his shots lapse in the belief that since he had had the illness before he could not get it again. Although not nearly as ill this time as he had been in the early 1930s in Paris, he was nonetheless confined to his bed for

314

several weeks. During the illness, Jane, who had by then moved into the house in the Medina, came each day to cook his meals at the hotel. To keep her company, Yacoubi moved in with her, but they maintained fairly separate existences.

During Bowles's convalescence, Williams and Frank Merlo came into town for two weeks, doing much to bolster both his and Jane's spirits. Another visitor came to see Bowles also, a man he didn't know: "My memory of him is that he was tall, thin, grey-faced. He had with him the publisher's contract for a book called *Junkie;* it was going directly into paperback and the terms were not good. We talked, he left, and I went back to bed." The man was William Burroughs, and *Junkie* was his first book. Burroughs also recalled that first meeting at the Massilia:

> I stayed very briefly, I would say about ten minutes, and that was the end of that. I had read his books, *The Sheltering Sky* and *Let It Come Down* and several short stories and I knew he lived in Tangier. There was a go between, a man named Dave Woolman. . . . He knew everybody. He worked for the *Tangier Gazette,* did a sort of gossip column. He had talked to Paul and Paul had said, "Yes, bring him around at such an hour," and so it was arranged. . . . He didn't ask me to come around again. He was certainly polite and I could see that he was unwell. He was in a dressing gown and so the conversation was quite brief. He was quite neutral, not surprisingly. We moved in completely different circles. Paul used to move around [socially] a great deal in Tangier, even went to all these fancy parties that were given by the Old Mountain crowd [Tangier's wealthy Europeans], was in solid with that group. I wasn't.

After that first, brief meeting, Bowles "caught glimpses of Burroughs now and then on the Boulevard Pasteur. . . . We nodded and went our respective ways." It would, in fact, be several more years before they would become friends.

Once recovered from typhoid, Bowles, Yacoubi, and Temsamany went up to Fez, as Bowles was curious about the effects of the political unrest on that city, the center of the independence movement. Although rumors and news bulletins had been circulating daily in Tangier about the political upheavals in other parts of Morocco, the city had been largely unaffected, as it was governed internationally. Bowles didn't even have to get to Fez to see that the country was under siege. On the road they had to pull over while a convoy of trucks, armored cars, and tanks roared by. In Fez, tanks circled the ancient walls; in the city itself, the residents looked at Bowles with hostile eyes. The daily newspaper printed body counts and stories detailing the latest atrocities.

A new book had been in Bowles's head for some time. He "wanted to write a novel using as backdrop the traditional daily life of Fez, because it was a medieval city functioning in the twentieth century." But by the time he had made this visit, he realized that the Fez he had known and loved was disappearing before his eyes: "If I had started it only a year sooner, it would have been an entirely different book. I intended to describe Fez as it existed at the moment of writing about it, but even as I started to write, events . . . had begun to occur there. I soon saw that I was going to have to write, not about the traditional pattern of life in Fez, but about its dissolution."

Returning to Tangier, Bowles rented a house on a hill overlooking the ocean, just beyond the walls of the Casbah, and he and Yacoubi moved in for the summer. There, he began working on the novel, establishing a strict routine of writing from dawn to noon. The book rapidly began to take shape. Although he had never wished to write a political novel, he found himself "embroiled in the controversy, at the same time finding it impossible to adopt either side's point of view. My subject was decomposing before my eyes, hour by hour; there was no alternative to recording the process of violent transformation."

Even in Tangier life was becoming ever more politicized, decidedly less pleasant. In August, Bowles wrote Oliver Evans of the changed environment:

Everyone is in a foul temper, people are throwing stones at my house and screaming: Nazarene! (No one answers but the parrot, who gives wolf calls, laughs like a hysterical old maid, and then caws like a flock of crows.) It isn't even amusing for the Arabs, who want nothing more than to see great bloodshed, and spend their time moping around the house in hunger strikes and ripping pictures of Mendès-France out of the papers after which they either spit on them or, which is more likely, put them into their mouths and chew them up, grinding the saliva-soaked paper between their teeth until it's nothing but paste. It's not amusing because it's not going anywhere and can never make anything.

By the fall, Bowles had moved again, this time to the well-protected Casbah. He was becoming increasingly aware that Morocco as he knew it was quickly vanishing; at the same time, he very much hated the idea of leaving. In October, he wrote his parents: "I've had too many years of pleasant living in foreign places ever to be satisfied to live in the United States again. (I may *have* to live there, naturally, if there is a war, but until then I prefer to use that precious time in places I love.)"

It was not just political uneasiness that was affecting Bowles that fall. He and Jane had come to something of an impasse over their respective relationships, hers with Cherifa, his with Yacoubi. At some point during the summer, using as bribes lavish gifts and money, Jane had finally seduced Cherifa into sleeping with her. As a consequence, Cherifa was spending more and more time at the house, often bringing a group of other Moroccan women with her, a matter which worried Bowles. Yacoubi had always disliked and distrusted Cherifa, and he now convinced Bowles that he should no longer go to the house, as Cherifa was sure to poison him. When Bowles agreed to Yacoubi's demand that only Jane visit them, Jane turned against Yacoubi. Things intensified when Jane told Bowles that she had found packets of *tseuheur*—small bundles, used for black magic purposes, containing blood, fingernails, pubic hair, and other personal excreta—under her pillow and mattress. This was all Yacoubi needed to convince him of Cherifa's malevolent intentions. Jane, although warned by both Bowles and Yacoubi, refused to believe that Cherifa had placed them there. Instead, she denounced Yacoubi to Bowles.

By the late fall, they had reached a standoff; Bowles would not visit her because of Cherifa; she would not come to see Bowles because of Yacoubi. As fall progressed into winter, Bowles hit on what he thought to be a solution: going to Ceylon. Curiously, he had not visited Taprobane since purchasing it nearly two years earlier. After much hedging, Jane agreed. In December, he booked first-class passage for him, Jane, and Yacoubi on a ship bound for Colombo. At the last minute, Jane persuaded Bowles to take along Temsamany, but Bowles insisted that he be booked in tourist class.

When the ship docked at Naples on December 13, the English writer Richard Rumbold came on board. He kept a diary of the trip, recording his observations of fellow passengers, in particular the Bowleses. In his entry for December 15, he noted, "I like Bowles very much. A wiry fellow with piercing blue eyes, a sort of crew cut, and a sort of wild-eyed candid look characteristic of certain Americans, and with much disinterested goodness and kindness in his character." He also found Jane intriguing. After sitting up late with her one night, drinking gin in her cabin, he wrote: "She is wonderfully stimulating to me, very much in touch with her intuitive self, like a deep sea diver. She has a quality of spiritual perception, a sort of feeling and seeing life, like an artist, and never thinking it; very fascinating, if one is prepared to let go and dive with her."

Arriving at Colombo two days before Christmas 1954, the Bowleses and company made their way to Weligama; Rumbold stayed for a while in Colombo, agreeing to visit them in March on Taprobane. Jane had never been terribly enthusiastic about Bowles's purchase of the island—had, in fact, told him, "I think you're crazy! . . . You'll never get *me* there." Now that she was there, she at first tried to make the best of it, but after a week or so found herself becoming increasingly depressed and anxious. The heat, which she never had been able to endure well, was oppressive. As the island did not have electricity, there was no possibility of installing electric fans. In addition, Taprobane was plagued by huge bats. Although Bowles had warned her about them, she was not prepared for their size—three-foot wingspreads and large teeth—or quantity. The strange and ample vegetation also worried her. Having developed a phobia of snakes, she was constantly afraid that a cobra might come slithering out of the dense undergrowth. Perhaps worst of all, she found it impossible to write.

Bowles, on the other hand, once again reestablished the regimen he had set for himself in Tangier, writing from dawn to noon. While he did not ignore Jane's difficulties in adapting, he tended to trivialize them, partly so as not to have to be interfered with in his work. But immersion in the novel also served as a convenient escape, enabling him not to have to take her complaints seriously. Publicly he declared that "she suffered in comparative silence." If she did, it might largely have been due to the fifth of gin that she consumed daily in an attempt to blur reality. Drinking this much was bad enough, but compounded by daily ingestion of a hypertensive medication, the effects were even more pronounced, leaving Jane depressed and nearly stupefied.

After they had been on Taprobane for about a month, Peggy Guggenheim came to visit, temporarily lifting Jane's spirits. But Guggenheim was appalled at Jane's condition: "I think she was having a nervous breakdown. Paul was working and he was occupied with that and with Ahmed." Guggenheim tried to convince Jane to go with her to India, but Jane refused, agreeing only to accompany her to Colombo, where they spent a week. When Jane returned to Taprobane, she felt that she could not endure Ceylon much longer. Within a few weeks, Bowles put her and Temsamany on a ship for Tangier; he and Yacoubi remained behind.

While Bowles may have seemed somewhat indifferent at the time, the residue of the joint visit lingered in his mind. Two years later he made the following entry in a notebook, a note for a novel that he would never write, at least in this form:

> Entire situation in Weligama 2 years ago minus civil status of wife and two Moslems. Set up should be fairly actual, wife about as Mrs. Copperfield, as far as character and compulsive behavior go, but motive can be left blank, with fear acting as backdrop and general emotions and atmosphere element: (Eventually it must become apparent that her fear is of him) if still irrational. He must face her with it, demand: But why? Why? She thinks: "If he doesn't know that he doesn't know anything in this world." She says: "If I knew why, I wouldn't be afraid."

This note is accompanied by a longer treatment of the idea:

> A painter and his wife set out to visit house he has bought in S.E. Asia on a previous solo trip there. First scene shown would be on ship, where a kind of inverted complaining is being done by the wife, under guise of friendliness. She hates the heat, the ocean, "primitive" places and people, is convinced that because they are Americans they will be the object of unfavorable criticism on the part of the natives. He methodically ridicules these fears. She admits that she equates being with him and being alone, and solitude in a

strange place is her idea of hell. If it is a house he liked well enough to buy, she knows privately that she will hate it, but her story to him is quite different. If he likes it well enough to buy it, she owes him the duty to go with him to it, because it is so seldom that he finds a place where he thinks he can work.

These fragments have far more reality than fiction about them, and reveal a great deal more about Bowles's awareness of Jane's feelings than any statements he ever made on the subject. Indeed, they fill in a great deal of emotional detail surrounding the visit. From this other evidence, it seems clear that Jane went to Ceylon out of loyalty to Bowles, knowing in advance that she would detest it. The wife's complaints and fears are those of Jane; the painter's ridicule of these, Bowles's way of dealing with them. Beyond being informative about the situation on Taprobane, however, the fragments also serve as an indication of the status of the Bowleses' marriage at the time. The old fear that Jane felt of being alone with Bowles was clearly still a factor. Her attempts to conceal it, to subsume it through a series of externally projected complaints and anxieties, were also characteristic.

In a long passage from the one finished chapter of the novel, Bowles described the couple's relationship through the wife's reflections on her husband. While a fictionalization, it is a very thin one; in some ways it is a tellingly accurate portrait of Bowles, as he imagined himself perceived through Jane's eyes:

She could not be submissive; she had to stand her ground, yet she hated it when he was displeased with her. Worse than this, she knew he thought it was all the same to her whether they were on good terms or bad; it hurt her that he could not see through her feigned indifference, that he should be so easily taken in by her pose of self-sufficiency. Sometimes she suspected that he was perfectly aware, that it was merely easier to pretend not to know. Of course the best way for him to have his way was to give in to her immediately, but this he did very seldom. She had never been able to decide whether he was extraordinarily insensitive to everything that went on outside his mind, or whether he just didn't give a damn. She was less sure about him now than she had been ten years before, an hour after she had met him for the first time. Even then she had known that he was divided against himself, but the division had seemed to exist within an entity: each of two opposing halves complemented the other. But during the years of being married to him she had examined him from so many angles and at such close range that now all she could see was a mass of contradictions. He was a savage fanatic, a sentimental cynic, hedonist in his asceticism; he always hoped for the worst, and when the worst actually happened, he went to pieces. From the beginning she had sensed something in his character which made it possible for her to witness its slow unveiling without intense surprise, but the one detail for which she had not prepared, was his ineffectiveness in a crisis. When a decisive moment arrived, his entire personality seemed to melt, to liquefy; she could see him disintegrate before her eyes; where there had been someone there was no one, and she was both ashamed for him and terrified by the phenomenon. He, however, could undergo it, come out the other side, and discuss it with bland objectivity, as though it had happened to someone in a book, not to him at all, and he could never understand why she was furious with him at such moments.

Bowles did not write more than half a dozen more notebook pages about this couple and their relationship. Perhaps he realized it was too autobiographical; perhaps he just couldn't find enough in the theme to interest him. Although elements from this work would find their way into his last novel, *Up Above the World,* that is really quite a different book. Commenting on the abandonment of this novel he has said rather enigmatically, "I had it all worked out and then? I don't know. It got heavy for me."

After Jane left, Bowles settled back into his writing routine and busied himself in the afternoons with instructing the servants, shopping on the mainland, and seeing to further household restorations. In the evenings, he and Yacoubi frequently wiled away the hours watching the "devil dancers" on the mainland. As Bowles explained, "Nominally a devil-dance is a magical observance with a therapeutic purpose; its aim is to banish the demons of pain, psychosis and general bad luck by inducing such terror in the subject that he will automatically expel them—a rudimentary shock treatment." Bowles quickly became fascinated by these dances and soon learned that the best place to watch them was not in the village of Weligama, but in the palm forest, "for here in the dark, without added artificial light, the howling masked figures leaping with their flames among the trees achieve their full dramatic effect."

When Rumbold came to visit in mid-March, Bowles, by now an aficionado, took him to see the dancers. Rumbold was enchanted; Bowles a bit disappointed, as it had been held in the village. Returning to the island, Rumbold, Bowles, and Yacoubi shared a pipe of kif. The effect on Rumbold's perception of Bowles was profound:

> I looked at Paul. Formerly I thought of him as a 'psychic' person, by which I mean a man with a mind, sensibilities, neuroses, fears, problems, and I had tried, in my normal everyday state, to enter sympathetically into his psyche and puzzle it out. But now that side of Paul vanished; it was as though his mind had disappeared and all that was left was the outline of his features; he was no longer a psychical but only a physical entity. At the same time everything grew very quiet and we seemed to sit . . . in silence for hours on end, like the four characters in *Huis Clos*—a sort of eternity. Then Paul arranged some cups and saucers round him and began drumming on them with a spoon, as though the rhythm of the drums at the devil dance had got into his head. And no one said anything; it was a neutral act, as meaningful or meaningless as any other, neither good nor bad. . . . "It's good for you," Paul told me later, "to face up to your unconscious."

"Kif abolishes no inhibitions; on the contrary it reinforces them, pushes the individual further back into the recesses of his own isolated personality, pledging him to contemplation and inaction," wrote Bowles in 1953. Given to producing effects of inwardness, kif only served to enhance the internalization in a man such as Bowles, enabled him to cut himself off from any external reality. In some ways the man Rumbold saw that night was the real Paul Bowles, an individual alone, isolated in his self-involvement, drumming out the music in his own head, for his own benefit.

CHAPTER 24

BOWLES FINISHED the novel on March 16, 1955, and mailed it off to New York from Weligama. Its title, *The Spider's House,* came from the *Koran:* "The likeness of those who choose other patrons than Allah is as the likeness of the spider when she taketh unto herself a house, and lo! the frailest of all houses is the spider's house, if they but knew." The title is appropriate for a novel that deals as much with the spiritual consequences of political change on the individual as with the physical aspects of the independence movement.

The Spider's House has the most complicated plot of any of Bowles's novels as it interweaves two basic stories and two worlds, that of the Moroccans and that of the foreigners. The principal Moroccan character is a fifteen-year-old boy, Amar. The foreign characters are John Stenham, an American writer who has lived for several years in Fez; Moss, an English painter, Stenham's friend and fellow lodger at the Merinides Palace Hotel (modeled on the Hotel Palais Jamai, where Bowles often stayed); and Polly (Lee) Veyron, née Burroughs, a divorced American tourist, formerly married to a Frenchman. Discounting the prologue, which features Stenham, the first third of the novel is concerned exclusively with Amar. Like Yacoubi, he is a descendant of the Prophet, a healer, possessor of *baraka* (white magic used for healing purposes), a devout Muslim. As the novel opens in the autumn of 1954, during Ramadan, Bowles uses Amar and his adventures dodging the two major factions vying for control of the city—the Istiqlal, or resistance, and the French secret police—as a way of showing the schism and distrust rampant within the Moroccan community. Although Amar has been brought up to hate the French, he is really fairly apolitical, truly uncomprehending of the situation. His world is disintegrating around him as rapidly as it is around that of the French.

About a third of the way through the novel, the narrative shifts to focus on Stenham and Lee, who have just met each other. Stenham is an "old hand," speaks Maghrebi, is in love with a Morocco that was, and, consequently, laments the encroaching Europeanization of the country: "When I first came here it was a pure country. There was music and dancing and magic every day in the streets. Now it's finished, everything. Even the religion. In a few more years the whole country will be like all the other Moslem countries, just a huge European slum, full of poverty and hatred." Lee, on the other hand, has a decidedly different view of Morocco: "For her the Moroccans were backward onlookers standing on the sidelines of the parade of progress; they must be exhorted to join, if necessary pulled by force into the march. Hers was the attitude of the missionary, but whereas the missionary offered a complete if unusable code of thought and behavior, the modernizer offered nothing at all, save a place in the ranks." Despite the differences in their attitudes, they are thrown together and, largely because of circumstance, become lovers after a few days. Their affair, however, is hardly a central focus of the narrative; indeed, it was added by Bowles after the novel's completion at the urging of Bennett Cerf and Donald Klopfer at Random House, who felt that the novel needed a love interest in order to entertain more readers.

Amar first notices Stenham and Lee in a sinister little café on the outskirts of the Medina. Realizing that they are not French, he muses: "What peculiar people they were . . . the most foreign of all the foreigners he had seen." The foreigners have also noticed Amar, and Stenham begins a brief conversation. Suddenly, a burst of machine gun fire is heard and the three escape the café, taking refuge in another café of Amar's choosing. The two story lines converge at this point, and the rest of the novel is concerned with this unlikely trio encountering the rapid, at times terrifying, collision of colonialism with revolution. Finally, after a further series of adventures in which all three of the characters in some ways lose their naïveté about their ordered universes, the novel ends on a rather painful note. Stenham and Lee go off to Casablanca, abandoning Amar, the understated message being that despite affinity and shared moments of danger, the worlds of the Muslim and the Nazarene are doomed to remain separate.

While Stenham and Bowles have a lot in common, Bowles claims that *The Spider's House* is not autobiographical: "I tried always very hard not to write about myself. . . . Naturally, I did put myself into the character in a certain sense, but it's certainly not I." Though Stenham is not Bowles, he did serve as a mouthpiece for many of Bowles's observations on the end of the French-dominated era in Morocco. Through the process of getting to know his protagonist, of articulating Stenham's insight (and lack of it), Bowles was also able to gain for himself a greater understanding of the changing Moroccan situation and its implications for him. Like Bowles, Stenham is of the opinion that traditional Morocco was vanishing before him, that once Fez crumbled to the resistance, Morocco as he knew and loved it would cease to exist: "When this city fell, the past would be finished. The thousand-year gap would be bridged in a split second." But for all of his longing for a preservation of the past, Stenham, like Bowles, was not sympathetic to the French. They, in fact, are the true enemy, as they were the ones to introduce initially the notion of "progress."

Stenham also shares Bowles's desire for being alone, loves to walk on the city's outskirts, primarily because he is conscious of its "outsidedness," which mirrors his own sense of being an outsider. But instead of being a victim of alienation, as are many of Bowles's other protagonists, Stenham prides himself on having struck a precarious balance between himself and involvement in the world: "A man must at all costs keep some part of himself outside and beyond life. If he should ever for an instant cease doubting, accept wholly the truth of what his senses conveyed to him, he would be dislodged from the solid ground to which he clung and swept along with the current, having lost all objective sense, totally involved in existence." Reaching this understanding has been a process:

> There could be no equality in life because the human heart demanded hierarchies. Having arrived at this point, he had found no direction in which to go save that of further withdrawal into a subjectivity which refused existence to any reality or law but his own. During these postwar years he had lived in solitude and carefully planned ignorance of what was happening in the world. Nothing had importance save the exquisitely isolated cosmos of his own con-

sciousness. Then little by little he had had the impression that the light of meaning, the meaning of everything, was dying. Like a flame under a glass it had dwindled, flickered and gone out, and all existence, including his own hermetic structure from which he had observed existence, had become absurd and unreal.

The Spider's House, for all its political overtones, is not a political novel in the usual sense. It is, like the majority of Bowles's work, a depiction of how people respond to stress. And inevitably, the Westerner, under pressure, fails the test. While often this results in physical doom, in The Spider's House one senses that Stenham's betrayal of Amar will condemn him to spiritual self-damnation. By rejecting humanity and by pulling out of Fez, the only place he feels at home, he is propelling himself into rootlessness, into the wasteland of his own self. As Bowles noted, "Not all the ravages caused by our merciless age are tangible ones. The subtler forms of destruction, those involving only the human spirit, are the most to be dreaded."

The Spider's House was published in New York on November 14, 1955. The reviews were laudatory, many critics extolling Bowles's "mature" style and sensibility. "The world and the people created by Mr. Bowles are completely convincing," wrote William Peden in the Saturday Review. "This is the work of a mature writer who has freed himself from the excesses and eccentricities of his earlier fiction, who has something significant to say, and who says it with authority, power, and frequently with beauty." But having "something to say" was apparently not as interesting to the vast majority of readers as had been Bowles's "excesses and eccentricities," for the book did not sell nearly as well. It was not published in England until 1957, when it was brought out by a small house, Macdonald & Co., John Lehmann having closed his press. Also, unlike the first two novels, which sold over 200,000 copies each in paperback, The Spider's House was not issued in paper until 1982, when Black Sparrow Press brought it out in the United States; in England, it has yet to appear in any reprinted form.

In June 1955, Bowles and Yacoubi returned to Tangier, after having spent some time in the Far East, mainly Hong Kong and Japan. They moved again into the Massilia, but Bowles rented, as well, a two-room cottage on the Old Mountain to use as a studio. Installing a piano, he began working again on *Yerma,* as Libby Holman, in letter after letter, was agitating for its completion. That summer another, rather unusual project also came his way: providing a commentary for a group of photographs of the Sahara. The request came from a Swiss publisher, Manesse Verlag; the reason that Bowles was called in was that the photographer, Peter Haeberlin, had been killed while on a photographic expedition in South America before he could complete the arrangement of the photos in book form. Although some of the photographs had captions on the back, the majority did not. As a result, Bowles had to reconstruct the photographer's trans-Sahara journey. It was no small task, as it turned out, for while Bowles had himself traveled through a great deal of the region, Haeberlin had penetrated farther than Bowles had ever gone. In the end, however, Bowles succeeded in providing an informative and interesting commentary for each photo and his introduction to the book is masterful in its evocation of the vastness of the Sahara and its diverse inhabitants.

He also used the opportunity to fire off a well-conceived salvo bemoaning the intrusion of European culture into the region:

> How greatly the West needs to study the religions, the music, and the dances of the doomed African cultures! How much, if we wished, we could learn from them about man's relationship to the cosmos, about his conscious connection with his own soul. Instead of which, we talk about raising their standard of living! Where we could learn *why,* we try to teach them the all-important *how,* so that they may become as rootless and futile and materialistic as we are. Perhaps this, at least, is not wholly inevitable. I cannot help interpreting the title of this book [*Yallah*] (which in Arabic means: Let us be off!) as an exhortation to those of us who are able, to salvage what is still intact and valuable in a part of the world which, more than any other at this point in history, needs our understanding and sympathetic guidance, if we wish to avoid seeing a world-shaking catastrophe take place before our eyes.

In October 1956, *Yallah* was published in German translation in Zurich; the following year McDowell, Obolensky brought it out in the United States.

* * *

The summer and fall of 1955 were tense times in Tangier. The independence movement was growing rapidly, Europeans were fleeing Morocco in droves, and the safety of other expatriate residents was becoming less assured. In September, Bowles wrote to Thomson of the situation:

> Here things seem to be going from bad to worse, although some people think such a thing is impossible. Obviously it isn't; the situation could be far more abject, and doubtless it will be before too long. We still come and go in the streets, and no one molests us. But the possibility of being attacked is uppermost in every non-Moslem's mind; that is made evident in a hundred different small gestures and reactions on the part of one's European and American friends. I have taken an apartment until the first of October next year, but whether I'll be able to stick it out that long remains to be seen. . . . My feeling is that the usefulness of Morocco as a place to work has worn thin; it could hardly be otherwise when one is unable to keep oneself from being drawn into the daily life of everyone in the street, and from drawing everyone into one's own daily life.

But Bowles did not leave that fall. As a kind of stasis had been reached, he instead continued to work sporadically on *Yerma* in his new apartment in the Nouvelle Ville. He progressed very little, however, and spent the summer and fall expanding his social circle in Tangier, cultivating friendships with the English painter Francis Bacon and with William Burroughs. Bacon struck Bowles as highly observant and articulate, but above all else, a man "about to burst from internal pressures." It was this bottled energy that he put into his paintings, bursting on canvas, rather than in life. Yacoubi was fascinated by him as well, and soon Bacon agreed to teach the Moroccan how to use oils, a turning point in Yacoubi's artistic career.

Of Burroughs, Bowles said: "I had decided that [he] was a true eccentric, thus very much worth knowing." Before Bowles had really become acquainted with Burroughs he "had been told about him: how he practiced shooting in his room down in the Medina, and all the rest of the legend. When I got to know him I realized the legend existed in spite of him and not because of him: he didn't give a damn about it."

Burroughs was working on *Naked Lunch* at the time. According to Bowles, "the manuscript . . . lay on the floor of Bill's room . . . being ground underfoot month after month." Burroughs disputes this: "I was probably sorting things out when he came in because I did not leave papers on the floor. He may have seen that; I was maybe trying to get some sequence and I'd spread them out to see where I was going, but it was certainly a special occurrence." He does, though, remember reading Bowles a section now and then from *Naked Lunch.* Bowles found the passages highly amusing: "When he read aloud from it, at random (any sheet of paper he happened to grab would do) he laughed a good deal, as well he might, since it is very funny, but from reading he would suddenly (paper still in hand) go into a bitter conversational attack upon whatever aspect of life had prompted the passage he had just read."

Shortly after getting to know Burroughs, Bowles told him that he ought to get acquainted with Brion Gysin, "thinking that each would appreciate the other." Burroughs was not so sure: "Brion had met me before and didn't approve of my way of life or my association with the Spanish since he was tied up with the Arabs. Or he thought I was incompatible with this Arab-oriented life he'd set up. But then Paul told Brion that he was missing something, that I was a special person that he should pay attention to, and since Brion listened to Paul that resulted in my getting to know him." Thus began a thirty-year collaboration, one of the richest in modern American letters.

At the time Gysin was running a restaurant in Tangier called the 1001 Nights, which, according to Bowles, was by that time "the only good one in town." Gysin's main interest in starting the restaurant, however, was not in culinary creations, but in showcasing the Jajouka musicians and their music. "For me," says Bowles, "Jajouka never had a great musical interest but Gysin went mad about it." Nonetheless, 1001 Nights, during the few years of its existence, was a major gathering spot in Tangier, and unlike many other restaurants, was patronized by both expatriates and Moroccans.

Jane, during the summer and fall of 1955, was even more involved with Cherifa than she had been previously. As a result, she and

Bowles maintained separate residences—Bowles in the hotel, Jane in the house in the Casbah—and would go for several days, sometimes over a week, without seeing each other. In the fall of 1955, however, Jane came to see Bowles. Cherifa, she informed him, demanded either money or the house if the relationship were to continue. As Jane had little money, she had promised to hand over the house to Cherifa. Bowles reluctantly agreed, feeling that she might at last be pacified; by the first of the year the house belonged to Cherifa, although it would take until March 1956 for the legal transfer to be completed.

By that time, Jane was back in the United States and Bowles was in Lisbon, where he stayed for several weeks, writing an article for *The Nation* on the Portuguese political situation. While still in Lisbon, Bowles received a wire in April from his parents announcing that they were coming to visit him in Tangier that summer. Bowles consequently returned to Morocco to prepare for their arrival; Jane, too, arrived back in Tangier in June.

Although Morocco had gained independence from France on March 2, 1956, Tangier was not immediately affected, as it was still governed internationally. Clearly, though, the situation was not the same. Writing an article for *The Nation* on Tangier, Bowles noted that despite official policy, the "integration" of Tangier with the rest of Morocco was already becoming a reality:

> Walk down into the Zoco Chico any night. In the little square lined with cafés you can see that in fact, if not officially, the integration of Tangier with the rest of Morocco has already taken place. Instead of the customary assortment of European tourists and residents, elderly Moslems in *djellabas* and native Jews from the nearby streets of the Medina, you are likely to see sitting at the tables no one but young Moslems in European dress—mostly blue jeans. . . . And the Europeans who used to be here every night, where are they? Safe in their houses, or sitting in the fluorescent glare of the French and Italian cafés of the Boulevard Pasteur. They know better than to wander down into the part of town where they are not wanted.

Despite Bowles's concern, though, life in Tangier went on very much as it always had. The change was subtle, mainly observable in the spirit of independence that had taken over the average

Moroccan. Although initially a bit worried over his parents visiting a country in strife, by the time of their departure from New York in June, Bowles felt at ease about their visit. He scurried about, making preparations for their arrival, to which he was actually looking forward.

Indeed, over the years, Bowles had developed a much more cordial relationship with his parents. They exchanged letters frequently, full of mutual concern about health, wealth, and happiness. Distance, of course, helped to make the relationship better, as they could not interfere in Bowles's life. Perhaps the best measure, though, of how far Bowles had come in restoring relations with his father can be seen in his dedication of *The Spider's House* to Claude. (*The Delicate Prey* had been dedicated to his mother.)

The visit went well. His parents seemed to enjoy themselves, abstained from criticism of him or his way of life, even smoked kif with him, although they still much preferred whiskey. While Bowles may not have felt, nor even desired to feel, that they now totally approved of him, the visit did serve to assure him that at least he had finally earned their respect. He still experienced, when reflecting on the past, a certain degree of animosity, but he also could realize that the instincts of self-preservation that he had learned in childhood had in maturity become a part of his character. Regardless of the hurts, of the terror endured by him as a child, he had managed to utilize the lessons from those early years to establish himself as an independent individual. The ability to invent a cosmos, originally a retreat from his father's menacing behavior, now served him publicly—had earned him, in fact, a reputation and a livelihood.

In November 1956, Bowles and Yacoubi headed for Ceylon again, Bowles having decided to sell Taprobane. Because of the Suez blockade, he and Yacoubi had to go to London to pick up a ship that would take them around the horn of Africa. In London, Bowles decided to inquire of his English publisher, Macdonald, about when *The Spider's House* would be out. He wrote Jane about the lack of reception he had received from the publishing house:

> They seemed completely uninterested in when or whether it would appear, also in whether I was in London or Kalamazoo. . . . I found

it difficult to get anything across to Macdonald. "What kind of book is it, they asked?" And when I said it was a novel, they said they'd look on their list and see. Then they announced: "Oh yes, scheduled for January. Is that all you wish to know?"

Getting a ship out of England, they finally arrived in Ceylon around Christmas. But Bowles's problems were far from being settled, for it proved considerably more difficult to sell the island than it had been to buy it. In January he wrote to Jane, "I am eager to sell the house and get out as quickly as possible, otherwise I shall have no money." In March, he was still saying very much the same thing:

> So far no one has bought the house, and it is quite clear that I will have to leave Ceylon without selling it, which I suppose means that it will be very difficult to sell it later. I've been running my legs off going from one agency of the government to the other, getting documents of all sorts which in the event of a sale will make it possible (conceivably at any rate) to get the money out of the country. . . . Each day the feeling of its utter futility becomes stronger. However, I intend to fix up everything that I can, so that there will be some sort of possibility of collecting the money should it be forthcoming. I can't afford not to, really.

Late that month Bowles did leave Ceylon with Yacoubi. When Taprobane was finally sold about a year later, despite all of the efforts he had made to ensure that he could remove the money from Ceylon, the new law prevented him from taking any of it out of the country. As a result, Bowles never recouped even a rupee from the sale.

He did manage to raise some cash at the time by placing an article on Tangier with *Holiday* and his short story "The Frozen Fields" with *Harper's Bazaar*. Telling Jane of the news, he added, "So I don't feel quite as useless as I did." Money, in fact, for the first time since 1950, was becoming something of a problem. Royalty payments were no longer pouring in as they had, *The Spider's House* having not yet sold enough copies even to exceed Bowles's initial advance of $6,000. And while he had received another advance from Random House earlier that year for a collection of travel essays, he did not yet feel that he had suitable material for a whole volume. In fact, the book would not appear until 1963.

From Colombo, Bowles and Yacoubi sailed to Kenya, where Bowles was to do a story for *The Nation*. The Mau-Mau uprising was still fresh in the minds of Westerners; Bowles was charged with the duty of penetrating its causes, illuminating in the process the actual political situation in Kenya. His article is a marvel of reportage. Although clearly sympathetic to the African struggle for self-determination, he manages at the same time to give an objective report on the current turmoil.

From Mombasa, he and Yacoubi sailed the long way around Africa, the Suez Canal still being blocked by the British, spent a few days in Capetown, then went on to the Canary Islands and finally to Morocco. Disembarking in Casablanca in mid-May, Bowles was handed a telegram. It was from Gordon Sager in Tangier. It said, quite simply, that Jane had suffered a slight stroke several weeks earlier and was recuperating.

Returning to Tangier as soon as he could—by this time almost six weeks after the stroke—he found Jane alert, but with her eyesight greatly diminished and suffering from a kind of aphasia that caused her to mix up pronouns. Accounts differ as to what actually happened, but certain details do mesh in all versions. Early in the evening of April 4, 1957, she had gone to Gordon Sager's apartment. She began drinking fairly heavily, but returned to her own apartment on the eighth floor. Cherifa was there, waiting for her to return. What happened next is unclear. According to Cherifa, Jane ran up the stairs, threw water on her face, and began vomiting. Shortly afterward, she became unconscious. Cherifa then called Christopher Wanklyn, a friend of the Bowleses who was staying next door in Bowles's apartment. By the time Wanklyn arrived, Jane was on the floor. According to him, Cherifa had tied a slice of lemon around her forehead. Jane was regaining consciousness, but did not know what had happened to her; Wanklyn immediately called Gordon Sager and a doctor.

As she became conscious, she was rumored to have muttered a strange sentence. "I don't know what Jane said when she came out of the coma," Bowles commented years later. "Apparently she said, 'What's worse than *baisar?' Baisar* is a kind of very thick porridge that's eaten here. She had lost her memory and she was thinking of something that was even worse. She couldn't remember the word, and Gordon Sager decided to ask her, 'Do you mean *majoun?*' And she said, 'Yes, that's it.' Later she claimed that she never said such a thing. I tried to help her remember what had happened and she said, 'I may have had a few pipes of kif, I don't know.' "

Bowles wrote Thomson a more clinical account of what had occurred: "In April she had what has variously been described as a 'syndrome confusionnel,' a 'spasme cérébral,' a 'small bleed,' a 'microlesion' and a 'gros accident cérébral.' Whatever it was it resulted in temporary amnesia and a permanent loss of one half of the visual field. The latter has naturally been a terrible shock."

But in Tangier society, a less clinical diagnosis of the cause of the seizure began to circulate quickly. Focusing on the story of Jane being fed *majoun,* suspicions began to mount that Cherifa had tried to poison her. Although Bowles claims now that he really has no idea whether it is true or not, in the past he did lean toward this theory. It should be noted that Jane was always highly susceptible to cannabis in any form, and was not a frequent user; had she taken *majoun* or even kif, she might very well have become disoriented. The combination of any cannabis substance with alcohol would not have been likely, in and of itself, to have produced a stroke; but at the time Jane was also taking hypertensive medication, and this, in conjunction with alcohol, might well have been sufficient.

"Cherifa certainly did not poison Jane," asserts Edouard Roditi. "No, in my opinion Jane destroyed herself. She drank to the point of being an alcoholic, and finally, drank herself into a stroke." Says the painter Buffie Johnson: "It's curious. Paul can't bear people who drink, can't even bear alcohol, won't have it in the house. And yet, he positively balks at the idea of Jane drinking herself to death. He'd rather call it magic, but that wasn't it. . . . Jane was a very delicate little creature. Her body just finally couldn't stand the mistreatment. All those years of drinking too much finally caught up with her."

Once Bowles was back in Tangier, he quickly realized that Jane needed professional care beyond that which could be obtained locally. In late June, he wrote to a London neurologist in an attempt to get Jane admitted to an English clinic.

In the meantime, word of Jane's stroke had crossed the Atlantic. Libby Holman immediately sent a letter expressing her concern, as well as a check for $500, with the further promise of a monthly allotment of $175. Oliver Smith, Katharine Hamill, and Natasha von Hoershelman each agreed to send Jane $25 a month to help with expenses. In addition, Virgil Thomson sent Bowles $1,000, with a note explaining its source: "I did get worried about maybe you might need money, and so I took the liberty of acquiring some for you from the Institute's [American Institute of Arts and Letters] revolving fund (which exists for the purpose of discreetly coming to the aid of artists in emergencies). . . . It is neither a loan nor an award. If you need it, use it. If not, send it back. In any case I should be ever so grateful to hear from you about Janie's state."

"Janie's state," in fact, was far from good. On July 21, with arrangements already made to have her examined in London, she suffered "two epileptiform attacks." Bowles, in a letter thanking Thomson for the money, wrote that the seizures "further impeded her ability to see; at which point she lost what was left of her morale, and became quasi-hysterical, which she has been more or less constantly since then." At the beginning of August, Bowles took Jane to London. She was first admitted to the Radcliffe Infirmary but within twenty-four hours begged Bowles to remove her from there. Two days later Bowles succeeded in moving her to Saint Mary's, also in London. He recapped the events in a letter to Thomson:

> During the ten days she was in St. Mary's she had all the essential tests: X-rays of brain and heart, various blood tests, electroencephalogram and arteriogram, and the possibility of brain tumor removed, as well as the necessity (that is, the feasibility) of surgery. But the facet of her emotional reactions to the illness were left untouched, and that is at least fifty percent of her present problem; that much should be apparent even to a neurologist. . . . The simple fact of the matter now is that Jane has lost her nerve and is at the brink of a mental breakdown. When things get to that point there is no end visible; a sort of spastic stubbornness puts her into direct opposition to any therapy a doctor can offer. She is convinced no one can diagnose her illness and that suicide is the only solution.

In late August, the Bowleses headed back to Tangier. On board the ship, Jane had another seizure, which resulted in "mental confusion, amnesia and complete hysteria." When the ship docked in Gibraltar, Bowles tried to get Jane to enter a clinic there, but she refused. Finally, they arrived back in Tangier, but almost from the moment they were back in Morocco, she became obsessed with returning to London. On September 10, Bowles wrote Thomson of the latest events:

> Jane's Tangier doctor came to see her immediately upon her arrival, and got hold of a psychiatrist named Pidoux who had written some monographs on black magic in the Haute Volta and such subjects. He talked each day to Jane for an hour, and seemed to calm her; his sedative properties, however, were most ephemeral, and within two or three hours after he had left she was back in the same awful state. Each succeeding day she appeared to retreat further into an inaccesible region of being. To communicate at all with her one was obliged to discuss her return to London; she could not hear anything else, literally. . . . At the same time she was increasing her intake of drugs at an alarming rate, and in spite of a daily absorption of a quantity and variety that would have put a horse out, failed to sleep or relax at all. There was also an undercurrent of violence in her behavior which worried me terribly, directed principally inward, but taking the form of unreasoned hostility to others at times, so that she was impelled to take hold of heavy objects with the idea of hurling them across the room.

Given Jane's condition, it was clear that something had to be done. That same week, Bowles arranged to have her accompanied on a flight to London, as he felt himself too exhausted to travel again so soon. In the same letter to Thomson, he said: "The last forty-eight hours were pretty awful for everyone; as the time drew near, Jane became worse. She was convinced she was being sent to be tortured, that she would never come back again, and her ability to describe and discuss her own state lucidly, at the same time being imprisoned by it, was perhaps the worst part." Once in London, Jane was admitted to a psychiatric clinic in the countryside. Bowles made arrangements to follow at the end of the month. Looking back on it in 1972, Bowles said sadly, "I did not know it, but the good years were over."

PART VI

Things Gone and Things Still Here

CHAPTER 25

Bowles ARRIVED in England in late September 1957. Yacoubi accompanied him, as he was to have a show at the Hanover Gallery in London that Francis Bacon had helped arrange. By this time Jane was in St. Andrews, a psychiatric clinic in Northampton. Bowles went immediately to visit her, staying in Northampton for a few weeks. On his return trip to London he wrote Thomson that "she seems a little better than she did last week; in fact, for long periods she appeared to be her usual self. It was only at moments of emotional stress that one could sense that anything at all was the matter with her." The doctors, however, were advising that Jane undergo electric shock treatment, as they felt it "more than likely to produce a beneficial result in the shortest possible time." Jane was adamantly opposed. "She sees its effect on the other patients around her and rejects it, without understanding that the others are manic-depressives, schizophrenics, and alcoholics on whom it is often tried without much hope of being successful."

Bowles's own state of mind during this period is difficult to assess. From letters, it is evident that he was under a great deal of strain, was enormously concerned about Jane, but, characteristically, he kept his emotions much to himself. He carried on with his usual sense of decorum, attending to the details of Jane's hospitalization as if they were ordinary events, not matters of crucial importance to their lives. A notebook entry from this period also serves to illuminate his mental state: "All you can do is behave only as you would like others to behave with you in a similar situation. I appreciate commiseration, but naturally I'd rather not have it. I suspect it's the same with almost everyone." Similarly, in a draft letter to an unknown correspondent, in the same notebook, Bowles reflected on the idea of meriting a happy life:

> I can't subscribe to your conviction that you have the "right" to a pleasant life merely because you can conceive of such a thing.

339

. . . God knows I think everyone has to try to find such a thing, but I know it is false to think that one "deserves" anything at all. Thinking that is equivalent to making the statement which is the ultimate in absurdity: "Life is (good) (bad) (inexplicable) (simple) (any other adjective). What quality can existence possibly have? How can one merit anything?

Back in London, Bowles suddenly became ill himself and was admitted to the hospital with a severe case of Asian flu. For nine days he languished in a kind of delirium brought on by high fevers. But rather than succumb to the fever he used it as a way of linking himself directly to a sensate subconsciousness. Over the next nine days he wrote one of his most powerful stories, "Tapiama," about an American photographer somewhere in the wilds of Central America who ends up in a bar in a tiny hamlet on a river. The place, menacing from the start, becomes even more so as the photographer falls under the spell of the local drink, the *cumbiamba.* By the ambiguous end of the story, he is as dazed as the professor in "A Distant Episode," afloat in a canoe with Indians, going nowhere down the river.

When Bowles finished the story, on the tenth day of being in the hospital, his temperature registered 98.6. He was released, but a few hours later the fever returned, and by that evening he was back in the hospital. Pneumonia had set in, followed by pleurisy, and for the next three weeks he did not leave his bed. Finally, at the end of the month he was released into the care of his friend Sonia Orwell, George Orwell's widow.

During the time he had been in the hospital, Jane had received seven electric shock treatments. They apparently produced some temporary relief from acute anxiety and on November 11, she too was judged fit to return to Tangier. Arrangements were made to travel at mid-month.

Before Bowles left London, however, he wanted to try to arrange for publication of a new book of short stories. Sonia Orwell made an appointment for him at the publishing house of Hamish Hamilton. Bowles, however, "through inattentiveness," went instead to the offices of William Heinemann. Although he noticed the error when he presented Orwell's letter of introduction, by then it was too late. After a discussion with one of Heinemann's editors, the book was accepted on the spot. When it was finally published, nearly two years later, it contained ten stories, including some of Bowles's best: "Tapiama," "The Frozen Fields" (his semiautobiographical story of a bullying father and his precocious son), and the novella "The Hours After Noon," which gave a title to the collection.

Bowles, Jane, and Yacoubi returned to Tangier in late November 1957. The day after their arrival, Yacoubi was arrested on a warrant that had been issued in September. What had happened was this: On June 24, shortly after his return with Bowles from Ceylon, Yacoubi had been arrested, according to Burroughs, "allegedly for taking indecent liberties with a 14-year-old German boy. The boy's parents kicked up a row, went to the police." Thirty-six hours later, after Bowles had posted bail of 200,000 francs (about $500), Yacoubi was released. In both July and August, Yacoubi was arrested again for short periods. On these occasions, he was questioned about the personal habits of various Europeans in Tangier. In September, as Bacon had arranged the show for him in London, he applied at the tribunal for a return of his passport, and to everyone's surprise, it was handed back to him.

Now, however, he had been rearrested. The charge, during his absence, had been changed to "assault with intent to kill." Bowles retained several lawyers while Yacoubi stayed behind bars. During the early days of his incarceration, Bowles went daily to visit him, taking him food, but as the months wore on, and the trial was postponed and postponed again, Bowles, Jane, and many others in the expatriate community began to feel increasingly more concerned about their own safety. Other Moroccans in the Bowleses' circle were called in for questioning.

By late in the year, it was clear that the local police were hoping to drive out as many expatriates as possible, using their "personal life-styles" as an excuse. Moroccans such as Yacoubi, who seemed to have close ties to the expatriate community, were also under increased suspicion, not only because of suspected "immorality," but, more importantly, because they were suspected of being pro-French, or at the very least, not 100 percent supportive of independence. While Yacoubi indeed appears to have been involved with the young German, the intense interest taken in him by the local authorities had as much to do with their doubts concerning his political stance as it did with his alleged improprieties.

During this period, Jane, while not well, was at least holding steady. Her vision had improved somewhat and she could read a little, and with great difficulty write a letter now and then. Heavily medicated, however, she was often semidazed.

In early February 1958, the Bowleses decided to leave Tangier indefinitely. The main reason was that the police had stepped up their investigation at the first of the year, and the inquiry had spread to Bowles. In late January, he was questioned once; now Jane's relations with Cherifa were being investigated. Bowles feared that Jane would be interrogated next. This particularly concerned him, as he felt she was neither physically nor emotionally able to undergo questioning. As a result, they locked up their apartments, Bowles gave the Jaguar to Temsamany, and the Bowleses left for Madeira, Portugal, around the tenth of the month.

Although often prone to excessive worry about the authorities, Bowles had in this instance been wise to leave. Two weeks after their departure, he received a letter from a Tangier lawyer informing him that the police had been trying to bring him in again for questioning. "The only matter they are concerned with," wrote the attorney, "is the nature of your relations with Yacoubi, and for that reason they wish to interrogate you, with a view to implicating you. One of your fellow citizens, named Murray, was similarly found guilty, and has suddenly left Tangier. . . . In any case, until the end of the Yacoubi affair, there can be no question of your returning here." In March, Temsamany was called in four times by the police and grilled about Bowles and Yacoubi, Jane and Cherifa. He said he knew nothing of their intimate lives, that Yacoubi and Bowles always had separate rooms, that Cherifa was Jane's maid. Cherifa, meanwhile, had fled Tangier for the mountains. A few months later, Temsamany sold the car, and with the money went to Germany to work.

Life in Tangier was clearly no longer the expatriate paradise it had been. The crackdown, in fact, was having a great impact on the foreign community. Although the process of disintegration had been noticeable for some time, it was now accelerating. Residents, whether they had anything to hide or not, were quickly selling out and moving on. By the end of the decade, Tangier would largely lose its former international flavor, its perceived decadence and—for many—its charm.

Despite her anxiety about the situation in Tangier, Jane, after an initial bout of depression, actually began to improve. With Bowles's constant encouragement, she was able to write a little for the first time in a year; but by the end of March that brief spurt of activity was over and she lapsed into anxious inactivity. Her blood pressure soared again; a local doctor told her she risked another stroke. She at first welcomed the news, thinking she would die, but when the doctor said that she would most likely only become paralyzed and be unable to speak, she relinquished her belief in that possibility as a way out of her dilemma.

By the first of April, things had gotten to a point where Bowles felt he could no longer cope. Jane clearly needed greater care than he could provide for her in Portugal. Finally, Bowles informed her that her passport, which had expired, would not be renewed by the American embassy until they could do a complete check on her communist history, and that she would have to go to the United States to sort it out. There is the possibility that this, in fact, was a ruse concocted by Bowles to get her to New York; according to the U.S. Department of State, such a practice would be highly irregular. On the other hand, given America's recent bout of McCarthyism, Bowles's version could indeed have been true.

In mid-April, Jane flew to New York, where Tennessee Williams met her, escorting her to her friends Katharine Hamill and Natasha von Hoershelman, who had agreed to take care of her. Bowles stayed on in Madeira, at once relieved to have her off his hands and concerned and guilty that he wasn't with her. Although he did manage to write a few articles for *The Nation* and *Holiday,* he had been largely unable to work on any fiction while ministering to her; now that she was gone, he still felt it difficult, if not impossible, to get on with his writing. In the past it had always served him as a retreat from reality, but reality had never before been quite so insistent.

The situation improved somewhat in mid-May, when Bowles heard from Francis Bacon that Yacoubi's case had finally come up for trial and that he had been acquitted in less than five minutes. Bacon, however, discouraged Bowles from returning, as the air was not yet completely clear. There was even some concern that

Yacoubi's release could have been part of a trap laid for Bowles. (It wasn't, but fears were rampant.)

In June, Bowles received a telephone call from Libby Holman. *Yerma* was to be produced, at last. Bowles boarded the next ship for New York, using the interlude during the crossing to complete the opera. In New York, he went first to see Jane, whose condition, to his relief, had somewhat improved. She was going daily for language therapy (both reading and writing) at Lenox Hill Hospital and was making slow but perceptible progress in both areas. Psychologically, however, she was still feeling very disconnected from herself, and often from everyone else around her. Guilt, anxiety, and a profound inability to understand what was happening to her were as pronounced as ever. In one writing therapy session at the hospital, she wrote a chilling document:

> There are three people in here. Mother . . . my mother myself and a monster. The monster is not to be reconned with. I cannot deal with the monster. It is is not my fault. It is not my fault. Even if I could explain what it is that is missing it would help because I would still be where I am . . . no better off. There are no accounts to settle. Just the accounts of decinsy . . . decency. If the words come I hont . . . dont know how. I have no control over them. It is as if they had not come. I don't think any n- nurologist can find the missing link in my brain. Nor any Psychiatris for that matter. The simples explaination is this that 3 and 6 make nothing. I cannot.

Jane's tragedy was perhaps the greatest a writer can experience, namely the loss of self-expression. It was clear that she had so much to say, but never had she been so unable to say it. Words, which formerly had occupied a central position in her life, now evaded her. She was left with the dreadful realization that the sum of all her thinking produced nothing, since she could not create sentences sufficient to convey the ideas forming themselves in her mind, ideas that too soon became chimeras, evaporated before she could capture them on paper.

At the end of July, after rehearsals in New York, Bowles went with Holman and the cast of *Yerma* to Colorado, where the opera was to be performed at the University of Denver. It premiered there on

July 29, 1958. A critic from the New York *World-Telegram and Sun,* who had been sent to Denver to review the show, praised Bowles's music, but was somewhat less enthusiastic about Holman:

> In *Yerma,* García Lorca has written a brooding, passionate drama of a Spanish peasant woman whose unfulfilled yearning for a child becomes a consuming obsession. The flame that gnaws within her is as hot and dry as the Andalusian country where the action is set. Paul Bowles, who translated the drama from the original Spanish, has created an outstanding musical score. His music is haunting, weird, mystical. The score is modern, but strongly flavored with the compelling music of Spain's Arabic background. . . . Miss Holman appears to advantage when singing, but displays uncertainty in her acting. She got off to a slow, stiff start in Act One, but warmed to the job as the show went on.

Bowles privately felt that he had delayed too long in finishing *Yerma,* that Holman's voice was not what it had been in 1947 when he had begun the opera. Furthermore, he found the Denver orchestra "lamentable." After ten performances in Denver, and ten more in Ithaca, New York, the opera closed, never having made it to Manhattan. Bowles had hoped that Jane could attend the opera's opening in Ithaca, but she was too ill. After conferring with Mrs. Auer, Bowles decided that Jane needed hospitalization. On October 1, over her weak protest, she entered a psychiatric clinic, the Cornell Medical Center, in White Plains, New York. Almost immediately after she was admitted, Bowles flew to California, where José Ferrer had commissioned him to write a score for a new play, *Edwin Booth.* Although Bowles did not care much for Hollywood, the distraction seemed to do him good. He plunged himself into the work, producing a score in a matter of weeks.

Back in New York, John Goodwin invited Bowles, Ned Rorem, and another friend to spend the weekend at his house in Crescoe, Pennsylvania, with the specific intention of introducing Rorem and Bowles to mescaline. Once ensconced in Goodwin's country mansion, he handed them each a pill. Rorem recalls that Bowles had the attitude of one who was "submitting to the experience as to a necessary operation." For the first hour there was no effect, but as the afternoon wore on a heightened perception seemed to overtake them both. At some point Rorem observed, through the mescaline optic, that Bowles, "without feeling it had a liver attack, his bony hands, luminous green and transparent, clutched at the organ and tore it out as he grinned, his face all molars." Later, menaced by buzzing flies which in Rorem's mind had taken on monstrous proportions, he called out for help. Bowles responded, killing them with a simple swat, but in the state Rorem was in the act loomed as monumentally heroic. "Of the four," wrote Rorem, "Paul appeared the validest human, especially after nightfall."

Rorem's observation on Bowles's humanity is interesting, for it reveals a side of Bowles that he often tried rather hard to hide behind a charming mask of genteel detachment. But at this point in his life, with Jane hovering on the verge of mental and physical collapse, his emotions were perhaps close enough to the surface to be glimpsed, at least for a moment. The Bowles who had once seemed to Rorem "unknowable" and "aloof" now was perceived as possessing another dimension. It took mescaline for Rorem to glimpse it; many others never managed to see it at all.

Aside from this brief interlude, Bowles was largely preoccupied with Jane or was busy attending to various other matters, mostly concerning his livelihood. For years—practically since the late 1930s—Bowles had been trying to get financial support in order to collect Moroccan music. Now, with the advent of portable tape recorders, he was again trying to obtain a grant to make a series of recordings. In October, he met with Harold Spivacke, chief of the Library of Congress's Music Division, who in turn wrote on his behalf to the Rockefeller Foundation. In a letter to John Marshall at the Foundation, Spivacke quoted extensively from Bowles's proposal, which laid out the project's basic rationale and method for collecting the music:

With regard to the material I hope to collect: a recording project in Morocco is a fight against time and the deculturizing activities of political enthusiasts, and because of that I want to get down both folk and art music. Even in the latter, to which on principle no one is definitely opposed, public apathy is destroying the performance traditions, and to me it is important to capture whatever examples I can of *andaluz* music. It is the folk music, however, which is most in danger of disappearing quickly, and it is upon that I should concentrate. It is already too late to embark on a program of recording folk music here without governmental permission (which will doubtless involve a certain amount of interference). . . .

A certain amount of the music I hope to be able to get by installing myself in strategic spots and capturing it without the knowledge of the people making it. . . . By far the greatest part of the material, however, would be performed by professionals, and would have to be paid for—after, needless to say, innumerable hours of haggling, gifts, offers and counter offers. Even if one had an unlimited purse from which to pay them, without the haggling there would be no true personal contact, and without that contact there would be no bringing forth of their best material or of their best performing efforts.

Despite Spivacke's efforts and the support of Virgil Thomson and Peggy Glanville-Hicks, he did not receive the grant before returning to Morocco two months later, although he was informed that it was likely the project eventually would be approved.

During the period that Bowles had been in California, Jane had been undergoing therapy on a daily basis. When he returned to New York in November, he went to visit her. Although she complained bitterly about her internment, and begged him to take her back to Tangier, she was visibly improving. By mid-December, Jane was judged well enough to be released. As word had been received that the Bowleses could return without fearing police persecution, Bowles booked passage for them, and in mid-December they sailed to Algeciras, Spain.

The trip over was difficult. "Jane was beset with every sort of symptom at all hours of the day and night," Bowles wrote to Thomson. "Her heart beat too fast. She felt her blood pressure in her temples. Her head ached. She was nauseated. She was jittery." But the voyage over was apparently a pleasure cruise compared to Jane's reaction upon arriving in Algeciras. Becoming totally distraught, Jane insisted that Bowles get assurance from the police that they could indeed return without fearing arrest. Bowles wired Tangier. After a couple of days, the American consul cabled back that they might return whenever they wished. By the end of December they were once again ensconced in Tangier, where, Bowles wrote Thomson, "Jane immediately became another person entirely. She began to laugh and take pleasure in food, and become her old normal self, more so than she has been at any time since the stroke."

Bowles had little time to enjoy the respite, however. He had hardly been back in Tangier a month when Cheryl Crawford, who was producing Tennessee Williams's new play, *Sweet Bird of Youth,* wired that she wanted him to return to New York to write the music for it; Elia Kazan was to direct. Bowles was pleased. Earlier, Kazan had influenced the selection of another composer for *Camino Real,* which Williams had very much wanted Bowles to do. The reason, apparently, was that the Kazans, particularly Kazan's wife, Molly, had been shocked by *The Sheltering Sky* and for that reason had turned against Bowles. Now, however, Williams had persuaded Kazan that his "phobia" about Bowles's writing should not extend to his music, and the director had finally given his approval.

Jane's condition began to stabilize. Though she still had difficulty with reading and writing, she was psychologically much improved. Bowles, therefore, decided to risk the trip. Before he left, he hired a Spanish woman, to look after her around the clock, as well as a full-time cook. Others, like David Herbert and Jane's Tangier physician, Dr. Roux, said they would look in on her daily. Cherifa was also back in the picture, which worried Bowles, but with all the others around, he felt that she could be prevented from having a detrimental influence on Jane.

Bowles arrived in New York in mid-February 1959, score more or less in hand. He had begun working on it immediately in Tangier, then continued to compose on the ship, using the piano in the ballroom in the late evening. *Sweet Bird of Youth* opened first in Philadelphia, in late February, just a few weeks after Bowles's arrival. It then went on to Broadway on March 10. Brooks Atkinson, reviewing the play in the *New York Times,* called it "one of [Williams's] finest dramas," praising the actors, particularly Paul Newman and Geraldine Page. Of Bowles's score, he said it was "spidery and tinkling music of exquisite texture."

While in New York, Bowles stayed with Libby Holman. Allen Ginsberg, whom he had first met in Tangier during the period immediately after Jane's stroke, was now back in New York, and he and Bowles saw quite a lot of each other. Bowles recalled one particularly riotous evening when Holman thought it might be interesting to bring some Soviets she'd met together with the

Beats. Bowles invited Ginsberg, Gregory Corso, and Peter Orlovsky to have dinner at Holman's; Holman invited three Soviet officials. It was not a good mix. When offered marijuana by Ginsberg, the Soviets were unsure of what to do, as they knew it to be illegal. After conferring a bit, they decided not to smoke it. As the evening wore on, denunciations were made of Eisenhower by Ginsberg, and Khrushchev by Corso, provoking aghast looks from the Soviets. With the steady consumption of drinks by the Russians and marijuana by Bowles and the Beats, things turned even worse. Holman attempted to mediate, while Bowles looked on amused. Finally, sometime after dinner, Ginsberg decided to make a pass at one of the Soviets. The Russians left quickly and in a huff.

Before leaving New York, Bowles learned that the Rockefeller Foundation had at last awarded him a grant. He went to the Foundation's headquarters and was given a crash course in how to operate the professional-quality Ampex tape recorder that they were also providing him. By late May he was back in Tangier, eager to begin his recording. As Jane was holding steady, he decided to set out in July, thinking that it would only take him a short while to arrange permission with the authorities to do his recording. He soon became entangled in Moroccan governmental procedures, however, and finally decided to dispense with trying to obtain formal permission. Instead, he went to the American consulate, which drew up a document stating that the U.S. government was behind the project. They affixed several seals, stamps, and signatures and attached Bowles's photograph; Bowles decided that it looked sufficiently official to enable him to begin the project.

In the interim, he had gathered two traveling companions: Christopher Wanklyn, who spoke good Maghrebi and owned a Volkswagen; and a Moroccan, Mohammed Larbi, who'd recently escorted a British expedition on a trans-Saharan journey. Together, over the next five months, on four separate trips, they would travel some 25,000 miles through some of Morocco's most remote and rugged locales. Of the second trip, made from August 29 to September 22, 1959, Bowles kept a detailed account; he later published a selection of the travel notes as an article, "Ketama Taza," reprinted in expanded form as "The Rif, to Music," in his book of travel essays, *Their Heads Are Green and Their Hands Are Blue.*

The journey was not without difficulties. First, there was the physical hardship of abysmal hotels, tortuous roads, heat, and ultimately, for Bowles, illness. Second, there was the problem of making recordings. Although Bowles had originally expected governmental hostility, the local authorities were for the most part quite cordial and helpful. This, however, could not compensate for the fact that the Ampex ran only on 110-volt AC current and was not equipped with a battery pack. As a result, recording could only be done where there was electricity, and of the correct voltage. Despite all the difficulties, however, Bowles managed to collect a huge variety of music, representative of nearly all of Morocco.

There would, in fact, have been even more music recorded, but in October 1959 the Moroccan government suddenly decided that since his project was "ill-timed" (whatever that meant), he would not be allowed to undertake it. Bowles recalled that "the American Embassy advised me to continue my work." He proceeded, but by December the government had become aware of what Bowles was doing. "They informed me summarily that no recordings could be made in Morocco save by special permission from the Ministry of Interior. . . . I had practically completed the project . . . however, from then on it was no longer possible to make any recordings which involved the cooperation of the government; this deprived the collection of certain tribal musics of southeastern Morocco." Even with the lack of this latter music, Bowles had recorded more than 250 separate selections by the end of December.

Curiously enough, Bowles's efforts have never been terribly appreciated in Morocco. According to him, the prevalent "official" Moroccan attitude these days is that traditional folk music is "degenerate." Indeed, in the 1960s the government engaged in an all-out effort to encourage the composition of "patriotic" music, which would contain a political message—specifically, singing the praises of Morocco and Moroccan progress. The gradual "development" of many of the remote regions of the country and an increased migration from the country to the cities had a profound impact on traditional musical forms. Many of the forms that Bowles recorded are now impossible to hear in Morocco; and those that are heard are often diluted or mixed with other forms.

In the United States, despite the sponsorship of the Rockefeller Foundation and the Library of Congress, the tapes went promptly into an archive, where for more than a decade they gathered dust.

Finally, in 1972, the Library of Congress did issue a superb, two-volume record set, containing a fine sampling of Bowles's collection. Nonetheless, countless hours of recordings have never been released to the public and most likely never will be.

CHAPTER 26

As the new decade began, Bowles was back in Tangier. By now, he and Jane were living in separate apartments in a new building on the outskirts of the city, the Inmueble Itesa. To Bowles's relief, Jane's health was much improved. "She has put on weight, and looks very healthy and well," wrote Bowles to his parents on January 9. Despite her physical improvement, however, she began to worry about a new development in Tangier—the loss of its status as an international city, scheduled for that April. The process had begun with Moroccan independence in March 1956, and by now a number of the old residents, particularly the wealthier ones, had left. Those that remained, including the Bowleses, were jittery about what Tangier's loss of international status would mean for them. In a letter to his parents Bowles commented on what he saw as the impact:

> We are losing our charter in Tangier in April, which will mean that money can no longer move in and out of Tangier; once it enters it will be frozen, and the rate will be fixed in Rabat. I suppose it means inevitably that prices will soar sky-high, but we'll have to wait and see just *how* high before we make any decisions. . . . In general the Americans and English are staying on, while the French and Spanish are leaving in droves. Which is all right, since the Moroccans like the Anglo-Saxons better than Latins anyway. Perhaps the latter have been here long enough!

Another concern among some of the expatriates was that the loss of the charter would result in a far less open society. As an international city, Tangier possessed a tolerance of diversity that few cities in the world could claim. Despite the Yacoubi incident, one's sexual preference, while still a matter of gossip in the European quarter, was not generally a concern of the authorities. As a result, the city spawned a fairly large gay community, many of whose members were writers. Indeed, in residence at various times in Tangier in the 1950s and 1960s were a number of American gay writers, including Burroughs, Gysin, Edouard Roditi, Tennessee Williams, Allen Ginsberg, Alfred Chester, and Capote.

It was with these writers that Bowles most associated. Like them, Bowles also wrote about homosexuality, but unlike them, despite his talent for exceedingly effective, even shocking description, he never wrote graphically about gay sex. Also, in contrast to many in this group who were intent on proclaiming their homosexuality to the world through their writing, Bowles declined to define himself in terms of his sexual identity. That he gravitated toward gay men is undeniable, but even in the company of homosexuals, Bowles maintained his long-standing position that one's own sexuality was not a subject for public discussion.

The feared repression once the city came under direct control of the Moroccan government never really materialized. When the change did go into effect, however, the economic impact was as great as Bowles had feared: "The net result of the integration here is that prices are jumping skyward and consumers' goods are disappearing from the shelves of the shops that are left running. Hundreds of stores have shut and the owners have departed for better climes," he wrote his parents. Bowles seriously began to fear that, if the situation continued to be so chaotic, he and Jane would not be able to stay on in Tangier. The problem was where to go. Not being able to come up with a better choice, although they were considering Mexico again, the Bowleses stayed on, watching the changes take place around them.

Suddenly a possible, if temporary, answer to the dilemma arrived in the form of a telegram. It was from the head of the English Department at Los Angeles State College, Byron Guyer, who was offering Bowles a probable appointment as visiting professor of English for the academic year 1961–62. Bowles cabled the college, expressing interest in the position and asking for more details. But on May 2, he wrote his parents that he had decided not to take the job, explaining that:

I had thought it would be an informal sort of literary program, but the academic demands were too stiff for someone who has received only a year of college training. The courses required were "Crane to Faulkner, Cooper to James, The American Renaissance: Emerson, Whitman, Thoreau and Dickinson. Also: The Imagist Poets and Their Ideological and Literary Antecedents, and Jefferson and de Tocqueville on Democracy." Even if I studied nothing but those subjects day and night between now and September (assuming books on them were available here) I wouldn't be capable of teaching them to a lot of bright students who are right in the middle of their college education at the moment. And I have been out of college for thirty-one years! Perhaps some day some institution will offer me a creative literature course which would not demand such a strict academic preparation. It's too bad, as I had rather looked forward to doing it.

With the possibility of a temporary escape eliminated, Bowles sank back into his preoccupation with how to go on living in Tangier in the present climate of uncertainty. In a letter to Oliver Evans, he wrote of the dilemma:

We are still here in Tangier, expecting everything to get "worse" which it does do, but so slowly that generally we aren't conscious of it, until on certain days everything seems askew and wrong, and one can make a list of all the things that have altered, and confront oneself with it and feel a wave of fury or hopelessness, or even apprehensiveness (for the worst is always yet to come, naturally) and on those days a definite departure seems the only sensible decision. Then of course there are the other days, when one feels that one ought not to be hysterical, and that in reality most other places are even worse, and as for trouble brewing, Morocco has no monopoly on that, and so on. Net result: todo sigue igual. Then, too, there is the Sahara.

During this period Bowles nonetheless did manage to escape Tangier fairly often. On assignment for *Life* he went to Marrakech; for *Holiday* he journeyed to Fez. But things were not as they had been. These articles did not bring him great satisfaction and yet they took up time that he could have otherwise devoted to his own fiction. Bowles was feeling restless, anxious, depressed, no longer in control of his destiny. Life, which he had always managed to seize for himself through action—a trip, a creative work—was passing him by. Uncertainty about the future had never before preoccupied him to such an extent, but clearly it was linked to an overall sense of ennui. In a notebook entry from the mid-1950s, he had anticipated the stasis of daily life, without direction, without invention: "One of the great problems with which a man in my circumstances has to deal is the problem of boredom. Once you have felt a twinge of it there is no hope of shaking it off—at least, not here in a place like this—and although you can invent a thousand ways of forgetting it or making its presence less unpleasant,—(best thing to accept and study it,)—a kind of repulsion of the spirit against meeting its image—against entering into mirror as it were."

This meditation had by 1960 become real. Bowles was struggling, as had so many of his characters, for a sense of meaning to attach to existence. It was an old dilemma, but now it had taken on a more profound form, had shaken him to the core. Before, the feeling of nothingness had always been able to be challenged, if not overcome, by its infusion into fiction. But fiction was not, at present, able to serve him. Never one to cut and run, Bowles opted instead to confront his despair, look headlong at the image of his spirit leering at him in the mirror. "Best thing to accept and study it," he'd written parenthetically. It was that study which engaged him during the first year of the new decade.

Tangier, now that it was a bona fide part of Morocco, began to change slowly but perceptibly during the early 1960s. Beatniks began to arrive, taking the place of many of the old residents. This influx created a certain amount of alarm in the expatriate community, most of whom were fairly affluent, well established, and prone to anxiety about their status in Morocco, particularly since independence. William Burroughs commented that the established residents "all felt that the beatniks were endangering their whole position, casting aspersions on the foreign colony. And the old settlers were terrified, outraged: 'The first thing you know they'll get us all thrown out.'" This panic extended to Bowles and Jane, as well. According to Burroughs, "Jane and Cherifa were trying to cast a spell on the beatniks. Jane would say, 'I don't want to really hurt any of them, just make them a little sick so they'll go away.' They were all hysterical that way, particularly the Bowleses. Both of them were always worried that they were going to be thrown out."

Bowles wrote his parents about the beatnik invasion: "Every day one sees more beards and filthy blue jeans, and the girls look like escapees from lunatic asylums, with white lipstick and black smeared around their eyes, and matted hair hanging around their shoulders. The leaders of the 'movement' have moved their head-quarters here and direct their activities from here. Allen Ginsberg, Gregory Corso, and Burroughs are all established in Tangier now, sending out their publications from here." Despite his disparaging remarks and anxiety about deportation, Bowles made a distinction between the literary beatniks and what Burroughs terms "the lesser beats," the hangers-on, the beatniks in style only. Indeed, during the early part of the 1960s Bowles spent a good deal of time in the company of the "movement's leaders."

At about this time Burroughs was experimenting with a device called the Orgone Box, which he had constructed following infor-mation gleaned from the writings of Wilhelm Reich. Burroughs kept trying to persuade Bowles to try it out. Bowles said that when he finally decided to give it a try it was a cold night: "I . . . almost froze to death. . . . [Burroughs] said, 'You've got to stay in it at least an hour.' And I said, 'But it's pitch dark in there, and freezing cold!' 'Well, you've got to stay in it, won't do you any good if you just stay 10 minutes.' So I sat in there and sat in there; it was a protracted agony. I didn't stay an hour, I can tell you that; I stayed about 25 minutes and came out. He said, 'Did you feel anything?' I said, 'No, just a lot of cold.' "

Burroughs was not able to interest Bowles in cut-ups* either. "It was always against the grain with him. He'd say, 'Writing is one thing and painting another.' I pointed out that there was a time when writing and painting were one. 'Well,' he said, 'it's been separated so long.' I did several cut-ups of *The Sheltering Sky*. He didn't express any opinion on them. From that I concluded that he just wasn't interested."

Burroughs also confirms that there was a distance between Bowles and the beatniks: "Among the lesser beats, or miscella-

---

*A technique of writing championed by Brion Gysin and Burroughs in which random elements of a text (or texts) are rearranged to produce a new whole without regard for external logic.

neous beats, the general impression was that he was kind of uptight and old maidish. I think they sort of missed him—this wouldn't be true of Allen or Gregory, of course—but the rest of them. I don't think they really knew who Paul was. Besides, he was in solid with people like Lord David Herbert, who was a great admirer of Jane, very solidly in with the Old Mountain crowd, that rather wealthy expatriate circle. Paul was a celebrity in that group, regarded as a celebrity, as well known as Tennessee Williams who came to visit occasionally. Everybody in that crowd knew who Paul was." With Burroughs and Ginsberg, however, and to a lesser extent with Corso, Bowles developed close friendships. Bound together by a common interest in kif, Morocco, and literature, they saw each other frequently.

Although Bowles had a much deeper and longer-lasting friendship with Burroughs, it was Ginsberg who began to work on Bowles's behalf, trying to hook him up with Lawrence Ferlinghetti, who, as the editor of City Lights Books, had published Ginsberg's *Howl*. Ginsberg felt that in Ferlinghetti, Bowles would find a sympathetic publisher for some new stories that he was writing, all inspired by kif. For almost a year Bowles resisted writing to Ferlinghetti. Finally, after numerous entreaties on Ginsberg's part, several while Ginsberg was resident in Tangier, several more after he and Orlovsky had set out for the Middle East, Bowles finally sent off a letter to City Lights. It read, in part:

> First I'd do well to explain why I'm writing: I've had three letters from Allen Ginsberg . . . directing me to do it. Perhaps he suspected that I wouldn't take him seriously the first time, and for that reason repeated his suggestion in each missive. In today's letter he managed to persuade me that I should. The reason I had hesitated before was that I believed I had nothing precise to offer; now he thinks I should suggest a group of three stories about kif in Morocco. It seems rather a small item, but perhaps that's what you want. . . . I . . . could be relied on to furnish an extra story to add to my three, if you felt that said three were insufficient to constitute a tome. . . . Whatever you say is fine with me; I'd be delighted to appear under your aegis.

Ferlinghetti responded immediately. Bowles, although delighted with Ferlinghetti's interest, was also a bit worried: "What I'd like to be sure of is that the word *Morocco* will be kept out of any blurb regarding the stories. The authorities here are touchy about the kif question, and since I live here and my wife is not well, I want to avoid any problems of that kind, naturally." Ferlinghetti wrote back assuring Bowles that he would keep Morocco out of the title or in any publicity material, but asked him to suggest a title for the collection. Bowles responded, after a short delay:

> The title business has kept me thinking, but not with any great degree of productivity. The difficulty with finding a word that has some reference, even oblique, to kif, is that the word will necessarily be a Moghrebi word, and thus will have no reference at all save to the few who know the region. (*Moghrebi* itself could be used, I suppose: *Four Moghrebi Tales,* for instance. But of course no kif is suggested there.) Do you like A HUNDRED CAMELS IN THE COURTYARD . . .? On the title page we could have the whole quote: "A pipe of kif before breakfast gives a man the strength of a hundred camels in the courtyard."
>
> . . . . . Moghrebi Proverb

> That would more or less capsulize the meaning, since the theme of all the stories is specifically the power of kif, rather than the subjective effects of it.

Ferlinghetti was as delighted with Bowles's title as he had been with the four stories. The tales, as Bowles points out, all revolve around kif. Kif smoking, of course, had played a significant role in the concluding section of *Let It Come Down* and was incidental to *The Spider's House,* but these are the first stories to show "the power of kif" in Moroccan society among the Moroccans themselves. Although Bowles had been smoking kif for years, it was only in the late 1950s that it became a regular habit. By the early 1960s, when this sequence of stories was written, Bowles was using cannabis not just as a stimulus for writing, but as "a way out of the phenomenological world." He had internalized the Moroccan concept of "two worlds, one ruled by inexorable natural laws, and the other, the kif world, in which each person perceives 'reality' according to the projections of his own essence, the state of consciousness in which the elements of the physical universe are automatically rearranged by cannabis to suit the requirements of the individual." In terms of writing, the stories in *A Hundred Camels in the Courtyard* represented an attempt to use kif, not just for inspiration, but as an integral part of the composition technique. Bowles explained the process this way:

> I began to experiment with the idea of constructing stories whose subject matter would consist of disparate elements and unrelated characters taken directly from life and fitted together as a mosaic. The problem was to create a story line which would make each arbitrarily chosen episode compatible with the others, to make each one lead to the next with a semblance of naturalness. I believed that through the intermediary of kif the barriers separating the unrelated elements might be destroyed, and the disconnected episodes forced into symbiotic relationships.

In order to comprehend fully the notion of the kif intermediary, it is essential to understand that for Bowles, kif functioned as a passageway to enlightenment, making visible certain connections that might otherwise have been overlooked by a writer grounded solely in the physical world. "For a dedicated smoker," he wrote, "the passage to the 'other world' is often a pilgrimage undertaken for the express purpose of oracular consultation." By the time he wrote these stories, Bowles, in fact, had become convinced that kif had such beneficial effects that he would make continual use of it. In some ways, kif smoking would become the one constant element in his existence from then on.

Others were not so sure of the efficaciousness of using kif to create. Gore Vidal, normally a great admirer of Bowles's work, noted that "these pieces strike me as entirely uninhabited and of no interest." Bowles, responding to this criticism, asserted that "there are plenty of people in those stories. [Vidal] claimed not to understand them, which I can only interpret as bias since they're all specifically about kif which he holds in low esteem. But we've disagreed on that for forty years." Vidal perhaps meant that he felt the characters were not terribly well drawn. If so, the reason might very well be that in these stories, all of the characters are Moroccans and the tales are told entirely from a Moroccan perspective. Although these are not the first stories that Bowles had written in which no Westerner or Western viewpoint figures, they are far more hermetic than many of his other stories that are populated largely by Moroccans. So immersed was Bowles in Morocco and in a Moroccan sensibility, that these tales read as if they could have been written by a Moroccan writer.

This, of course, was partially what Bowles was aiming at, but in addition he was attempting to convey the central role and natural-ness of using kif within Moroccan culture; had the stories featured kif-smoking Westerners, particularly in 1961, they would have of necessity been flavored with a high degree of exoticism. This was exactly the opposite of Bowles's intention. In some respects, his goal was to show by way of implied contrast the difference between a society which relies on cannabis as a release from the pressures of daily life, and one in which alcohol fulfills that function. For Bowles, the major difference is that "alcohol blurs the personality by loosening inhibitions. The drinker feels, temporarily at least, a sense of participation." Kif, on the other hand, pushes the individ-ual into "contemplation and inaction."

While Bowles was personally enamored of kif smoking, he was also around this time beginning to politicize kif by viewing it as a traditional part of Muslim society. In an article in *Kulchur,* written in 1961, he explained this concept:

> The last strongholds of cultures fashioned around the use of sub-stances other than alcohol are being flushed out. In Africa particu-larly, the dagga, the ganja, the bangui, the kif, as well as the dawamesk, the sammit, the majoun and the hashish, are all on their way to the bonfires of progressivism. They just don't go with pre-tending to be European. The young fanatics of the four continents are furiously aware of that. They are, incidentally, also aware that a population of satisfied smokers or eaters offers no foothold to an ambitious demagogue. The crowd with a little alcohol in it behaves in a classical and expected fashion, but you can't even get together a crowd of smokers: each man is alone and happy to stay that way. . . . The user of cannabis is all too likely to see the truth where it is and to fail to see it where it is not. Obviously few things are poten-tially more dangerous to those interested in prolonging the status quo of organized society.

Although here Bowles is denouncing the Europeanization of the Third World and holding up kif as an element of traditional North African society, the theme of "progress" as a destroying factor is a major concept in his fictional work of the period. Indeed, this theme is implicit—and sometimes explicit—in almost all of his fiction about Morocco written from the 1960s on. In "The Hyena," a fable, Bowles tells of a hyena who lures a stork into its cave through promises of peace and friendship. Once the stork is inside the cave, however, the hyena quickly kills her. "The stork represents tradition, the hyena represents progress," explains Bowles. "Progress normally wins out. Tradition isn't strong enough."

Another story, "The Time of Friendship," written between 1960 and 1962, is one of Bowles's most poignant meditations on the way in which politics interferes in the daily life of individuals. Like *The Spider's House,* this story shows the pernicious effects of progress from the angle of the independence movement. Set in Algeria during the early days of the war against the French, it is essentially a story of friendship between a spinster Swiss schoolteacher, Fräulein Windling, and a young Algerian, Slimane. The model for Fräulein Windling was the woman Bowles met in 1947 while traveling in the Sahara when working on *The Sheltering Sky.* At the time Bowles had been impressed by her sympathetic relationship with the local Algerians. In light of the bitter war for independence, Bowles began to think of her, wondering what would have become of her once the war had actually begun. In the story, he worked out her inevitable fate: the French order her to leave the oasis, meaning, naturally, that she must also leave behind Slimane.

Through this simple plot, Bowles creates perhaps his most tender story. Early on, he labors to paint a rather idyllic picture of the oasis as seen through Fräulein Windling's eyes: "Everything was made by the people themselves out of what the desert had to offer. They lived in a world of objects fashioned out of baked earth, woven grass, palmwood and animal skins." In love with their simple way of life, their goodwill, she has spent each summer holiday there since the end of World War II.

But this summer, the "virus of discontent" is sweeping Algeria. The French have made mass arrests; war is being waged in the north. In spite of the rumors of war, Fräulein Windling feels that the fighting is too distant to disturb her idyll. As usual, she has a visitor, Slimane, a young man she has known over the years. And, as usual, she has brought him a little gift. The first month or so goes by as it has always gone by: in little excursions, in long conversations with Slimane. But then, suddenly, the French authorities tell her she must leave. Instinctively she knows that life in this simple, peaceful remote region of the Sahara will never be the same; that she will never be back. Her thoughts turn to her young friend: " 'He's too young to be a soldier,' she told herself. 'They won't take him.' But she knew they would. . . . 'Another year, perhaps,' the captain had said. She saw her own crooked, despairing smile in the dark window-glass beside her face. Maybe Slimane would be among the fortunate ones, an early casualty."

"The Time of Friendship" is, aside from *The Spider's House,* Bowles's most sustained fictional treatment of how the wars for independence had such personal consequences for Arabs and Europeans alike. On the surface, the power of the story comes precisely from his unrelenting focus on the ramifications of the war for the individual, but the larger theme is that of the end of an era. Without being didactic or sentimental, Bowles makes the reader slowly aware of the way in which war destroys not only simple friendships, but also a culture, a society, an entire way of life. Ultimately, this is for Bowles the greater consequence of it all. This should not be construed as merely thinly veiled nostalgia on Bowles's part for the colonial era. It is, rather, a sober record of a small tragic moment in history in which a country and a people, who have survived intact throughout the decades of foreign occupation, suddenly are on the verge of losing themselves in the forced march of "progress."

It was preoccupations like these, witnessing the daily endangerment of traditional North African culture—its music, folktales, kif, its simple way of living—that so adversely affected Bowles. He had spent six months in 1959 and another month in 1961 working assiduously to preserve its music from the post-independence rush to modernize and politicize it; he was now about to embark on a similar effort that would occupy him from then on: the preservation of its oral literature through translation.

As early as 1952 Bowles had begun to record a few of Ahmed Yacoubi's tales, but it wasn't until the 1960s that he began to think seriously about translating stories told to him in Maghrebi. Part of the reason was that the tape recorder made the work more feasible (Bowles had rapidly transcribed Yacoubi's first tales in a notebook as Yacoubi told them). Then Bowles became acquainted with Larbi Layachi, a young man with a powerful story to tell. They met when the Moroccan was working as a watchman at a café Bowles frequented on Merkala Beach, near his apartment. One day in the spring of 1962, following a conversation they had about storytelling, Layachi came to see him, saying that "he wanted to make a book." Bowles replied that "making a book is a lot of work," but that he'd be willing to see what he could do with it "if it were really good." The next night Layachi came to Bowles's apartment. Bowles sat him in front of the tape recorder; after a long pause, the Moroccan began to speak. "Immediately I knew," recalls Bowles, "that whatever the story might turn out to be, his manner of telling it left nothing to be desired. It was as if he had memorized the entire text and rehearsed the speaking of it for weeks."

Several other recording sessions followed. As each episode unfolded, Bowles became more enchanted with the story, which was turning out to be essentially Layachi's autobiography. Working closely with the storyteller, Bowles went over each spoken text, word by word, clarifying for himself the exact meaning and nuance of each sentence: "At the outset I had seen that the translation should be a literal one, in order to preserve as much as possible of the style. Nothing needed to be added, deleted or altered."

Bowles worked that spring and over the summer with Layachi. Once he had finished translating a few segments, he decided to send them out for publication. Since he had previously published several Yacoubi translations in *Evergreen Review,* he now sent them the opening chapter from Layachi's work, "The Orphan." It was not only accepted by them, but Richard Seaver, then an editor at Grove Press, wrote Bowles asking if he would consider giving Grove the completed work. A small advance was also promised. Bowles responded enthusiastically.

Through immersion in these translations of the early 1960s, Bowles began to feel less dissatisfied with his existence. Although still prone to pessimism, he had once again found that creative work gave him a sense of purpose. In addition, Tangier had stabilized politically, which greatly alleviated his concern about needing to leave Morocco. Jane's health, too, though sustained by a battery of drugs, had generally been good, despite several small problems—shingles and hernia operations—and mentally she was much improved. She was also writing a little again, spurred on by a $3,000 grant from the Ingram-Merrill Foundation for a new play. More money was also coming her way, an inheritance of $35,000 from her Aunt Birdie, who had recently died. For the first time since her marriage she was relieved from worry about finances. Although still managed by Cherifa, she had a number of other friends, and a new lover, an Englishwoman. While those who had known her well before the stroke noticed that she was far more prone to bouts of depression and melancholy than she had been previously, those meeting her for the first time saw only a delightful, somewhat odd, but thoroughly engaging personality. And while the Bowleses' life in Tangier was not perfect, it was far better than it had been since Jane's stroke.

But for Bowles, it was a very different life from the one he had led before. His earlier bouts of wanderlust had largely abated, as had his quest for the limelight, which was already beginning to elude him. Now, at fifty years old, he was more content to work quietly, enjoying what he could about Morocco without being quite so despairing about the changes wrought by the rapid move of the country from benignly neglected colony to developing country. His articles for *Holiday* and other magazines brought in a steady income, allowing him to write about places he liked, while also affording him the opportunity to make astute, often critical observations on the customs and culture of various peoples. His translations from Maghrebi were well received in the West and in demand by various publications. Translations, furthermore, kept him in tune with Morocco and the Moroccans, and gave him an insider's perspective on the workings of the Moroccan mind, a perspective he had been learning about since his first encounter with the country thirty years before. In short, Bowles had entered a new phase in his life: it was a time of productivity, of relative content, of quiet accomplishment.

CHAPTER 27

Dᴜʀɪɴɢ ᴛʜᴇ summer of 1962 Bowles had a visit from an English publisher, Peter Owen, who asked him for a manuscript to publish. Bowles initially told him that though flattered by his offer, he had nothing to give him. A day or so later, however, he decided to offer him a collection of travel essays. Although nearly ten years earlier he had gotten an advance from Random House for just such a book, he now felt that he had finally written a few essays worth collecting in book form. Out of more than twenty published pieces he made a selection of nine essays to give to Owen. When he mailed the book, he included, as well, a number of photographs he had taken in Morocco and the Sahara. The title he chose for the collection, *Their Heads Are Green and Their Hands Are Blue,* was taken from a poem called "The Jumblies" by Edward Lear:

> Far and few, far and few
>   Are the lands where the Jumblies live;
> Their heads are green, and their hands are blue
>   And they went to sea in a Sieve.

Bowles was wise to wait until 1962 to collect these essays in book form, as he was able to include several of his best articles, including "The Road to Tassemist," written only that year, and a reworked version of "The Rif, to Music." In the foreword to the collection, he explained the underlying concept of the book:

If people and their manner of living were alike everywhere, there would not be much point in moving from one place to another. With few exceptions, landscape alone is of insufficient interest to warrant the effort it takes to see it. Even the works of man, unless they are being used in his daily living, have a way of losing their meaning, and take on the qualities of decoration. What makes Istanbul worthwhile to the outsider is not the presence of the mosques and covered *souks,* but the fact that they still function as such. . . . And North Africa without its tribes, inhabited by, let us say, the Swiss, would be merely a rather more barren California.

This premise, the virtue of differences between peoples, is in fact the thread that links all of these essays together. Whether remarking on the religions and religious practices of South India, or on the Berbers of North Africa, Bowles is continually in quest of the essence of a particular culture. Although *Their Heads Are Green* is not travelogue, Bowles does not keep himself out of the narrative; indeed, in many ways these are the most personal pieces of writing Bowles has ever done. As such, he stands in the tradition of the great travel writers of the earlier part of the century—D. H. Lawrence, Robert Byron, J. R. Ackerley, Graham Greene, and André Gide, among others—in his ability to provide an unblinking account of the culture he is examining, while also creating a memorable portrait of himself as a "Jumblie hunter."

Bowles had just finished assembling the articles for *Their Heads Are Green* when he was summoned to New York to write the music for a new Williams play, *The Milk Train Doesn't Stop Here Anymore.* At the beginning of September he made the voyage over, accompanied by Jane, who had not been back to the States since 1958. In general, it was a busy trip for Bowles. Not only did he have to produce a score, he was also completing arrangements with Grove Press, and picking up an advance of $2,000 ($1,250 for Layachi, $750 for himself) for the translation, which he had now entitled *A Life Full of Holes.* Although the book is ostensibly a record of Layachi's various misadventures on the way to manhood, Richard Seaver wanted to enter it for the Formentor Prize, given for the best international fiction book of the year, and as a result decided to publish it as a novel. While in New York, Bowles also went to Random House to offer them *Their Heads Are Green.* He wrote to Jane of their reaction:

They weren't very nice about their contract which I signed ten years ago with them; their position was that since I had not held to my side of it with regard to time of delivery . . . they were not bound to observe their side of it, which is purely financial. However, they are giving me half the advance they should have given me according to the terms. And since Helen Strauss had already insisted (in 1955) upon getting fifty percent of the original sum for me, I shall have been paid 75 percent of the promised advance before the book is published.

Before giving Random House the book, Bowles decided to remove one essay, "Mustapha and His Friends," that was in the original collection he had given Owen. He also provided a different set of photographs for the American edition. Otherwise, the text is identical to that of Owen's.

While in New York, Bowles also recorded "The Delicate Prey" and "A Distant Episode" for Spoken Arts Records. His reading of the stories, plain and unemotional, is at the same time almost musical, revealing the carefully compacted rhythmic pattern of his prose.

On that same trip to the States, he squeezed in a visit to Florida to see his parents, who had moved to Gulfport a few years before. Jane, meanwhile, visited with her mother, who now resided in Florida as well, but had come up to New York to see her. Jane also spent a good deal of time with Libby Holman, with Natasha von Hoershelman and Katharine Hamill, and with the English lover she had met in Tangier. Bowles disapproved of the latter relationship, primarily because when with her Jane drank a great deal. As Bowles knew that Jane would not respond to his admonitions to stop drinking, he characteristically did not object too strenuously. Instead, he tried to persuade her to return to Tangier ahead of him so that she could get some writing done. Although his strategy was undoubtedly somewhat transparent to Jane, she nonetheless did leave New York around the middle of November.

But being back in Tangier did not mean Jane was able to write. She was, in fact, blocked again. In December Bowles wrote to urge her on, from New Haven, where *The Milk Train Doesn't Stop Here Anymore* was being tried out. "No work depends on the ability to find the perfect adjectives while one is writing it. And any process or formula which will make it possible to get the skeleton constructed . . . any method or trick or manner is valid, as long as the thing gets on paper." Jane responded that she couldn't write because of the "mess" surrounding her daily life. Bowles again tried to bolster her, while also prescribing a method for removing herself from the "mess":

> I was sorry to hear that as you put it, everything has got to be a mess in Tangier and therefore you haven't worked. That was the very thing we were making great resolves about while you were still here. . . . that you wouldn't *allow* the mess-tendency to take over, because that has always been the pattern, and that has been exactly what has always got in your way. Of course everything's a mess, but *please* forget the mess now and then each day, because otherwise you won't ever work. The mess is just the decor in which we live, but we can't let decor take over really. I know you agree in principle, but does that help you to leave the mess outside regularly for a while and get inside to work? Also, I know it's easy to talk about and hard to do, but pretend you really live here in New York instead of there, and it might help. I mean, that you're only over there for a short while.

By the first of the year Bowles too was back in Tangier. On January 29, 1963, he wrote his parents that "Jane is working every day too, on her new play." Bowles was also working intensely, trying to finish *A Life Full of Holes* in time for an April submission for the Formentor Prize. Although he did manage to deliver it on schedule, the book did not win. Bowles was not terribly disappointed; the deadline had provided the necessary impetus to finish the translation.

In early May, the Bowleses rented a beach house on the Atlantic coast south of Tangier in the town of Asilah, the model for Cabeza de Lobo in Tennessee Williams's play *Suddenly Last Summer.* That summer a young American writer whom Bowles had known in New York, Alfred Chester, arrived in Morocco, partly through Bowles's invitation. Talented and more than a little mad, Chester quickly became a part of the Bowleses' circle, spending time with them in Tangier and Asilah. He was particularly fond of Jane, and Jane of him.

At first, Bowles also welcomed Chester to Morocco, introducing him to the English writer Norman Glass, who was also living at that time in Asilah, as well as to Layachi and a young Moroccan fisherman and small-time hustler named Dris, who would become Chester's lover. But almost from the beginning of his stay, Chester had a very uneven relationship with Bowles. At some point in the summer, according to Glass, they quarreled over Bowles's refusal to lend Chester some blankets. Seeing Glass in the street, Chester immediately began to question the Englishman about Bowles. He particularly wanted to know if Bowles had been saying nasty things about him. When Glass told him no, Chester seemed disappointed. By this time he had in fact developed a strange love-hate relationship in his own mind with Bowles. On one hand, he clearly admired Bowles's work, praised it constantly, and wrote a splendid review of *A Life Full of Holes;* on the other, he seemed to detest Bowles's refinement, sense of decorum, and calm, qualities exactly opposite those of Chester.

By the end of the summer, Chester had worked up a grudge against Bowles, somehow believing that he was conspiring against him. Just how, no one was apparently ever sure, including probably Chester, but he made it clear to everyone at the time that he feared Bowles. The fear turned to animosity over another incident that summer, one that involved Glass. It started out innocently enough: Glass, who was thinking of doing a translation, went to see Bowles to get some details regarding contracts. On the way back to his hotel, he stopped off at Chester's and related the conversation to him. Suddenly, Chester became furious, began screaming that he was going to get Bowles this time and insisted on marching over to Bowles's house with Glass in tow. Once there, he began to fulminate incoherently against Bowles, until finally Bowles asked him and Glass to leave. Outside, Chester apparently told Glass that he now regretted what he had said, blaming it all somehow on his dead father; he did not, however, return to apologize. Later that week, Bowles wrote a letter to an acquaintance of both his and Chester's, Ira Cohen, saying that he and Glass had

just broke[n] off diplomatic relations for all time. If he comes back here, I'll throw him out. I've finally had enough of his nonsense, as well as that of his friend Alfred Chester. I'm arranging to have them both bumped off in Tangier, incha'Allah . . . What a shame all these people have to be born and give forth their stench to an unsuspecting world! But now that they exist, one has to do something about cleaning the place up, obviously.

In late February 1964, Chester found the letter at Cohen's and went into a tirade. Glass was in Sicily at the time, but remembers receiving a letter from Chester denouncing Bowles and asking him to sign an anti-Bowles petition. Glass responded by telling Chester that he felt it was all a joke, the proof of it, if nothing else, being that such a long interval had passed and both he and Chester were still alive.

The matter did not end there, however, for in his literary magazine, *Gnoua,* Cohen planned to run a piece by Irving Rosenthal, another expatriate Tangier writer, which contained the following line: "Some of the campiest queens I've known had cocks drier than Paul Bowles' mouth caught between Tafraout and Taroudant [two cities in the Sahara] with kif and without water." Bowles asked Cohen to delete the offending phrase. Chester, who was proofreading the magazine for Cohen, was torn over the matter. As he wrote to a friend, "Of course, Paul brings the wish to expose him out in everyone. . . . At first, I said no no, you mustn't print that, it doesn't matter even if Paul does want to be exposed, we have no right to be judges."

But despite his reservations, Chester soon decided to see if he could profit from the situation. Nearly broke, he had written to a number of people (including Jacqueline Kennedy) asking for money. He also attempted to get $10,000 from wealthy Tangier expatriate Rex Henry, who was a close friend of Jane's. As Chester had gotten no response from Henry, he went to Jane and tried to blackmail her into interceding with Henry on his behalf, offering in return to have the line removed from Rosenthal's story. Much to Chester's dismay, Jane answered, "Oh I love you, Alfred," and he abandoned the scheme. Suffering by this point from rather extreme paranoid delusions, Chester then went to the American consul for protection. Subsequently, Bowles was called in for questioning by the Tangier police, but the case was quickly dropped. Finally, several months later, Chester wrote a letter to Jane, who had also been urging him to see the whole business as a joke, allowing that she was probably right, that Bowles had not been serious.

To Bowles, however, he did not write; instead, still obsessed with him, he wrote of him. According to Norman Glass, Chester's story "Safari" and his novella *The Foot* both contain portraits of Bowles as seen through Chester's eyes. In "Safari" Bowles is Gerald, a scorpion hunter, of whom Chester writes: "Sometimes I think Gerald is God, at least a local god, or more exactly a local demon." In *The Foot,* Bowles is written into the very minor character of Peter Plate, whom the narrator considers his "magic father."

The "Chester episode," as it came to be known in Tangier, was ultimately far more significant for Chester than for Bowles (although the legend, at least in certain circles, has demonstrated a longevity far in excess of the event's actual importance). In the heat of the moment, Bowles did find it a source of concern—the main concern being that Chester's madness might not be perceived as such, and that Chester could endanger his reputation, if not his situation in Tangier, by calling him to the attention of the authorities. In the end, however, most everyone else in Tangier, including the American consul, came to believe that Chester was simply unbalanced. Aside from a certain amount of unpleasantness, the incident had few repercussions for Bowles. By 1965, in fact, Bowles, who had never lost respect for Chester's fiction, was once again on fairly friendly terms with the author, enthusiastically praising his new novel, *Jamie Is My Heart's Desire.* He wrote to bookseller Andreas Brown asking him to try to locate a copy—even two copies—for him, as he was "delighted with it," adding that "the copy I have belongs to Alfred." Chester, on the other hand, continued his descent into lunacy. After some months in a London mental institution he drifted from country to country, finally moving to the Arab quarter of Jerusalem, where in 1971 he committed suicide.

Bowles did little writing during that summer of 1963 in Asilah. He did, however, compose one letter that has all the hallmarks of his best fiction. Written to Ned Rorem, it was composed under mescaline. The apparent reason he wrote to Rorem was that the only other time he'd used the drug was in 1958, in the company of the composer. A tremendously poetic letter, it not only evokes the texture of a summer's night in a blighted resort town by the sea, but also reveals Bowles's recurring preoccupation with the nature of reality and the self-examination of the dark soul laid bare. As such, it is worth quoting at length.

Dear Ned:

Not that it's germane to anything but the writing of this letter. But since the only other time I've taken mescaline was your fly-horror evening in the Poconos, it seems important to say that I'm writing from somewhere down there. Eight hours have gone past and I've felt nothing more than the sensation of being a tiny human rowboat with a huge motor attached to it. Much energy, inability to sit still, to eat or drink. Capable of talking at length, but inclined to be polemical, and, probably unpleasant although I haven't asked the opinion of anyone. I imagined that forcing myself to write you a letter would focus my energies sufficiently to keep me in one place. It seems to be doing that at least. Yes, it's unpleasant, I suppose. A supremely unpleasant experience, naturally. And, I shouldn't think, of any use to anyone, save in retrospect. And even then! Is it really of interest to make up one's mind about a segment of reality? Today the whole summer has opened up, like an enormous abscess, and spewed out its essence. How did it happen? A breathless day, thick with fog from dawn on. Hot fog. It came up out of the water, and with an enveloping stench that caught one's breath; everyone was saying: The air smells of shit. I walked two miles up the beach, and it was just as thick and cloying as back here by the house where the waves are stiff with black crust of rotted seaweed, and only now and then lick into the pools in the rocks where the sewage has lain these several months. Just as bad everywhere. Instead of coming with its water to clean away our filth, the ocean has decided to cover us with its own corruption. So the sweat runs down the chest inside the shirt, and the fog collects on the hairs of the jacket, and drips, and one doesn't know whether one is hot or cold. One shivers. It got to be quite awful about seven o'clock. The fog had turned black, and was moving around the rooftops in tatters, and the smell of excrement was vast and sweet all around. What is it? I asked the Moslems. Kharra, they said calmly. No reconoces la mierda cuando la hueles? [Can't you recognize shit when you smell it?] I knew there would come a bad day eventually, and so I'm astonished to be examining it. Perhaps the interesting thing about mescaline is the fact that it enables one to look closely and calmly at pure horror without feeling anything at all, save perhaps a vague desire to repair to another world as quietly as one can. But it makes me cantankerous. In all my conversations I find myself leading the inquisition. Oh? Yes? When? Why? Aha, and how? I see, But why? Oh, you think so? And what makes you think so? I went to see Alfred Chester and quizzed him for a while. When I came out into the street it was as though the play had been finished for a good half hour, and only a work light was burning, and the play was over forever, and the sets had been struck, and the doors were open onto the street. Probably Fifty-Third

Street. Whatever mescaline does, it doesn't seem to make one coherent. But neither does it supply any feeling of there being an interior, unreachable cosmos. It says: See where you are? Look around. This is what it's like. Can you stand seeing it? Touching it, smelling it? Fortunately one draws no conclusions, since everything is far too real to be able to mean anything. As I say, you examine horror very closely, without even any interest. Disgust is what one would feel if one were alive. Instead of that, one knows that it's all artificial, the structure of reality itself. Disgust is something that ought to be felt *for* one by someone. But of course, there is not even anyone to experience the disgust, so it remains there, unfelt, but all around one—unregistered loathing, unattainable nausea, as wide as the smile of the sea while it belches up its corruption. So then I tried to eat dinner. Not possible. Yes, salad and soup and melon and Coca Cola and Vichy, but not beef! And we agreed that this is the season of polio and meningitis and uncharted fevers, because it always is when the cherqi blows it all up into dust towers and scatters it over the land. . . . If only it would rain for an hour and wash out the sweet smell of urine that fills the alleys. Each day since the first of May, when I came to Asilah, the smell has got a little stronger, the stains on the cement have grown blacker and thicker as layer dries on layer. The fishheads crawl with maggots and bristle with flies. Sometimes I take out a litre of gasoline and pour it over a particularly lively pile of garbage beside the front door. When I light it, the neighbors stick their heads out of the windows above and watch. They think it has something to do with my religion, and very likely it has. Yes, yes, of course. Don't we all want to be cremated? We who no longer have any connection with the earth. I took a lot of wild walks at top speed around the Medina trying to lose the motor that was inside, or at least to run it down for a while. Nothing changed. I came back and lay down and read Robbe-Grillet for an hour, running with sweat and sometimes shivering with what I thought was cold. At twilight the fog lifted itself right out of the sea and rose into the air several hundred metres up, and there was the moon, and all the rest of the spots in the sky the same as always. But the heat was worse than ever, and the stench stronger because the tide had risen further. The waves were having difficulty breaking against the side of the house, they were so laden with the putrefaction they had found inside. Although the slaughter-house is outside the ramparts, it is not more than two hundred feet from here, and the blood runs down among mountains of garbage, because the town dump is also right here at the same spot. Four months of living here, and being aware of it, and

amused by the fact, and it took mescaline to convince me of its
existence, to make me be able to say: But of course. You knew that
all the time. And you knew the people were all as loathsome as the
sea and the air. They smooth the lapels of your jacket while they tell
you their lies. . . . A large grasshopper just sprang into my face. How
it got into the Medina at all, I don't understand. Give my best to you,
if you see you.

Masterful and strangely lyrical, the letter reveals Bowles's continual fascination with the darker aspects of Morocco—putrefaction, horror, the unreality of reality. Asilah is seen through
Bowles's mescaline lens as a nightmarish embodiment of pervasive
rot, as a grand metaphor for the state of society itself. He quite
obviously takes a certain delight in evoking the seamier side of
things, as if by doing so he can make visible his thesis of the
putrefying consequences of civilization.

In the spring of 1964 Bowles rented "a property up on the Old
Mountain which had twenty-four acres of forest land at the top of
a cliff." There he began work on a new novel, composing it
"peripatetically, with a notebook in my hand wandering through
the forest breathing in the eucalyptus." He characterized the book,
tentatively titled *Where the Slades Went,* as "a murder mystery about
beatniks, decidedly light." Although it is to some extent a murder
mystery, and does feature a couple of beatniks, it is not "light" in
the usual sense of the word. The novel, in many ways, is another
version of Bowles's primary theme: American innocents abroad
bumbling toward their death in an exotic locale.

While Bowles began the novel in earnest in May, it actually had
its genesis, as critic Lawrence Stewart perceptively points out, in
his two earlier abandoned novels: *Almost All the Apples Are Gone* and
the untitled sketch of the painter and his wife in Ceylon. But unlike
the previous three finished novels, written mainly on location, this
book was truly a novel from memory, this time from very distant
memory—the Bowleses' honeymoon trip of 1938. As noted earlier, the itinerary, much of the landscape description, and the character of Mrs. Rainmantle were drawn from their travels in the late
1930s.

Set in an unnamed Central American country that combines

attributes of Costa Rica and Guatemala, it is the story of the Slades, an elderly doctor and his young wife, who set out on an extended trip through the tropics. On board the boat that is taking them up the Central American coast, they meet Mrs. Rainmantle, a corpulent, disagreeable character, loathed by the doctor, but upon whom the wife, Day Slade, takes pity. Once the boat docks, the three of them end up for the night in a nasty hotel near the water. The Slades are waiting for the train to the capital the next morning; Mrs. Rainmantle is waiting for her son, a resident of the country, to pick her up. As there are only two "habitable" rooms in the hotel, and one of them is dank, dark, and closetlike, without a lock on the door, Mrs. Rainmantle and Day end up sharing one room, while Dr. Slade spends the night in the other. The next morning, when about to depart in the predawn darkness, Day shines her flashlight beam for an instant on the sleeping, but strangely contorted figure of Mrs. Rainmantle, who seems to Day "like a chromolithograph of Jesus where the closed lids suddenly flew open and the eyes were there, looking straight ahead."

In the capital, Day meets a young man named Grover (a.k.a. Grove, Grovero, Vero), half English, half Latin American, who offers to show her the city. Later, he invites the Slades to his penthouse, where he lives with a seventeen-year-old woman named Luchita and her baby by another man. There, he spikes Dr. Slade's drink, carries him off to his ranch and begins to inject him with drugs in order to alter his memory, all under the guise of taking care of him. Day also falls victim to a drug-laced drink. The reason for Vero's strange behavior is that he has murdered his mother, Mrs. Rainmantle, while she slept in the same room with Day, and suspects that somehow the Slades may know of it. The Slades, of course, have no idea what is happening to them, nor are they aware of Vero's connection to the odious Mrs. Rainmantle. In fact, only Dr. Slade is even aware that Mrs. Rainmantle is dead, having read of her "accidental" death in a fire at the hotel after their departure, set to cover up the crime.

Vero, though, is hell-bent on making sure that they know nothing and continues his course of LSD-like treatments combined with tape-recorded messages to alter their memories. Naturally, however, his suspicious mind continues to convince him that the Slades do know the truth, particularly after he observes Day looking at some semicharred notes relating to his brainwashing techniques. But while she does not understand the implications, the Slades are nonetheless doomed. As the book ends, Bowles conjures up a series of scenes, more hallucinatory than any drug-induced vision, in which Day sets out to look for Dr. Slade. In the nearby town of San Felipe, caught up in a festival complete with fireworks and streets thronged with parading locals, she wanders in a daze seeking a doctor to treat her husband. Dr. Slade, ignorant and innocent, has already been killed, just as Day will soon be. There is, however, one further ironic twist left in the novel. Vero's right-hand man, Thorny, a beatnik hanger-on and former classmate who has been a party to all three murders, suddenly realizes that it is he who is now in control of the situation; for all of Vero's homicidal conniving, he has simply ended up Thorny's victim.

While this summary only hints at the elaborate twists in the novel, the book, as a murder mystery must be, has a very intricate plot. At times, in fact, the effect on the reader is one of disorientation, but unlike Bowles's other work, particularly the early surrealist-inspired pieces such as "The Scorpion" or "By the Water," the dislodging of logic is not due to the disappearance of a recognizably rational universe. It stems, rather, from the structure of the narrative itself in which a combination of devices, including the withholding of certain information and the raising of false leads and false hopes, create a kind of continual puzzle within a puzzle. Not until late in the novel, in fact, does Vero's motivation become clear. And while his scheming can hardly be thought of as rational, the scenes themselves, conveyed in Bowles's chillingly detached style, are always grounded in the realm of reality, albeit a rather perverse one.

Bowles has always regarded this novel as "light," referring to it also as an "entertainment," in the manner of Graham Greene, or as a *sotie,* after Gide. It is not, of course, the subject matter that is light, but, instead, the lack of philosophical preoccupation. Unlike in the other three novels, and in many of the stories, the protagonists in this work do not muddle over their fates nor posit cosmic consequences for their action or inaction. While the familiar theme of sexual tension—between old Dr. Slade and his young wife—is again present, it is by no means a central concern. Indeed, the Slades are lacking a philosophical dimension, and the occasional philosophical reflection that Bowles allows Vero is almost always closer to being a parody of true thought rather than any kind of substantive musing on man's fate. Vero, in fact, is a classic victim of self-deception; wallowing in self-pity, he is a master at conjuring up a slapdash stance in order to justify his actions.

The inherent amorality in Bowles's position, which had previously served him so well, is much closer to Poe's or Machen's misanthropic tales of the supernatural; but unlike either of these predecessors, Bowles does not fully enter a gothic realm so great as to create in the reader a lingering sense of horror. The difficulty is not with his ability to create an unrelenting notion of irrational victimization. Indeed, Bowles adroitly sets up the Slades as victims of circumstance from the beginning and leaves them no way out; it is this single premise that guides the entire narrative, as it did much of Bowles's other fiction. But the essential problem here is that the characters are so insufficiently drawn that the reader really does not particularly care what happens to them.

Bowles worked daily on the novel throughout the late spring, the summer, and into the fall. In mid-October he wrote his mother that the book was "just about done, save for retyping the entire manuscript. . . . (Of course, it's not merely a question of retyping, but rewriting as I go.)" By December, he was back in Tangier, and had finished reworking the book.

He was also busy saying good-bye to Burroughs, Gysin, and Layachi, who were leaving Tangier for New York. Gysin was trying to market an invention of his called the Dream Machine. Bowles wrote to his parents:

> Brion thinks he may make a fortune with an invention of his called the Dream Machine. He has signed a contract with a manufacturing firm which will produce them en masse. It's like the nineteenth-century "whirligig" . . . although the principle is different, his machine benefitting from modern science. It turns electrically and produces what neurologists call the "alpha wave," which corresponds to nineteen flashes per second and hits the optic nerve in such a way that it induces hallucinations (not to mention frequent epileptic seizures!). Anyway, it promises a new kick to the juvenile delinquents. So far there is no law against such a contraption. If

people want to knock themselves out with the alpha wave, they're at liberty to do it, I suppose.

Layachi, however, was leaving because a French translation of *A Life Full of Holes* had just appeared and he was afraid that when the book arrived in Morocco he would be arrested. As Burroughs and Gysin were willing to take him along, and since Bowles paid for his passage, it seemed to Layachi an opportunity not to be missed. (When *A Life Full of Holes* was finally published in French translation, it was, in fact, seized by the Moroccan authorities.)

In early January 1965 Bowles learned that his father had suffered a cerebral hemorrhage. Although his condition was not critical, Bowles felt that he should be there. But Jane was reluctant to cross the Atlantic because of the likelihood of storms, and so the Bowleses did not leave for New York until April. Upon arrival, Bowles immediately went to Florida, where he was relieved to find his father up and around. After a couple of weeks, Bowles returned to New York, but didn't stay long, as John Goodwin, then living part of the year in Santa Fe, New Mexico, invited Bowles to visit him there.

Bowles accepted the invitation; Jane stayed in New York. For Bowles, the trip was more than a vacation. As he explained to his parents in a letter written from Santa Fe on May 6, 1965, "Jane and I had wanted to come out here . . . to look around at the place as a possible settling-spot once we have to leave Morocco (which will come sooner or later, everyone is sure)." While there, he even looked at a few houses, "not with any idea of choosing those particular ones . . . but just to get a general idea." The prices, while lower than any in New York, were far higher than even a villa in Tangier. Bowles simply noted what he could get for his money, and postponed the decision indefinitely.

Before he had left for Santa Fe, Bowles had given his book to Helen Strauss, who had in turn sent it to Random House. On his return a couple of weeks later, he was disappointed to learn that the publisher was "still reading" the manuscript, to which he had now given the title *Up Above the World.* Bowles had expected a decision by that point. On May 31 he wrote his mother, grumbling about the protracted decision-making process: "Nothing can possibly be settled while I'm still here, which is too bad, but everyone takes so long to do anything here in New York; I should have to stay here indefinitely. What I've been trying to do while I was here is to get at least some of my books (which are out of print, mostly) reprinted so they will be available again. . . . Even on that I have nothing definite, but I think something will develop later out of my efforts." In fact, he had no success in getting any of his books reissued. Worse, Random House decided to turn down *Up Above the World,* leaving Bowles without a publisher.

There is always a certain whimsical quality to an artist's popularity, but Bowles's decline has some demonstrable causes. Perhaps the major reason for his inability to excite publishers or readers about his work, either new or old, had to do with the fiction itself. The American expatriate as an interesting character, in life or in art, milked so well by the "lost generation" of the 1930s, was no longer in vogue. Even Hemingway, the leader of that generation, had fallen temporarily from grace; and while others, like Mailer or Capote or Vidal, changed their styles to fit the times, Bowles did not.

At the same time, Bowles was no longer receiving the kind of support formerly provided by friends. In the past, Williams, Thomson, Copland, and others had consistently endeavored to draw public attention to Bowles's work. Williams's important reviews of *The Sheltering Sky* and *The Delicate Prey* had played a large role in creating a climate for popular success. Now, however, no one rushed forward to call on editors or to write articles. It wasn't that Bowles had fallen out of favor with his creative allies but rather that, by this point, many of them had stopped writing reviews, while others had simply gotten out of the habit of helping him. Nor was Bowles in a position to help himself, as his prolonged absence from America prevented him from appearing on talk shows, signing books, or going to the right literary parties. His self-imposed exile had begun to exact its price.

In June, Bowles and Jane returned to Tangier. Aside from seeing his parents and learning of the shocking real estate prices in Santa Fe, Bowles had accomplished little on the trip.

CHAPTER 28

Back in Tangier, Bowles learned from his agent that she had found a publisher for *Up Above the World.* "I finally got a fairly good contract on my new book from Simon & Schuster, so it is they who will be publishing the work, instead of Random House, who didn't understand it and consequently wanted changes made," Bowles wrote his mother, adding: "Grove Press was eager to publish it as it stood, but my agent didn't want to deal with them; agents always prefer to deal with what they call 'big houses.'"

With that issue settled, he was beginning to tape a new novel for translation, this one by another young Moroccan, Mohammed Mrabet. Mrabet had actually met Bowles and Jane several years earlier while working as a cook and bartender for an American who had a house on the Old Mountain, but it wasn't until 1964 that he became truly friendly with them. One day in the spring of 1965, while visiting Bowles, Mrabet saw a copy of *A Life Full of Holes* with Layachi's photo on the cover. "I began to laugh when I saw it, because I knew Larbi could not write. How can that be Larbi's book? He can't even sign his name." Bowles explained to him that Layachi had simply taped the stories, adding that he'd even made some money doing it. That convinced Mrabet that he too had some tales to tell. In his autobiography, *Look and Move On,* translated by Bowles, he recounted how it was that he came to tell stories: "I began to go see [Bowles] several times a week, and each time I spent two hours or so recording stories. Finally I had a good collection of them. Some were tales I had heard in the cafés, some were dreams, some were inventions I made as I was recording, and some were about things that had actually happened to me."

One day, Mrabet recalls, he told Bowles that he had a story that he thought Bowles would especially like. "Of course, he said: Let's hear it. So I told him a very long one that went on for many nights. ... I started to talk and he was sitting opposite me, and every little

380

while I would fill my pipe [with kif]. And it went on that way until I finished the book." Mrabet's "long story" turned out to be a novel, *Love with a Few Hairs,* a fascinating tale of obsessional love. As the book begins, a young Moroccan, also named Mohammed, is being kept by a rich Englishman named Mr. David, while at the same time infatuated with a young woman named Mina, who at first spurns him. Through magic, she eventually falls in love with him and they marry. For the first several months of marriage they are both in bliss, but Mina's mother, opposed to the marriage from the beginning, divines that Mina is under a spell. She breaks it; Mina falls out of love with Mohammed and has an affair. Eventually, after much soul-searching and vacillation, Mohammed leaves her and goes back to live with Mr. David.

Although the plot is simple, *Love with a Few Hairs* is a masterful book, a deft chronicle of life in Tangier, with its dual society of Moroccans and expatriates. It is in many ways the same world that Bowles gave us, but the difference is that this Tangier is seen through the eyes of a Moroccan. Mr. David, who dotes on Mohammed, is easily recognizable as a typical "old settler," in love with a colonial Morocco and with Moroccans who faithfully serve him. But Mohammed, who engages our sympathies from the beginning, is no fool. While he is genuinely fond of Mr. David, he also makes use of him, extracting gifts from the more than willing Nazarene. And while Mohammed's family disapproves of his life with the Englishman, they are not contemptuous of the presents Mr. David hands over to "his Moslem" and the family. In some ways, *Love with a Few Hairs* is a variation on the old picaresque theme of the sympathetic trickster, who uses his wits to survive in a society not of his own making.

In Mrabet, Bowles found not only an astonishingly gifted storyteller, but a friend as well. Over the years, in fact, Mrabet would doubtlessly become the single individual closest to Bowles, his most faithful friend, a continual source of delight. In some ways, Mrabet's friendship can be seen as replacing the deep relationship that Bowles had had with Yacoubi, without the probable sexual component of that earlier relationship. This is not to say that Bowles was no longer fond of Yacoubi, but in the late 1950s and early 1960s, the two of them had gradually drifted apart. Although there was for a time some difficulty between them, apparently over

Yacoubi's willingness to tell tales while in jail, the main reason for
the change in the relationship was that Yacoubi had married, fa-
thered a child, and consequently was living a far more independent
life. While Yacoubi was still a frequent visitor to Bowles's home,
the relationship was not nearly so close as it had been.

Once Mrabet came on the scene, however, Yacoubi became far
more distant. Mrabet and Yacoubi never liked each other, forcing
Bowles, in essence, to choose between them. To some extent it was
jealousy on the part of the two Moroccans, but in addition, an
incident occurred in the mid-1960s that served to fuel the animosity that they felt for each other. In 1965 Mrabet was working as a
bartender at the Tangier Inn, a small hotel in Tangier run by an
American (the model for Mr. David's hotel in *Love with a Few Hairs*).
Yacoubi was living there with his wife and baby and over the
months had run up a considerable bill. As he wanted to move back
to Fez, he decided to sneak out without paying. Little by little he
began surreptitiously to bring down his possessions. In fact, Mrabet was watching the entire thing. Finally, with his wife and baby
in a taxi outside, Yacoubi brought down the last suitcase. Mrabet
quietly went over, grabbed Yacoubi by the shirt, dragged him over
to the cash register and presented him with a bill. Yacoubi had no
choice but to pay. Although Yacoubi always feigned forgetfulness,
Mrabet never allowed the incident to go unremembered. Even
years later, when Mrabet and Yacoubi would occasionally meet at
Bowles's at the same time, Mrabet would sit silently and glare at
Yacoubi, who would speak mainly to Bowles. As soon as Yacoubi
would leave, Mrabet would turn to Bowles and say, usually
apropos of nothing specific to the conversation, "See what a son-
of-a-bitch he is!"

Mrabet was also fond of Jane, and she of him, despite his violent
opposition to the ever-present Cherifa. Mrabet recalls that he was
continually trying to persuade Bowles that Jane was giving Cherifa
far too much money and that he should interfere on Jane's behalf,
since she clearly could not resist Cherifa's demands. Bowles would
only reply that since it wasn't his money, there was nothing he
could do about it. Mrabet, however, claims that Bowles was afraid
of Cherifa. There seems to have been good reason for it. Bowles
recalls that one day he and Jane had an argument over the usual
matter: money for Cherifa. Jane had given her 50,000 francs that

morning; by the afternoon Cherifa was demanding more. Bowles became angry, but in the end decided there was little he could do. As he walked to the door, Cherifa, who had been watching the scene, lunged at him, her fingers splayed in an attempt to put out his eyes. Bowles narrowly escaped through the door and upstairs to his own apartment.

Incidents like these, in combination with various stories and rumors that circulated around Tangier, served to abet the creation of Cherifa in Bowles's mind as an almost larger-than-life villainess. In October 1965 he wrote to Andreas Brown: "As you know, Cherifa carries a switch-blade always, in order to castrate any male who may say good evening to her. Never knew a woman who hated men so violently. I'm told she makes a specialty of stealing brides on the eve of their weddings. Hadn't known before, but occasionally I get the low-down on her from somebody. And always I'm more appalled by her than before."

Jane, although alternately still attended or managed or dominated by Cherifa, had in fact fallen in love with a European, a resident of Tangier since 1949, Princess Marthe Ruspoli, about ten years her senior. Separated from an Italian prince, Ruspoli was wealthy, aggressively intelligent, and prone to drama. Jane fell into Ruspoli's orbit in late 1963; by 1965, she had apparently become as dependent on Ruspoli as she had earlier been on Cherifa or Helvetia Perkins. Edouard Roditi remembers that Ruspoli always tried to control Jane: "She was a rigid authoritarian, very opinionated and decisive." She was also a devout Catholic, and frequently talked to Jane about religion. It was in large part her intelligence that attracted Jane, her ability to hold serious conversations on a variety of topics, particularly literature, art, and religion. "Marthe, of course, hated Cherifa," recalls Roditi. "She was always advising Jane to get rid of her." But Jane, although no longer sexually involved with Cherifa, would not hear of it. Cherifa, in fact, continued to live with Jane even during the years in which she was involved with Ruspoli. Their bond, as perverse as it seemed to onlookers, was stronger than steel.

It was these relationships that occupied center stage in Jane's life. Although she worked intermittently on her play and stories, she could bring nothing to fruition. The stroke had had a good deal to do with it, but even before that she was having considerable difficulty getting words she felt worth keeping onto paper, from which she could get enough satisfaction to go on with her work. Even the reissuing of *Two Serious Ladies* by Peter Owen in England, in January 1965, and the publication of her stories, *Plain Pleasures,* also by Owen in 1966, did not provide an impetus to write, despite their garnering excellent reviews this time around.

Edouard Roditi posits that Jane might simply have been cut off from the milieu that had originally provided her with inspiration:

> Had Paul, all these years, been dragging Jane away from her own familiar world on a wild-goose chase to Central America, Ceylon and Morocco, in his romantically outdated quest for the Eldorado of a doomed exoticism? The natural setting of Jane's finest writing had indeed been middle-class American suburbia, whether on the East Coast of the United States or in Southern California. Her ability to depict her few exotic environments and characters even seems to have been borrowed to some extent from Paul's writings. Her few and generally sketchily depicted exotic characters are all much of the same class as those who appear in Paul's fiction, and one can detect, in the relationship between Jane and Paul as writers, a curious phenomenon of literary osmosis.

Jane herself, about this same time, made the following statement: "From the first day, Morocco seemed more dreamlike than real. I felt cut off from what I knew. In the twenty years that I have lived here I have written only two short stories, and nothing else. It's good for Paul, but not for me." Commenting on this statement, Bowles noted that feelings are not "monolithic, as though they never shifted and altered throughout the years. I know Jane expressed the idea frequently toward the end of her life, when she was bedridden and regretted not being within reach of her friends. Most of them lived in New York, of course. But for the first decade she loved Morocco as much as I did."

It is, naturally, pure speculation as to whether Jane would have written more if she had remained in America, but clearly Morocco did have a debilitating effect on her, removing her from the context of her fictional fabrication. Isolated from publishers, agents, literary friends, and acquaintances, and stung by the initial critical reception accorded both her novel and play, by the mid-1960s she was at the point of devaluing her own work. It was Bowles who saw to it that *Two Serious Ladies* was republished, and only because he had held on to her stories and was willing to retype them for publication was *Plain Pleasures* made possible.

That Jane, for all of her strong-mindedness, ultimately followed Bowles, acquiescing to his desires, at least in terms of living in Morocco, is fairly self-evident. In a fragment of a story, "The Iron Table," she records a conversation between a husband and a wife that goes a long way toward explaining her own attitude:

> "Why do you ask me if I wouldn't love to go into the desert, when you know as well as I do I wouldn't. We've talked about it over and over. Every few days we talk about it." Although the sun was beating down on her chest, making it feel on fire, deep inside she could still feel the cold current that seemed to run near her heart.
>
> "Well," he said. "You change. Sometimes you say you *would* like to go."
>
> It was true. She did change. Sometimes she would run to him with bright eyes. "Let's go," she would say, "into the desert." But she never did this if she were sober [. . . .]
>
> "Do you think I ought to go?" she asked him.
>
> "Go where?"
>
> "To the desert. To live in an oasis." She was pronouncing her words slowly. "Maybe that's what I should do, since I'm your wife."
>
> "You must do what you really want to do," he said. He had been trying to teach her this for twelve years.
>
> "What I really want. . . . Well, if you'd be happy in an oasis, maybe I'd really want to do that." She spoke hesitantly, and there was a note of doubt in her voice.
>
> "What?" He shook his head as if he had run into a spiderweb. "What is it?"
>
> "I meant that maybe if you were happy in an oasis I would be too. Wives get pleasure out of making their husbands happy. They really do, quite aside from its being moral."

The dialogue could quite clearly have been lifted from an actual conversation between the Bowleses. All of the familiar elements in their relationship are recorded here: Bowles's passive-aggressiveness; Jane's indecisiveness; her ultimate acquiescence through the dual rationale of believing that what was good for her husband might also be good for her, as well as its being a "moral" course. While it does not explain her entire reasoning for remaining in Morocco, Jane very definitely tried to convince herself, for more than a decade, that any place Bowles liked so much must also be good for her. And despite her sexual independence, as Buffie Johnson has said, "Jane very much liked the idea of being Mrs. Bowles."

As for Bowles, he believed that Jane was making a free choice in being with him in Morocco, that, in fact, she had chosen it as much as he had. At first, it seems, she had indeed exercised her own free will, but as the years went by, and as she ceased more and more to write, it became increasingly clear to many around her that Morocco did not serve her in the way it did Bowles. That she was relatively content there socially is indisputable, but so is the fact that she was largely unable to draw on the country as a source of inspiration. And unlike Bowles, who could conjure up from memory the sights, sounds, atmosphere, and texture of places seen in the distant past, Jane, to some extent, depended upon proximity to the milieu that she was writing about in order to have a sense of how and what to write. After nearly twenty years of living largely outside the United States, as Roditi points out, she no longer was in touch with the culture from which sprang her creativity.

And yet Bowles was truly unwilling to compromise his own need to remain in Morocco, and continually made it known to her how much he abhorred the idea of living in the United States. As such, either unconsciously or consciously, he put Jane in a position of having to exert her own initiative, knowing full well that she sorely lacked the ability to take action herself. Like the husband in "The Iron Table," he believed that he had been trying to teach her for years that she had to act independently from him, while fully expecting her not to exercise her choice in regard to staying in Morocco.

Perhaps he felt he had made enough compromises already. He had put off many of his own plans in order to be with her, had taken time away from his own work to see that her writing went back into print, had continually exhorted her to write more, had sold Taprobane because she loathed it, and had consistently tolerated her lesbian life-style and neurotic involvement with Cherifa. Because of his attentiveness to her and his own decision not to interfere in her love affairs or social life, he may have believed that he was entitled to hold out for staying in the locale where he was the happiest. Most likely, though, Bowles never fully realized the adverse effect that living in Morocco possibly had had on her writing. It was easier to blame the stroke, to point to the fact that even before her illness she was writing little. Whatever the reason, Jane would remain in Tangier until such time as she was no longer physically or psychologically capable of doing so, or as some think, until Bowles could no longer cope with her being there.

On March 15, 1966, *Up Above the World* was published by Simon & Schuster; in January 1967 it was brought out by Peter Owen in London. Just before the American publication of the novel, in February, Helen Strauss sold the film rights to Universal Studios for $25,000. In a letter to his mother, Bowles explained that although there had been some hesitation on his agent's part to accept the offer, thinking she might be able to get more later, Bowles was pleased: "It seemed to me that she might easily not have been made a better offer later, particularly if the book should get less than enthusiastic reviews when it comes out."

The reviews, in fact, were mixed, but none praised the novel without some qualification. Even the most laudatory critics noted that Bowles's amorality was bothersome. Webster Schott, writing in the *New York Times Book Review,* commented that "the author's own attitude is as anti-moral as a tombstone. He values situations, possibilities pushed to extreme. . . . As with his music the author may prefer his fiction to be as thesis-free as chords. But words form ideas. The lacking idea here is of a morally uninhabitable world, created by an artist robbed of compassion and endowed with such gifts as to make the loss seem irrelevant." Another reviewer noted that "Bowles performs like a musician who has fallen in love with one tune which he plays magnificently, but over and over again. The novel is lopsided, 193 pages of tension and 26 pages of relief. When it does finally come, the relief is so banal that it is an anti-climax." But no review was as scathing as that in the *New Yorker:* "A dull story, designated on the cover as a novel, about an unamiable couple who are incessant nap-takers. . . . Although Mr. Bowles is inordinately vague about his characters' motives or lack of motives, he is always ready with precise descriptions of minor mental processes, tones of voice, types of yawns, and unpleasant Latin-American hotel rooms."

Despite some of the more negative reviews, another offer had meanwhile come Bowles's way. He wrote his mother about it: "[It] involves my going to Bangkok to write a book about the city, and that I may possibly do. I've never been there, and from all I've heard and read, it's fascinating. . . . Anyway, I've written back to the publishers, (Little, Brown) to ask for details on the sort of book they'd like, and so forth. They pay $5,000 on signing of contract and $5,000 on delivery of manuscript, which seems to me good pay." Bowles accepted the offer, signed a contract a month later and began to make preparations for his trip.

Suddenly, during the first week in June, Bowles received a wire from Florida. His mother had died, and his father, now largely an invalid, had to be confined to a nursing home. Bowles accelerated and altered his departure plans to include a stop in Florida, but shortly before leaving for New York on July 9, another wire came, telling him that his father, too, was dead. Whatever emotion Bowles felt, he kept it largely to himself, noting only that "for some reason the death of my parents diminished my unwillingness to leave Tangier; very likely the shock made itself felt by leaving me in a state of indifference. I can only deduce that I felt profoundly guilty for having excised them from my life."

But was it Bowles who had "excised" his parents, or was it, in fact, the reverse? Perhaps in the case of his mother, he had indeed cut her out of his life, but with Claude, this hardly seems to be true. If Bowles excised his parents, particularly his father, he did so in reaction to their cutting him off emotionally. As such, his withdrawing from them was quite obviously a necessary condition for his own development as an individual and as an artist. Indeed, in order to survive his childhood and adolescence with any semblance of wholeness, it had probably been essential for him to exile himself emotionally from his parents. Why guilt, therefore? One explanation is offered by Edouard Roditi: "Paul, being someone who always felt guilt, naturally felt guilty."

Beyond that, though, one senses from Bowles's letters to his parents over the years that he desired, and had managed to achieve, some sort of rapprochement, if only a superficial one.

While to be sure the letters generally contain mostly news bulletins, with little or no emotional investment, they do nonetheless represent some degree of the concern Paul felt for his parents. The guilt, therefore, may not have been due to feeling that he had excised them, as he surmised, but because he did, in reality, feel fairly indifferent to their passing, despite the frequent exchanges of letters and his own attempts to report dutifully to them.

In letters to friends, written before learning that his father had died, he mentions his mother's death only in passing, in the context of having to change his plans. To Thomson, for instance, he wrote: "Now I have got to undo my plans for going eastward, and instead go to New York. My mother died last week, and I must go and see my father. Later I'll take a westward ship through the canal." And to Andreas Brown: "My mother died last week and I have got to go back to the States briefly; I'll continue from New York to Bangkok." To novelist James Purdy, commenting on the deaths of both his parents, he wrote: "My parents died and I have got to go sometime this year to Florida to take care of the house."

As the true emotional bonds between Bowles and his parents had been broken so many years before and never been repaired sufficiently, he may not have experienced any profound sense of loss. Then again, as an expert at hiding emotions, even from himself, it is also quite possible that he was not at the time truly sure of how he felt: indifference can mask depression. What is clear is that Bowles kept his emotions tucked well away and allowed "indifference" to be projected to the outside world.

The Bowleses arrived in New York the third week in July. On the 28th, Bowles sailed for Bangkok via Panama, Los Angeles, San Francisco, Hong Kong, and Manila. Jane, meanwhile, stayed a few weeks in New York in order to see friends and her editor, Hal Vursell, at Farrar, Straus, & Giroux, who was preparing for publication that fall *The Collected Works of Jane Bowles,* with an introduction by Truman Capote. She also went to Florida to visit her mother, then back to Tangier in late August.

Bowles's voyage to Bangkok took almost two months. When he arrived in mid-September, he discovered it was hardly the mysterious tropical city of canals and temples and exotic vegetation that he had expected it to be. Instead, with the Vietnam War raging, it was clogged with American soldiers and was overpopulated, dirty, and hot. In addition, Bowles was having trouble with his knee. While in San Francisco during a stopover, he had cut it when he accidentally walked into a plate glass door at the St. Francis Hotel. It had been stitched up and the wound had healed, but he was in pain whenever he moved it.

On the second of October, he wrote Virgil Thomson his impressions:

> Have been here now a fortnight, and am not sure I want to stay six months! In any case, the government so far has not granted me permission to remain more than one month, although I have various irons in the fire which may or may not heat up sufficiently. For one thing, it's too hot to lead one's life easily, and I doubt that I could get used to it in so short a period of time. Probably a year would do the trick, but who wants to be stuck in such a place for a year. If you've been here, you must remember that the air is well-nigh unbreathable with exhaust fumes, and that the noise in the streets is more shattering than anything in any American city. . . . Taxis are equipped with ladies who lean out and suggest massage. Never knew it was possible to be accosted so many times per hour. . . . Unless one is looking for ladies to massage one, the place is not an amusing one. At the same time, if a man kisses a woman in public, he can be imprisoned, even, my informants insist, though they be man and wife. The Mystelious East. Scleam, scleam! No one will heal you. Dilectly beneath loom is glotto full of hungly lats.

By mid-October Bowles was still finding little to like about Thailand, except for the prevalence of marijuana and the presence of an old acquaintance, Oliver Evans, who was spending the year there as a Fulbright exchange professor. Language, furthermore, was a major barrier for Bowles. In a story he wrote in 1971, "You Have Left Your Lotus Pods on the Bus," inspired by a ride on a Bangkok bus during that fall of 1966, he recounts an amusing tale of miscommunication. Two Americans, Brooks (modeled on Evans) and the narrator board a bus. In the back, a man screams continually throughout the journey. The Thai passengers pay him no mind but the Americans, bothered by his howls, decide that he must be mad or drunk. Finally, after leaving the bus, they ask a Thai companion what the man was shouting about. He said, " 'All the buses must have a driver's assistant. He watches the road and tells the driver how to drive. It is hard work because he must shout loud enough for the driver to hear him.' "

In mid-November, Bowles quit Bangkok for Chiengmai, north of the capital. Although he found it more agreeable in some respects, he was very isolated there. He wrote to Evans, in Bangkok, asking him to come up and bring with him some more marijuana ("my pot is running low, God forbid!"), then went on to say that he was seeking to find out more about the opium trade: "I'll inquire about the opium dens if I find anyone to inquire from. Haven't met a soul here, either Thai or otherwise. . . . The U.N. have estimated that 75% of the world's supply of illicit opium passes through Chiengmai, a ton at a time, and that there are whole warehouses full of it here! Junk headquarters of the world! . . . Had a letter from Jane's doctor in Tangier who says she isn't well. I may have to curtail my sojourn here by a month or more, and return to Tangier in January."

In fact, Jane was not doing well at all, and Bowles was forced to leave sooner than he had expected. Just before his departure, he wrote Andreas Brown that Jane was described by her doctor as having "fallen into an excessively depressed state in which she only eats, sleeps and sits silently all day waiting for night. . . . It seems she does not even telephone anyone anymore. . . . Whenever I disappear Cherifa takes over with her potions, and Jane goes into a tailspin."

When Bowles arrived in Tangier in late February, he found Jane in a deep depression. By early April, with no improvement in Jane's condition, Bowles was forced to hospitalize her. To Thomson, he provided details in a letter of April 27:

Jane is in Malaga in hospital. I took her over two weeks ago. It was painful, but there was no possible way of allowing her to stay here in the state she was in when I got back from Bangkok. No amelioration appeared during the month and a half I waited, watching her. She could be lucid only if one managed, for a minute or two, to get her mind away from her "illness." Behind it all she seemed to be quite clear about her state, and could discuss it rationally now and then in moments of stress. Fundamentally the trouble was that she did not seem to care one way or the other. It was all happening in someone else about whom she didn't give a damn, and so she shrugged her shoulders. I'm hoping the hospital can get her interested in something, even if only in getting out.

Bowles's decision to place Jane in a psychiatric hospital, excruciatingly difficult for him, was made even worse by the criticism he received for it by some in Tangier. Cherifa, naturally, but Ruspoli as well, denounced Bowles; stories began to circulate in Tangier that Bowles had gotten rid of Jane because he didn't want to bother with her. Roditi recalls that "people in Tangier liked to think of Jane as the charming, witty, eccentric lady she'd been. But that, she wasn't any longer. She was a pathetic mess. There was really nothing else that Paul could do but institutionalize her. She could not be looked after properly in Tangier and certainly not by Paul alone. It was all very unfair."

Perhaps the worst part of the ordeal for Jane was that she was fully cognizant of the fact that she had deteriorated so severely. And yet, there was nothing that she could do to rise above it, to use her consciousness of her situation to improve it. Shortly after she was institutionalized, David Herbert came to visit her. He had made a collection of the reviews of the recently published *Collected Works,* which were generally glowing, and thinking to cheer her up, decided to present her with them. "As reading was such an effort, Janie made me read them to her," Herbert later recalled. "She looked very sad and, for a little while, said nothing, then hopelessly, she said: 'I know you meant this kindly, darling, but you couldn't have been more cruel. . . . It all makes me realize what I was and what I have become.' I was terribly upset. Janie, seeing this, looked up with a ghost of a smile. 'Give me the book,' she said. I handed her *The Collected Works.* With a trembling hand she picked up a pencil and added *'of Dead Jane Bowles.' "*

Herbert also remembers that the effect on Bowles was devastating: "Paul was unable to write, compose, or accomplish anything." This was largely the case, although he did find that he could work a bit on translation, in particular a new book by Mrabet, a coming-of-age story which would eventually be called *The Lemon.* "I have to do something," Bowles wrote Oliver Evans, "and with the thunderheads of Jane's illness on the horizon, I can't get into anything which requires true concentration." Even translation, though, was clouded by the fact that the book was likely to be banned in Morocco. Both *A Life Full of Holes* and *Love with a Few Hairs* had been seized in Tangier and their distribution prevented. But as the intended audience for the books was clearly not Moroccans anyway, Bowles pressed on; translation could be worked on for a few hours at a stretch, was less affected by interruption, either physical or mental.

In the meantime, his first American collection of stories since *The Delicate Prey* was about to be issued in New York by Holt, Rinehart & Winston. It contained thirteen stories, including the four from *A Hundred Camels in the Courtyard,* and several that were printed in *A Little Stone.*

Published in July 1967, *The Time of Friendship* was enthusiastically received. "He is American fiction's leading specialist in melancholy and insensate violence. . . . At his best, Bowles has no peer in his sullen art," wrote *Time* magazine. Melvin Maddocks, in *Life,* noted that Bowles "survives, a unique trader in African Gothic, because he is a superb storyteller and because he avoids the one unforgivable sin of his genre: voyeurism. He extends to his characters a frail but consistent humanity they do not extend to one another or to themselves. Like Virgil and Dante before him, he has the common compassion to go to hell with the children of his imagination." Bernard Bergonzi, however, writing in the *New York Review of Books,* sounded a somewhat less positive note: "He places his characters before us and then destroys them in an unerring way: It is a remarkable performance, but one expects something more from literature."

Despite the generally excellent reviews, the book did not sell terribly well, nor was it reprinted in paperback. One possible explanation for the lack of public reception was offered by John Gray, an English critic: "Bowles has not adapted his style to the changing years, with the result that he now seems old-fashioned. . . . It is not a question of a lack of contemporary facts, but of a basic disharmony with the prevailing *geist.* This is always a problem for the expatriate writer (as has recently been evidenced by Lawrence Durrell); and in Bowles this problem seems to be focused on an inability to deal simultaneously with two cultures." Maureen Howard, writing in *Partisan Review,* noted similarly that Bowles's "bleak modernity" had "worn thin."

The remarks are interesting in that they reflect as much on the readers of the late 1960s as they do on Bowles. Alienation, particularly existential alienation, had peaked as a theme; readers were demanding a greater degree of entertainment from their writers, or at the very least, books relevant to their social, psychic, or libidinous concerns: thus the dominance of writers like Jacqueline Susann, Irving Wallace, and Harold Robbins on the best-seller lists, followed by a plethora of self-help books, ranging from *The Games People Play* to Masters and Johnson. For horror, there was *Rosemary's Baby,* and for murder, *In Cold Blood,* both vastly more appealing to American audiences with their overwhelming "Americanness." The exotic was restricted to Vietnam, as interpreted by Robin Moore in his best-selling *The Green Berets* or to the Israel in James Michener's *The Source.* To be sure, serious fiction was still being published and read, but the public was far more interested in Norman Mailer, William Styron, Saul Bellow, or John Barth than in even a writer such as Graham Greene, who had recently offered up *The Comedians,* possibly the novel of that period closest to sharing Bowles's vision of expatriates abroad—that is, if Bowles had had a sense of humor.

Bowles, it seems, had indeed lost touch, or perhaps American readers had simply lost touch with Bowles. His message was not welcome, if even understood. Despite the critical acclaim, Bowles's work had begun to fall into obscurity, was beginning to be forgotten as quickly as had his music. Indeed, when *The Time of Friendship* went out of print in 1969, there was no book of Bowles's still in print from a major house. The only works available were the Layachi and Mrabet translations, a small book of poems from the 1920s issued in 1968 by Black Sparrow Press in an edition of 250 copies, and *A Hundred Camels in the Courtyard.* It would take another decade for Bowles to be "rediscovered," and even then the "rediscovery" would be slow in developing, made only by a few.

Bowles himself was aware of the situation, but he'd been an expatriate too long to change his mode. In 1985 he acknowledged that despite the personal advantage he feels he has gained from living in Tangier, "because I like it better," popular acceptance of his work probably would have been greater had he spent more time in the United States: "I should think it a disadvantage to write only about exotic peoples and Americans abroad. The work might be more important if it were about contemporary America. But it's not and I'm still here." Indeed, Bowles, by the late 1960s and into the 1970s, was becoming even further distanced from the American *geist*. American characters began to drop out of the narratives altogether; the stories began to resemble the translations more and more. In essence, Bowles had made a decision to follow his own vision rather than make even the slightest compromise to the prevailing taste. Predictably, his work became less and less read by mainstream readers (and critics). Bowles's subjective universe, which had once been of such interest to American readers, no longer was so compelling. In some ways, he had become a "foreign" writer.

PART VII

*The Hiss
of Time*

CHAPTER 29

In April of 1967 Bowles received an inquiry from Oliver Evans, asking if he would be interested in spending a year as a visiting writer/professor at San Fernando State University, in California, the college where Evans himself taught. Bowles replied that while he had reservations about the job, he was intrigued by the offer:

> I'm sure that one day sooner or later I shall find myself teaching somewhere, but I ought to be eased into it psychologically, with a post that consists only of seminars, and for a short-term the first time. It's really a matter of learning to take for granted the new *état civil*. At the moment I can't believe that I could really teach anyone anything. And you'll admit that I *am* pretty ignorant of general literature. Or perhaps you don't know that. You didn't mention when the putative year at San Fernando would begin. I certainly can't go this autumn. I don't even know whether Jane will be over her depression by then, and I'm the only person who can take care of her.

Evans responded that Bowles could more or less set his own terms and could start whichever semester he wished.

As for Jane, she wasn't doing well at all. By June, Bowles was forced to consider whether he should allow her to undergo shock treatments again. To Thomson, he wrote of his quandary: "My feeling is that it blots out whole departments of memory permanently, which isn't so good. Of course, she is dead set against it. But if she can't get well without it . . . ?" Later that month, Jane did undergo the shock therapy. There was some improvement and Bowles was told that she could possibly return to Tangier later that summer.

In the interim, Bowles had gotten rid of Cherifa. According to Mohammed Mrabet, the events leading to her departure were

399

quite dramatic. They centered on a philodendron plant that had been in Jane's apartment for several years. One day, in the late spring of 1967, Mrabet remarked to Bowles that it was curious that the plant had never grown, and that furthermore, he had divined the reason: it had something planted in it, something magical. Bowles apparently refused, at least at first, to believe Mrabet's diagnosis, but Mrabet persisted, finally persuading Bowles to go with him down to Jane's apartment where Cherifa was still staying. "Watch Cherifa," he told Bowles, "when I go to take the plant." Mrabet then proceeded to walk over and pick up the plant. Bowles stood in the doorway. As soon as Mrabet lifted it, Cherifa began to scream, attempting to prevent him from taking the plant upstairs. Bowles came over, Mrabet forcefully pushed Cherifa aside, and they rushed for the door. Upstairs, they began to excavate the soil surrounding the roots. Suddenly a black cloth packet appeared, the roots wrapped around it.

Bowles recounted: "Cherifa had it manufactured by somebody who told her that this mess, with the right words said over it, would entwine with the roots of the plant and enable her to give instructions to the plant which the plant would carry out. . . . The plant was her guardian; it wouldn't let anything happen that would injure her when she wasn't in the house. The thing she feared most was that she wouldn't get any money. The plant was her protection." Although it was Mrabet who had uncovered Cherifa's plot, he wouldn't touch the packet, which contained "pubic hairs, dried blood, fingernails, antimony, and various other things." Bowles decorously extracted the packet containing the *tsuheur* concoction and flushed it down the toilet. When they went back downstairs, Cherifa was gone.

Bowles brought Jane back from Málaga in early July. She was extremely weak, having lost over twenty pounds during her stay in the hospital; her psychological state, however, was at least stabilized, if not improved. When Bowles told her about the plant episode and Cherifa's dismissal, Jane at first didn't really react, being, as Bowles recalled, "so ill she didn't care." But soon she was meeting Cherifa in town and continued to pay her a salary. The situation continued that way until one day, in September, Cherifa moved back in with Jane. Mrabet urged Bowles to bar Cherifa from the building but Bowles felt he could really do nothing about it;

he feared that making a scene could cause Jane to relapse into her previous depression. In August, Jane had been operated on for hemorrhoids; the stitches tore, and in October she had to undergo the operation again. Bowles wrote to Evans that "she lies screaming all night, and there doesn't seem to be anything the doctors can do for her. No injection calms the pain. This preoccupation has kept me from doing much of anything."

In fact, with all of the uncertainty about Jane's condition, Bowles was finding it impossible to work on his book on Bangkok. During Jane's convalescence it was clear to him that he simply couldn't come up with it. "The Bangkok book I have abandoned wholly, and am returning Little, Brown's advance," wrote Bowles to Evans. "It's impossible for me to work, no matter how hard I try, and it has been that way since I returned from Thailand. . . . As you know, I never give up on writing projects. But this was one that didn't interest me in the beginning; I accepted it out of greed, and I hope I've learned better, so that I shan't get myself into that sort of thing again." In the same letter he told Evans that he wasn't sure whether he could accept the new offer of a one-semester appointment to teach at San Fernando in the fall of 1968, though "the idea of going there does interest me."

Part of Bowles's hesitation stemmed from concern about his own lack of academic preparation. In letter after letter he expressed this concern to Evans with statements such as, "If only I could believe that someone as truly ignorant as I could actually fill such a teaching position. What could I do, knowing nothing except how to write my own material?" or, "I'm really a composer with a composer's mind, and I don't even have the normal cerebral functioning of a writer." This is not false humility; Bowles felt genuine panic about the idea of teaching. "I'm not worried about academic credits," he explained, "but I do wonder what will be the reaction of a student who asks me something about WAR AND PEACE or LE ROUGE ET LE NOIR or BUDDENBROOKS, and I am obliged to say that I don't know the books." He did finally agree to accept a one-semester position, with the reservation that he could pull out if Jane suddenly took a turn downward.

Toward the end of the year, Jane seemed to be doing much better. Bowles was beginning to feel optimistic, but abruptly she moved out of the apartment and into the Hotel Atlas. Even this didn't bother Bowles too much until it became clear that the proximity of the Parade Bar was the main reason for her move. Alcohol, in combination with the potent medication, produced an almost immediate reaction of mental instability. At the beginning of the year, she began totally to lose control. On February 5, 1968, Bowles wrote Evans about it:

> At the moment I am in something of a state about Jane, who suddenly became wholly unbalanced, and caused an uproar in town which lasted for almost a month, steadily increasing in volume and pitch, until, together with an intern from the psychiatric hospital here, I got her back to Spain to the sanatorium, where she now is. . . . Jane seemed to believe that she was Barbara Hutton, and threw away large amounts of money constantly. In order to be able to do that, she had to borrow from everyone in the city—individuals and shops alike. Then she issued checks without provision (having emptied the bank account here without my knowledge) and the Moroccan government moved in, claiming it was my fault, since the account was a joint one. I've already sent for three thousand dollars, to pay off the debts, but they keep cropping up, and I can see that it won't be enough.

The money and the checks had been issued to anyone who happened to be around her—to those she knew, but most especially to those she didn't—as she sat at the bar in the Atlas Hotel or at the Parade Bar. Diagnosed as being manic-depressive, Jane, once in the Spanish clinic, was given a variety of drugs to "stabilize" her precarious state of mental health, but there was little real improvement in her condition. In June, however, Bowles made arrangements to have her cared for in a private pension in Granada, run by Americans. Within ten days, though, Bowles received a phone call informing him that they were not in a position to care for a woman in Jane's condition. According to Mohammed Mrabet, who went with Bowles to Granada, the expatriates were quite angry with Bowles, claiming he had never explained to them how poor Jane's mental health was and accusing him of trying to pawn her off on them. Jane was readmitted to the clinic in Málaga; Bowles sadly returned to Tangier, realizing that it was very likely Jane would have to be hospitalized indefinitely.

Meanwhile, he began to make plans for his one-semester teaching stint. He had agreed to teach two classes, one on the existential novel, the other in creative writing, but as the September starting date grew nearer, he became increasingly nervous: "I'm stumped, because I don't know what is expected of me," he confided to Evans. "Try to envisage my ignorance and explain to me what goes on in a classroom, what is a course? a lecture course? a seminar? a class? Who does the talking in each? What is the teaching process? Does one tell students one's own reactions to books, or does one remain wholly objective in approach? Does one interpret?" Evans responded, reassuring him that he would not have to write out lectures, that simply he would be responsible for leading discussions. Much relieved, Bowles sent Evans his reading list for the existential novel: Camus's *The Stranger* and *Exile and the Kingdom,* Sartre's *Intimacy* and *Nausea,* and Simone de Beauvoir's *The Blood of Others.*

In September, with Jane's condition stable but unimproved, Bowles sailed for New York, then went by train to California. Before leaving Morocco, he explained to Thomson his reason for accepting the position: "I imagine it's pretty awful, and I have no desire to go there, (or to go anywhere in the U.S.) or to teach anywhere, for that matter. However, it seems a practical solution to as yet undeclared financial difficulties. The cost of keeping Jane in hospitals and with doctors and medicine grows, whereas my income doesn't."

Despite Bowles's initial anxiety about teaching, he actually found the task relatively easy, if not terribly satisfying. "The classes seem a farce, in that I don't feel I'm 'teaching' at all, and very probably I'm not," he wrote Thomson from California. "However, the students seem satisfied, and I suppose that's what matters." While in Santa Monica, he also looked up old friends. Christopher Isherwood lived nearby; so did Tennessee Williams. Mohammed Mrabet also came over to keep Bowles company, but left after three weeks: "He hated the place, which struck him as uncivilized. 'No está civilizado,' he reiterated constantly. 'New York está civilizado, Los Angeles no!' "

One major reason for Mrabet's discontent had to do with a wild night he and Bowles had endured that began with a party at Tennessee Williams's. Bowles recalls that "Tennessee had these very strong bodyguards who instead of protecting him were plying him with liquor, trying to keep him quiet. . . . Anyway, during dinner everyone except Mrabet and myself was drinking." When it was time to leave, Oliver Evans, although extremely drunk, refused to let either Bowles or Mrabet drive. "We were going down the mountainside and Mrabet kept saying, 'Please tell him to stop. I want to get out. I don't want to die like this. I'd rather walk." But Evans refused to stop. Finally a police car came up behind them, and Evans eventually pulled over to the side. He was promptly arrested, the car locked, and Bowles and Mrabet (in djellaba) were left standing on the side of the road somewhere on the outskirts of Los Angeles at 3:00 A.M.

They began walking down the road until they eventually found a phone. Suddenly, while Bowles was trying to arrange for a taxi to pick them up, another police car arrived on the scene. "They saw Mrabet," Bowles recalls, "and out came the police, pointing their guns at him." Bowles hurried out of the telephone booth and they pointed a gun at him, too, then began to fire off questions: " 'What are you doing? Why are you here? . . . Where's your car?' 'Haven't got one,' I said. It's a great mistake in Los Angeles not to have a car. They found it very suspicious. Also, they looked at Mrabet and said, 'Whaddayou supposed to be?' Not understanding English he didn't know what they were asking but he assumed they were insulting him. So he just said, 'Pasaporte?' and pulled out his passport." Bowles finally satisfied the police as to their respective innocence. Eventually a taxi came and Bowles and Mrabet arrived back around dawn at Bowles's motel in Santa Monica. Mrabet left within a couple of days for Tangier.

By the end of the term in January 1969, Bowles was more than ready to leave California himself. "I must get back and take Janie back to Tangier," he wrote Thomson. One of the first things he did upon his return was to evict Cherifa and another Moroccan woman from Jane's apartment, over their strong protests. Then, despite the concern of her doctor, he removed Jane from the clinic and brought her back to Tangier. But Jane was in no condition to be home. Edouard Roditi, who visited her shortly after her return, recorded his impressions of her: "I called on her in her apartment, but she failed to recognize me and huddled in sheer terror against the wall at the head of her bed, concealing all but her eyes beneath a blanket." David Herbert also witnessed Jane's deteriorated self:

"Janie lay on the floor most of the day, staring at [Bowles]. She would not eat and hardly spoke. There were still flashes of the old wit, but it was obvious that she would have to return to the home."

Within four months, in fact, Jane had to be taken back to Málaga. Roditi attempted to see her there: "I tried to visit her some months later. The nuns then assured me that she might fail to recognize me and that such a visit might only disturb her throughout the following few days. I was told that she was becoming increasingly incontinent and often attempted instinctively to remedy this by refusing to absorb any food." Jane was also beginning to talk more and more about becoming a Catholic, a matter that according to Buffie Johnson had actually begun to arise before she returned to the clinic: "The Princess Ruspoli said that Jane walked down her stairs one day saying, 'I want to be baptized. I insist on being baptized. I've always wanted to be baptized.' " Now that she was in a Catholic hospital, there was likely also some pressure on her to convert. Despite her occasional talk about it, she did not become a Catholic convert at the time. Bowles, however, did quarrel with Ruspoli over the matter, as he felt that she was the one who had instigated this. They also, according to Johnson, were divided again on Bowles's returning Jane to the clinic in Málaga: "The Princess Ruspoli again blamed him for it. It was truly impossible for him to care for her, but there were those in Tangier who just didn't understand that."

Meanwhile, in April 1969, Bowles had signed a contract with Putnam for an autobiography with a delivery date in two years' time. But with constant concern about Jane's health and frequent trips to Málaga to visit her, he found it difficult to write. In addition, before he could write he had to organize his recollections. To do this, he began to compile a chronology of his life, which occupied him for the first year: "I had no diaries or letters to consult, so I had to go back over my entire life, month by month, charting every meaningless meander of its course."

In May 1970, this work was suddenly interrupted when Bowles received word that Jane had suffered another stroke that caused her to deteriorate even further. She became largely comatose, failing to recognize practically anyone who came to see her. She had to be fed, a spoonful at a time, and was rapidly becoming

blind. There were moments, even days, of relative lucidity, but
these were hardly the norm. That fall, she converted to Catholi-
cism. According to Buffie Johnson, "Paul was positively appalled
because he belongs to that old generation that is terrified by religion. He also just didn't believe that Jane could have come to this
on her own. It was terrible for him, but there was nothing he could
do." Roditi recalls that upon her baptism, Jane became more and
more "obsessed by what she believed to have been her past sins.
. . . Poor Jane had thus become like one of her own fictional
characters now that the magic of her art as a writer no longer
protected her against her obsessions by allowing her to exorcize
them in print." In the end, Bowles was forced to accept her "con-
version," although he still does not believe that it was sincere. By
this point Jane was totally blind, helpless, only occasionally lucid.

"In the midst of this," recalls Roditi, "Paul was trying to write
that autobiography. But because he was so filled with pain and
torment he had to shut off his emotions lest it consume the book.
The result is that it's a very impersonal memoir." Many others
agreed. When *Without Stopping* was published in 1972, Virgil
Thomson, reviewing it in the *New York Review of Books,* wrote:

> His life, as told, unrolls like a travelogue. I would not have expected
> out of him either "confessions" or true-story gossip, anything indis-
> creet or scabrous. But Paul has always been so delicious in talk,
> games, laughter and companionship, so unfailingly gifted for both
> music and letters, so assiduous in meeting his deadlines with good
> work, so relentless in his pursuit of authenticity among his own
> ethnic associates (and all others) that it is a bit surprising to find
> oneself in the same flat pattern of casual acquaintance that includes
> everybody else he ever knew.

Ned Rorem, too, was critical of Bowles's effort:

> Scores of names are dropped with no further identification than
> their spelling, while close acquaintances vanish and die without so
> much as an editorial sigh from their friend. He displays no envy of
> competitors, no sign of carnal or intellectual passion. His one obses-
> sion would seem to be for investigation—not of the heart, which
> even his fiction avoids, but of the body as affected by foreign cul-
> tures, by the implacability of nature, exotic cuisine, ill health, hard
> drugs, but never, never by sex. If his novelist's reputation qualifies

this printing of his journal, his novel's morosely powerful voice remains mute.

Privately, others who had known Bowles over the years agreed. William Burroughs, for instance, referred to the autobiography as "Without Telling." Bowles, however, felt he had written what he could write, was annoyed with the poor reception, with what he perceived as attacks by old friends: "Why should I write about my feelings? I don't think they should be written about. What difference does it make?" He does, on the other hand, acknowledge that the book is a bit lacking in personal emotion, but feels that the circumstances under which he wrote it need to be taken into consideration: "Actually, I think the first half was personal enough, but the last half was hurried. Time was coming to an end and I had to meet the deadline. . . . I rushed it off."

Bowles returned to translation following the completion of the autobiography. Indeed, Bowles's output over the year following *Without Stopping* was as diverse as it was prolific. Not only were there half a dozen stories by Mrabet, but works by new authors as well, including another young Moroccan, Mohamed Choukri. Choukri, however, presented Bowles with special difficulties. Unlike Mrabet, Layachi, or Yacoubi, Choukri wrote his works in Classical Arabic rather than speaking them in the Maghrebi dialect. Bowles commented:

Had I known how difficult it would be to make English translations of Mohamed Choukri's texts, I doubt that I would have undertaken the work. The stories were typed in Arabic script (which I cannot read), and the language used was Classical Arabic (which means something to me only in the case of words that have been carried over more or less intact to the local North African dialect). It was Choukri himself who was obliged to do the translating, sometimes working through the medium of the colloquial *darija,* but generally through Spanish and occasionally even French, if the sought-for word did not come. When we were translating his autobiography *For Bread Alone,* he sat beside me, in order to see that I was making a word-for-word version of his text. If he noticed an extra comma he demanded an explanation. I was driven to reiterating: But English is not Arabic! Finally we devised a modus operandi which involved our sitting on opposite sides of the room.

Despite the difficulties, Bowles managed over the course of a few years to present admirable translations of Choukri's work. Choukri's two short portraits, *Jean Genet in Tangier* and *Tennessee Williams in Tangier,* are compelling, charming, and insightful. The direct narratives, which recount Choukri's relatively brief encounters with these writers, are filled with astute and honest observations; in a certain sense Choukri's books demythologize both Genet and Williams, render them as individuals in a way that many full-length portraits have not. As William Burroughs noted in his introduction to *Jean Genet in Tangier,* "As I read Choukri's notes, I saw and heard Jean Genet as clearly as if I had been watching a film of him. To achieve such precision simply by reporting what happened and what was said, one must have a rare clarity of vision. Choukri is a writer."

Choukri's autobiographical *For Bread Alone* is a powerful, often brutal tale of growing up destitute in Morocco, but in the end is a remarkable testimony to a young man's determination to become more than his circumstances might have dictated. Although sociology is not what Choukri is about, the book could also be read profitably as a piercing account of Moroccan society in the latter part of the twentieth century.

But for Bowles, it was "smooth-rolling" Mrabet who continually entranced him the most. As he noted, "[Mrabet] has no thesis to propound, no grievances to air, and no fear of redundant punctuation. He is a showman; his principal interest is in his own performance as a virtuoso story-teller." With a seemingly inexhaustible supply of stories to tell, Mrabet kept Bowles well supplied with tapes. His impressive output now includes more than a dozen published books.

Another author who began to intrigue Bowles in the early 1970s was Isabelle Eberhardt, a turn-of-the-century Swiss writer whose life was as much of an adventure story as anyone could possibly concoct. Born in Geneva in 1877, she went with her mother to Algeria in her late teens, became a convert to Islam, and fell fully under the spell of North Africa. After the death of her mother, she lived in dire poverty in Tunis, then later in Marseilles and Algeria. In 1902 she married an Algerian soldier and went to live in the Sahara; in 1904 she was killed in a flash flood. When her body was recovered in what was left of her house, among the debris surrounding her was a muddy manuscript. It was that book, eventually published as *Dans l'Ombre Chaude d'Islam,* that first captured Bowles.

Bowles recalled that he first read about Eberhardt in Jean Cocteau, "just a paragraph or so about how extraordinary she was." Then, in Paris in 1931, during the period in which he was living with Dunham and Abdelkader, he learned more about Eberhardt through his upstairs neighbor, Lucie Delarue-Mardrus, who had known Eberhardt and visited her in Algeria. At some point Bowles acquired Eberhardt's biography and a few of her books. In 1972, when he began to do the first translations, he picked and chose freely from among her numerous writings, culling what he thought to be the most interesting pieces. "She wasn't a great writer," says Bowles, "but she was an extraordinary person in every way and led an extraordinary life. She had a certain ability to penetrate the emotional reality of a country and to describe it beautifully, too— but her pieces are light sketches." Having translated a dozen or so selections over the course of a few years, Bowles decided he finally had a sufficient number for a small volume, which he called, after one of the stories, *The Oblivion Seekers.* He sent the book to City Lights, which published it in 1975.

Bowles's involvement with translation was to some extent a way to keep his mind occupied, without having to dwell on the personal. Translation afforded distance, allowed him to become immersed in the words and thoughts of others. Escaping into the universe of Mrabet, Choukri, or Eberhardt, he could temporarily flee from his concern over Jane, banish for a few hours now and then the anxiety, the fear, and the sadness. Still, while there was no fiction for Bowles during these years, he did return to poetry. The poems of this period are dark, filled with an overwhelming sense of doom, of nothingness, of unanswered questions:

> Is it appropriate to offer suggestions?
> Ways of walking in the spring,
> ways of sleeping in the summer
> (forbidden unless marked otherwise),
> autumn starving, winter dying
> and two porters to carry your guilt
> across the strip of no-man's land

that flanks the eastern border.
Does anyone imagine this will throw them off the track?

"It was a horrendous period for Paul," remembers Edouard
Roditi. "It was terrible to have to bear witness to his suffering
without being able to do anything. . . . Not that he said much about
it, but you could feel it. He was draped in sadness."

On May 3, 1973, Bowles received a telegram from the clinic in
Málaga. Jane had suffered another stroke and was unconscious.
The next morning he boarded the first ferry from Tangier, arriving
in Málaga at mid-day. In a letter to Virgil Thomson, he wrote of
Jane's last hours: "I . . . spent the afternoon with her. She was still
in a coma, and seemed to be breathing with difficulty. I left the
hospital to go and have dinner. At nine I received a call saying she
had just died."

The following day she was buried in the Catholic cemetery, San
Miguel, in Málaga. Her grave is not marked, for Bowles refused to
erect a cross over her burial place. "I couldn't care less about
what's in that grave or all those conventions," Bowles explained
to Buffie Johnson.

Although Bowles had naturally expected Jane to die for some
time, the reality of her death was not mitigated by anticipation. To
Thomson he wrote: "You may be sure that for a good many years
I've reflected on the possibility of being left alone by Jane, and now
that it has happened, I think of it a great deal more. The principal
difference between then and now is that my degree of interest in
everything has been diminished almost to the point of nonexist-
ence. That makes a great difference, since there is no compelling
reason to do anything whatever."

The feeling of emptiness would remain with him for a long
while—perhaps, to some degree, forever. Although their relationship had often been difficult, and was undoubtedly odd when measured against conventional norms, there was an intense bond
between them. That they had always allowed each other the freedom to be must be seen in retrospect as a measure of the devotion
they felt for each other, a devotion largely free from possession.
"Paul told me that he'd only loved three people in his life. One of
them was Jane," recalls Buffie Johnson. "In his own way he was

absolutely devoted to her, and she to him. And Jane is not at all
forgotten by Paul. His face lights up any time Jane is mentioned."

Life, though altered, would go on for Bowles. There would be
new fiction, new translations. But sorrow would linger, would remain a presence:

> I have no idea of what is going to happen
> or in which parts the pain will be.
> We are only in spring, and spring has a twisting light.
> Spring's images are made of crystal and cannot be recalled.
> There will be suffering, but you know how to coax it.
> There will be memories, but they can be deflected.
> There will be your heart still moving
> in the wind that has not stopped flying westward.
> and you will give a signal. Will someone see it?

We thought there were other ways.
The darkness would stay outside.
We are not it, we said. It is not in us.

> Yes, yes, go with her. The old man smiled.
> You will be back. You will not find me.

There was a time when life moved on a straighter line.
We still drank the water from the lake,
and the bucket came up cold
and sweet with the smell of deep water.
The song was everywhere that year, an absurd refrain:
It's only that it seems so long, and isn't.
It's only that it seems so many years,
and perhaps it's one.
When the trees were there I cared that they were there,
and now they are gone.
On our way out we used the path that goes around the swamp.
When we started back the tide had risen.
There was another way, but it was far above and hard to get to.
And so we waited here, and everything is still the same.

There were many things I wanted to say to you
before you left. Now I shall not say them.
Though the light spills onto the balcony
making the same shadows in the same places,

only I can see it, only I can hear the wind
and it is much too loud.

The world seethes with words. Forgive me.
I love you, but I must not think of you.
That is the law. Not everyone obeys it.
Though time moves past and the air is never the same
I shall not change. That is the law, and it is right.

CHAPTER 30

O N THE SURFACE, the world seemed to change little for Bowles after Jane's death. He remained in the Inmueble Itesa, largely internalizing the emotional upheaval that he was experiencing, revealing it only occasionally to a few very close and trusted friends. But internally, life was decidedly different. The major struggle now was to make sense of things, to have a rationale for his own existence. He remembers feeling "disconnected" from his own existence: "I think I lived vicariously largely and didn't know it. And when I had no one to live through or for, I was disconnected from life."

But as on so many other occasions in which he found himself in crisis, he retreated into words. He had not written any fiction for almost four years. Suddenly, in 1974, he began writing short stories again, not about himself, but about Moroccans. In the process, though, his life had become more and more routine. Dividing his creative time between his own fiction and translations, he also devoted a certain portion of the day to his voluminous correspondence and to entertaining his numerous visitors. Mrabet was by far the most constant, but others came too. Tennessee Williams still occasionally came to Tangier; the painter Maurice Grosser, long a part-time resident of Tangier, took Jane's apartment for the winter; in the summer, Buffie Johnson sublet it from Grosser. Christopher Wanklyn was still in Morocco, though he had moved permanently to Marrakech. And of the Old Mountain crowd, Bowles still had David Herbert, Margaret McBey, and several others. Roditi was there for a while before moving to Paris in the mid-1970s. Cherifa, now that Jane was dead, never came around to disturb Bowles, though he occasionally glimpsed her in passing on the street. It was perhaps the continuity that helped Bowles through the first years following Jane's death. "Perhaps the best thing about [Tangier]," Bowles wrote Thomson, "is the feeling it gives one of being in a pocket of suspended time and animation. Nothing happens for such long periods of time that one dreads any change which might upset the stasis. That's the way it affects me, at least."

Stasis, in fact, is the word that best described Bowles's life in Tangier. In a 1977 poem, "Far from Why," he wrote the following lines:

> There is a way to master silence
> Control its curves, inhabit the dark corners
> And listen to the hiss of time outside

Characteristically, the way he "mastered silence" was to listen to the voice within and follow its fictional dictates. Though there will not be another novel, there have been nearly as many stories written in the years following Jane's death as in the thirty preceding years, a number of them ranking with the best of Bowles's short fiction.

"Here to Learn," written in 1978, is one of his most interesting stories of the 1970s because it reverses the usual theme of the expatriate American or European adrift in North Africa, telling instead the story of a young Moroccan woman, Malika, who goes abroad. Entertaining and wonderfully ironic, "Here to Learn" takes jabs, almost playfully, at both the West and Morocco. Malika, who grows up in poverty in a town in the Rif, suddenly finds herself an object of attraction to a variety of Nazarenes; thus begins her "upward ascent." Over a period of time she is passed from one man to another, goes to Paris, Lausanne, Los Angeles, and Beverly Hills. At the end of the story, she arrives back in Morocco after an absence of two years. Dressed in blue jeans, she goes to visit her mother, but to her surprise discovers that her whole neighborhood has been leveled by a bulldozer. Her mother is dead, and her sister has gone to Casablanca.

Decidedly light despite the bitter ending, "Here to Learn" is at the same time an enunciation of a familiar Bowles theme, the difficulty both of becoming a member of another culture and, once a resident abroad, of returning home. Malika goes back to Morocco precisely to show off her worldly "success," never suspecting that Morocco itself has also rapidly changed: "The idea that the town might change during her absence had never occurred to her; she herself would change, but the town would remain an unmoving backdrop which would help her define and measure her transformation." Thus, when confronted with the remains of her former neighborhood, tears well up in her eyes. But: "It was not for her mother that she felt like weeping; it was for herself. There was no longer any reason to do anything."

In reversing the usual theme, Bowles at times almost seems to be parodying himself: "She was assailed afresh by the sensation . . . of having gone too far for the possibility of return." Reading this kind of reflection, one can't help but be reminded of so many other statements of this sort—in *The Sheltering Sky* or *Let It Come Down*—but in those books the gravity was so much greater. This is not to imply that Bowles is not serious about his theme, or that Malika does not deserve a certain amount of sympathy, but clearly Bowles is playing with some old philosophical ideas, and by extension with his readers who know those ideas in a different, more consequential context.

The ironic, even humorous quality of "Here to Learn" is also present in a number of Bowles's other stories of the late 1970s. "Rumor and a Ladder" is a delightful tale of the octogenarian Monsieur Ducros, who ingeniously outwits the Moroccan authorities in regard to exporting currency. "Kitty" is a tale of transformation, about a young girl who becomes a cat. Unlike many of the stories of the 1940s and 1950s, which were published in magazines such as *Harper's Bazaar* or *Mademoiselle,* Bowles's new work, as has been the case since the 1960s, was for the most part published in "little magazines."

With one of these magazines, *Antaeus,* Bowles had a very close relationship. Started by Daniel Halpern in Tangier, in 1970, the magazine quickly began to earn a reputation as an important literary journal; much of this was initially due to Bowles's assistance, which included writing to many of his old literary colleagues asking for contributions. Although his name appears on the masthead as "founding editor," a position he still holds, Bowles discovered that the title was largely honorary. "It entitled me to read page proofs and place a certain amount of work in *Antaeus,*" he recalled. Bowles was genuinely delighted with the quality of the magazine, though he did eventually stop reading galleys.

It was also through Halpern that Bowles's fiction began to reappear in print, when Halpern, with the financial backing of heiress Drue Heinz, started Ecco Press. The first title printed in their series, appropriately called "Neglected Books of the 20th Century," was *The Delicate Prey,* which had long been out of print. This was followed shortly by reissues of *The Sheltering Sky* and *Up Above the World.* In Black Sparrow Press, which had published Bowles's poems and translations of Mrabet's work, he also found a publisher willing to put out a volume of *Collected Stories,* which was followed by reissues of *Let It Come Down* and *The Spider's House.* Bowles also continued to have a productive relationship with City Lights; and in England, Peter Owen was his only publisher, bringing out an occasional translation and reprinting the novels.

But while Bowles's work was beginning to reappear in bookstores, he could hardly be regarded as a popular writer. The Ecco, Black Sparrow, City Lights, and Owen editions were small, usually less than three thousand copies. In a curious way he was becoming, in his relative obscurity, a kind of "cult" figure. Because of his expatriate status, his association with drugs, his cruel, often macabre stories, those who knew of Bowles delighted in creating, then perpetuating a mystique, if not a myth, confusing in many cases the writing with the writer. It is to some extent a legend that still prevails: "The swami of the dark side," he was dubbed in a 1987 commentary on National Public Radio.

In Tangier, relatively isolated from American literary currents, Bowles continued to live largely unaware that he was becoming a writer of somewhat legendary proportions, even if such fame was restricted to a few avid fans. Throughout the 1970s and into the 1980s, as his books began to be reprinted his following grew, not just in the United States and in England, but in France and Spain as well, where his books appeared, or reappeared, in translation. He was hailed in those countries as one of the great contemporary American writers, a title that does not usually spring to mind among most Americans. For Bowles none of this was terribly meaningful. "I think [fame] only means something if you live in the place where you're famous," he says. And in Tangier, outside of a few in the expatriate community, Bowles clearly was not famous. Indeed, he claims that despite all of the translations he has done, he really has never had a reputation in Morocco, except perhaps, from time to time, a negative one:

> I've been attacked various times in the paper for being a neo-coloni-
> alist. First of all they claimed that I wrote all the translations that I
> do and that the Moroccans don't exist. Mrabet doesn't exist. And,
> of course, he got pretty angry about that. And then they said that yes,
> Mrabet exists, but he's just a *pantin,* a marionette being manipulated
> by the Americans and implying practically that the C.I.A. was behind
> it. Idiotic! They didn't really like what he does because for them it's
> a Morocco of the past. They don't want to admit that there's any
> magic today. There is, and he knows it, but officially there's no such
> thing. And there's no kif so you can't write about that. Mrabet just
> writes about what he sees without any political overtones whatever.
> But for them it's very reactionary, practically wicked. They consider
> a writer really a journalist, and he's supposed to write about present
> day topics. A fiction writer is looked upon askance, as telling a bunch
> of lies.

Still, Bowles has continued to translate Mrabet and to write about the country he adopted nearly half a century ago. In late 1980 he began to work on a new book, neither fiction nor entirely nonfiction, "perhaps lyrical history," suggests Bowles. When completed in 1981 it would be called *Points in Time.* Bowles recalls its genesis: "I wanted to write a story about Morocco as I imagined it and as it seems to have been written about. . . . It's not a novel. . . . It's a sort of trip through the centuries." Bowles's designation of the genre is extremely accurate, for though *Points in Time* is based on historical fact, the book reads more like a series of poetic vignettes, at times approaching a meditation on the past. The points in time range over more than two thousand years, from the period of Roman exploration to the present.

"Whatever I wrote was actually part of history. I gave it flesh, naturally," says Bowles. "Flesh" in this case meant more than just injecting dialogue into some of the various incidents that he se-lected for retelling. Indeed, the triumph of the book is the absolute artistry with which he depicts the diverse events from Morocco's history. In terms of sheer craft and beauty of language, *Points in Time* is very likely Bowles's greatest achievement.

As lyrical history, the book is also exceedingly rich, for while it continues Bowles's grand attempt to present Morocco to the West, with all its beauty, intolerance, horror, and passion, it also provides a context, lacking in many of his other works, namely that of an historical continuum through which the reader can gain a perspective of what is inherently Moroccan about Morocco. Bowles's selection of incidents naturally mirrors his own interests; often they revive the familiar theme of the Westerner failing to come to an understanding of the Moroccan and Muslim mind. It is as if Bowles is writing about his predecessors, who like him were lured by Morocco's siren song. Thus, in his story of Fra Andrea, an Italian monk who journeys in the sixteenth century to Fez in order to have religious discussions with several Muslim intellectuals, we meet the classic Bowles hero: Fra Andrea goes to Morocco to seek enlightenment; he finds death. Other incidents are linked to some of Bowles's other predominant concerns: the extraordinary Moroccan landscape, mad Islamic holy men, tricksters, and the continual inability of Christians to understand Muslims, of Muslims to understand Christians, of Moroccan Jews to understand or be understood by either group. In some ways *Points in Time* can be seen as the ultimate synthesis of all of Bowles's previous musings on Morocco, as an attempt to unify within less than a hundred pages his preoccupations of half a century.

When Peter Owen published the book in England in 1982 it was widely acclaimed: *"Points in Time* seems to insert a needle into the country's heart and draws off its life-blood for us. . . . Like Flaubert, the author at once cauterizes and augments his horrors by a style which can recount a sunset or a beheading with equal disposition," said one reviewer.

In 1984 the book was published in the United States by Ecco Press. It was barely noticed by the American media. Sales were small, less than 5,000 copies in hardback. For all of the "rediscovery" of Paul Bowles, he was still a writer for the happy few.

The 1980s also saw Bowles's brief return to teaching, this time as a creative writing professor in the Tangier program set up by the School of Visual Arts in New York. Regina Weinreich, who taught in the same program with Bowles, recalls that "in class, Bowles was more presence than performance. He does not consider himself a teacher but he gave both encouragement and conference time most generously. Still, students were eager for definitive statements on their own work; instead he insisted obsessively on proper language."

In his first class, in the summer of 1982, however, he found a new protégé in a young Guatemalan, Rodrigo Rey Rosa. Rey Rosa recalls that he signed up for the class precisely because Bowles was the teacher. He wrote a few pages in English, sufficient for him to be accepted into the program. When he arrived in Tangier and discovered that Bowles was as fluent in Spanish as in English, he was overjoyed. Thereafter, he wrote in Spanish. Many of these stories so impressed Bowles that he decided to translate them into English. He convinced City Lights to publish them, and the collection, *The Beggar's Knife,* appeared in 1985. Bowles is currently at work translating a second volume of Rey Rosa's stories; as with the first book, most of the stories have not yet appeared in their original Spanish versions.

The School of Visual Arts program lasted only two summers. It was closed, not because of lack of enthusiasm on the part of students, but because the New York school became worried when news reports reached them that there had been anti-American disturbances (greatly exaggerated) during 1984. Bowles was not sad to see it go. "It took up a lot of my time," he recalls, "and little of the writing was much good."

Bowles's most recent fiction reflects his exile in a stylistic way, namely that he has begun to use his major medium of communication with the outside world, letters, as a way of telling a story. Two recent epistolary pieces, "Unwelcome Words" and "In Absentia," read very much as if they were actual letters to real recipients. Indeed, particularly in "Unwelcome Words," the borderline between fact and fiction is very narrow; in general, except for a few minor details, the story is fiction only because the letters were not actually sent to anyone. "In Absentia," while on the surface far more fictional, nonetheless reflects Bowles's current view of himself as being cut off from participating in the lives of those he cares (or cared) about. Since he lives without a telephone, his only true communication with the world beyond Tangier is through letters, which are only as good as the correspondents' ability to provide sufficient information. "In Absentia," in fact, is really a story about how letters can fail to convey understanding.

Despite the drawbacks, Bowles adamantly refuses to have a telephone installed. To some, this seems a quaint eccentricity; to others it reveals a desire to keep the unpredictable outside world at a distance. The post can be controlled; Bowles can choose not to answer a letter, or to answer it in his own fashion. Whether a result of whim or deep-held belief, Bowles clearly is interested in maintaining his privacy, his exile. Although uniformly courteous to visitors who bother to trek to the Inmueble Itesa to see him, he is careful about letting them intrude on his self-imposed schedule, which over the years has become increasingly more strict. The routine is nearly unvarying: Mrabet arrives early in the morning, around 8:00, to fix Bowles's breakfast. After rising, Bowles works for a while, at fiction or translation, usually spending an hour or two in the early afternoon answering his correspondence. Visitors usually begin arriving around 2:00 or 3:00, as does his maid; at 4:30 his driver, Abdelouahaid Boulaich, comes to take Bowles to the post office. By 6:00 Mrabet returns to fix dinner for Bowles. They frequently talk for a couple of hours, smoke kif together. Bowles then retires for the night, most often eating dinner in bed. Mrabet returns then to his own family, leaving Bowles alone.

With the exception of a brief trip to Switzerland for an operation in late September 1984, Bowles has remained in Morocco almost exclusively since Jane's death. While generally in good health, he did undergo another operation for a blocked artery in his leg in September 1986; this surgery, however, was performed in Rabat. As a result of his condition, he was forced to give up cigarette smoking, a habit he had indulged in since his university days. He also cut down on smoking kif, but still smokes half a dozen or so kif cigarettes a day.

He has not returned to the United States since his teaching stint at San Fernando State, nor does he have any desire to see his native land again. He claims that part of the reason he disdains travel these days is that he immensely dislikes flying. And as the days of ship travel have passed, he does not see himself leaving Morocco for any distant point. Even a trip to Europe does not interest him. In April of 1988 an all–Paul Bowles Concert was performed at the Festival MANCA in Nice. Although Bowles toyed with the idea of going to France for the concert, he decided ultimately to stay in Tangier. "I don't feel up to making such a trip, and am afraid of arriving there ill, which would be hell," he commented.

Financially, Bowles is fairly well off, although he continues to live very modestly, resenting expenses of any sort. He refuses to expand on where he derives his income, but is quick to point out that it has not been from sales of his writing. In October 1989, however, even this situation changed when Vintage Books acquired the paperback reprint rights for *The Sheltering Sky*. The deal, according to Bowles's agent, Ned Leavitt, was in the low six figures. The reported reason for the high price was that Vintage was banking on Bertolucci's film of the novel to reawaken readers' interest in *The Sheltering Sky*. Yet despite this handsome sale, it is unlikely that Bowles will alter his longstanding habit of frugality.

When Bowles first moved into the Inmueble Itesa, his five-story apartment house was one of the few buildings in the area, but the neighborhood is now rapidly being developed. The American consulate (now practically closed) and the American School are just across the street. With the exception of Bowles's building, most of the housing consists of new, spacious single-family homes on tree-lined streets. If it were not for an occasional figure glimpsed on the street in a caftan or djellaba, it would be difficult to locate the quarter in any country, for there is little there that speaks of Morocco. It is, in fact, not terribly different from any upper-class suburban neighborhood in a gentle climate.

But for Bowles, the pageant of Morocco is still present, always lying beneath the everyday facade:

> I relish the idea that in the night, all around me in my sleep, sorcery is burrowing its invisible tunnels in every direction, from thousands of senders to thousands of unsuspecting recipients. Spells are being cast, poison is running its course; souls are being dispossessed of parasitic pseudo-consciousness that lurks in the unguarded recesses of the mind.
>
> There is a drumming out there most nights. It never awakens me; I hear the drums and incorporate them into my dream, like the nightly call of the muezzins. Even if in the dream I am in New York, the first *Allah akbar!* effaces the backdrop and carries whatever comes next to North Africa, and the dream goes on.

For more than half a century now, Bowles has been living his dream of North Africa, chronicling its shadow and light, using it again and again as a fertile backdrop for charting the darkest regions of the human psyche. No other geography has lent itself so keenly to the task.

Bowles claims to have felt upon first glimpsing North Africa that this was the magic territory he had been awaiting all his life to enter, a place "that in disclosing its secrets would give . . . wisdom and ecstasy—perhaps even death." That Bowles has gained wisdom and ecstasy from his long Moroccan exile is unquestionable; it seems inevitable that it will also give him death, as it is inconceivable that he shall ever leave. In the interim, his quest to divine the secrets of his adopted country continues unabated. The dreamer and the dream go on.

A SELECTED BIBLIOGRAPHY OF BOOKS, COMPOSITIONS, AND RECORDINGS BY PAUL BOWLES*

BOOKS

Novels

The Sheltering Sky. London: John Lehmann, 1949; New York: New Directions, 1949. Reprint, New York: The Ecco Press, 1978; London: Peter Owen, 1981.

Let It Come Down. London: John Lehmann, 1952; New York: Random House, 1952. Reprint, Santa Barbara, California: Black Sparrow Press, 1980; London: Peter Owen, 1984.

The Spider's House. New York: Random House, 1955; London: Macdonald & Co., 1957. Reprint, Santa Barbara, California: Black Sparrow Press, 1986.

Up Above the World. New York: Simon & Schuster, 1966; London: Peter Owen, 1967. Reprint, New York: The Ecco Press, 1982; London: Peter Owen, 1982.

Short Stories

A Little Stone. London: John Lehmann, 1950.

The Delicate Prey. New York: Random House, 1950. Reprint, New York: The Ecco Press, 1982.

The Hours After Noon. London: Heinemann, 1959.

*For a complete bibliography of books, music, and recordings by Paul Bowles, see Jeffrey Miller, *Paul Bowles: A Descriptive Bibliography.* Santa Barbara, California: Black Sparrow Press, 1986.

A Hundred Camels in the Courtyard. San Francisco: City Lights Books, 1962.

The Time of Friendship. New York: Holt, Rinehart & Winston, 1967.

Pages from Cold Point and Other Stories. London: Peter Owen, 1968.

Things Gone & Things Still Here. Santa Barbara, California: Black Sparrow Press, 1977.

Collected Stories 1939–1976. Santa Barbara, California: Black Sparrow Press, 1979.

Midnight Mass. Santa Barbara, California: Black Sparrow Press, 1981; London: Peter Owen, 1985.

Unwelcome Words. Bolinas, California: Tombouctou Books, 1988.

Call at Corazón and Other Stories. London: Peter Owen, 1988.

Non-Fiction

Yallah. New York: McDowell, Obolensky, 1957.

Their Heads Are Green and Their Hands Are Blue. London: Peter Owen, 1963; New York: Random House, 1963. Reprint, New York: The Ecco Press, 1984.

Without Stopping. New York: G. P. Putnam's Sons, 1972; London: Peter Owen, 1972. Reprint, New York: The Ecco Press, 1985.

Points in Time. London: Peter Owen, 1982; New York: The Ecco Press, 1984.

Poetry

Next to Nothing: Collected Poems 1926–1977. Santa Barbara, California: Black Sparrow Press, 1981.

Translations

R. Frison-Roche, *The Lost Trail of the Sahara.* New York: Prentice Hall, 1951.

Jean-Paul Sartre, *No Exit.* New York: Samuel French, Inc., 1958.

Driss ben Hamed Charhadi (Larbi Layachi), *A Life Full of Holes.* New York: Grove Press, 1964; London: Weidenfeld & Nicolson, 1964.

Mohammed Mrabet, *Love with a Few Hairs.* London: Peter Owen, 1967; New York: George Braziller, 1967. Reprint, San Francisco: City Lights Books, 1986.

Mohammed Mrabet, *The Lemon.* London: Peter Owen, 1969; New York: McGraw-Hill, 1972. Reprint, San Francisco: City Lights Books, 1986.

Mohammed Mrabet, *M'Hashish.* San Francisco: City Lights Books, 1969; London: Peter Owen, 1988.

Mohamed Choukri, *For Bread Alone.* London: Peter Owen, 1974; San Francisco: City Lights Books, 1987.

Mohammed Mrabet, *The Boy Who Set the Fire.* Santa Barbara, California: Black Sparrow Press, 1974. Reprint, San Francisco: City Lights Books, 1988.

Mohamed Choukri, *Jean Genet in Tangier.* New York: The Ecco Press, 1974.

Mohammed Mrabet, *Hadidan Aharam.* Santa Barbara, California: Black Sparrow Press, 1975.

Isabelle Eberhardt, *The Oblivion Seekers.* San Francisco: City Lights Books, 1975; London: Peter Owen, 1987.

Mohammed Mrabet, *Look and Move On.* Santa Barbara, California: Black Sparrow Press, 1976.

Mohammed Mrabet, *Harmless Poisons, Blameless Sins.* Santa Barbara, California: Black Sparrow Press, 1976.

Mohammed Mrabet, *The Big Mirror.* Santa Barbara, California: Black Sparrow Press, 1977.

Mohamed Choukri, *Tennessee Williams in Tangier.* Santa Barbara, California: Cadmus Editions, 1979.

Abdeslam Boulaich, et al., *Five Eyes.* Santa Barbara, California: Black Sparrow Press, 1979.

Mohammed Mrabet, *The Beach Cafe & The Voice.* Santa Barbara, California: Black Sparrow Press, 1976.

Mohammed Mrabet, *The Chest.* Bolinas, California: Tombouctou Books, 1983.

Rodrigo Rey Rosa, *The Beggar's Knife.* San Francisco: City Lights Books, 1985; London: Peter Owen, 1988.

Jean Ferry, et al., *She Woke Me Up So I Killed Her.* San Francisco: Cadmus Editions, 1985.

Mohammed Mrabet, *Marriage with Papers.* Bolinas, California: Tombouctou Books, 1986.

MAJOR COMPOSITIONS

For Piano and Orchestra

Sonata for Oboe and Clarinet, 1931.

Sonata No. 1 for Flute and Piano, 1932.

Sonata for Violin and Piano, 1934.

El Bejuco, 1934.

Music for a Farce, 1938.

Huapango No. 1 and No. 2, 1939.

La Cuelga, 1946.

Orosí, 1946.

Sayula, 1946.

Six Preludes for Piano, 1947.

Sonatina for Piano, 1947.

Concerto for Two Pianos and Orchestra, 1949.

Night Waltz, 1958.

Cross Country, 1976.

For Voice

Scènes d'Anabase (text by St.-John Perse), 1932.

Blue Mountain Ballads (text by Tennessee Williams), 1946.

A Picnic Cantata (text by James Schuyler), 1954.

Many of Bowles's songs are collected in *Selected Songs,* Santa Fe, New Mexico: Soundings Press, 1984.

Operas

Denmark Vesey (libretto by C-H Ford), 1939.

The Wind Remains (based on the play by García Lorca), 1943.

Yerma (based on the play by García Lorca), 1958.

Ballets

Yankee Clipper, 1937.

Johnny A., 1939.

Pastorela, 1941.

Colloque Sentimental, 1944.

INCIDENTAL THEATER MUSIC

Horse Eats Hat, 1936.

Who Fights This Battle?, 1936.

The Tragical History of Dr. Faustus, 1937.

Too Much Johnson, 1938.

My Heart's in the Highlands, 1939.

Love's Old Sweet Song, 1940.

Twelfth Night, 1940.

Liberty Jones, 1941.

Watch on the Rhine, 1941.

South Pacific, 1943.

'Tis Pity She's a Whore, 1943.

The Glass Menagerie, 1944.

Jacobowsky and the Colonel, 1944.

Ondine, 1945.

Cyrano de Bergerac, 1946.

The Dancer, 1946

Land's End, 1946.

Twilight Bar, 1946.

On Whitman Avenue, 1946.

Summer and Smoke, 1948.

The Tempest, 1950.

In the Summer House, 1953.

Edwin Booth, 1958.

Sweet Bird of Youth, 1959.

The Milk Train Doesn't Stop Here Anymore, 1962.

Oedipus the King, 1966.

The Garden, 1967.

Wet and Dry/Alive, 1968.

The Bacchae, 1969.

Bachelor Furnished, 1969.

Caligula, 1978.

Birdbath, 1981.

FILM MUSIC

Bride of Samoa, 1933.

Venus and Adonis, 1935.

145 W. 21, 1936.

Seeing the World, 1936.

America's Disinherited, 1937.

Chelsea through the Magnifying Glass, 1938.

How to Become a Citizen of the U.S., 1938.

The Sex Life of the Common Film, 1938.

Film Made to Music, 1939.

Roots in the Soil, 1940.

Congo, 1944.

Dreams That Money Can Buy, 1947.

MAJOR RECORDINGS

Sonata for Flute & Piano/Two Mexican Dances, Art of This Century Recordings, 1943.

Concerto for Two Pianos, Winds and Percussion, Columbia Masterworks, 1948.

Night Waltz, Columbia Masterworks, 1949.

Sonata for Two Pianos, Concert Hall Society Inc., 1949.

Music for a Farce/Scènes d'Anabase, Columbia Masterworks, 1954.

A Picnic Cantata, Columbia Masterworks, 1955.

The Wind Remains/Music for a Farce/Letters from Morocco (Letters from Morocco, music by Peggy Glanville-Hicks, text by Bowles), MGM, 1958.

Blue Mountain Ballads, Music Library Release, 1964.

American Piano Music: Copland, Thomson, Bowles, Barber, Bernstein, Ramey. Bennett Lerner, piano. Etcetera Records, 1984. (Contains the following pieces by Bowles: Six Preludes for Piano, *Huapango No. 1, El Bejuco, Tierra Mojada, Orosí, La Cuelga, Huapango No. 2*).*

American Piano Music: Copland, Blitzstein, Harris, Barber, Schuman, Ramey, Bowles. Bennett Lerner, piano. Etcetera Records, 1986. (Contains the following pieces by Bowles: *Dance, Cross Country,* Sonatina for Piano).*

*Currently available.

NOTES

INTRODUCTION

xi AMERICA OR AMERICAN THEMES: Gore Vidal, Introduction in Paul Bowles, *Collected Stories 1939–1976* (Santa Barbara, Calif.: Black Sparrow Press, 1979), p. 1.

xii "AS GOOD AS ANYTHING IS NOW": Tennessee Williams quoted in Dotson Rader, "The Art of Theater V: Tennessee Williams," in *Paris Review,* Vol. 23, No. 81, Fall 1981, p. 162.

xii "SHORT STORIES WRITTEN BY ANYONE": Norman Mailer, *Advertisements for Myself* (New York: Perigee Books, 1959), p. 429.

xii "COMPOSER HE MOST LOVED: PAUL BOWLES": Ned Rorem, "Pulitzer," in *An Absolute Gift* (New York: Simon & Schuster, 1978), p. 74.

xiii "SECOND HALF OF THE TWENTIETH CENTURY": Vidal, Introduction in Bowles, *Collected Stories,* p. 6.

xiii "FIND IT OLD-FASHIONED": Bowles to author, February 3, 1986.

xiv "FROM ALL PARTICIPATION IN THE PROJECT": Letter of Agreement, Bowles to author, June 20, 1986.

xiv "I DON'T ENVY YOU YOUR TASK": Bowles to author, August 2, 1986.

xiv "WITH A MOST DIFFICULT SUBJECT": Burroughs to author (book inscription), April 28, 1987.

PART I: THE INVENTED COSMOS

Chapter 1

3 MOTHER'S BROTHERS, PAUL AND FRED WINNEWISSER: Bowles, Conversation with author, January 14, 1987.

3 SEEMED NORMAL AND HEALTHY: On birth, Bowles, Conversation with author, January 14, 1987. Paul Bowles, *Without Stopping* (New York: G. P. Putnam & Sons, 1972; reprinted New York, The Ecco Press, 1985), pp. 10, 42–43.

4 "BUT THOSE BLACK CAPES!": Bowles, *Without Stopping,* p. 43.

4 "OVER MY DEAD BODY": *Ibid.,* p. 39.

4 "EATS HIS OWN KITTENS": *Ibid.,* p. 39.

5 "LODE OF SPLEEN AGAINST DADDY": *Ibid.,* p. 38.

5   FOUND THE ACCOUNT "EXCITING": *Ibid.,* p. 39.

5   "YOUNG MAN. REMEMBER THAT": *Ibid.,* p. 10.

6   FOR HIS OUTDOOR "PLAY": *Ibid.,* p. 14.

6   DICTATES OF HIS PARENTS: *Ibid.,* p. 14.

6   ANIMAL STORIES, IS DATED 1915: Notebook, Bowles, Personal collection, Tangier.

7   "FRIGHTENED ME EVEN MORE": Bowles, *Without Stopping,* p. 33.

7   TO HAVE REPEATED NIGHTMARES: Bowles quoted in Daniel Halpern, "Interview with Paul Bowles," in *TriQuarterly,* No. 33, Spring 1975, p. 161. Bowles quoted in Oliver Evans, "An Interview with Paul Bowles," in *Mediterranean Review,* Vol. 1, No. 2, Winter 1971, p. 6.

7   "STORIES OF POE": Paul Bowles, Dedication in *The Delicate Prey and Other Stories* (New York: Random House, 1950; reprinted New York: The Ecco Press, 1972), n.p.

7   "AS FAR AS YOU LET HIM": On philosophy of child rearing, Bowles, *Without Stopping,* p. 23.

8   "APPLES, AND DAMP EARTH": *Ibid.,* p. 11.

8   "HE WAS LIVING IN IT": Bowles, "The Frozen Fields" in *Collected Stories,* p. 262.

9   A FAR GREATER EVIL: On maternal grandparents, Bowles, Conversation with author, January 14, 15, 1987. Bowles, *Without Stopping,* pp. 11–13.

10   MID-SEVENTEENTH CENTURY: On the Bowles family history, Samuel Bowles, *Genealogical and Historical Notes of the Bowles Family* (Springfield, Mass.: n.p., 1851).

10   "WAR OF THE REBELLION": Bowles, *Without Stopping,* p. 18.

10   KEYS TO BUILDING CHARACTER: On paternal grandparents, Bowles, Conversation with author, January 14, 15, 1987. Bowles, *Without Stopping,* pp. 15–19.

11   "IT'S NOT NATURAL": Bowles, *Without Stopping,* p. 18.

12   "EVERY VOLUME I SELL": Henry James quoted in Harvey Green, *Fit for America: Health, Fitness, Sport, and American Society* (New York: Pantheon Books, 1986), p. 297.

12   "CHEWED THE FIRST PROPERLY": Undated fragment (Notes for *Without Stopping*), Paul Bowles Collection, the Harry Ransom Humanities Research Center, the University of Texas at Austin (HRC).

12   "MODEL PUPILS": Bowles quoted in Evans, "Interview with Bowles," p. 3.

12   SPOKEN TO ANOTHER CHILD: Bowles, *Without Stopping,* p. 23.

13   "UNREMITTING WARFARE": *Ibid.,* p. 27.

13   "BRING HIM DOWN TO EARTH": *Ibid.,* p. 28.

13   "BUT BACKWARD": Bowles, Conversation with author, June 20, 1987. Bowles, *Without Stopping,* p. 29.

13   "FOR ONLY OLD. 1": Undated childhood notebook, HRC.

14   CORRECT GEOGRAPHICAL LOCATIONS: *Ibid.*

14   ASHES INTO THE MUD: Bowles, *Without Stopping,* p. 21.

15   "THIRD PERSON, ME": Bowles quoted in Jeffrey Bailey, "The Art of Fiction LXVII: Paul Bowles," in *Paris Review,* Vol. 23, No. 81, Fall 1981, p. 71.

15   CASE OF HYPOCHONDRIA: Bowles, Conversation with author, June 21, 1987.

Chapter 2

16   *ROOTABAGA STORIES:* Bowles, *Without Stopping,* p. 31.

17   NOT MENTION ADELAIDE'S NAME: *Ibid.,* p. 31.

17   LATIN AMERICAN PIECES: *Ibid.,* p. 28.

17   "GOD HIMSELF TO ME": Bowles to Bruce Morrissette, February 15, 1930, Personal collection, Morrissette.

17   PIANO TECHNIQUE: Bowles, *Without Stopping,* p. 34.

18   OF A NINE YEAR OLD: Bowles, Conversation with author, January 16, 1987.

18   "LIKE A STARVING PUSSYCAT": Bowles, *Without Stopping,* p. 36.

19   "RECOVERS THE BONES": Undated fragment, HRC.

21   "BLUEY LABER DOZLEN": *Ibid.*

21   "WRITING OF MOST ADULTS": Charles-Henri Ford, Preface to "Bluey: Pages from an Imaginary Diary," in *View,* Vol. 3, No. 3, October, 1943, p. 1.

22   "31 DEGREES": *Ibid.,* p. 82.

24   "IN THE BITTER TOWN": Undated childhood notebook, HRC.

24   "REALIZED UNTIL THAT DAY": Bowles, *Without Stopping,* p. 44.

25   "PREOCCUPY ME FOR MANY YEARS": *Ibid.,* p. 45.

25   "SURFACE OF THE SNOW": Bowles, "The Frozen Fields," in *Collected Stories,* p. 265.

26   "OR QUESTIONING IT": *Ibid.,* p. 275.

26   "ACROSS THE FIELDS": *Ibid.,* p. 276.

27   "RESPECT FOR THE UNFORESEEN": Bowles, *Without Stopping,* p. 40.

28   "YOUNG MEN DANCING TOGETHER": On visit to Uncle Guy Ross, Bowles, *Without Stopping,* pp. 40–42.

29   TO LICK HIS WOUNDS: *Ibid.,* p. 51.

30   "RATIONALLY MOTIVATED COSMOS": On cut screen incident, Bowles, Conversation with author, August 26, 1987. Bowles, *Without Stopping,* pp. 55–56.

30   "MY SWEET, SWEET AIR!": Bowles, "Air," in unpublished mss, *Air to the Sea,* 1927, HRC.

31 WRITING TO HIS PEERS: Evans, "Interview with Bowles," pp. 2–3. Bowles, *Without Stopping*, pp. 46–47.

31 READINGS WERE CANCELED: Bowles, *Without Stopping*, p. 47.

31 "SNOB FACTORY": On Exeter, *Ibid.*, p. 53.

32 "RUSTLING OUTSIDE MY WINDOWS": *Ibid.*, p. 52.

32 "MY OWN EXISTENCE": *Ibid.* p. 53.

Chapter 3

34 DEATH OF GRANDMOTHER WINNEWISSER: Telegram, August Winnewisser to Rena Bowles, January 30, 1924, HRC.

34 SORT OUT HIS EMOTIONS: Bowles *Without Stopping*, p. 58.

34 PROOF HE NEEDED: *Ibid.*, p. 58.

34 "THREATENING AND TRUE": On Roth's soda fountain incident, *Ibid.*, p. 59.

35 DO SO AS WELL: On the Hoaglands and Mrs. Crouch, *Ibid.*, pp. 65–66. Bowles, Conversation with author, January 11, 1987.

36 TO DO WITH THE DEATH: Bowles, Conversation with author, August 26, 1987. Bowles, *Without Stopping*, p. 66.

36 ANYTHING HE HAD DONE: On Aunt Mary, Bowles to Bruce Morrissette, July 22, 1930, Personal collection, Morrissette, and Bowles, *Without Stopping*, pp. 61–65.

37 "THE WORMS OF RUIN": Bowles, "A Chatting as of Unfetters," unpublished mss, December 9, 1927, HRC.

37 "DAMNED FOOL HE IS": Bowles, *Without Stopping*, p. 67.

37 "AWAY FROM ME": Bowles, Conversation with author, July 5, 1986.

38 ENGLISH WRITER ARTHUR MACHEN: Bowles, Conversation with author, January 10, 1987.

39 "NEVER CEASED TO WONDER": Arthur Machen, *Far Off Things* (New York: Alfred A. Knopf, 1923), p. 35.

39 STRANGER FOR NO PURPOSE: On Gide's appeal, Bowles, Conversation with author, July 4, 1985.

40 "LOSE ITS INTEREST": André Gide, *Les Caves du Vatican*, excerpt trans. CS-L (Paris: Gallimard, 1950), p. 206.

40 COMPREHENDING GOLDBERG'S POINT: Bowles, *Without Stopping*, p. 67.

41 NAME WAS FULLER: *Ibid.*, p. 68.

41 FAILED GEOMETRY: Bowles, Conversation with author, January 16, 1987.

41 THE IDEAL FATHER: On Burns, Bowles, *Ibid.*, Morrissette, Conversation with author, February 13, 1987.

42 STRAVINSKY'S *FIREBIRD:* Bowles, Conversation with author, January 12, 1987. Bowles, *Without Stopping*, p. 69.

42 "HOWTH CASTLE & ENVIRONS": Janet Flanner, "Paris Letter" in *New Yorker*, April 30, 1927, pp. 106–7.

43 "ON THE SACRED SPOTS": Bowles, *Without Stopping*, pp. 69–70.

43 "REALLY A SINCERE ONE": Eugène Jolas, in *transition*, Vol. 2, No. 13, Summer 1928, p. 276.

44 "YOUR SPIRE SONG": Eugène Jolas to Bowles, March 30, 1928, HRC.

44 "DRIBBLE RESIN": Paul Bowles, "Spire Song," in *Next to Nothing: Collected Poems 1926–1977* (Santa Barbara, Calif.: Black Sparrow Press, 1981) p. 14.

44 "PAST THE THICKET": *Ibid.*, p. 14.

45 "BEYOND LIME RINDS": *Ibid.*, p. 20.

46 "ANYTHING BEYOND THAT": Bowles, *Without Stopping*, pp. 72–73.

46 "SHOW IT TO YOU?": Paul Bowles quoted in Mark Dery, "Talking to a Stranger: Paul Bowles Interviewed in Tangier, Morocco" (unpublished), 1983.

46 "FLUSHING HIGH SCHOOL": *The Oracle* (Senior Number), January, 1928, p. 11.

46 "HIS SPARE TIME": *Ibid.*, p. 40.

47 "HOBBY/LITERATURE": *Ibid.*, p. 47.

47 POE, HAD GONE THERE: On decision to attend the University of Virginia, Bowles, Conversation with author and Jonah Raskin, July 7, 1985. Bowles, *Without Stopping*, p. 70.

48 AT 212 CENTRAL PARK SOUTH: Bowles, *Without Stopping*, p. 71.

48 "WITH BODY HAIR": *Ibid.*, p. 72.

49 "GIVE IT FOR QUALITY": *Ibid.*, p. 73.

49 WHOLLY PLATONIC: *Ibid.*, p. 73.

50 "SEXUALLY. NEVER": Morrissette, Conversation with author, February 13, 1987.

50 "IMPORTANT TO HIM": Virgil Thomson, Conversation with author, March 6, 1986.

50 COULD GET AWAY WITH: Bowles, *Without Stopping*, pp. 73–74.

51 "IS THE TRUTH": Bowles to Daniel Burns, undated (Summer 1928), HRC.

52 "TO WRITE UNINTELLIGIBLY": Bowles to Burns, undated (Summer 1928), HRC.

53 "READING SPENGLER": Bowles to Burns, undated (Summer 1928), HRC.

53 "BELOVED BELOVED": Bowles to Burns, undated (Summer 1928), HRC.

53 FULL OF MOTHERS AND SONS: Bowles, *Without Stopping*, p. 74.

Chapter 4

54   190 FACULTY MEMBERS: *The University of Virginia* (Information pamphlet and calendar) (Charlottesville, Virginia: The Michie Company, 1928), p. 3.

54   "RUN UP AGAINST HERE": Bowles, *Without Stopping,* p. 74.

55   "BLACK QUARTER OF CHARLOTTESVILLE": *Ibid.,* p. 76.

56   OPPORTUNITY PRESENTED ITSELF: *Ibid.,* p. 75.

56   "FELT WELL PHYSICALLY": Undated fragment (Notes for *Without Stopping*), HRC.

57   "LITTLE PROVINCIALITIES?": Bowles to Burns, undated (Fall 1928), HRC.

57   "HIS LATER STYLE": Bruce Morrissette, Untitled memoir, in *Twentieth-Century Literature,* Vol. 32, Nos. 3–4, Fall–Winter 1986, p. 282.

57   "ATTENTION ON MY PART": Undated fragment (Notes for *Without Stopping*), HRC.

58   "WHISKEY WAS AGED": Bowles, *Without Stopping,* p. 75.

58   "AMONG SOME CIRCLES": Bowles to Burns, undated (Fall 1928), HRC.

58   " 'ÉPATER LE BOURGEOIS' ": Morrissette, Conversation with author, January 5, 1987.

59   "ASSURE YOU OR NO?": Bowles to Burns, undated (Fall 1928), HRC.

59   ANTHEIL'S *SECOND STRING QUARTET:* Aaron Copland and Vivian Perlis, *Copland: 1900 through 1942* (New York: St. Martin's Press, 1984), p. 157.

59   "COMPOSER IN THE UNITED STATES": Bowles, *Without Stopping,* pp. 98–99.

59   HANDS STRAPPED TO HIS SIDES: *Ibid.,* p. 77.

60   "WANTED TO LEARN": Undated fragment (Notes for *Without Stopping*), HRC.

60   "BUNCH OF FUDDY-DUDDYS": Morrissette, Conversation with author, January 5, 1987.

61   "OVERCOAT AND WENT OUT": Undated fragment (Notes for *Without Stopping*), HRC.

62   "ONE FELL SWOOP": Bowles, *Without Stopping,* p. 78.

62   "REMAIN HERE LONG ENOUGH": Bowles to Morrissette, March 20, 1929, Personal collection, Morrissette.

62   "IT'S A FREE COUNTRY": Bowles, *Without Stopping* p. 78.

63   NEXT TRANSATLANTIC STEAMER: On assistance from Hoaglands and Mrs. Crouch, *Ibid.,* pp. 78–79.

63   PERMITTED HIM TO STAY ON: *Ibid.,* pp. 79–80.

63   BID HIM BON VOYAGE: *Ibid.,* p. 80.

64   AWAY FROM THE DOCK: "Outgoing Passenger and Mail Steamships," in *New York Times,* March 29, 1929, p. 58.

PART II: A MANUFACTURED SAVAGE
Chapter 5

67   "IN THE STREETS OF PARIS": Paul Bowles, "André Gide's *The Counterfeiters,*" in *The Oracle* (Thanksgiving Issue) November 1927, p. 22.

68   "WRONG ENVIRONMENT OR A MISANTHROPE": Bowles to Morrissette, undated (April 1929), Personal collection, Morrissette.

68   SERENADE OF THE PARIS STREETS: On arrival in Paris, Bowles, *Without Stopping,* p. 82.

69   FOR A WORK PERMIT: On finding *Herald Tribune* job, *Ibid.,* p. 83.

70   CONCERNED ABOUT MAKING A MISTAKE: *Ibid.,* p. 83.

70   "GIVE ANYONE A WRONG NUMBER": *Ibid.,* p. 83.

70   TO ANNOUNCE HIS PRESENCE: Bowles, Conversation with author, June 20, 1986. Bowles, *Without Stopping,* p. 84.

70   "SWIFTLY AS A RESULT": Bowles, *Without Stopping,* p. 85.

71   "PLACE WHERE IT IS FED": *Ibid.,* p. 84.

71   "COLON SEE YOU SATURDAY": Morrissette, Untitled memoir, in *Twentieth-Century Literature,* p. 283. Morrissette, Conversation with author, October 29, 1987.

71   "WOULD NOT FORGIVE": Bowles, *Without Stopping,* p. 86.

72   GO AWAY FOR A "CURE": *Ibid.,* p. 86.

72   "MUST ACCOMPANY TRANSGRESSION": *Ibid.,* p. 86.

73   LOOK FOR ANOTHER: Bowles to Morrissette, April 28, 1929, Personal collection, Morrissette.

73   TO SEE THE SIGHTS: Bowles to Morrissette, June 20, 1929, Personal collection, Morrissette.

74   "ONE WAY OR ANOTHER": Bowles, *Without Stopping,* p. 89.

75   "BECOMES INVOLUNTARILY EMBITTERED": Bowles to Morrissette, June 27, 1929, Personal collection, Morrissette.

75   "DINT OF TALKING ABOUT IT": Bowles, *Without Stopping,* p. 89.

75   "BEDTIME TO ANOTHER": Bowles to Morrissette, June 20, 1929, Personal collection, Morrissette.

76   QUIT THE JOB THAT DAY: Bowles, *Without Stopping,* p. 90.

76   PAINFULLY SUNBURNED: *Ibid.,* pp. 90–91.

77   "COLD-BLOODED AND RIDICULOUS": On Hubert's arrival, *Ibid.,* pp. 92–93.

78   "HUBERT IS RESPONSIBLE FOR IT!": On trip with Hubert, *Ibid.*, p. 95.

78   EMBARKED FOR NEW YORK: Bowles to Morrissette, July 14, 1929, Personal collection, Morrissette.

Chapter 6

79   "SEE ANYTHING AROUND YOU": On return, Bowles, *Without Stopping*, p. 96. Bowles to Morrissette, August 1, 1929, Personal collection, Morrissette.

79   "ENTIRELY MY FAULT": Bowles to Morrissette, September 19, 1929, Personal collection, Morrissette. The letter, written in French, a fairly common practice for Bowles when writing to French-speaking correspondents, reads in the original as follows: "C'est fini. Je vais rester ici pour devenir raffiné. . . . J'ai honte. Je n'ai pas assez de caractère pour dédaigner les prières de ma mère. Je ne la blâme pas. C'est tout-à-fait ma faute."

80   "A CIVIL STATUS": Bowles, *Without Stopping*, p. 98.

80   "ENTIRELY IN YOUR HANDS": Bowles to Morrissette, September 4, 1929, Personal collection, Morrissette.

80   INQUIRING IF HE HAD GOTTEN MARRIED: Bowles, *Without Stopping*, p. 97.

81   "ONLY! ONLY!": Bowles to Morrissette, October 23, 1929, Personal collection, Morrissette.

81   RETURN FROM WORK: Bowles, *Without Stopping*, p. 97.

82   "I CAN FORM": Bowles to Morrissette, February 24, 1930, Personal collection, Morrissette.

82   "HAVE IT THUS": Bowles to Morrissette, February 28, 1930, Personal collection, Morrissette.

82   "NEW ENGLAND PURITANISM": Bowles to Morrissette, February 28, 1930, Personal collection, Morrissette.

82   "GUESSED IT AS LOW": Thomson, Conversation with author, March 6, 1986.

82   "IDEA OF SEX": Morrissette, Conversation with author, February 13, 1987.

83   "SOMEONE WITH IMPUNITY?": Bowles to Morrissette, February 28, 1930, Personal collection, Morrissette.

84   DECLINED THE OFFER: Bowles to Burns, undated (Fall 1929), HRC.

84   "BOHEMIAN" ATMOSPHERE: Bowles, *Without Stopping*, p. 98.

84   "THE BOOK INDEFINITELY": Morrissette, Conversation with author, January 5, 1987. The reference to Gide is to *The Counterfeiters*,

where George Molineux does not allow a lack of funds to deter him from appropriating a book from a bookstall.

85 COUNTRYSIDE OUTSIDE OF PARIS: Bowles, Conversation with author, June 19, 1986. Bowles, *Without Stopping,* pp. 97–98.

85 "FOR THE OLD WOMAN": Paul Bowles, "In the Creuse," unpublished mss., 1930, HRC.

87 "PREFER SUBSTANTIAL FOOD": Bowles to Morrissette, February 23, 1930, Personal collection, Morrissette.

87 "MIGHT INTEREST YOU": Bowles, *Without Stopping,* p. 98.

88 "BENEVOLENT AND SCHOLASTIC GRASSHOPPER": Paul Rosenfeld, "The Newest American Composers," in *Modern Music,* Vol. 15, No. 3 (March–April, 1938), p. 153.

88 "A MINUTE," AND CONTINUED WORKING: Bowles, *Without Stopping,* p. 99.

88 "THE ENTIRE DAY": Bowles to Morrissette, March 9, 1930, Personal collection, Morrissette.

88 "WHICH I COULD WORK": Bowles, *Without Stopping,* p. 99.

89 "ONLY THE BLUE RIDGE": Bowles to Morrissette, March 9, 1930, Personal collection, Morrissette.

89 CONTEMPORARY MUSIC AND LITERATURE: On isolation at the University of Virginia, Bowles to Morrissette, April 10, 1930, Personal collection, Morrissette.

89 DEBUT IN THE STRAVINSKY MASTERPIECE: Bowles, *Without Stopping,* pp. 100–101.

90 MEETING HARRY DUNHAM: Bowles, Conversation with author, January 14, 1987. Bowles, *Without Stopping,* p. 101.

90 HIS *JAZZ CONCERTO:* Bowles, *Without Stopping,* pp. 99–100.

91 TWO-HOUR PRACTICE SESSION: Bowles to Morrissette, July 22, 1930, Personal collection, Morrissette.

91 SMITH AND HER TWO SONS: Bowles, *Without Stopping,* p. 101.

92 "ISN'T IT A PITY": Bowles to Burns, October 19, 1930, HRC.

92 "DESTRUCTIVE INFLUENCE OVER THEIR SON": Bowles, *Without Stopping,* p. 103.

92 OF *THE MESSENGER*: Morrissette, Conversation with author, October 30, 1987.

93 "TO SPARE FOR US": Bowles to Gertrude Stein, undated (December 1930), Gertrude Stein Collection, The Beinecke Rare Book and Manuscript Library, Yale University Library (Yale).

93 "WITH THESE PEOPLE, BOY": Bowles, *Without Stopping,* p. 166.

93 "TO COME AFTER YOU": *Ibid.,* p. 104.

94 "ASK TO BE BORN": *Ibid.,* p. 105.

94 "DID NOT MATTER MUCH": *Ibid.,* p. 105.

94   "KEPT TO HIMSELF": *Ibid.,* p. 105.

95   "AFFINITY FOR IT": Bowles, Conversation with author, June 16, 1986.

95   SAW HIM OFF: Bowles to Burns, undated (March 1931), HRC.

Chapter 7

96   " 'MAKE SONGS OF' ": Bowles to Burns, undated (March 1931), HRC.

96   PLACE TO STAY: Edouard Roditi, Conversation with author, April 30, 1987.

96   "A PERFECT GUEST": Suarès, quoted in Edouard Roditi, "Works and Days of the Young and Evil," Unpublished memoir of Paul Bowles.

97   "GENTLEMAN," ADDED TOKLAS: Bowles, *Without Stopping,* p. 106.

97   "BE AS THEY ARE": Gertrude Stein, *Four in America* (New Haven: Yale University Press, 1947), p. 3.

97   WAS A "FREDDY": Bowles, Conversation with author, June 16, 1986. Bowles, *Without Stopping,* p. 106.

97   WERE OPENED TO HIM: Bowles to Burns, undated (Spring 1931), HRC.

98   "LAURENCIN'S PORTRAIT OF HIM": *Ibid.*

98   "REACTIONARY IN SUCH RESPECTS": *Ibid.*

98   A *"LANCER-*ING": Bowles, *Without Stopping,* p. 106.

99   THEIR BRIEF ENCOUNTER: Bowles, Conversation with author, June 16, 1986. Bowles, *Without Stopping,* p. 108.

99   "SOMETHING I CARED ABOUT": Bowles quoted in Bailey, "The Art of Fiction LXVII: Bowles," p. 75.

99   "BECAUSE IT'S NOT POETRY": On Stein's rejection, Bowles, *Without Stopping,* pp. 121–22. Bowles, Conversations with Author, June 14, 1986, and August 28, 1987.

100   "POET, WHO KNOWS": Stein to Bowles, [May 1931], Gertrude Stein Collection, Yale.

100   "THINGS LOOK UP": Bowles to Stein, May 20 [1931], Yale; Excerpt published in Donald Gallup, ed., in *The Flowers of Friendship: Letters Written to Gertrude Stein* (New York: Alfred A. Knopf, 1953), p. 251.

100   "EAST END OF THE CITY": Bowles quoted in Bailey, "The Art of Fiction LXVII: Bowles," p. 73.

100   SCULPTOR, RENÉE SINTENIS: Roditi, "Works and Days of the Young and Evil."

101   "HAVE YOU MAD EYES?": Bowles quoted in *Ibid.*

101   "AVAILABLE TO OUTSIDERS": Bowles, *Without Stopping,* p. 110.

101   "RATHER THAN DISSIMULATE IT": *Ibid.,* p. 110.

101 "PERHAPS MERELY UNINTERESTING": *Ibid.*, pp. 110–111.

101 "NOT ONE LIKE PAUL": Roditi, Conversation with author, April 30, 1987.

101 ATTRACTIVE BUT "ALOOF": Christopher Isherwood, *Christopher and His Kind* (New York: Farrar, Straus, & Giroux, 1976), pp. 60–61.

102 "CITY AFTER TODAY": Bowles to Burns, undated (Summer 1931), HRC.

102 "TYPICAL GERMAN" MENTALITY: Bowles, *Without Stopping*, p. 114.

103 "BEGIN TO SCREAM INSANELY": Bowles to Burns, undated (Summer 1931), HRC.

103 "BUT WHAT OF IT?": Bowles to Burns, undated (Summer 1931), HRC.

103 "*JE SUIS DÉJÀ ROMANTIQUE*": Bowles to Roditi, quoted in Roditi, "Works and Days of the Young and Evil."

103 "PAUL WAS NOTHING SPECIAL THERE": Roditi, Conversation with author, April 30, 1987.

104 "NEVER HEARD OF GERTRUDE STEIN": Bowles to Burns, undated (Summer 1931), HRC.

104 "TZUUKA. TZUUKA": Bowles, *Without Stopping*, p. 115.

104 VOCAL INFLECTIONS, THE FORM: Bowles, Conversation with author, January 17, 1987.

105 "SUMMER HOUSES, ALL": Bowles to Burns, undated (Summer 1931), HRC.

105 "PERSONAL KIND OF RELATIONSHIP": Bowles, *Without Stopping*, pp. 120–21.

105 "NOR SENSIBLE IN WINTER": Gertrude Stein, *The Autobiography of Alice B. Toklas* (New York: Harcourt, Brace, 1933), p. 309.

106 "AS A SOCIOLOGICAL EXHIBIT": Bowles, *Without Stopping*, p. 119.

106 "A MANUFACTURED SAVAGE": *Ibid.*, p. 119.

106 "ABOUT THE ENTIRE MATTER": Bowles to Burns, undated (Summer 1931), HRC.

107 "NEVER BE ANY MORE POEMS": *Ibid.*

107 "EVEN LOOKED AT THEM": Bowles, *Without Stopping*, pp. 123–24. Conversation with author, June 14, 1986.

107 "ARRIVES IN THE SILENCE": Paul Bowles, "Ed Djouf," excerpt trans., CS-L, in *Next to Nothing*, p. 48.

108 "OTHERWISE FROM KNOWING HER": Bowles to Morrissette, undated (August 1935?) Personal collection, Morrissette.

108 "I AM LAZY. SHE KNOWS": Bowles quoted from letter in Roditi, "Works and Days of the Young and Evil."

108 "LIFE OF CRIME TOO YOUNG": Bowles, *Without Stopping*, p. 123.

108 "WHEN YOU ARE THIRTY": Gertrude Stein, *The Autobiography of Alice B. Toklas*, p. 309.
109 "SHINES EVERY DAY": Bowles, *Without Stopping*, p. 123.

Chapter 8

110 "WHICH BYPASSED THE MIND": Bowles, *Without Stopping*, p. 125.
110 "BEAUTIFUL AND TERRIBLE": *Ibid.*, p. 125.
110 WITH THE ODD NAME: Bowles, Conversation with author, August 24, 1987. Bowles, *Without Stopping*, p. 126.
110 "MUCH WILDER," REPLIED BOWLES: *Ibid.*, p. 126.
111 "ASSET TO THE COMMUNITY": *Ibid.*, p. 128.
111 "CONTINUOUS PERFORMANCE, ANYWAY": *Ibid.*, p. 193.
112 "BUT UNREPRODUCIBLE SOUND": On acquiring a piano, Bowles, Conversation with author, January 15, 1987. Bowles, *Without Stopping*, pp. 127–28.
113 "MOUNTAINS IS ÉPATANT": Bowles to Burns, undated (July 1931), HRC.
113 "GO ON THE WARPATH": Bowles to Stein, undated (July 1931), Gertrude Stein Collection, Yale.
113 "ALWAYS PLEASANTLY SHOCKED": *Ibid.*
114 "CANVASES ONE BY ONE": Bowles, *Without Stopping*, p. 129.
114 "IN THE WIND IN THERE SOMEWHERE": *Ibid.*, p. 130.
115 PARIS LATER IN THE FALL: On Fez trip and Dunham, Bowles, Conversation with author, January 15, 1987. Bowles, *Without Stopping*, pp. 130–31.
115 "BRIGHTER" THAN IN TANGIER: Bowles, *Without Stopping*, p. 130.
115 "MAKE MY HOME SOME DAY": Bowles to Morrissette, November 2, 1931, Personal collection, Morrissette.
115 "AND *VERY* BEAUTIFUL": Bowles to Stein, October 9, 1931, Gertrude Stein Collection, Yale.
115 BEAT A HASTY RETREAT: Bowles, Conversation with author, January 15, 1987.
115 "HARRY TOOK IN EVERYTHING": Thomson, Conversation with author, March 6, 1986.
115 "WHICH INTERESTED HIM": Bowles, *Without Stopping*, p. 131.
115 "STRIVE FOR INVISIBILITY": *Ibid.*, p. 132.
116 "FROM MYSELF AS WELL": *Ibid.*, p. 132.
116 "I WAS ALL TOO EVIDENT": *Ibid.*, p. 131.
116 SLEEVE OF HIS DJELLABA: On the Drissi brothers: Bowles, Conversation with author and J. Raskin, July 7, 1985. Bowles, *Without Stopping*, pp. 132–33.

117   MOROCCANS TO LIVE IN POVERTY: Thomson, Conversation with author, March 6, 1986.

117   "INSTINCT FOR FINDING THEM": *Ibid.*

118   BRING THE BOY TO PARIS: On Abdelkader, Bowles, Conversation with author, June 15, 1986. Bowles, *Without Stopping*, pp. 133–34.

118   DAMAGED THE DRAWING: On Bowles's departure from Tangier, Bowles, *Ibid.*, pp. 137–38.

119   "ASKED NO QUESTIONS": *Ibid.*, p. 125.

119   "EVER SEEN IN MY LIFE": Bowles quoted, in Evans, "Interview with Bowles," p. 4.

119   "I WAS AT PRESENT": *Ibid.*, pp. 4–5.

119   "POCKET OUTSIDE THE MAINSTREAM": Bowles quoted in Halpern, "Interview with Bowles," p. 159.

119   "ALL THAT NONSENSE": Bowles quoted in John Bainbridge, *Another Way of Living: A Gallery of Americans Who Choose to Live in Europe* (New York: Holt, Rinehart & Winston, 1968), pp. 243–44.

120   "BETTER IDEA OF YOURSELF": *Ibid.*, p. 239.

120   MADE BY SATAN: Bowles, *Without Stopping*, p. 139.

120   "OF LACK OF TIME": Bowles to Copland, quoted in Copland and Perlis, *Copland: 1900 Through 1942*, p. 191.

121   SUSPICIONS ABOUT HER CONFIRMED: Bowles, *Without Stopping*, p. 140.

121   "SCHOOL OF RAVEL": Thomson, Conversation with author, March 6, 1986.

121   REHEARSING THE PLAYERS: *Ibid.*

122   "TALL, SUAVE AND POLYGLOT": Bowles, *Without Stopping*, p. 141.

122   "HIS MATERIAL PROBLEMS": Roditi, "Works and Days of the Young and Evil."

122   "WAS GOING TO RAPE HIM": Roditi, Conversation with author, April 30, 1987.

122   "SUPERFICIAL MODE OF THOUGHT": Henry Boys, "America in London," in *Modern Music,* Vol. 9, No. 2 (January–February 1932), pp. 92–93.

122   "GOT HOSPITAL TREATMENT": Bowles, *Without Stopping*, p. 142.

Chapter 9

124   CLOSE TO HER BROTHER: Virgil Thomson, *Virgil Thomson* (New York: Alfred A. Knopf, 1966), p. 206.

124   "ANYTHING IN THE WORLD": Roditi, Conversation with author, April 30, 1987.

124   "DIED IN THE WAR": Thomson, Conversation with author, March 6, 1986.

124 "EXCEPT PAUL, I THINK": Roditi, Conversation with author, April 30, 1986.

124 "IN HIS CHARACTER": Thomson, Conversation with author, March 6, 1986.

125 "LEAD PAUL INTO ANYTHING": *Ibid.*

125 "DAINTY AND DEVOTED": Thomson, *Virgil Thomson,* p. 206.

125 "WITH ANNE MANHEIM": Bowles to Morrissette, January 21, 1932, Personal collection, Morrissette.

125 "DIDN'T HAVE IT": Thomson, Conversation with author, March 6, 1986.

125 "OCCASIONAL DESPERATE EXCITING THOUGHTS": Bowles to Stein, January 10 [1932], Gertrude Stein Collection, Yale.

126 "MY REQUEST. WHY NOT?": Bowles to Morrissette, January 26, 1932, Personal collection, Morrissette.

126 TO PLEAD OUTRIGHT FOR MONEY: Bowles to Thomson, undated (January? 1932), Virgil Thomson Collection, Music Library, Yale University (Yale).

126 "YOU OUGHT TO DO": Stein to Bowles, published as lyric to "Letter to Freddy," (New York: G. Schirmer, 1946), pp. 2–3.

126 "LOOKING QUITE WELL": Thomson, Conversation with author, March 6, 1986.

126 "VIRTUOSO AT BEING TAKEN CARE OF": *Ibid.*

127 CURE FOR SYPHILIS: Bowles, *Without Stopping,* p. 144.

127 "EARS OF AMELIA DUNHAM": Roditi, Conversation with author, April 30, 1986.

127 "LOSE THINGS, DON'T YOU?": Bowles, *Without Stopping,* p. 145.

128 "DISCIPLINE OUT OF HIM THAN NADIA": Thomson, Conversation with author, March 6, 1986.

128 "CHEAPER AND BETTER": Thomson to Aaron Copland, November 26, 1931, Yale.

129 "WHOM HE STUDIES WITH": Copland to Thomson, quoted in *Copland: 1900 Through 1942,* p. 195.

129 "INVITED AND PAID FOR": Thomson, Conversation with author, March 6, 1986.

129 "HAD LONG BEEN FAMOUS": Roditi, "Works and Days of the Young and Evil."

129 "SAFETY OF THE LOUNGE": *Ibid.*

129 "CAME TO AN UNDERSTANDING": *Ibid.*

130 "PREDILECTION FOR HANDSOME YOUNG MEN": On Copland's homosexuality, Joan Peyser, *Bernstein: A Biography* (New York: Beech Tree Books–William Morrow, 1987), p. 56.

130 COPLAND'S "PET": Bowles to Thomson, June 24, 1933, Yale. Bowles to Stein, July 17, 1933, Yale.

130 THIS WAS NOT THE CASE: Thomson, Conversation with author, November 4, 1987. Roditi, Conversation with author, April 30, 1986.

130 "IN THE PHYSICAL SIDE": Thomson, Conversation with author, March 6, 1986.

130 "IT WAS ALL MENTAL": Roditi, Conversation with author, April 30, 1986.

130 "SO LONG AS HE ENJOYED IT": Morrissette, Conversation with author, February 13, 1987.

130 "SUCH A THING AS TOO MUCH FUN": William Burroughs, Conversation with author, April 28, 1987.

131 TO HELP BOWLES OUT: Roditi, Conversation with author, April 30, 1987.

131 "DANCING IN EACH *PLAZUELA*": Bowles, *Without Stopping*, p. 147.

132 "EXACTLY LIKE A MOROCCAN," *Ibid.*, p. 148.

132 BECOME MCKAY'S LITERARY AGENT: Wayne F. Cooper, *Claude McKay: Rebel Sojourner in the Harlem Renaissance: A Biography* (Baton Rouge and London: Louisiana State University Press, 1987), p. 277.

132 PLEASANT EXILE, UNTIL 1934: On the McKay-Bowles imbroglio, see Cooper, *Claude McKay*, pp. 277–78.

132 "REALLY TO HEAR": Paul Bowles, "Africa Minor," in *Their Heads Are Green and Their Hands Are Blue* (New York: Random House, 1963; reprinted New York: The Ecco Press, 1984), pp. 35–36.

133 "MEMBERS OF HIS CULTURAL GROUP": Bowles, *Without Stopping*, p. 151.

133 "SO OFTEN IN EGYPT": *Ibid.*, p. 152.

PART III: ON THE MAP

Chapter 10

137 "EYES WOULD SHUT": Paul Bowles, *The Sheltering Sky* (New York: New Directions, 1949; reprinted New York: The Ecco Press, 1978), p. 227.

137 "JUST LIKE JESUS": Bowles, *Without Stopping*, p. 153.

137 TO VISIT HIM AGAIN: *Ibid.*, pp. 152–53.

137 "LOOKED POSITIVELY SKELETAL": Morrissette, Conversation with author, October 30, 1987.

137 THE MARQUIS DE VILLENEUVE: Bowles, *Without Stopping*, p. 153.

138 "AND DON'T YOU FORGET IT": *Ibid.*, p. 153.

138 "THAN HEARING SOUND": Alfred H. Meyer, "Yaddo—A May Festival," in *Modern Music*, Vol. 9, No. 4 (May–June 1932), p. 74.

138   DELIGHTED TO SEE "FREDDY": Morrissette, Conversation with author, January 2, 1987.

138   "MATERNALLY TOWARDS HIM": *Ibid.*

138   "ABSOLUTELY INTENT ON MEETING THEM": *Ibid.*

139   " 'OH, YOU DON'T SAY?' ": *Ibid.*

139   "BEING A CHILD ALL OVER AGAIN": Bowles, *Without Stopping,* p. 154.

139   "GETTING MOST IMPATIENT": *Ibid.,* p. 154.

140   WHO WERE SUMMERING THERE: Thomson to Bowles, October 17, 1932, Yale.

140   "ALL RIGHT AFTER SUNSET": Bowles, *Without Stopping,* p. 155.

140   "MARSEILLES AND POINTS SOUTH": Bowles to Thomson, undated (September? 1933), Yale.

141   "THAN ANYTHING ELSE": Bowles quoted in Jeffrey Miller, *Paul Bowles: A Descriptive Bibliography* (Santa Barbara, Calif.: Black Sparrow Press, 1986), p. 233. [Quote incorrectly attributed to Bowles, *Without Stopping*]

141   "EVEN WHEN OBVIOUSLY A TRICK": Bowles to Morrissette, December 10, 1932, Personal collection, Morrissette.

142   AFRICAN SIDE OF THE MEDITERRANEAN: Bowles, Conversation with author, August 26, 1987.

142   TO DO THE COOKING: On getting settled in Ghardaïa, Bowles to Morrissette, January 12, 1933, Personal collection, Morrissette. Bowles, *Without Stopping,* pp. 156–57. Bowles, Conversation with author, August 24, 1987.

142   NEWLY LIGHTED BRAZIER: Bowles, *Without Stopping,* p. 157.

143   CHECKING THEM LATER FOR ACCURACY: Bowles, Conversation with author, January 14, 1987. Bowles, *Without Stopping,* p. 165. Margot Miflin, "Through a Colored Lens: Paul Bowles Talks About His Dreams," unpublished, 1984.

143   TWENTY-THREE YEARS OLD: Bowles, *Without Stopping,* p. 158.

144   "ESTHETICALLY SATISFYING": *Ibid.,* p. 159.

144   ARRIVING IN THE TOWN OF QAIROUAN: Bowles to Stein, March 7, 1933, Gertrude Stein Collection, Yale. Bowles, *Without Stopping,* p. 161.

144   TRAIN TICKET TO ALGIERS: Bowles to Morrissette, March 13, 1933, Personal collection, Morrissette.

145   SET OUT FOR TANGIER: On trip to Algiers, Bowles to Morrissette, undated (April? 1933), Personal collection, Morrissette. Bowles, *Without Stopping,* pp. 162–64.

145   "REMAINED WITH ME AND TAKEN ROOT": Bowles, *Without Stopping,* p. 166.

146   CONVINCED OF HER TALENT: On Ford and Barnes, Bowles to Morris-

sette, undated (Spring 1933), Personal collection, Morrissette. Bowles, *Without Stopping*, p. 167.

146 "INDEFINITELY OUTSIDE AMERICA": Bowles, *Without Stopping*, p. 165.

147 "ONE DOLLAR FIFTY CENTS A DAY": Bowles to Morrissette, June 27, 1929, Personal collection, Morrissette.

Chapter 11

148 "IN THE LAST MOVEMENT": Copland to John Kirkpatrick, May 29, 1933, quoted in Julia Smith, *Aaron Copland: His Work and Contribution to American Music* (New York: E. P. Dutton, 1955), pp. 148–49.

148 "ARE IN EUROPE. QUEL MENSONGE!!": Bowles to Thomson, June 24, 1933, Yale.

149 NAMED ORVILLE FLINT: Bowles, *Without Stopping*, p. 168.

149 "MASSACHUSETTS 1932": Paul Bowles, "Massachusetts 1932," in *Unwelcome Words: Seven Stories* (Bolinas, Calif.: Tombouctou Books, 1988), pp. 33–42.

149 TITLED "A PROPOSITION": "A Proposition," unpublished mss., undated, HRC.

149 "SEEMS TO HIM UNBEARABLE": All quotes, *Ibid.*

150 "AMERICA IS AMERICA": Bowles to Thomson, undated (September? 1933), Yale.

150 "TELLING THE TRUTH": Stein quoted in, Bowles to Burns, undated (Summer 1931), HRC.

151 EXCISED FROM HARRY'S LIFE: Bowles, *Without Stopping*, p. 168.

151 OCCASIONALLY, MARC BLITZSTEIN: Aaron Copland, *Copland: 1900 Through 1942*, p. 192.

151 "OF THE AMERICAN COMPOSER": *Ibid.*, p. 192.

151 "VALUE OF THE VENTURE": Bowles, *Without Stopping*, p. 168.

151 "IN NO UNCERTAIN TERMS": *Ibid.*, p. 168.

152 MEETINGS OF AN AMERICAN PLACE: *Ibid.*, p. 193. Bowles to Stein, undated (February 1934), Yale. Gertrude Stein Collection, Excerpt quoted, in Gallup, ed., *The Flowers of Friendship*, p. 276.

153 POSSIBLY AUTHENTIC IN BOWLES": Marc Blitzstein, "Mid-Season in New York," in *Modern Music*, Vol. 11, No. 2 (January–February 1934), p. 101.

153 BOHEMIAN PERSONALITIES AND ATMOSPHERE: On Latouche, Morrissette, Conversation with author, January 2, 1987. Bowles to Morrissette, December 13, 1933, Personal collection, Morrissette. Bowles, *Without Stopping*, p. 169.

153 *SIVA* (LATER *BRIDE OF SAMOA*): Bowles, *Without Stopping*, p. 172.

154 "TICKETS FOR IT": Bowles to Stein, undated (February 1934), Gertrude Stein Collection, Yale. Excerpt quoted in Gallup, ed., *The Flowers of Friendship*, p. 276.

154 "WOULD LIKE THEM VERY MUCH": *Ibid.*, p. 276.

155 "BUT I'M STILL WORRIED": Bowles to Morrissette, February 23, 1934, Personal collection, Morrissette.

155 "I WILL PLAY TO HIM": Bowles to Morrissette, March 29, 1934, Personal collection, Morrissette.

155 IN GIBRALTAR IN AUGUST: On American Fondouk employment, Bowles, *Without Stopping*, pp. 170–171.

156 RETIRED BRITISH ARMY OFFICER: On firing of Brown, Bowles, *Without Stopping*, pp. 174–75.

157 "WAS MORALLY INVOLVED": Paul Bowles, *Let It Come Down* (New York: Random House, 1952; reprinted Santa Barbara, Calif.: Black Sparrow Press, 1980), p. 170.

157 "AS A QUE GUAPO": Bowles to Burns, November 2, [1934], HRC.

158 "FROM ALGERIA AND EGYPT": *Ibid.*

158 "I GOT NO EFFECT": Bowles, *Without Stopping*, p. 179.

158 "WHEN THEY WERE OFFERED": *Ibid.*, p. 179.

159 "FINCA IN THE SELVA": Bowles to Burns, undated (December 1934), HRC.

160 "IN THE WAY AT THE ANTIPODES": *Ibid.*

Chapter 12

161 AUSTRIAN'S GRAND PIANO: On employment with Fuhrman, Bowles, *Without Stopping*, p. 185. Morrissette, Conversation with author, October 30, 1987.

162 PROVIDE A FULL SCORE: Bowles, *Without Stopping*, p. 185.

162 CELLAR IN BUCKETS: Bowles, Conversation with author and J. Raskin, July 7, 1985.

162 SOME TOKEN CONSIDERATION: Bowles, *Without Stopping*, p. 186.

163 SENT THEM TO THOMSON: Bowles to Thomson, February 10, 1935, Yale.

163 A SUITE OF HIS OWN: Thomson, *Virgil Thomson*, p. 251.

164 LORING ASSIGNED TO CHOREOGRAPH IT: Bowles, *Without Stopping*, p. 192.

164 WOULD CAUSE HIM CONSIDERABLE PROBLEMS: Bowles, Conversation with author, January 15, 1987.

164 BARTÓK'S *CONCERTO FOR ORCHESTRA*: *Ibid.* and Bowles, *Without Stopping*, p. 191.

165 "THE IMAGES WOULD HAVE BEEN": Bowles, *Without Stopping*, p. 192.

165   "MELODIC INDIVIDUALITY": Colin McPhee, "New York's Spring Season, 1936," in *Modern Music,* Vol. 13, No. 4 (May–June 1936), p. 40.

165   "MEMBERS OF CAFÉ SOCIETY": Bowles, *Without Stopping,* p. 192.

165   "DIGGING THEM UP AGAIN TOMORROW": *Ibid.,* p. 192.

166   " 'WELL-TRAINED' CONSERVATORY PRODUCT": Aaron Copland, "America's Young Men—Ten Years Later," in *Modern Music,* Vol. 13, No. 4 (May–June 1936), p. 10. Republished in Copland, *Copland on Music* (New York: Doubleday, 1960), p. 162.

166   "AS PART OF THE MUSIC": Bowles, *Without Stopping,* p. 192.

167   PROVIDED BOWLES WITH FREE MEALS: Bowles, Conversation with author, June 15, 1987.

167   "IT WOULD NEED A LOT OF MUSIC": Thomson, Conversation with author, March 6, 1986.

168   SUPPLYING MOSTLY THEIR OWN MUSIC: *Ibid.* and John Houseman, *Unfinished Business* (London: Chatto & Windus, 1986), p. 109. Thomson, *Virgil Thomson,* p. 265.

168   "FIT WHAT INTO THE PLAY": Thomson, Conversation with author, March 6, 1986.

168   "WRITTEN FOR A SHOW EVER IS": *Ibid.*

168   EVEN SANG A SONG: *Ibid.*

169   "KEEP THIS IN THE SHOW": Thomson, *Virgil Thomson,* p. 265.

169   "TIME WE WANT IT": Frederick Jacobi, "In the Theater," in *Modern Music,* Vol. 14, No. 2 (November–December 1936), p. 42.

169   "PLAY THEM FOR US ON THE PIANO": Thomson, Conversation with author, March 6, 1986.

169   "BEING ABLE TO ORCHESTRATE": *Ibid.*

169   "ALL BY YOURSELF THIS TIME": Thomson quoted in Bowles, *Without Stopping,* p. 195.

170   "ENTRY INTO MUSICAL BIG-TIME": Virgil Thomson, "In the Theater," in *Modern Music,* Vol. 14, No. 2 (January–February 1937), p. 105.

170   "MILITANT-SOUNDING MUSIC": Bowles, *Without Stopping,* p. 195.

170   "WAS NOT COMMUNICATIVE": *Ibid.,* p. 196.

170   "HE'S MY ENEMY": Jane Bowles quoted in "Jane Bowles," in John Wakeman, ed., *World Authors 1950–1970* (New York: H. W. Wilson, 1975), p. 203.

171   "DON'T YOU THINK?": Bowles, *Without Stopping,* p. 196.

172   RETURN FROM SWITZERLAND: On biographical information on Jane Bowles, "Jane Bowles," in Wakeman, ed., *World Authors 1950–1970,* pp. 202–3. Millicent Dillon, *A Little Original Sin: The Life and Work of Jane Bowles* (New York: Holt, Rinehart & Winston, 1981).

172   "RATHER FULL LIPS": Edouard Roditi, "The Fiction of Jane Bowles as a Form of Exorcism," Unpublished memoir of Jane Bowles.

172 "FULL OF MISCHIEF": Thomson, Conversation with author, November 3, 1987.

173 "BECOME EXTREMELY NERVOUS": Jane Bowles quoted in "Jane Bowles," in Wakeman, ed., *World Authors 1950–1970,* p. 203.

173 LEFT-WING "WELFARE" ORGANIZATION: Bowles, *Without Stopping,* p. 197.

173 EXILE'S PRESENCE THERE: *Ibid.,* p. 197.

Chapter 13

174 BOWLES WAS READY TO CONTINUE SOUTH: Bowles, *Without Stopping,* p. 197.

174 REMAIN SO UNTIL MARRIED: *Ibid.,* p. 199.

174 KNEW LITTLE ABOUT MUSIC: Jane Bowles to Miriam Levy, undated (February 1937) in Millicent Dillon, ed., *Out in the World: Selected Letters of Jane Bowles 1935–1970* (Santa Barbara, Calif.: Black Sparrow Press, 1985), p. 18.

174 "TONNY'S SCORNFUL REMARKS": Bowles, *Without Stopping,* p. 198.

175 "WE WEREN'T SORRY TO LOSE HER": Bowles to Morrissette, undated (March? 1937), Personal collection, Morrissette.

175 TO GO TO BED WITH HIM: Bowles, *Without Stopping,* p. 199.

175 "HIS ARMS ALWAYS OUTSTRECHED": Bowles, Conversation with author, January 14, 1987.

176 "PERFORMANCE OF *HOMENAJE A GARCÍA* LORCA": Paul Bowles, "Sylvestre Revueltas," in *Modern Music,* Vol. 18, No. 1 (November–December 1940), p. 12.

176 "FILLED WITH LUMINOUS TEXTURE": *Ibid.,* p. 12.

176 "BABIES WAS INFERNAL": Bowles, *Without Stopping,* p. 199.

176 "ON AROUND HIM IN HIS COUNTRY": Bowles, "Sylvestre Revueltas," in *Modern Music,* p. 12.

177 "WITH QUIET PRIDE: *HE DICHO*": *Ibid.,* p. 13.

178 AT ANY MALE INTRUDERS: On trip to Tehuantepec, Bowles to Thomson, May 17, 1937. Bowles, *Without Stopping,* pp. 200–201.

179 "THORNY TREES AND CACTI": Bowles, *Without Stopping,* p. 201.

179 BEFORE RETURNING TO MEXICO CITY: On Guatemala trip, Bowles to Thomson, May 17, 1937, Yale. Bowles, *Without Stopping,* p. 203.

179 WIRE FROM LINCOLN KIRSTEIN: Bowles, *Without Stopping,* p. 204.

179 ARTIST'S MONEY HAD NOT YET ARRIVED: On loans to Tonny, Bowles to Thomson, May 17, 1937, Yale.

180 ALWAYS PREFERRED THE PIANO VERSION: Bowles, Conversation with author, January 14, 1987.

180 "PASTICHES OF THE EXOTICA": Elliott Carter, "With the Dancers," in *Modern Music,* Vol. 15, No. 2 (January–February 1938), p. 122.

180 "A BRIGHT LITTLE SUITE": Paul Rosenfeld, "The Newest American Composers," in *Modern Music,* Vol. 15, No. 3 (March–April 1938), p. 158.

181 IN DEAL BEACH, NEW JERSEY: Bowles to Morrissette, undated (Summer 1937), Personal collection, Morrissette.

181 AN OLD FRIEND, GENEVIEVE PHILLIPS: On reunion with Jane, Dillon, *A Little Original Sin,* p. 49.

181 JANE WAS "WILD": Bowles, *Without Stopping,* p. 321.

181 "A STALINIST TRAP": *Ibid.,* p. 206.

182 " 'OH, LENNY, NE RAVELONS PLUS' ": Leonard Bernstein quoted in Copland, *Copland: 1900–1942,* p. 337.

182 "BOWLES-THOMSON WAR": Thomson to Bowles, Draft letter, undated (Fall–Winter 1938), Yale.

183 "RUINING IT, I'M SURE": Bowles to Thomson, February 7, 1938, Yale.

183 "IN YOUR MUSICAL INSPIRATION": Thomson to Bowles, Draft letter, undated (February 1938), Yale.

183 NEVER HAD ANY LASTING CONSEQUENCES: Thomson, Conversation with author, November 2, 1987.

183 "SHORTER DISTANCE THAN ONE IMAGINES": Bowles, *Without Stopping,* p. 207.

184 "MARRYING A CRIPPLE": Bowles quoted in Dillon, *A Little Original Sin,* p. 50.

184 TO SAIL ON MARCH 1: "Shipping and Mails," in *New York Times,* February 28, 1938, p. 81.

184 INEVITABLE CONSEQUENCE OF EXISTENCE: Bowles statement reported in Dillon, *A Little Original Sin,* p. 50.

184 WERE QUITE CLOSE TO HER: David Diamond statement reported in *Ibid.,* p. 50.

184 AFTER HER DAUGHTER HAD: Jane Bowles, "Jane Bowles," in Wakeman, ed., *World Authors 1950–1970,* p. 203. Thomson, Conversation with author, March 6, 1986.

184 SUM ONCE SHE HAD MARRIED: Thomson, Conversation with author, March 6, 1986.

185 "INIMICAL TO ME AS YOU": Jane Bowles quoted in Dillon, *A Little Original Sin,* p. 89.

185 "WASN'T TRUE": Paul Bowles quoted in *Ibid.,* p. 89.

185 "THAT WAS HER WAY OF LIFE": Thomson, Conversation with author, March 6, 1986.

185 "MANY AT THAT TIME WERE DOING IT": Roditi, Conversation with author, April 30, 1987.

185 WERE SHORT-LIVED: Dillon, *A Little Original Sin,* p. 80.

186 PLAYING THE DRUMS: Bowles, *Without Stopping,* p. 206.

PART IV: ENTRANCES AND EXITS

Chapter 14

189 SWARM OF PEOPLE IN THE STREETS: Bowles to Morrissette, April 28, 1938, Personal collection, Morrissette.

189 STORY OF THEIR HONEYMOON: Thomson, Conversation with author, March 6, 1986.

190 "BUT OF NO GREAT IMPORTANCE": Jane Bowles, *Two Serious Ladies,* in *The Collected Works of Jane Bowles* (New York: Farrar, Straus & Giroux, 1966); expanded edition, *My Sister's Hand in Mine: The Collected Works of Jane Bowles* (New York: The Ecco Press, 1978), p. 201.

190 "IS WHOLLY NON-AUTOBIOGRAPHICAL": Bowles quoted in Bailey, "The Art of Fiction LXVII," p. 84.

191 "COMFORTABLE, NOTHING MORE IS NECESSARY": Jane Bowles, *Two Serious Ladies,* in *My Sister's Hand in Mine: The Collected Works of Jane Bowles,* p. 37.

192 "YOU COULD IF YOU WANTED": Paul Bowles, "Call at Corazón," in *Collected Stories,* p. 68.

192 "ON TOP OF THEM": *Ibid.,* p. 74.

192 "PAST THE WINDOW": *Ibid.,* p. 75.

192 AS AN INTERCOASTAL FERRY: Bowles, *Without Stopping,* p. 208.

193 "AS WELL AS THE ESTATE MANAGER": Dillon, *A Little Original Sin,* p. 53.

193 "EARTHQUAKES AND MONKEYS": Bowles to Stein, [April 1938], Gertrude Stein Collection, Yale.

194 "PARROT-CONSCIOUS": Paul Bowles, "All Parrots Speak," in *Their Heads Are Green,* p. 146.

194 "COULDN'T BEAR TO BREAK UP THE FAMILY": *Ibid.,* p. 147.

194 "OF COURSE WE BOUGHT IT": *Ibid.,* p. 147.

194 "FELT RATHER THAN BELIEVED": *Ibid.,* p. 146.

194 TO GET BACK INTO HIS CAGE: Dillon, *A Little Original Sin,* p. 54.

195 "FOR THE OTHER VOYAGERS": Paul Bowles, "All Parrots Speak," in *Their Heads Are Green,* p. 148.

195 TO LIVE ON HIS MANOR: Bowles to Morrissette, April 28, 1938, Personal collection, Morrissette.

196 "DRIVE HER INTO THE JUNGLE": Bowles quoted in Lawrence D. Stewart, "Up Above the World So High," in *The Mystery and Detection Annual* (Beverly Hills: Donald Adams, 1973), pp. 258–59.

197 "FOUR YEARS. MAGNIFICENT": Bowles to Morrissette, April 28, 1938, Personal collection, Morrissette.

198 WHAT HAD OCCURRED THAT NIGHT: On whorehouse incident, Dillon, *A Little Original Sin,* pp. 54–55.

198 "ONLY IN OUR CABIN": Bowles, *Without Stopping,* p. 210.

198 BECOME *TWO SERIOUS LADIES:* Halpern, "Interview with Bowles," p. 173.

199 TO VARIOUS LESBIAN BARS: Thomson, Conversation with author, March 6, 1986.

199 "THOUGHT IT WAS INTERESTING": Bowles quoted in Dery, "Talking with a Stranger: Paul Bowles Interviewed in Tangier, Morocco."

200 "THERE WERE NO REPERCUSSIONS": Bowles, *Without Stopping,* p. 211.

200 "FIND THE ROOM STILL EMPTY": *Ibid.,* p. 210.

201 "URGED JANE TO COME TO CANNES": *Ibid.,* p. 211.

201 FOUND A LITTLE HOUSE TO RENT: Bowles to Stein, undated (Summer 1938), Yale.

202 THE WILLIAM GILLETTE FARCE: Bowles, Conversation with author, August 26, 1987.

Chapter 15

203 BOWLESES WERE NEARLY BROKE: Bowles, *Without Stopping,* p. 213. Bowles, Conversation with author, August 26, 1987.

204 PUT ON A TRAGEDY, *DANTON'S DEATH:* Bowles, *Without Stopping,* p. 213.

204 BOWLES STORMED OUT OF THE OFFICE: Bowles, Conversation with author, August 26, 1987.

204 "ODD CHARACTERS FROM THE NEIGHBORHOOD": Bowles, *Without Stopping,* p. 213.

205 GOING RATE OF $23.86 A WEEK: On getting on relief, Bowles to Morrissette, January 19, 1939, Personal collection, Morrissette. Bowles, *Without Stopping,* pp. 213–214.

205 "NOT WE WHO PAID, HOWEVER": Bowles to Morrissette, January 19, 1939, Personal collection, Morrissette.

205 "TO SHOCK [HIS] FATHER": Bowles quoted in Paula Chin, "Stories of Violence," [Interview with Bowles], in *Newsweek* (International Edition), August 4, 1986, p. 8.

206   "WAS STALINIST": Thomson, Conversation with author, November 2, 1987.
206   "KNOW WHAT I'M READING": Bowles, *Without Stopping*, p. 215.
206   CHIEF AMONG THEM, THOMSON AND COPLAND: Buffie Johnson, Conversation with author, March 6, 1986.
206   " 'ASKED TO THE ASKEW SALON' ": Jane Bowles quoted in *Ibid.*
207   WROTE THE ENTIRE SCORE: Bowles, *Without Stopping*, p. 215.
207   AT LEAST FOR THE INTERIM: Bowles, *Ibid.*, p. 216.
208   "A FEW LITTLE OIL STOVES": Jane Bowles, *Two Serious Ladies*, in *My Sister's Hand in Mine*, pp. 112–13.
208   FULLY HETEROSEXUAL: Thomson, Conversation with author, November 2, 1987.
208   BERNSTEIN DECLINED TO STAY ON: Bowles, *Without Stopping*, p. 216.
209   RIGHT TO STAY THERE AT ANY TIME: Jane Bowles to Mary Oliver, undated (Summer 1939) in Dillon, ed., *Out in the World: Selected Letters of Jane Bowles*, p. 23.
210   "SHARE IT WITH ANYONE": *Ibid.*, p. 23.
210   PAY FOR ALL THE BOOZE: Bowles, *Without Stopping*, p. 217.
211   "NAGGING EX-DRINKER AT HIS SIDE": *Ibid.*, p. 218.
211   WOULD RUIN HER HEALTH: On Bowles's reaction to Jane and Mary Oliver, *Ibid.*, pp. 218–19.
213   MANIFESTATION OF PSYCHIC POWER: On Oliver's decline, Bowles, *Without Stopping*, pp. 219–20.
213   TO THE NEW SITUATION OR ATMOSPHERE: Bowles, Conversation with author, June 18, 1986.
213   "I AM AWARE": William Saroyan, "Note to *Love's Old Sweet Song*," in *Three Plays* (New York: Harcourt, Brace & Co., 1940), p. 15.
214   "NOT IN PRESENT NEED": Bowles, *Without Stopping*, p. 222.
214   BE FUNDED FOR AN OPERA: Bowles, Conversation with author, August 27, 1987.
214   SOME SORT OF LIBRETTO: *Ibid.* Bowles, *Without Stopping*, pp. 223–24.
214   RIO GRANDE VALLEY OF NEW MEXICO: Bowles, *Ibid.*, p. 222.
215   "CARE WHO CAME ALONG WITH US": *Ibid.*, p. 223.
215   "JANE WANTED HIS PRESENCE": *Ibid.*, p. 223.
215   "SHE DID NOT DRINK TOO MUCH": *Ibid.*, p. 223.

Chapter 16

216   "SAND, DRIFTWOOD AND PEBBLES": Bowles, *Ibid.*, p. 225.
217   BY THAT OF THE BOKES: *Ibid.*, p. 225. For a slightly different version of the Desert Rose episode, see Dillon, *A Little Original Sin*, p. 83.

217   "was a libretto": Bowles, *Without Stopping*, p. 226.

217   "i lost a whole opera": William Saroyan, "*The Alphabet Opera* by Paul Bowles and William Saroyan," in *Sons Come and Go, Mothers Hang in Forever* (New York: McGraw-Hill, 1976), pp. 169, 171.

218   on the brink of civil war: Bowles, Conversation with author, January 16, 1987.

218   could not work at all: Bowles, *Without Stopping*, p. 226.

218   "more insidious, more corrosive": *Ibid.*, p. 227.

219   welfare of the party: *Ibid.*, p. 227.

219   frequently nestling in her hair: On the Bowleses' menagerie, *Ibid.*, pp. 228–29. Dillon, *A Little Original Sin*, p. 85.

219   never disturb bowles in his room: Bob Faulkner quoted in Dillon, *A Little Original Sin*, p. 85.

220   "saw him after that a few times": Bowles, Conversation with author and J. Raskin, July 7, 1985.

221   "very merry personality": Kenward Elmslie, Conversation with author, September 1, 1988.

221   a possible love affair: On Helvetia Perkins, Thomson, Conversations with author, March 6, 1986; November 2, 1987. Dillon, *A Little Original Sin*, pp. 88–89.

222   "without robbing shakespeare": S. L. M. Barlow, "In the Theater," in *Modern Music*, Vol. 18, No. 2 (January–February 1941), p. 126.

223   "no drama in these affairs": Thomson, Conversation with author, March 6, 1986.

223   much more mature than jane: Thomson, Conversation with author, November 2, 1987.

224   "heat is there but no love": S. L. M. Barlow, "In the Theater," in *Modern Music*, Vol. 18, No. 3 (March–April 1941), p. 190.

224   acknowledge his contribution: Bowles, Conversation with author, June 19, 1986. Bowles to Thomson, undated (November 1943), Yale.

224   a member of the party: Bowles, *Without Stopping*, pp. 230–31.

225   the remaining room on that floor: Bowles, *Without Stopping*, p. 233. Humphrey Carpenter, *W. H. Auden: A Biography* (Boston: Houghton Mifflin, 1981), pp. 304–6.

225   "when it was due": Bowles, *Without Stopping*, p. 233.

225   "keep us all in order": *Ibid.*, p. 233.

226   moved to his own house nearby: Bowles to Thomson, June 27 [1941], Yale.

226   "you never see them": *Ibid.*

226   "directly beneath me": *Ibid.*

227   "HOMEMADE PATCHOULI": Ned Rorem, to author, October 24, 1988.
227   "SUCH INTIMACY!": *Ibid.*
227   "LIKE THAT TO EACH OTHER": *Ibid.*
227   "TOUCH CONDESCENDING PERHAPS": *Ibid.*
227   "PLATONIC PALS": *Ibid.*
228   "UPHEAVALS BACK IN CHICAGO": On Rorem and "Pages," *Ibid.*
228   "HIS PRESENCE SEEN AT ALL": Paul Bowles, "Pages from Cold Point," in *Collected Stories,* p. 83.
229   "HAVE HAPPENED AT ALL": Bowles to Thomson, July 27 [1941], Yale.
229   IT WAS "LOUSY, TERRIBLE": Kirstein quoted in Bowles to Thomson, June 27 [1941], Yale.
229   "GET IT FOR NOTHING": Bowles to Thomson, July 27 [1941], Yale.
229   "OF DEFERRED SETTLEMENTS?": *Ibid.*
230   JANE AND PERKINS TO ACAPULCO: *Ibid.*
230   LATEST NEW YORK "NEWS AND GOSSIP": Bowles to Thomson, undated (1942), Yale.
231   " 'OF THOSE THINGS,' SHE ASSURED ME": Bowles, *Without Stopping,* p. 240.
231   "I HOPE SO": *Ibid.,* p. 240.
231   EVEN HAD THAT WORKING TITLE: Dillon, *A Little Original Sin,* p. 105.

Chapter 17

232   WITH SPOKEN DIALOGUE AND DANCE: On *The Wind Remains,* Bowles, Conversation with author, August 27, 1987. Bowles, *Without Stopping,* p. 249.
233   "TO BE STILL ALIVE": Bowles to Thomson, undated (April 1942), Yale.
233   OVERDOSE OF NEMBUTAL: Bowles, *Without Stopping,* p. 242.
233   BY SLASHING HER WRISTS: Dillon, *A Little Original Sin,* p. 108.
234   "SCHWAB CLAIMS NOT IN BODEGA": Bowles, *Without Stopping,* p. 243.
234   MORE ROUNDS OF QUESTIONING, FINALLY LEFT: *Ibid.,* p. 243. Bowles, Conversation with author, January 15, 1987.
234   "THOUGHT I WAS GERMAN!": Bowles, Conversation with author and J. Raskin, July 7, 1985.
235   14TH STREET AND SEVENTH AVENUE: *Ibid.*
235   "I LIKED HIM": Bowles quoted in Dery, "Talking to a Stranger: Paul Bowles Interviewed in Tangier, Morocco."
236   "COMEDY OF MANNERS": Roditi, "Works and Days of the Young and Evil."

236 "REFUSING TO LIVE OR SLEEP WITH HIM": Thomson, Conversation with author, March 6, 1986.

236 SUCH A SHORT AMOUNT OF TIME: Bowles, Conversation with author, August 28, 1987.

237 HALF AN HOUR OR LESS: *Ibid.*

237 "CONTINUED MY WORK": On selective service exam, Bowles, *Without Stopping,* p. 248.

237 "AND WENT NOWHERE": Bowles, *Without Stopping,* p. 249.

238 "ONE'S OWN SANITY," Edith H. Walton, "Fantastic Duo," in *New York Times Book Review,* May 9, 1943, p. 14.

238 IN ITS FIRST YEAR OF PUBLICATION: Alfred A. Knopf to Jane Bowles, Royalty statement, March 1, 1944, HRC.

239 SCHEME TO WHICH HE READILY AGREED: Peggy Guggenheim, *Out of This Century* (New York: The Dial Press, 1946), p. 345.

239 "DIDN'T EXIST FOR JANE": Miriam Levy quoted in Dillon, *A Little Original Sin,* pp. 73–74.

240 ANY MEMORY OF WHAT HAD HAPPENED: Bowles, *Without Stopping,* p. 251.

240 CONTRIBUTED TO HER ANXIETY: Dillon, *A Little Original Sin,* p. 113.

240 "QUEBEC WAS NEARBY": Bowles, *Without Stopping,* p. 251.

240 "NOSTALGIA FOR PREWAR PARIS": *Ibid.,* p. 265.

241 "INGENIOUS *BAL-MUSETTE* SCORE": S. L. M. Barlow, "Music and Dancing on Broadway," in *Modern Music,* Vol. 22, No. 2 (January–February 1945), p. 133.

242 "AND SAID: *'Vraiment?'* ": Bowles, *Without Stopping,* p. 255.

242 "DALÍ'S USUAL OUTLANDISH WEIRDNESS": Quoted in Miller, *Paul Bowles: A Descriptive Bibliography,* p. 244.

242 "STRAY FISH, MORE AND MORIBUNDIA": S. L. M. Barlow, "Music and Dancing on Broadway," in *Modern Music,* Vol. 22, No. 2 (January–February 1945), p. 133.

243 "EVEN IF MADE TO AN AILUROPHOBE": Bowles, *Without Stopping,* p. 234.

243 "IT WAS MARVELOUS": Bowles quoted in Mike Steen, *A Look at Tennessee Williams* (New York: Hawthorn Books, 1969), p. 145.

244 "OF THE NOCTURNE ON STAGE": S. L. M. Barlow, "In the Theater," in *Modern Music,* Vol. 22, No. 4 (May–June 1945), p. 277.

Chapter 18

245   "CENTRAL AMERICA AND THE CARIBBEAN": John Bernard Myers, Untitled memoir, in *Twentieth-Century Literature,* Vol. 32, Nos. 3–4, Fall–Winter 1986, p. 284.

246   "INCANTATIONS, RITUALS, HORSEPLAY": *Ibid.,* p. 285.

246   OF A CONTEMPORARY MEXICAN MAGAZINE: On Bowles's "hoax," Bowles, Conversation with author, January 16, 1987.

246   PERPETRATOR OF THE POSSESSION: Juan de la Cabada, "Nicodemus," in *Cuadernos Americanos,* March 1944, pp. 237–50.

247   "LAND OF FICTION WRITING": Bowles, *Without Stopping,* p. 261.

248   "YOU MAKE A STORY": On "The Scorpion," Bowles, Conversation with author and J. Raskin, July 7, 1985.

248   "CALLED THAT THE END": Bowles to Graham T. Ackroyd, May 21, 1950, HRC.

249   "STORY OF THE PROFESSOR": Bowles quoted in Evans, "Interview with Bowles," p. 11.

249   PERKINS AND JANE, THE SECOND: On 28 West 10th Street, Bowles, *Without Stopping,* pp. 257–58.

250   "GO AMONG THE OTHERS": Jane Bowles, "A Quarreling Pair," in *My Sister's Hand in Mine,* p. 416.

250   WITH A WOMAN FROM BOSTON: Dillon, *A Little Original Sin,* p. 126.

250   " 'I'M NOT. SO STOP IT' ": Bowles quoted in Bailey, "The Art of Fiction LXVII: Paul Bowles," p. 84.

251   "DISCUSSING IT WITH HER FIRST": *Ibid.,* p. 82.

251   "WRITE MY OWN FICTION": *Ibid.,* p. 82.

251   "AFRAID TO DISCOURAGE ME": Jane Bowles to Paul Bowles, undated (September 1947), HRC. Also in Dillon, ed., *Out in the World: The Selected Letters of Jane Bowles,* p. 46.

251   "MUSIC PUBLISHED AND RECORDED": Thomson, Conversation with author, March 6, 1986. On Peggy Glanville-Hicks, Bowles, *Without Stopping,* pp. 259–60.

251   "ALMOST CONSTANT COMPANION": Bowles, *Without Stopping,* p. 259.

253   "WHICH WILL SURROUND HIM": Unknown author, "Bowles's Fortune," undated fragment (1945), HRC.

253   SIGNED OVER LUNCH: Bowles, Conversation with author and J. Raskin, July 7, 1985.

254   "SATISFACTION OF THE PRODUCERS": Bowles, *Without Stopping,* p. 269.

254   PRINTED WORDS, "NO EXIT": Bowles, *Ibid.,* p. 270.

255   "DEXTERITY" OF SARTRE'S WRITING: Brooks Atkinson, "Lost Souls

Tortured by Being in Each Other's Company," in *New York Times*, November 27, 1946, p. 21.

255 "YOU'LL BE BETTER OFF": Bowles, *Without Stopping*, p. 271.

255 "ENOUGH OF A CATHARTIC": Bowles quoted in Harvey Breit, "Talk with Paul Bowles," in *New York Times Book Review*, March 9, 1952, p. 18.

255 "I HAD BECOME INVOLVED": Bowles, *Without Stopping*, pp. 273–74.

255 "LIVE IN NEW YORK ANY LONGER": Bowles, Conversation with author, July 5, 1985.

256 "MAKE MORE MONEY WRITING": Thomson, Conversation with author, March 6, 1986.

256 "COULD HANDLE WAS RAVEL": *Ibid.*

256 YEARS HE HAD BEEN COMPOSING: Rorem, Conversation with author, April 19, 1986. Ned Rorem, "Come Back Paul Bowles," in *New Republic*, April 22, 1972; republished as "Paul Bowles," in Rorem, *Pure Contraption: A Composer's Essays* (New York: Holt, Rinehart & Winston, 1974), p. 34.

256 IN TOUCH WITH HIM SOON: Bowles, Conversation with author, June 16, 1986.

256 "INEFFABLE SWEETNESS AND CALM": Bowles, *Without Stopping*, p. 274.

256 "THAN ANYWHERE ELSE": *Ibid.*, p. 274.

257 "TRIP TO TANGIER": *Ibid.*, p. 274.

257 "SEEMED IMPORTANT TO ME": Bowles quoted in Halpern, "Interview with Bowles," p. 162.

257 "WOULD BE *THE SHELTERING SKY*": Bowles, *Without Stopping*, p. 275.

PART V: ". . . AND MOROCCO TOOK OVER"
Chapter 19

261 "AND NOT YOURS": Jane Bowles to Paul Bowles, undated (August 1947), HRC. Also in Dillon, ed., *Out in the World: Selected Letters of Jane Bowles*, p. 37.

261 "AND MOROCCO TOOK OVER": Bowles, *Without Stopping*, p. 276.

261 "STATE OF PERPETUAL EXCITEMENT": *Ibid.*, p. 277.

261 "THROUGH THE DAY": *Ibid.*, p. 278.

262 "WOULD HAPPEN," HE SAYS: Bowles, Conversation with author and J. Raskin, July 7, 1985.

262 "BIGGEST FLAW": *Ibid.*

262 "DIFFERENT SET OF PAINTS": *Ibid.*

262 PRACTICALITY OF THE PURCHASE: Oliver Smith to Bowles, Telegram, October 18, 1947, HRC.

263 "IS ALL WRONG FOR ME": Jane Bowles to Paul Bowles, undated

(October 1947), HRC. Also in Dillon, ed., *Out in the World: Selected Letters of Jane Bowles,* pp. 61–62.

263   "ARRIVE SUDDENLY IN TANGIER": Jane Bowles to Paul Bowles, undated (December 1947), HRC. Also in Dillon, ed., *Out in the World: Selected Letters of Jane Bowles,* p. 64.

263   "WITHOUT EXACTLY SHUDDERING": Jane Bowles to Paul Bowles, undated (December 1947), HRC. Also in Dillon, ed., *Out in the World: Selected Letters of Jane Bowles,* p. 74.

263   "WILL BE JUST THE OPPOSITE": Jane Bowles to Paul Bowles, undated (October 1947), HRC. Also in Dillon, ed., *Out in the World: Selected Letters of Jane Bowles,* p. 64.

264   ACCOMPANY HER TO NORTH AFRICA: Jane Bowles to Paul Bowles, undated (December 1947), HRC. Also in Dillon, ed., *Out in the World: Selected Letters of Jane Bowles,* p. 66.

264   HER HOUSE IN CONNECTICUT: On Libby Holman, John Bradshaw, *Dreams That Money Can Buy: The Tragic Life of Libby Holman* (New York: William Morrow, 1985), p. 279.

264   "GENERATIONS OF MANIACS": Jane Bowles to Paul Bowles, undated (October 1947), HRC. Also in Dillon, ed., *Out in the World: Selected Letters of Jane Bowles,* p. 60.

264   "SPACE IN THE MIDDLE!": *Ibid.*

264   "OVER TO THE SUBCONSCIOUS": Bowles, *Without Stopping,* p. 279.

265   "SHOULD HAVE FOUND WITHOUT IT": *Ibid.,* p. 279.

265   "HAS TO GO ON": Bowles, Conversation with author and J. Raskin, July 7, 1985.

265   "MAKING IT SATISFACTORY": *Ibid.*

266   "HANDKERCHIEF AFTER BLOWING HIS NOSE": Paul Bowles, *The Sheltering Sky,* p. 84.

266   "IT WOULD ENTAIL": *Ibid.,* p. 105.

266   "THEY BE ALONE TOGETHER": *Ibid.,* p. 105.

267   "BE ALONE WITH HER": *Ibid.,* p. 106.

267   "A NOVEL FROM MEMORY": Bowles quoted in Evans, "Interview with Bowles," p. 11.

267   "POETIC SPOT I'VE EVER SEEN": Bowles, *Without Stopping,* p. 282.

268   WHEN THE SUN WENT DOWN: *Ibid.,* pp. 283–84.

268   "ARRIVE FROM GIBRALTAR": Jane Bowles to Paul Bowles, undated (July 1948), HRC. Also in Dillon, ed., *Out in the World: Selected Letters of Jane Bowles,* p. 79.

268   COME IN AND MURDER HER: Bowles, *Without Stopping,* p. 286.

269   "VIEW ME WITH SUCH DISGUST": Jane Bowles to Paul Bowles, undated (October 1947), HRC. Also in Dillon, ed., *Out in the World: Selected Letters of Jane Bowles,* p. 63.

269 "TURNED OUT SO DIFFERENTLY": Jane Bowles to Paul Bowles, undated (July 1948), HRC. Also in Dillon, ed., *Out in the World: Selected Letters of Jane Bowles*, p. 79.

270 "WITHOUT YOUR THINKING OF IT": *Ibid.*

271 "MORE THAN ANYTHING": *Ibid.*

271 "TRIANGLE LAID IN THE SAHARA": Bowles to Peggy Glanville-Hicks, quoted in Dillon, *A Little Original Sin*, p. 158.

272 WHICH ONE CAN REMAIN: Bowles to James Laughlin (draft), Notebook, HRC.

272 "WANTED TO FORGET": Paul Bowles, *The Sheltering Sky*, p. 14.

272 "WHEN HE WAS STATIONARY": *Ibid.*, p. 105.

272 "WITH KIT . . . INTO THE UNKNOWN": *Ibid.*, p. 105.

273 "FROM THE EXPERIENCE ITSELF": Bowles quoted in Paula Chin, "Stories of Violence," p. 8.

273 "KEEPING THE EVIL OUTSIDE": *Ibid.*, p. 8.

Chapter 20

274 "UNHESITATINGLY REJECTED IT": Bowles, *Without Stopping*, p. 292.

274 "PRODUCED SOMETHING ELSE": *Ibid.*, p. 292.

274 "IN ENGLAND EXCEPT YOURS!": John Lehmann, *The Ample Proposition: Autobiography III* (London: Eyre & Spottiswoode, 1966), p. 82.

274 "WHAT I SAW IN IT": John Lehmann, Untitled memoir, in *Twentieth-Century Literature*, Vol. 32, Nos. 3–4, Fall–Winter 1986, p. 292.

275 DETESTED EACH OTHER: Bowles, Conversation with author, June 18, 1986.

276 THROUGH BOWLES EARLIER THAT YEAR: Dillon, *A Little Original Sin*, pp. 157–58.

276 "NOTHING SEEMS TO MOVE": Jane Bowles to Paul Bowles, undated (August? 1948), HRC. Also in Dillon, ed., *Out in the World: Selected Letters of Jane Bowles*, p. 88.

276 "WHEN I CHOSE TO": Jane Bowles to Paul Bowles, undated (August 1948), HRC. Also in Dillon, ed., *Out in the World: Selected Letters of Jane Bowles*, p. 93.

276 "GET MORE OF IT": Jane Bowles to Paul Bowles, undated (August 1948), HRC. Also in Dillon, ed., *Out in the World: Selected Letters of Jane Bowles*, p. 93.

276 "HOPELESS, HOPELESS SITUATION": Jane Bowles to Paul Bowles, undated (October 1948), HRC. Also in Dillon, ed., *Out in the World: Selected Letters of Jane Bowles*, p. 103.

277   "AN ENEMY OF TETUM": Jane Bowles to Libby Holman, in Dillon, ed., *Out in the World: Selected Letters of Jane Bowles*, p. 132.

277   "FUN AGAIN SOME DAY": *Ibid.*, p. 131.

277   "IDEA WITHOUT YOU, I MEAN": Jane Bowles to Paul Bowles, undated (August? 1948), HRC. Also in Dillon, ed., *Out in the World: Selected Letters of Jane Bowles*, p. 86.

277   "I DON'T EXIST INDEPENDENTLY": *Ibid.*, p. 86.

278   "MUTE ABOUT EVERYTHING": Jane Bowles to Libby Holman in Dillon, ed., *Out in the World: Selected Letters of Jane Bowles*, p. 127.

278   DECIDED ON THE EXACT AMOUNT: Jane Bowles to Paul Bowles, undated (August 1948), HRC. Also in Dillon, ed., *Out in the World: Selected Letters of Jane Bowles*, p. 94.

279   "LETTER BUT YOU DIDN'T": Jane Bowles to Paul Bowles, undated (November 1948), HRC. Also, in a slightly edited version, in Dillon, ed., *Out in the World: Selected Letters of Jane Bowles*, p. 120.

279   "LEFT HIM TO DIE": Bowles, *Without Stopping*, p. 283.

279   "UNTIL IT DISAPPEARED": Paul Bowles, "The Delicate Prey," in *Collected Stories*, p. 170.

280   "THE WRONG IDEA": Williams quoted in Steen, *A Look at Tennessee Williams*, pp. 155–56.

280   "YOU SHOULD PUBLISH IT": *Ibid.*, p. 156.

280   "LIKE AN ELECTRIC VIBRATOR!": Tennessee Williams to Donald Windham, in Windham, ed., *Tennessee Williams' Letters to Donald Windham 1940–1965* (New York: Holt, Rinehart & Winston, 1977), p. 228.

281   "CONFISCATED IT ALL": Bowles quoted in Steen, *A Look at Tennessee Williams*, p. 147.

281   "PREVENT A SERIOUS CRASH": Tennessee Williams to Donald Windham, in Windham, ed., *Tennessee Williams' Letters to Donald Windham 1940–1965*, p. 229.

281   "THEN NO MORE!": Tennessee Williams to Donald Windham, in Windham, ed., *Tennessee Williams' Letters to Donald Windham 1940–1965*, p. 229.

281   "I'M NOT NEUROTIC ANYMORE": Jane Bowles to Katharine Hamill and Natasha von Hoershelman, in Dillon, ed., *Out in the World: Selected Letters of Jane Bowles*, p. 133.

282   "RAILING FOR SEVERAL SECONDS": Bowles, *Without Stopping*, p. 291.

284   "TO KILL HIM. HE DOES": All quotations, pp. 283–84, from Paul Bowles, "Almost All the Apples Are Gone," novel fragment (unpublished) in Notebook, HRC.

284   *"TOURNÉE GASTRONOMIQUE,"* ACCORDING TO BOWLES: Bowles, *Without Stopping*, p. 293.

284   "CONSTITUTED A KIND OF TORTURE": *Ibid.*, p. 294.

285   "ENORMOUS AMOUNT OF GOOD": Jane Bowles to Libby Holman, in Dillon, ed., *Out in the World: Selected Letters of Jane Bowles*, p. 141.

285   "COULD GIVE VERY FUNNY IMITATIONS": John Lehmann, *The Ample Proposition: Autobiography III*, p. 111.

285   "RATHER THAN A TALKER": *Ibid.*, p. 111.

285   "COMPOSER-WHO-ALSO-WRITES-WORDS": Ned Rorem, "Paul Bowles," in *Pure Contraption: A Composer's Essays*, p. 34.

Chapter 21

286   "ALREADY TAKEN A LOSS": Bowles, Conversation with author, June 18, 1986.

286   BEST-SELLER LIST AT NUMBER 15: *New York Times Book Review,* January 1, 1950, p. 8.

287   "REALLY FIRST-RATE WRITER": Tennessee Williams, "An Allegory of Man and His Sahara," in *New York Times Book Review,* December 4, 1949, p. 38.

287   "BEST BOOKS I'VE READ THIS YEAR": William Carlos Williams, "The Best Books I've Read This Year," *Ibid.*, p. 4.

287   "REMARKABLE JOB OF WRITING": "Sex and Sand," in *Time,* December 5, 1949, p. 112.

287   "HIT A FINANCIAL JACKPOT": "Our New Writers," in *Life,* January 30, 1950, p. 35.

288   "SHADE OF GIANT TREES": Paul Bowles, "Taprobane," mss, HRC.

288   RATHER THAN A COLLECTION OF SHORT STORIES: Helen Strauss to Paul Bowles, October 12, 1950, HRC.

289   "CLIFFS AND BEGAN THERE": Bowles quoted in Halpern, "Interview with Bowles," p. 162.

289   "MELODRAMATIC TO GO ON WITH IT": Bowles quoted in Richard F. Patteson, "Paul Bowles: Two Unfinished Projects," *Library Chronicle of the University of Texas at Austin,* New Series, No. 30, 1985, p. 60.

290   "NOTHING CHANGES EVERYTHING": Bowles, Notebook, HRC.

290   "WORK ON IT LATER ON": Paul Bowles, "Introduction: Thirty Years Later," *Let It Come Down* (Santa Barbara, Calif.: Black Sparrow Press, 1980), pp. 7–8.

291   "SONG IN THE AIR": Bowles, Notebook, HRC.

291   "PLANTED FOR SHADE": Paul Bowles, "From Notes Taken in Ceylon," in Themistocles Hoetis, ed., *Zero Anthology* (New York: Zero Press, 1956), p. 112.

291   "A LITTLE FRIGHTENING": Paul Bowles, "Notes on a Visit to India," in *Harper's Magazine,* July, 1957, p. 71.

292   PIANO IN THE FIRST PLACE: Bowles, *Without Stopping,* p. 303.

292   WOULD INDEED GO ON BEYOND WESTPORT: Jane Bowles to Libby Holman, in Dillon, ed., *Out in the World: Selected Letters of Jane Bowles,* pp. 157–59.

293   "SEEMED TO BE AT LOOSE ENDS": Bowles, *Without Stopping,* p. 304.

293   "AT THAT PARTICULAR TIME": Brion Gysin, quoted in Terry Wilson, "Here to Go: Planet R-101," *Re/Search #4/5,* 1982, p. 46.

293   WORK ON *LET IT COME DOWN:* Bowles, *Without Stopping,* p. 310.

294   "PARAPHRASING THE KORAN": Paul Bowles, *Gallery Announcement for Ahmed Yacoubi Exhibit* (New York: Amici Gallery, 1964), p. 4.

294   "FROM HIS FAMILY": Bowles, Notebook, HRC.

295   IN THE EARLY 1950s: On sexual component of Bowles's relationship with Yacoubi: Tennessee Williams, in Windham, ed., *Tennessee Williams' Letters to Donald Windham 1940–1965,* p. 281. Thomson, Conversation with author, March 6, 1986. Edouard Roditi, Conversation with author, April 30, 1987. William Burroughs, conversation with author, April 28, 1987.

295   "THOUGHT TO BE DOING SOMETHING": David Herbert, *Second Son* (London: Peter Owen, 1972), p. 124.

295   "ANYTHING TOO, FOR THAT MATTER": Bowles, *Let It Come Down,* p. 26.

295   "COLONIAL LIFE IN MOROCCO": Bowles, *Without Stopping,* p. 305.

296   "SHORT FICTION—'A DISTANT EPISODE' ": Tennessee Williams, "The Human Psyche—Alone," in *Saturday Review of Literature,* December 23, 1950, p. 20.

296   "BEST OF FITZGERALD HAS UNTIL YOURS": Alice B. Toklas to Bowles, in Edward Burns, ed., *Staying on Alone: Letters of Alice B. Toklas* (New York: Liveright, 1973), pp. 188–89.

296   "IS NOT TO MY TASTE": Alice B. Toklas to Bowles, December 7, 1950, HRC.

297   "IS ANYONE'S GUESS": Bowles to Peggy Glanville-Hicks, quoted in Dillon, *A Little Original Sin,* p. 212.

297   "CONTINUE BEING AN ARTIST": Bowles, Undated fragment, HRC.

297   "BECOME ENGROSSED IN": Paul Bowles to Rena Bowles, July 26, 1951, HRC.

298   "WITHDRAWAL IS LOGICAL": Tennessee Williams, "The Human Psyche—Alone," in *Saturday Review of Literature,* December 23, 1950, p. 19.

299   "CAVERN OF HIMSELF": *Ibid.,* p. 19.

299   "CRACKS ABOVE YOUR HEAD": Bowles quoted in Harvey Breit, "Talk with Paul Bowles," in *New York Times Book Review,* March 9, 1952, p. 18.

299   "YOU CAN AFFORD IT": Bowles, *Without Stopping,* p. 307.

300   SERVICE AS A CHAUFFEUR: *Ibid.,* pp. 307–8.

Chapter 22

301   TO WORK IN PEACE: Paul Bowles to Rena Bowles, July 26, 1951, HRC.

301   THE FINAL SECTION "WRITE ITSELF": Bowles, Conversation with author and J. Raskin, July 7, 1985.

301   "SUPPLYING ANY CONSCIOUS DIRECTION": Paul Bowles, "Introduction: Thirty Years Later," *Let It Come Down* (Santa Barbara, Calif.: Black Sparrow Press, 1980), p. 8.

301   "END OF THE BOOK": *Ibid.,* p. 8.

301   "GAINED ON HIM CONSTANTLY": Bowles, *Let It Come Down,* p. 21.

302   "ANY LIFE WOULD BE BETTER": *Ibid.,* p. 21.

302   "GIVE YOU ANY PURPOSE": *Ibid.,* p. 34.

302   "VICTIM INTO A WINNER": *Ibid.,* p. 169.

303   "AND I'VE GOT IT": *Ibid.,* p. 195.

303   " 'MERRY MABEL DUNE' ": *Ibid.,* p. 284.

303   "SECURITY IS A FALSE CONCEPT": Bowles quoted in Halpern, "Interview with Bowles," p. 165.

303   "DETERMINED LARGELY BY ITS INHABITANTS": Paul Bowles, "Tangier," in *Gentlemen's Quarterly,* October 1953, p. 54.

304   "SITUATION AT THE END": Bowles quoted in Evans, "Interview with Bowles," p. 11.

304   "HE'S HIS OWN VICTIM": Bowles, Conversation with author and J. Raskin, July 7, 1985.

304   " 'TO A WORK OF ART' ": Leonard Amster, "In No Country," in *Saturday Review of Literature,* May 5, 1952, p. 18.

304   "OF BOWLES'S SHORT STORIES": Robert Gorham Davis, "A Relentless Drive Toward Doom," in *New York Times Book Review,* March 2, 1952, p. 1.

305   "SPYING FOR INTERNATIONAL": Bowles, Conversation with author, August 26, 1987.

306   "YEARS SINCE CHILDHOOD": Bowles, "Taprobane," mss, HRC.

306   "IT WAS MEANINGLESS": Bowles quoted in Bailey, "The Art of Fiction LXVII," p. 79.

306   "WIRE MONEY IMMEDIATELY": Bowles, "Taprobane," mss., HRC.

307   "WERE ALL MINE": *Ibid.*

307   "TYPED PICNIC RECIPES": Kenward Elmslie, Conversation with author, September 1, 1988.

308   SHIP CROSSING THE ATLANTIC: On the Bowles-Holman-Yacoubi incident, Jon Bradshaw, *Dreams That Money Can Buy: The Tragic Life of Libby Holman,* pp. 311–13.

309   "DO A GOOD JOB ON THE FILM": Tennessee Williams, in Windham, ed., *Tennessee Williams' Letters to Donald Windham 1940–1965*, pp. 281–83.

309   "WHICH HE DID": Bowles to Andreas Brown, January 3, 1966, HRC.

310   "MASTER AT BARGAINING": Bowles, "A Man Must Not Be Very Moslem," in *Their Heads Are Green*, pp. 60–61.

310   "GETTING TO KNOW US": Bowles quoted in Breit, "Talk with Paul Bowles," in *New York Times Book Review*, March 9, 1952, p. 18.

311   "ASSEMBLED ON A STAGE": Harvey Taylor, in Detroit *Times*, May 24, 1953.

312   JANE REWRITE HER PART: Dillon, *A Little Original Sin*, p. 231.

312   "IN A POETIC STYLE": Brooks Atkinson, "At the Theater," in *New York Times*, December 30, 1953, p. 17.

312   "REFRESHINGLY BITTER BEVERAGE": Truman Capote, "Introduction," in Jane Bowles, *My Sister's Hand in Mine: The Collected Works of Jane Bowles*, p. viii.

312   "REACH MORE PEOPLE": Jane Bowles quoted in "Confessions of an Honest Playwright," in *Vogue*, May 1, 1954, p. 137.

313   "HER HAPPY PRONOUNCEMENT": Walter Kerr, *Pieces of Eight* (New York: E.P. Dutton, 1968), p. 156.

Chapter 23

314   FROM HER ARDENT SUITOR: Jane Bowles to Katharine Hamill and Natasha von Hoershelman, in Dillon, ed., *Out in the World: Selected Letters of Jane Bowles*, pp. 170–81.

314   "WE ARE ALL WOMEN": *Ibid.*, p. 179.

315   "WENT BACK TO BED": Bowles, "William Burroughs in Tangier," unpublished memoir, Personal collection, Bradford Morrow.

315   "WITH THAT GROUP. I WASN'T": Burroughs, Conversation with author, April 28, 1987.

315   "WENT OUR RESPECTIVE WAYS": Bowles, "William Burroughs in Tangier," unpublished memoir Personal collection, Bradford Morrow.

316   CARS, AND TANKS ROARED BY: Bowles, *Without Stopping*, p. 323.

316   "IN THE TWENTIETH CENTURY": Paul Bowles, "Preface," in *The Spider's House* (Santa Barbara, Calif.: Black Sparrow Press, 1982), p. i.

316   "ABOUT ITS DISSOLUTION": *Ibid.*, p. i.

316   "PROCESS OF VIOLENT TRANSFORMATION": *Ibid.*, p. i.

317   "CAN NEVER MAKE ANYTHING": Bowles to Oliver Evans, August 24, 1954, HRC.

317 "IN PLACES I LOVE": Bowles to Rena and Claude Bowles, October 11, 1954, HRC.

317 DENOUNCED YACOUBI TO BOWLES: Dillon, *A Little Original Sin,* pp. 255–56.

318 "KINDNESS IN HIS CHARACTER": Richard Rumbold, *A Message in Code: The Diary of Richard Rumbold 1932–60,* ed. William Plomer (London: Weidenfeld & Nicolson, 1964), p. 156.

318 "AND DIVE WITH HER": *Ibid.,* pp. 156–57.

318 "NEVER GET *ME* THERE": Bowles, "Taprobane," mss., HRC.

318 ALSO WORRIED HER: Bowles, *Without Stopping,* p. 325.

318 "SUFFERED IN COMPARATIVE SILENCE": Bowles, "Taprobane," mss., HRC.

319 "THAT AND WITH AHMED": Peggy Guggenheim quoted in Dillon, *A Little Original Sin,* p. 262.

319 "I WOULDN'T BE AFRAID": Bowles, Notebook, HRC.

320 "THINKS HE CAN WORK": *Ibid.*

321 "WITH HIM AT SUCH MOMENTS": *Ibid.*

321 "GOT HEAVY FOR ME": Bowles quoted in Lawrence Stewart, "Paul Bowles: Up Above the World So High," in *Mystery and Detection Annual,* p. 260.

321 "RUDIMENTARY SHOCK TREATMENT": Bowles, "Taprobane," mss., HRC.

322 "FULL DRAMATIC EFFECT": *Ibid.*

322 "UP TO YOUR UNCONSCIOUS": Richard Rumbold, *A Message in Code: The Diary of Richard Rumbold 1932–60,* ed. William Plomer, pp. 171–72.

322 "CONTEMPLATION AND INACTION": Bowles, "A Man Must Not Be Very Moslem," in *Their Heads Are Green,* pp. 71–72.

Chapter 24

323 "IF THEY BUT KNEW": Bowles, Epigraph to *The Spider's House* (New York: Random House, 1955; reprinted Santa Barbara, Calif.: Black Sparrow Press, 1982), n.p.

323 PALAIS JAMAI, WHERE BOWLES OFTEN STAYED: Bowles, Conversation with author, June 20, 1986.

324 "FULL OF POVERTY AND HATRED": Bowles, *The Spider's House,* p. 188.

324 "SAVE A PLACE IN THE RANKS": *Ibid.,* p. 252.

324 TO ENTERTAIN MORE READERS: Lawrence D. Stewart, *Paul Bowles: The Illumination of North Africa* (Carbondale: Southern Illinois University Press, 1974), p. 161.

324   "FOREIGNERS HE HAD SEEN": *Ibid.,* pp. 137–38.

325   "CERTAINLY NOT I": Bowles, Conversation with author and J. Raskin, July 7, 1985.

325   "IN A SPLIT SECOND": Bowles, *The Spider's House,* p. 167.

325   "INVOLVED IN EXISTENCE": *Ibid.,* p. 203.

326   "BECOME ABSURD AND UNREAL": *Ibid.,* pp. 195–96.

326   "ARE THE MOST TO BE DREADED": Bowles, "Preface" in *The Spider's House* (Santa Barbara, Calif.: Black Sparrow Press), p. ii.

326   "FREQUENTLY WITH BEAUTY": William Peden, "French Islam," in *Saturday Review,* November 5, 1955, p. 18.

327   OF THE PHOTOS IN BOOK FORM: Bowles, *Without Stopping,* p. 330.

327   "TAKE PLACE BEFORE OUR EYES": Paul Bowles, *Yallah* (New York: McDowell, Obolensky, 1957), p. 17.

328   "ONE'S OWN DAILY LIFE": Bowles to Thomson, November 22, 1955, Yale.

328   "BURST FROM INTERNAL PRESSURES": Bowles, *Without Stopping,* p. 331.

328   "VERY MUCH WORTH KNOWING": Bowles, "William Burroughs in Tangier," unpublished memoir, Personal collection, Bradford Morrow.

329   "GIVE A DAMN ABOUT IT": Bowles, "Burroughs in Tangier," in *Big Table,* No. 2, Summer 1959, p. 42.

329   "UNDERFOOT MONTH AFTER MONTH": Bowles, Conversation with author and J. Raskin, July 7, 1985.

329   "A SPECIAL OCCURRENCE": Burroughs, Conversation with author, April 28, 1987.

329   "HE HAD JUST READ": Bowles, "Burroughs in Tangier," in *Big Table,* p. 43.

329   "WOULD APPRECIATE THE OTHER": Bowles, Conversation with author, January 16, 1987.

329   "MY GETTING TO KNOW HIM": Burroughs, Conversation with author, April 28, 1987.

329   "ONLY GOOD ONE IN TOWN": Bowles quoted in Dery, "Talking with a Stranger: Paul Bowles Interviewed in Tangier, Morocco."

329   "GYSIN WENT MAD ABOUT IT": *Ibid.*

330   LEGAL TRANSFER TO BE COMPLETED: Paul Bowles to Jane Bowles, March 25, 1956, HRC.

330   "WHERE THEY ARE NOT WANTED": Bowles, "View from Tangier: The Spreading Arab Tide," in *The Nation,* June 30, 1956, p. 549.

331   THE VISIT WENT WELL: Bowles, Conversation with author, August 24, 1987.

331   MUCH PREFERRED WHISKEY: *Ibid.*

332 " 'IS THAT ALL YOU WISH TO KNOW?' ": Paul Bowles to Jane Bowles, undated (December? 1956), HRC.

332 "SHALL HAVE NO MONEY": Paul Bowles to Jane Bowles, January 11, 12, 1957, HRC.

332 "AFFORD NOT TO, REALLY": Paul Bowles to Jane Bowles, March 2, 1957, HRC.

332 "USELESS AS I DID": Paul Bowles to Jane Bowles, March 18, 1957, HRC.

333 GORDON SAGER AND A DOCTOR: On Jane's stroke, Dillon, *A Little Original Sin*, pp. 285–86. Dery, "Talking with a Stranger: Paul Bowles Interviewed in Tangier, Morocco." Bowles to Thomson, August 31, 1957, Yale. Bowles, Conversation with author, August 27, 1987.

334 " 'PIPES OF KIF, I DON'T KNOW' ": Bowles quoted in Dery, "Talking with a Stranger: Paul Bowles Interviewed in Tangier, Morocco."

334 "BEEN A TERRIBLE SHOCK": Bowles to Thomson, August 31, 1957, Yale.

334 TRIED TO POISON HER: This rumor still persists among many in Tangier. Several of the long-term residents expressed this opinion to the author in the course of conversations in 1986 and 1987.

334 "DRANK HERSELF INTO A STROKE": Roditi, Conversation with author, April 30, 1987.

334 "CAUGHT UP WITH HER": Johnson, Conversation with author, March 6, 1986.

335 $25 A MONTH TO HELP WITH EXPENSES: On financial assistance, Bowles to Thomson, August 31, 1957, Yale. Dillon, *A Little Original Sin*, p. 289.

335 "ABOUT JANIE'S STATE": Thomson to Bowles, August 3, 1957, Yale.

335 "TWO EPILEPTIFORM ATTACKS": Bowles to Thomson, August 31, 1957, Yale.

335 "LESS CONSTANTLY SINCE THEN": *Ibid.*

335 "SUICIDE IS THE ONLY SOLUTION": *Ibid.*

336 "AMNESIA AND COMPLETE HYSTERIA": *Ibid.*

336 "HURLING THEM ACROSS THE ROOM": Bowles to Thomson, September 10, 1957, Yale.

336 "PERHAPS THE WORST PART": *Ibid.*

336 "GOOD YEARS WERE OVER": Bowles, *Without Stopping*, p. 336.

PART VI: THINGS GONE AND THINGS STILL HERE

Chapter 25

339 "THE MATTER WITH HER": Bowles to Thomson, October 2, 1957, Yale.

339 "SHORTEST POSSIBLE TIME": *Ibid.*

339 "HOPE OF BEING SUCCESSFUL": *Ibid.*

339 "SAME WITH ALMOST EVERYONE": Bowles, Notebook, HRC.

340 "CAN ONE MERIT ANYTHING?": Bowles, Draft letter to Irving [Rosenthal?] in Notebook, HRC.

340 TEMPERATURE REGISTERED 98.6: Bowles to author, June 20, 1986.

340 JUDGED FIT TO RETURN TO TANGIER: Bowles to Thomson, November 11, 1957.

340 WILLIAM HEINEMANN: Bowles, *Without Stopping,* p. 339.

341 "WENT TO THE POLICE": Burroughs, Conversation with author, April 28, 1987.

341 "ASSAULT WITH INTENT TO KILL": Unknown author (Bowles?), Fragment detailing chronologically the entire Yacoubi affair, HRC.

341 CALLED IN FOR QUESTIONING: *Ibid.*

341 SUPPORTIVE OF INDEPENDENCE: Bowles, Conversation with author, August 25, 1987.

342 "YOUR RETURNING HERE": Ney Bensadon to Bowles, February 24, 1958 (in French), HRC. The letter reads in the original: "Le seul point qui figure . . . est l'état et la nature de vos relations avec Monsieur Yacoubi, et c'est à ce propos que l'on désirait vous interroger, voire vous inculper. Un de vos concitoyens du nom de Murray a été inculpé pour un fait similaire, et a quitté précipitamment Tanger. . . . En tous cas, jusqu'à la fin de l'affaire Yacoubi, il n'est pas question que vous retourniez ici."

342 CHERIFA WAS JANE'S MAID: Christopher Wanklyn to Jane Bowles, March 21, 1958, HRC.

342 WENT TO GERMANY TO WORK: Bowles, Conversation with author, August 25, 1987.

343 TO SORT IT OUT: Bowles, *Without Stopping,* p. 339.

343 LESS THAN FIVE MINUTES: Francis Bacon to Paul Bowles, May 14, 1958, HRC.

344 FEARS WERE RAMPANT: *Ibid.*

344 "3 AND 6 MAKE NOTHING. I CANNOT": Jane Bowles, undated fragment, HRC.

345 "AS THE SHOW WENT ON": Quoted in Bradshaw, *Dreams That Money Can Buy: The Tragic Life of Libby Holman,* p. 329.

345 WHEN HE HAD BEGUN THE OPERA: Bowles, Conversation with author, January 14, 1987.

345 WHITE PLAINS, NEW YORK: Dillon, *A Little Original Sin,* p. 315.

345 INTRODUCING ROREM AND BOWLES TO MESCALINE: Ned Rorem, *The New York Diary of Ned Rorem* (New York: George Braziller, 1967), p. 161.

345 "A NECESSARY OPERATION": Ned Rorem, *The New York Diary of Ned Rorem,* p. 161.

346 "FACE ALL MOLARS": *Ibid.,* p. 163.

346 "ESPECIALLY AFTER NIGHTFALL": *Ibid.,* p. 164.

347 "THEIR BEST PERFORMING EFFORTS": Bowles letter to Harold Spivacke, quoted in toto in Spivacke to John Marshall, October 17, 1958, HRC.

347 "SHE WAS JITTERY": Bowles to Thomson, December 27, 1958, Yale.

348 "SINCE THE STROKE": *Ibid.*

348 HAD TURNED AGAINST BOWLES: Tennessee Williams to Bowles, undated (1958?), HRC.

348 "MUSIC OF EXQUISITE TEXTURE": Brooks Atkinson, "Sweet Bird of Youth," in *New York Times,* March 11, 1959, p. 39.

349 QUICKLY AND IN A HUFF: On Ginsberg and the Russians, Bowles, *Without Stopping,* pp. 343–44.

350 THE CORRECT VOLTAGE: For a detailed account of the trip, see Bowles, "The Rif, to Music" in *Their Heads Are Green,* pp. 83–127.

350 "CONTINUE MY WORK": *Ibid.,* p. 85.

350 "MUSICS OF SOUTHEASTERN MOROCCO": *Ibid.,* p. 86.

350 FOLK MUSIC IS "DEGENERATE": Bowles, Conversation with author, June 20, 1986.

Chapter 26

352 "HEALTHY AND WELL": Paul Bowles to Claude and Rena Bowles, January 9, 1960, HRC.

352 "HAVE BEEN HERE LONG ENOUGH!": *Ibid.*

353 "FOR BETTER CLIMES": Paul Bowles to Claude and Rena Bowles, April 19 [1960], HRC.

354 "LOOKED FORWARD TO DOING IT": Paul Bowles to Claude and Rena Bowles, May 2 [1960], HRC.

354 "THERE IS THE SAHARA": Bowles to Evans, December 29, 1960, HRC.

355   "MIRROR AS IT WERE": Bowles, Notebook, HRC. When Lawrence
      Stewart (*Paul Bowles: The Illumination of North Africa,* p. 151) asked
      Bowles about this notebook entry, Bowles told him that this was
      intended to be made into a journal entry for "Pages from Cold
      Point." Based on the surrounding material in the notebook, how-
      ever, which all dates from the mid-1950s, it seems unlikely that this
      was the case.

356   "TO BE THROWN OUT": Burroughs, Conversation with author, April
      28, 1978.

356   "PUBLICATIONS FROM HERE": Paul Bowles to Claude and Rena
      Bowles, June 12 [1961?], HRC.

356   " 'JUST A LOT OF COLD' ": Bowles quoted in Dery, "Talking to a
      Stranger: Paul Bowles Interviewed in Tangier, Morocco."

356   "JUST WASN'T INTERESTED": Burroughs, Conversation with author,
      April 28, 1978.

357   "KNEW WHO PAUL WAS": *Ibid.*

357   "UNDER YOUR AEGIS": Bowles to Lawrence Ferlinghetti, December
      11, 1961, Bancroft Library, University of California, Berkeley
      (Berkeley).

358   "OF THAT KIND, NATURALLY": Bowles to Ferlinghetti, December 28,
      1961, Berkeley.

358   "SUBJECTIVE EFFECTS OF IT": Bowles to Ferlinghetti, January 12,
      1962, Berkeley.

358   "A WAY OUT OF THE PHENOMENOLOGICAL WORLD": Bowles, Conver-
      sation with author, July 7, 1985.

358   "REQUIREMENTS OF THE INDIVIDUAL": Bowles (A note on mode of
      composition, in inside cover of record sleeve), in *Paul Bowles Reads
      a Hundred Camels in the Courtyard* (Santa Barbara, Calif.: Cadmus
      Editions, 1981), phonodisc. Published as "Preface," *A Hundred
      Camels in the Courtyard* (San Francisco: City Lights, 2nd ed., 1986),
      p. ix.

359   "INTO SYMBIOTIC RELATIONSHIPS": *Ibid.,* p. ix.

359   "PURPOSE OF ORACULAR CONSULTATION": *Ibid.,* p. ix.

359   "AND OF NO INTEREST": Gore Vidal, "Introduction" in Paul Bowles,
      Collected Stories 1939–1976, p. 11.

359   "FOR FORTY YEARS": Bowles quoted in Miflin, "Through a Colored
      Lens: Paul Bowles Talks About His Dreams."

360   "SENSE OF PARTICIPATION": Bowles, "A Man Must Not Be Very
      Moslem," in *Their Heads Are Green,* p. 71.

360   "CONTEMPLATION AND INACTION": *Ibid.,* p. 72.

360   "STATUS QUO OF ORGANIZED SOCIETY": Bowles, "Kif—Prologue and
      Compendium of Terms," in *Kulchur,* No. 3, 1961, p. 36.

361 "TRADITION ISN'T STRONG ENOUGH": Bowles, Conversation with author and J. Raskin, July 7, 1985.

361 WHEN WORKING ON *THE SHELTERING SKY:* Bowles, Conversation with author, June 20, 1986.

361 "PALMWOOD AND ANIMAL SKINS": Bowles, "The Time of Friendship," in *Collected Stories 1939–1976,* p. 337.

362 "AN EARLY CASUALTY": *Ibid.,* p. 361.

362 TOLD TO HIM IN MAGHREBI: Bowles, Conversation with author, June 19, 1986.

363 "IF IT WERE REALLY GOOD": Bowles, "Introduction" in Driss Ben Hamed Charhadi (Larbi Layachi), *A Life Full of Holes,* trans. Paul Bowles (New York: Grove Press, 1964; reprinted, 1966), p. 8.

363 "OF IT FOR WEEKS": *Ibid.,* p. 8.

363 "DELETED OR ALTERED": *Ibid.,* p. 8.

363 CONSIDER GIVING GROVE THE COMPLETED WORK: Bowles, Conversation with author, June 19, 1986.

364 INGRAM-MERRILL FOUNDATION FOR A NEW PLAY: Paul Bowles to Claude and Rena Bowles, January 17 [1962], HRC.

364 AUNT BIRDIE, WHO HAD RECENTLY DIED: *Ibid.*

Chapter 27

365 COLLECTION OF TRAVEL ESSAYS: Bowles, *Without Stopping,* p. 351.

366 "MORE BARREN CALIFORNIA": Bowles, "Foreword," in *Their Heads Are Green,* p. vii.

367 "THE BOOK IS PUBLISHED": Paul Bowles to Jane Bowles, undated (December 1962), HRC.

367 GET SOME WRITING DONE: Paul Bowles to Jane Bowles, December 5 [1962], HRC.

367 "THING GETS ON PAPER": *Ibid.*

368 "THERE FOR A SHORT WHILE": Paul Bowles to Jane Bowles, December 11 [1962], HRC.

368 "ON HER NEW PLAY": Paul Bowles to Claude and Rena Bowles, January 29, 1963, HRC.

368 THROUGH BOWLES'S INVITATION: The account of the Chester-Bowles imbroglio is drawn largely from Norman Glass, "The Decline and Fall of Arthur Chester," in *Paris Review,* Vol. 18, No. 71, 1977, pp. 89–125. Other incidental information obtained from Burroughs, Conversation with author, April 28, 1987. Roditi, Conversation with author, April 30, 1987. And Alfred Chester letters, Personal collection, Edward Field.

369   "THE PLACE UP, OBVIOUSLY": Paul Bowles to Ira Cohen, undated (fall 1963), Personal collection, Edward Field.

370   "WITH KIF AND WITHOUT WATER": Irving Rosenthal, quoted in Alfred Chester to Edward Field, February 28, 1964, Private collection Edward Field.

370   "NO RIGHT TO BE JUDGES": *Ibid.*

370   ABANDONED THE SCHEME: Alfred Chester to Norman Glass, May 3, 1964, Private collection Edward Field.

371   "MORE EXACTLY A LOCAL DEMON": Chester quoted in Glass, "The Decline and Fall of Arthur Chester," p. 101.

371   "MAGIC FATHER": Alfred Chester, *The Foot* in Ted Solotaroff, ed., *New American Review,* No. 9, 1970, p. 19.

371   "COPY I HAVE BELONGS TO ALFRED": Bowles to Andreas Brown, October 15, 1965, HRC.

374   "IF YOU SEE YOU": Bowles to Ned Rorem, August 27, 1963, Personal collection, Rorem.

374   "TOP OF A CLIFF": Bowles, Conversation with author and J. Raskin, July 7, 1985.

374   "BREATHING IN THE EUCALYPTUS": *Ibid.*

374   "ABOUT BEATNIKS, DECIDEDLY LIGHT": Paul Bowles to Rena Bowles, November 23, 1965, HRC.

375   "LOOKING STRAIGHT AHEAD": Bowles, *Up Above the World* (New York: Simon & Schuster, 1966; reprinted New York: The Ecco Press, 1982), p. 40.

376   AS A *SOTIE,* AFTER GIDE: Bowles, Conversation with author, June 20, 1986.

377   "BUT REWRITING AS I GO": Paul Bowles to Rena Bowles, October 18, 1964, HRC.

377   FINISHED REWORKING THE BOOK: Paul Bowles to Claude and Rena Bowles, December 12, 1964, HRC.

378   "LIBERTY TO DO IT, I SUPPOSE": *Ibid.*

378   HE WOULD BE ARRESTED: Bowles, Conversation with author, August 24, 1987. Bowles to Andreas Brown, January 3, 1966, HRC.

378   VISIT HIM THERE: Paul Bowles to Claude and Rena Bowles, May 17, 1965, HRC.

378   "EVERYONE IS SURE": Paul Bowles to Claude and Rena Bowles, May 6, 1965, HRC.

378   "TO GET A GENERAL IDEA": Paul Bowles to Claude and Rena Bowles, May 17, 1965, HRC.

379   "OUT OF MY EFFORTS": Paul Bowles to Claude and Rena Bowles, May 31, 1965, HRC.

Chapter 28

380 "THEY CALL 'BIG HOUSES' ": Paul Bowles to Rena Bowles, July 29, 1965, HRC.

380 "CAN'T EVEN SIGN HIS NAME": Mohammed Mrabet, *Look and Move On*, trans. Paul Bowles (Santa Barbara, Calif.: Black Sparrow Press, 1976), p. 90.

380 "HAD ACTUALLY HAPPENED TO ME": *Ibid.*, p. 91.

381 "UNTIL I FINISHED THE BOOK": Mrabet quoted in Daniel Halpern, "Mohammed Mrabet Talking to Daniel Halpern" (Interview in Spanish, trans. Paul Bowles), in *Transatlantic Review 39*, Spring 1971, p. 127.

382 SO CLOSE AS IT HAD BEEN: Bowles and Mrabet, Conversation with author (in Spanish), August 26, 1987.

382 "SEE WHAT A SON-OF-A-BITCH HE IS!": *Ibid.*

383 TO HIS OWN APARTMENT: *Ibid.*

383 "APPALLED BY HER THAN BEFORE": Bowles to Brown, October 15, 1965, HRC.

383 "OPINIONATED AND DECISIVE": Roditi, Conversation with author, April 30, 1987.

383 LITERATURE, ART, AND RELIGION: Johnson, Conversation with author, May 6, 1986.

383 "TO GET RID OF HER": Roditi, Conversation with author, April 30, 1987.

384 "PHENOMENON OF LITERARY OSMOSIS": Roditi, "The Fiction of Jane Bowles as a Form of Exorcism."

384 "GOOD FOR PAUL, BUT NOT FOR ME": Jane Bowles, "Jane Bowles," in Wakeman, ed., *World Authors 1950–1970*, p. 203.

384 "AS MUCH AS I DID": Bowles quoted in Bailey, "The Art of Fiction LXVII: Paul Bowles," p. 88.

385 WAS *PLAIN PLEASURES* MADE POSSIBLE: Bowles, *Without Stopping*, pp. 356–57. Bowles to Thomson, June 21, 1965, Yale.

385 " 'FROM ITS BEING MORAL' ": Jane Bowles, "The Iron Table," in *My Sister's Hand in Mine: The Collected Works of Jane Bowles*, pp. 466–67. I am indebted to Edouard Roditi for pointing out the similarity in style and substance between this fictional dialogue and dialogues typical of the Bowleses during this period.

386 "IDEA OF BEING MRS. BOWLES": Johnson, Conversation with author, March 6, 1986.

387 "WHEN IT COMES OUT": Paul Bowles to Rena Bowles, February 21 [1966], HRC.

387   "MAKE THE LOSS SEEM IRRELEVANT": Webster Schott, in *New York Times Book Review,* March 20, 1966.

387   "IS AN ANTI-CLIMAX": Conrad Knickerbocker, "Books of the Times," in *New York Times,* March 12, 1966, p. 25.

388   "LATIN-AMERICAN HOTEL ROOMS": in *New Yorker,* July 9, 1966, p. 90.

388   "SEEMS TO ME GOOD PAY": Paul Bowles to Rena Bowles, February 21 [1966], HRC.

388   "EXCISED THEM FROM MY LIFE": Bowles, *Without Stopping,* p. 359.

388   "NATURALLY FELT GUILTY": Roditi, Conversation with author, April 30, 1987.

389   "SHIP THROUGH THE CANAL": Bowles to Thomson, June 15, 1966, Yale.

389   "NEW YORK TO BANGKOK": Bowles to Andreas Brown, June 15, 1966, HRC.

389   "TAKE CARE OF THE HOUSE": Bowles to James Purdy, May 3, 1967, HRC.

389   BACK TO TANGIER IN LATE AUGUST: Jane Bowles to Gordon Sager, undated (July–August 1966) in Dillon, ed., *Out in the World: Selected Letters of Jane Bowles,* pp. 283–84.

390   WAS IN PAIN WHENEVER HE MOVED IT: Bowles to Andreas Brown, January 4, 1967.

390   "FULL OF HUNGLY LATS": Bowles to Thomson, October 2, 1966, Yale.

391   " 'DRIVER TO HEAR HIM' ": Bowles, "You Have Left Your Lotus Pods on the Bus," in *Collected Stories 1939–1976,* p. 399.

391   "TO TANGIER IN JANUARY": Bowles to Evans, November 29, 1966, HRC.

391   "GOES INTO A TAILSPIN": Bowles to Brown, January 18, 1967, HRC.

392   "IF ONLY IN GETTING OUT": Bowles to Thomson, April 27, 1967, Yale.

392   "IT WAS ALL VERY UNFAIR": Roditi, Conversation with author, April 30, 1987.

392   " 'OF DEAD JANE BOWLES' ": David Herbert, *Second Son,* p. 127.

392   "COMPOSE, OR ACCOMPLISH ANYTHING": *Ibid.,* p. 126.

392   "WHICH REQUIRES TRUE CONCENTRATION": Bowles to Evans, April 11, 1967, HRC.

393   AND THEIR DISTRIBUTION PREVENTED: Bowles to Brown, June 9, 1967, HRC.

393   "NO PEER IN HIS SULLEN ART": "Specialist in Melancholy," in *Time,* August 4, 1967, p. E-3.

393   "WITH THE CHILDREN OF HIS IMAGINATION": Melvin Maddox, "Brilliant Hobbyist of Modern Infernos," in *Life,* July 21, 1967, p. 8.

393 "SOMETHING MORE FROM LITERATURE": Bernard Bergonzi, "Not Long Enough," in *New York Review of Books,* November 9, 1967, p. 33.

393 "DEAL SIMULTANEOUSLY WITH TWO CULTURES": John Gray, "Indefinite Futures," in *Books and Bookmen,* June 1968, p. 34.

393 HAD "WORN THIN": Maureen Howard, in *Partisan Review,* Winter 1968, p. 149.

394 IN JAMES MICHENER'S *THE SOURCE: The Bowker Annual of Library and Book Trade Information* (New York & London: R. R. Bowker, 1967), p. 134.

394 "BECAUSE I LIKE IT BETTER": Bowles, Conversation with author and J. Raskin, July 7, 1985.

395 "I'M STILL HERE": *Ibid.*

PART VII: THE HISS OF TIME

Chapter 29

399 "CAN TAKE CARE OF HER": Bowles to Evans, April 11, 1967, HRC.

399 "CAN'T GET WELL WITHOUT IT": Bowles to Thomson, May 1, 1967, Yale.

400 "WHEN I GO TO TAKE THE PLANT": Mrabet and Bowles, Conversation with author (in Spanish), August 25, 1987.

400 ROOTS WRAPPED AROUND IT: *Ibid.*

400 "PLANT WAS HER PROTECTION": Bowles quoted in Dery, "Talking to a Stranger: Paul Bowles Interviewed in Tangier, Morocco."

400 "VARIOUS OTHER THINGS": *Ibid.*

400 "SO ILL SHE DIDN'T CARE": *Ibid.*

401 "FROM DOING MUCH OF ANYTHING": Bowles to Evans, November 13, 1967, HRC.

401 "IDEA OF GOING THERE DOES INTEREST ME": *Ibid.*

401 "HOW TO WRITE MY OWN MATERIAL?": Bowles to Evans, August 15, 1967, HRC.

401 "FUNCTIONING OF A WRITER": Bowles to Evans, January 8, 1968, HRC.

401 "I DON'T KNOW THE BOOKS": *Ibid.*

402 "IT WON'T BE ENOUGH": Bowles to Evans, February 5, 1968, HRC.

402 TO PAWN JANE OFF ON THEM: Mrabet and Bowles, Conversation with author (in Spanish), August 25, 1987. For a slightly fictionalized account of the incident, see Mohammed Mrabet, "What Happened

in Granada," in *The Boy Who Set the Fire,* trans. Paul Bowles (Santa Barbara, Calif.: Black Sparrow Press, 1974), pp. 28–40.

403   "DOES ONE INTERPRET?": Bowles to Evans, May 15, 1968, HRC.

403   *THE BLOOD OF OTHERS:* Bowles to Evans, May 23, 1968, HRC.

403   "WHEREAS MY INCOME DOESN'T": Bowles to Thomson, August 5, 1968, Yale.

403   "THAT'S WHAT MATTERS": Bowles to Thomson, November 26, 1968, Yale.

403   "LOS ANGELES NO!": *Ibid.*

404   WITHIN A COUPLE OF DAYS FOR TANGIER: On Williams and the post-party arrest, Bowles and Mrabet, Conversation with author, August 25, 1987. All quotes and similar account in Dery, "Talking to a Stranger: Paul Bowles Interviewed in Tangier, Morocco."

404   "TAKE JANIE BACK TO TANGIER": Bowles to Thomson, November 26, 1968, Yale.

404   "HER EYES BENEATH A BLANKET": Roditi, "The Fiction of Jane Bowles as a Form of Exorcism."

405   "RETURN TO THE HOME": David Herbert, *Second Son,* p. 127.

405   "ABSORB ANY FOOD": Roditi, "The Fiction of Jane Bowles as a Form of Exorcism."

405   " 'I'VE ALWAYS WANTED TO BE BAPTIZED' ": Johnson, Conversation with author, March 6, 1986.

405   "WHO JUST DIDN'T UNDERSTAND THAT": *Ibid.*

405   "MEANDER OF ITS COURSE": Bowles quoted in Bailey, "The Art of Fiction LXVII: Paul Bowles," p. 77.

406   "THERE WAS NOTHING HE COULD DO": Johnson, Conversation with author, March 6, 1986.

406   "EXORCIZE THEM IN PRINT": Roditi, "The Fiction of Jane Bowles as a Form of Exorcism."

406   "A VERY IMPERSONAL MEMOIR": Roditi, Conversation with author, April 30, 1987.

406   "EVERYBODY ELSE HE EVER KNEW": Virgil Thomson, "Untold Tales," in *New York Review of Books,* May 18, 1972, p. 35.

407   "POWERFUL VOICE REMAINS MUTE": Ned Rorem, "Paul Bowles," in *Pure Contraption: A Composer's Essays,* pp. 36–37.

407   AS "WITHOUT TELLING": Burroughs, Conversation with author, April 28, 1987.

407   "WHAT DIFFERENCE DOES IT MAKE?": Bowles quoted in Regina Weinreich, untitled memoir, in *Twentieth-Century Literature,* Vol. 32, Nos. 3–4, Fall–Winter 1986, p. 271.

407   "I RUSHED IT OFF": Bowles quoted in Bailey, "The Art of Fiction LXVII: Paul Bowles," p. 77.

407   "SIDES OF THE ROOM": Bowles, "Notes on the Work of the Transla-
      tor" in Abdeslam Boulaich et al., *Five Eyes,* trans. Paul Bowles
      (Santa Barbara, Calif.: Black Sparrow Press, 1979), p. 8.

408   "CHOUKRI IS A WRITER": William Burroughs, "Foreword" in
      Mohamed Choukri, *Jean Genet in Tangier,* trans. Paul Bowles (New
      York: The Ecco Press, 1974), n.p.

408   "A VIRTUOSO STORY-TELLER": Bowles, "Notes on the Work of the
      Translator," in Abdeslam Boulaich et al., *Five Eyes,* trans. Paul
      Bowles, p. 8.

409   "HOW EXTRAORDINARY SHE WAS": Bowles quoted in Dery, "Talking
      to a Stranger: Paul Bowles Interviewed in Tangier, Morocco."

409   VISITED HER IN ALGERIA: *Ibid.*

409   "HER PIECES ARE LIGHT SKETCHES": *Ibid.*

410   "THROW THEM OFF THE TRACK?": Bowles, "Etiquette," in *Next to
      Nothing: Collected Poems 1926–1977,* p. 64.

410   "DRAPED IN SADNESS": Roditi, Conversation with author, April 30,
      1987.

410   "SHE HAD JUST DIED": Bowles to Thomson, May 25, 1973, Yale.

410   "CARE LESS ABOUT ALL THOSE CONVENTIONS": Johnson, Conversa-
      tion with author, March 6, 1986.

410   "COMPELLING REASON TO DO ANYTHING WHATEVER": Bowles to
      Thomson, June 26, 1973, Yale.

411   "ANY TIME JANE IS MENTIONED": Johnson, Conversation with author,
      March 6, 1986.

412   "THAT IS THE LAW, AND IT IS RIGHT": Bowles, "Next to Nothing," in
      Next to Nothing: Collected Poems 1926–1977, pp. 69–71.

Chapter 30

413   "I WAS DISCONNECTED FROM LIFE": Bowles quoted in Dillon, *A Little
      Original Sin,* p. 421.

414   "THE WAY IT AFFECTS ME, AT LEAST": Bowles to Thomson, March 29,
      1974, Yale.

414   "THE HISS OF TIME OUTSIDE": Bowles, "Far from Why," in *Next to
      Nothing: Collected Poems 1926–1977,* p. 72.

415   "ANY REASON TO DO ANYTHING": Paul Bowles, "Here to Learn," in
      Midnight Mass (Santa Barbara, Calif.: Black Sparrow Press, 1981),
      p. 96.

415   "THE POSSIBILITY OF RETURN": Bowles, *Ibid.,* p. 84.

415   "A CERTAIN AMOUNT OF WORK IN *ANTAEUS*": Bowles, Conversation
      with author, July 6, 1985.

416   "SWAMI OF THE DARK SIDE": Carter Coleman, Profile of Bowles, National Public Radio, June 1987.

416   "IN THE PLACE WHERE YOU'RE FAMOUS": Bowles, Conversation with author and J. Raskin, July 7, 1985.

417   "AS TELLING A BUNCH OF LIES": *Ibid.*

417   "PERHAPS LYRICAL HISTORY": *Ibid.*

417   "TRIP THROUGH THE CENTURIES": *Ibid.*

417   "GAVE IT FLESH, NATURALLY": *Ibid.*

418   "A SUNSET OR A BEHEADING WITH EQUAL DISPOSITION": *Sunday Telegraph,* September 17, 1982.

419   "HE INSISTED OBSESSIVELY ON PROPER LANGUAGE": Regina Weinreich, Untitled memoir, in *Twentieth-Century Literature,* Vol. 32, Nos. 3–4, Fall–Winter 1986, p. 268.

419   IN SPANISH AS IN ENGLISH, HE WAS OVERJOYED: Rey Rosa, Conversation with author, January 16, 1987.

419   "LITTLE OF THE WRITING WAS MUCH GOOD": Bowles, Conversation with author, June 17, 1986.

420   "WHICH WOULD BE HELL": Bowles to author, February 29, 1988.

421   IN THE LOW SIX FIGURES: Edwin McDowell, "A Reprint May Lead to Rediscovery of Author," in *New York Times,* October 17, 1989.

421   "AND THE DREAM GOES ON": Bowles, *Without Stopping,* p. 366.

422   "WISDOM AND ECSTASY—PERHAPS EVEN DEATH": *Ibid.,* p. 125.

INDEX

481

ABOUT THE AUTHOR

CHRISTOPHER SAWYER-LAUÇANNO was educated at the University of California, Santa Barbara, and at Brandeis University, where he received his doctorate in Literary Studies. His books include *Destruction of the Jaguar: Poems from the Books of Chilam Balam,* a forthcoming volume of translations of García Lorca, and more than half a dozen books written while employed as a staff writer for Time-Life Books in Japan. Since 1982 he has taught in the Foreign Languages and Literatures section at MIT.